Britain's First Worker-Priests

Britain's First Worker-Priests

Radical Ministry in a Post-War Setting

John Mantle

SCM PRESS

0 334 02798 5

This edition first published 2000 by
SCM Press
9–17 St Albans Place London N1 0NX

SCM Press is a division of
SCM-Canterbury Press Ltd

Printed in Great Britain by
Biddles Ltd, Guildford and Kings Lynn

Dedicated to my parents

Rupert and Jean

whose loving and costly priesthood
on the Mid-Craigie housing estate and beyond
embraced all things human

and remembering
their contemporaries
Michael Gedge, John and Veronica Strong
and
all the men and women of the
Worker Church Group
who in priesthood laboured for the same humanity

Contents

A Simple Worker-Priest Chronology

1943	Henri Perrin sets off to Germany as worker-priest
	Michael Gedge begins as worker-priest in London armaments factory
1944	Sheffield Industrial Mission begins
1945	Worker-priests return to France to begin work there
1954	Vatican bans French worker-priest movement
1955	Michael Gedge/John Strong begin underground at Eyethorne
1956	John Rowe begins work in the East End of London
1957	Worker Church Group founded
1958	BCC Publishes *The Church and Industry* – mentions French worker priests only – not the British
1959	Worker Church Group publishes its *Statement*
	French worker-priest ban reiterated by Vatican
1959	Church Assembly publishes *The Task of the Church in Relation to Industry*
1960	The Southwark Ordination Scheme (later known as Course) begins. Anne Grubb's article on British worker-priests appears in *Frontier*. *Part-Time Priests?* edited by Robert Denniston is published
1961	*Priests and Workers* by David Edwards is published
1963	First Southwark ordinations
1965/66	Other part-time courses begin
1965	*Priests and Workers: A Rejoinder* by John Rowe is published
1966	'Go ahead' for more part-time courses
1970	Ted Wickham publishes Audenshaw paper – praises first worker-priests
1982	Worker Church Group becomes Shop Floor Association
1990s	SFA near collapse

Abbreviations

ABM	Advisory Board of Ministry
AEU	Amalgamated Engineering Union
ACCM	Advisory Council for the Church's Ministry
APM	Auxiliary Pastoral Ministry
BCC	British Council of Churches
CACTM	Central Advisory Council for the Ministry
GME	General Ministry Examination
GOE	General Ordination Examination
IM	Industrial Mission
LNSM	Local Non-Stipendiary Ministry
MO	Mass Observation
MSE	Minister in Secular Employment
NSM	Non-Stipendiary Ministry
NUM	National Union of Mineworkers
SFA	Shop Floor Association
SIM	Sheffield Industrial Mission
SLIM	South London Industrial Mission
TGWU	Transport and General Workers Union
WCG	Worker Church Group
W-P	Worker-Priest

Acknowledgments

A broad range of people have helped me in this study, and I have tried to mention everyone in text, footnotes or sources. In particular, my most grateful thanks go to the men and women of the Worker Church Group, without whose critical eye and substantial support this project would not have been possible. I must specially mention Fr Michael Gedge, who, in his late eighties, and two or three years before his death, gladly told me more about his early factory life, and his time underground with John Strong, who died a few years before Michael. I also need to thank John's widow Veronica, who has been so helpful in telling me her own account of the Group and especially about John. David Wilson has been particularly kind in allowing me to see his papers and those relating to the Southwark priest-worker chapter and his contacts with self-supporting ministries all over the world. Southwark's priest-worker chapter was different from the Worker Church Group, but it was nevertheless enormously important and successful in upholding ministry at work. At all times the support has been warm and generous, but I need to add, of course, that where interpretations of certain events are mine, and where on occasion views may not be shared, I need to ask for understanding and forbearance; I am fully aware that other interpretations are possible.

I am grateful for the support and advice of a range of scholars and others who have made their own contributions to this period, in particular to Dr Alistair Mason of the Department of Theology and Religious Studies at the University of Leeds, who throughout the course of this research has been at pains to oversee my efforts. Also to Professor Oscar Cole-Arnal, of the Wilfrid Laurie University and Waterloo Seminary, Ontario, who read my study of the French worker-priests; to the Revd Dr John Lowerson, Reader in Modern History at the University of Sussex, who scrutinized the post-war section; to Professor Howard Davis, of the University of Wales, Bangor, who originally taught me sociology; to Paul Bagshaw, who helped me understand the Sheffield Industrial Mission; to Dr Alan Suggate, formerly a Reader at the

University of Durham, who also discussed the background; to Fr Roland Walls and John Halsey, who had lived and worked in Sheffield and who have been deeply involved in the whole period; and to Patrick Vaughan, whose own fascinating study of the history of non-stipendiary ministry deserves publication in this country.

I am glad to acknowledge the help of Cynthia Wood-Higgs and a relation, Anne Mantle, for proof-reading at an early stage and latterly Anna Hansford and Peter King. I also acknowledge the financial assistance I received in the early stages from the Bishop of Chichester, the Rt Revd Dr Eric Kemp, the Chichester Diocesan CME funding, and the Crewdon Trust in Oxford.

I must also offer thanks to John Bowden, Managing Director of SCM Press, who all along has shown marvellous support for what I have tried to write and who has always assured me of his genuine fascination in my attempt to tell a story of a period he has lived through himself.

Finally I must also thank my own family, particularly my daughter Anna, who helped with the word-processing of the bibliography. But chief love and thanks go to my wife Gill and my son Tim who put up with what I seemed to become during the course of this enterprise: a brooding and detached member of the household. After a time – and it can be a short time – research of this size takes possession of the soul. It is not so much the time spent reading and researching – though that can be hard enough for a family – but the lengthy mental preoccupation with the subject which can disable an individual from maintaining relationships with those who are closest; it should remain a salutary warning to others.

'. . . it is only by living completely in the world that one learns to have faith'

Dietrich Bonhoeffer, *Letters and Papers from Prison*

Preface

The feel of country childhood, suggests Raymond Williams, is partly about a 'delighted absorption in our own world, from which eventually, in the course of growing up, we are distanced and separated'.[1] My earliest childhood in Bucksburn, near Aberdeen's airport, and in Inverness, where I first went to school, were the nearest thing to village life. Inverness, to be true, is a large town, but in Southside Road where we lived in a Scottish Episcopal rectory next door to our church with school and shops nearby and the distant countryside in view, life seemed idyllic.

However, my father believed he was called to something much tougher. After only five years in Inverness and at the age of nine, with mum, sister and brother, my rather sheltered and naïve little world was completely shattered by my father's move to the city of Dundee over one hundred miles to the south-east. I hated that move. Dundee is a city, not a town, and I viewed the area in which my father came to serve at the invitation of Bishop Eric Graham, as a hell-hole. The Mid-Craigie housing estate – sometimes known as 'little Moscow' because of the prevalence of communist sympathizers – lay on the eastern edge of the city bordered by what to me was a terrifying dual carriageway exposed to sub-zero north-easterly gales. This had originally been a 1930s slum-clearance area, and was itself now bounded by other sprawling post-war estates including pre-fabs. The pre-war concrete mission – a dank hall-church – stood virtually on the carriageway. To the left of this building is the Church of Scotland parish church, better built in brick. Today it works hand-in-hand in an important ecumenical partnership. But it is the little Episcopal concrete St Ninians, built in 1937, which was recently listed, but a listing unlikely to save it from eventual demolition.

I can still recall the damp and cheerless winter night my father was licensed. Here in this ghastly concrete hall with its badminton court painted on the floor, leaky radiators and in a fug that made you feel ill and faint, my father, in the company of supporting clergy from the city, was duly 'demoted' (it seemed to me) to priest-in-charge, when once he had been a rector.

I was bitter and angry. My childhood absorption in my Inverness back garden and bedroom view of distant Scottish farmland seemed to have been snatched away. I missed the stained glass of St John's with its saints and gospel scenes, its colourful stonework and brightly polished brass where my dad had taught me to serve at the altar. Now, here, in the strangeness of the city and in a dingy, stuffy and smelly hall, I felt lost and frightened.

Daylight brought little relief. A few yards behind the little concrete church were the brown tenements of the estate, and a rather squalid parade of shops where I would later catch a glimpse of my first 'teddy boy'. But worst of all, directly across the road, was the largest factory I'd ever set eyes on. Bonar Long's electrical engineering works, which built massive electrical transformers, stood amid a heavy-industrial factory complex. Then, horror of horrors, within a couple of years, we moved from a temporary suburban haven a mile away to a purpose-built house alongside the church and effectively on the Mid-Craigie estate. My parents would now live there – without the luxury of central heating and in windswept freezing conditions – for more than a decade, my father ending up as the longest-serving incumbent of that mission.

Of all the sights which never failed to astonish me was the mass exodus from the factory opposite when the 'hooter' went off. Workers, literally hundreds of them, would pour across the main carriageway as if heading directly for our house. Friday evenings would see them running, often through the church grounds and out into the estate beyond.

Sunday worship was happy, colourful and catholic, and it seemed to me that, accompanied by cross and lights, the gospel stories, read at every eucharist, actually mirrored the human life all around us. But as the years went by and we were visited from afar by Scottish and English clergy – including a Cowley dad or two – I began to be aware, even as a child, of an almighty chasm fixed between our culture and the industrial world that lay opposite. Few who worked there ever darkened the door of our church, or presumably that of our Christian brothers and sisters in the kirk next door.

Very slowly, however, the factory began to have a strange fascination for me. In my teenage years, I discovered that one or two of my classmates had gone to work there; one I think, was killed early on in a horrifying accident. Yet I still could not see how the Christian community with its story of Jesus Christ could have any relevance to or impact upon the workforce of any of the factories opposite, even though the gospel stories suggested that it did.

I did not know then that growing up can be puzzling and painful. It was only after several years that I became accustomed to our new world in the shadow of the these works. I was later able to develop a real fascination for Dundee and its history, for the things boys were interested in then: dockyards and ships, railway stations, bridges and ferries, and eventually the pop scene and girls; above all the city's spectacular location on the banks of the river Tay overlooking the county of Fife.

After a few years as an apprentice illustrator, I moved from Mid-Craigie to Edinburgh as a theological student, now much more at ease with the Dundee I left behind. Although I would later return to the city as a curate at Broughty Ferry (part of Dundee) and later still to Dundee's College of Education, I knew that a part of me lived on – and lives on still – on the very edge of that estate where I'd first heard of rock 'n roll, Suez, Russia's 1957 Sputnik, and the Beatles. I also knew, in a funny sort of way, that the story of Jesus Christ somehow lived on – and lives on still – often unknown, in the humanity of ordinary men and women, employed and unemployed, who may not have known or ever spoken his name – except to swear – but whose own lives, though sometimes apparently uncouth, had colour, richness, saintliness, sadness, and all the compassion and skullduggery of the gospel stories' own characters.

But more importantly, as I had gazed in childlike wonder at the factories opposite our home, I had not known that in places such as these, and greater than these; into engineering workshops, mines, dam sites, dockyards and railway sidings especially in France but also in Britain, some priests, laity and religious, had specifically chosen to live a presence that others would later describe as a 'golden page' in the history of the church.

For while my father and mother laboured tirelessly on, utterly devoted to their poor flock on the estate, caring as much for their worldly as their spiritual needs, others in other industrial locations knew that a wider flock could only be known by working and labouring directly alongside them, and in this case usually outside the parochial system. Following the French, a small but dedicated group of mainly Anglican clergy went to work in parts of industrial Britain – just like ours – because sharing that working life was their vocation too. It was only later as a theological student that the full story began to emerge for me and I would meet my first 'worker-priest', John Halsey, member of a community in Roslin, near Edinburgh, and an underground worker at the nearby colliery.

My discovery of the worker-priests has haunted my ministry ever since. In those days talk was sometimes about the 'failure' or 'ending' of the French experiment or the so-called 'collapse' of the Sheffield Industrial Mission (and what I already knew was a mistake – the 'non-existence' of worker-priests in Britain). I very occasionally came across an article about the British or French worker-priests, but it was all history, and I lost interest.

Then, in the mid 1980s I made an educational visit to Arras in northern industrial France with theological students whom I was then teaching from the Canterbury School of Ministry. To my astonishment I found on the very day we arrived that our host, Fr Léon Hamain, had arranged a meeting with French worker-priests for the next afternoon. And so, in a rather shabby little Arras back street, the *rue de Jérusalem*, I met the genuine article for the first time. There were some in our company of nearly forty, students and others, puzzled, bemused, even a little cynical about this rather ageing bunch of radicals. But I was deeply moved by their stories of the past: of one whose entire anti-clerical family had violently disowned him when he became a seminarian, only to be baptized, one and all, when he returned as a worker-priest to his own home docks; of another who as a youngster had seen his own caring *curé* constantly hounded by the Gestapo; of others who knew the very first worker-priests – 'the old wave' – who, in the face of Vatican threats that they must leave their place of work or face possible excommunication in 1954, refused to abandon their workmates and their families.

The worker-priests then gave accounts of their work today in the Nord de Calais region: work with the poor, the unemployed, with disenchanted youth, the socially excluded, and of their commitment still to be a presence, living the gospel of Jesus Christ in everyday life. Of course it was all too easy to be romantically swayed. But here they were before our very eyes. My interest was at once revived and I have met them again on regular occasions since then. They remain lively, socially and theologically articulate and alert, looking beyond the year 2000, and still totally committed to ordinary men and women who normally have nothing to do with the most institutionalized church in western Europe. They may appeared to some as 'has-beens', but they are rather important 'has-beens'; and where could I find such people in my own church today? The answer is in a handful of former British worker priests, alive and well, sometimes disengaged from the institutional church but still engaged in the communities where they live.

I fully endorse and warm to those who believe in the importance of parochial ministry. My father, after all, was and remains a devoted parish priest, who never knew of the worker-priests as he laboured, usually alone, in that dingy industrial estate. But it was devoted catholic clergy like my father, who, with the same understanding of sacrificial calling, introduced me to the story of the worker-priests (often in whispers) and who had grasped their deep sense of incarnational mission; that if a 'chasm' between ordinary working men and women and the Christian gospel really existed, then they would just have to put their boots on and cross it.

Introduction

Issues and the contexts

The story of the 1940s and 1950s worker-priests of France and Belgium is a well-documented episode in which 'Ted' Wickham suggested they wrote one of the 'golden pages' of church history. It has often been assumed, however, that at a time when industrial society was a focus for mission, that episode took place in isolation. Yet, in the early 1950s and 1960s, a handful of British priests (and sometimes their wives and supportive laity) went out to work in factory and mine in the context of post-war austerity and would remain there up to and beyond the 'white heat' of Harold Wilson's technological revolution in the 1960s. Most survived the 1980s and 1990s and now live beyond the year 2000 in the working districts where they began. How did this ministry come about, and what did it have to say about the life and mission of the established church?

By the late 1950s, it had dawned on a few churchmen and women, even in Britain, that one of the most extraordinary experiments ever in Christian ministry had recently taken place in France. There, in the decade following the Second World War, a relatively small number of priests and religious, with the blessing of cardinals and bishops, had, as an alternative to traditional parish ministry, entered docks, factories and many other industrial work-sites. They did this to share the working life of ordinary men and women, and in order to be a Christian presence simply where they found themselves. David Edwards would later describe this as 'the most courageous and extensive experiment undertaken by any Christian church anywhere to bridge the gulf fixed since the nineteenth century between organized religion and the working classes' (*Priests and Workers*, SCM Press 1961).

But by this time in the Church of England there were already anxieties about a shortage of clergy. Perhaps some kind of 'part-time' ministry might be the solution. And so, by the 1970s, non-stipendiary ministries –

that is, self-supporting ministries where clergymen and women earned their own living in secular jobs – were almost commonplace. To many people, then as now, these ministries – mainly but not exclusively in the Church of England – represented an exciting new departure in Christian ministry that seemed to have something in common with the dimly remembered French worker-priests of previous decades. So when accounts of the rise of these non-stipendiary ministries have been offered, the French are often cited as precursors of a kind. Rod Hacking, for example, in a valuable study entitled *On the Boundary – A Vision for Non-Stipendiary Ministry* (Canterbury Press 1990) suggested that the story of French worker-priests had 'significant consequences for the practice of the Church of England'. In a review of a book by M. A. H. Melinsky, Philip Welsh (*Church Times,* 20 November 1992) suggested that Melinsky had mentioned something which ought to be questioned: that 'non-stipendiary ministry meant a kind of worker-priest'. And the editors of *Tentmaking – Perspectives on Self Supporting Ministry,* James Francis and Leslie Francis (Gracewing 1998), have felt it right to include accounts of the French. Even the Church of England's own website has casually described non-stipendiary clergy as 'worker-priests'. In short, whenever the origins of self-supporting ministries are noted, the French are dragged in. It is as if their very inclusion somehow sanctifies and hallows the work of these ministries everywhere.

The popular notion, however, that can derive from such juxtapositions – that non-stipendiary ministries are simply a kind derivative of French worker-priests – illustrates a fundamental misunderstanding of worker-priests in France and, more significantly, those who gave themselves to this same ministry in Britain. The fact was, that while the story of the French began to unfold in some detail, the activities in Britain of a devoted handful of worker-priests, their wives and friends, went relatively unknown and have never been explained or explored in their historical or sociological contexts. This study attempts to put that right.

Britain's 'worker-priests' may have been thought of as the precursors of the later developing non-stipendiary ministries, and there are some parallels where that ministry has been focussed 'at work'. But the strands that led to non-stipendiary ministry weave something of a tangled web, and if there was thought to be a logical or inevitable step from worker-priests to the development of such ministries, worker-priests did not always share it. In practice, Britain's first worker-priests had much more in common with their counterparts in France; they were theologically well-educated and conventionally trained clergy, 'priests turned workers', who had resolved, as a priestly vocation, to live and work alongside their fellow men and women in manual labour.

And the 1950s and 1960s were a good time to do this. For all their divisions and ecumenical shortcomings, groups within the established churches in Britain, sometimes through the British Council of Churches, were beginning to share a common vision that may be said to have approached some kind of consensus: that the Christian gospel, the story of Jesus Christ, was for men and women everywhere, including those who, in that industrial society, were now totally estranged from the established churches.

This study introduces the British worker-priests, their families and friends, their lives and work. It documents the occasional indifference and hostility which they met, and will argue that they deserve a place alongside the French. They were utterly committed to sharing the lot of ordinary working men and women in manual labour, to organizing themselves, and to making explicit through the most serious social and theological reflection why they had chosen this particular 'way of Jesus Christ' as an alternative to working exclusively in parochial ministry. Finally, and most importantly, it was they (together with industrial chaplains) who took to heart the claims of the institutional church: that it must somehow speak to the men and women who earned their living in the heat of modern industrial life.

Early hopes had been raised when the church seemed to endorse the radical new outreach of industrial missions, including the Sheffield Industrial Mission and, in some instances, even the work of these first worker-priests. But it was a relatively short-lived support. By the mid- to late-1960s it was becoming clear that the institution's main agenda was beginning to shift away from this outreach, and inward towards its own domestic concerns. As a shortage of 'manpower' to staff the parishes fuelled the cry for a new and more flexible 'non-stipendiary ministry', so the issues became blurred. New non-stipendiary ministries did indeed appear, but rather than being – as the rhetoric so often argued – a dynamic connection with the 'world of work', they were viewed (more often by the non-stipendiary ministers themselves) as essential support 'for the vicar'. The institution meanwhile saw it as the quickest, cheapest and most expedient way of propping up the parochial system; and this, it must be added, has never really changed.

In France, the worker-priest ministry, in complete contrast, was a deliberate venture into another territory, the working world, offering a radical and demonstrable alternative to clericalism and parochialism.

The original movement, albeit small, had been encouraged by the hierarchy, and though attacked by the Vatican in the mid- and late-1950s was eventually revived and strengthened after Vatican II. It Britain, it failed to take off.

The handful of British worker-priests, their wives and lay associates who remained committed to understanding and sharing working life as a vocation were effectively shunned by an institution whose understanding and ministry 'to all people everywhere' was nevertheless locked in the culture of parochialism. For generations the territorial parish had been viewed as the only proper context for mission and ministry – the only way of being the church – and the handful of worker-priests, and some industrial chaplains who believed otherwise, were voices crying in the wind. Rather, the institution, which implicitly refused the worker-priests recognition, threw its weight behind the burgeoning non-stipendiary ministries, especially where these supported the parochial system, and where participants remained in middle-class and professional occupations, occasionally appropriating the title 'worker-priest' or 'priest-worker' for themselves. And the same institution, which for a moment in that post-war world had appeared to sanction an engagement with industrial society by new and radical means, gradually abandoned even that, and returned to its true focus of concern: internal debates and the maintenance of the territorial parish.

The historical and sociological setting

This book comprises a historical analysis of the emergence and contribution of Britain's first worker-priests, their wives and lay associates, by placing them in the context of a post-war Church of England. It uses primary and secondary historical material, including oral history, and allows some sociological interests to inform the study. The period it covers is an exciting one, but one that has received scant attention. So often, for the student of church history, reading modern history still means an exclusive attention to the nineteenth century.

The story begins in 1945 in a Britain shattered by six years of war. It introduces the reader to some of the political and cultural issues that make up a context where it was believed by many churchmen and women that the British people might be anti-church, anti-clerical, or even 'pagan'. But successive surveys showed that the British people were far from uniformly hostile. Rather, the British were ambivalent, 'puzzled', it was said at the time, about religion: 'believing,' suggests

Grace Davie, 'without belonging'. In some respects, this was perhaps the ideal setting for a worker-priest ministry, as the average parson could still be received with a measure of affection. The roots of this radical engagement are traced back to a variety of strands in Anglican theology and practice, and an indication of the parson's place in popular culture is noted.

The second chapter details the attempts made by the French and British churches in particular to engage directly with this post-war industrial world. The story of the French worker-priests – which is not as well understood as some assume – is outlined. Then, what is sometimes thought of as the Church of England's 'alternative strategy' – industrial mission with its origins in evangelical movements – is briefly sketched. The Sheffield Industrial Mission in particular is traced from its successful peak to its near collapse in the mid-1960s.

Chapters 3 and 4 – the heart of the study – turn their attention to the handful of British worker priests who took to heart the church's call that it must somehow engage directly with ordinary men and women, and who went beyond the methods of industrial mission. It begins with Michael Gedge in 1943 entering a munitions factory, feeling vindicated when he discovers the story of the French worker-priests, and traces the story of others in Britain who eventually made up the Worker Church Group years before the advent of non-stipendiary ministries.

Chapter 5 shows how the Church of England's shifting agenda on ministry began to cause confusion. Though serious consideration was given to self-supporting 'auxiliary ministries', especially with the introduction of the Southwark Ordination Course under Bishop Mervyn Stockwood, which produced its first clergy in 1963, none of these ministries came as a 'relief column' to the worker-priests' rather beleaguered Worker Church Group. Rather, SOC exemplified what would happen to virtually all other part-time courses thereafter. Despite the initial hopes of Stockwood that they would train some worker-priests, they ended up preparing men (and later women) who would either opt for traditional stipendiary ministry or remain firmly in middle-class jobs and professions. And some of the latter, frustrated in their world of work, or distressed by the feeling that they were marginalized by the church's stipendiary clergy, would eventually join the ranks of the stipendiary parochial ministry themselves. As a correspondent, Hugh Valentine, commented in the *Church Times* in October 1995, '. . . the NSM cause has not been greatly helped by those NSMs who see their ministry as confined to parish and altar'.

It had become clear early on, however, that there was a world of difference between the original worker priests and their little Worker Church Group on the one hand, and the new non-stipendiary ministries on the other. Although the new ministries had been introduced as new and dynamic within a 'missionary context' – or so it was often argued – sadly, they soon appeared to be the most expedient way of dealing with clerical shortages in the parishes and keeping the traditional system going. Ironically, and in complete contrast, it was the Worker Church Group which lived out one of the very reasons which the institution gave for special work in industrial areas:

> . . . [a] deep rift (has) developed between the Church and the common life of the people in the industrialized areas of the country, which the Church must seek to repair.[2]

From past stories to present realities

Britain's first worker-priests, their wives and lay associates, remained loyal to their original vocation, especially in working-class communities, and as successive Labour governments staggered on after Harold Wilson, only to end in exhaustion under Jim Callaghan, so the worker-priests found themselves marginalized. Even though non-stipendiary ministers vastly outnumbered them, few NSMs, rooted in the middle-class culture of the institution, took any interest in the Worker Church Group or, if truth be told, understood what they were about. Nevertheless, the Group remained committed to their vocation, organized, articulate and prophetic. Under the policies of Margaret Thatcher, and in what some believed was a deeply divided Britain developing its own underclass, the Worker Church Group evolved into something different. But it was late in the day; the institutional church had no room for 'radicals' of this kind, and even when it was able to produce its *Faith in the City* (1985), it did so without any evidence that it was aware that they even existed. The Commission, as it were on behalf of the church, confirmed, as the church had done nearly thirty years before, and as it continues to do today, that:

> The alienation between Church of England and the majority of working class people must cause us all to be greatly disturbed. . . [the Church] cannot persist in the way of self preservation and the 'institutional self-interest' which so often preoccupies it.[3]

The story of Britain's worker-priests and their supporters – which began in the mid-1940s – has been one of the judgments on and challenges to such ubiquitous institutional rhetoric.

I

Post-War Britain 1945–1967: A Context for Radical Ministry

'A considerable potential religious revival is knocking around. The trouble – for the Churchmen – is that it definitely is not going to tie itself to the old forms, and might tie itself to something utterly different, possibly not even Christian . . .'

(Tom Harrison of Mass Observation, in a paper 'Religious Feeling', 1944)

'It is plain that the worker will not come to the Church . . . The Church then must go to the worker and that involves identification at the deepest level.'

(A. Skevington Wood, Paisley minister in *The Expository Times*, March 1956)

'What I'm out for is a good time – all the rest is propaganda.'

(Arthur Seaton, in Alan Sillitoe, *Saturday Night and Sunday Morning*, 1957)

1. In the aftermath of war: society

(i) Politics and people

In 1945, members of the Conservative Party sat in shock and horror when the newly elected Labour Government stood in the House of Commons to sing 'The Red Flag', though there were a few, it appeared, who were rather unsure of the words. It mattered not. It was a symbolic moment. After fifteen years of Conservative rule, and a six-year war presided over by a coalition government, Churchill was defeated. The Conservatives lost a massive 203 seats with Labour gaining 227; a new age seemed to have been inaugurated, and Sir Hartley Shawcross could later announce '. . . we are the masters at the moment – and not only for the moment but for a very long time to come'.[4] The opportunity had at last arrived, and the country now sought a change of direction and looked to Labour to lead it.

Among some churchmen, too, there was hope, fuelled by years of war, that some kind of religious revival might begin, and to that end evangelistic enterprises began to be planned. But after the most devastating of European conflicts, neither Britain nor other countries in Europe were in a position to initiate policies that would make for rapid recovery – industrial, social or, for that matter, religious. The damage and disruption of the conflict were severe with hundreds of thousands of homes destroyed, industry exhausted and in decline, raw materials in scant supply, and whole communities devastated.

If the material condition of Britain's people was poor, morale threatened to be poorer still. After the euphoria of victory in Europe, the shock of what had actually been suffered slowly became apparent.[5] There would be those who would never come home, and those who did might find homes destroyed, family and friends scattered. In 1947 divorce rates went up to 60,000, ten times the pre-war figure. During the war, between 1941 and 1945, the number of divorce petitions filed was 16,075, but by 1951, with the conflict over, the number had risen to 38,382.[6] The Bishop of Norwich (Dr Percy Herbert) claimed in 1948 that 'public opinion is shocked by the growing number of divorces'.[7] Women who had fought the war at home bringing up children and taking a place in war-work now found themselves faced once again with the soul-destroying task of trying to keep a family together and make ends meet, when rationing – and it even included bread in 1946 – continued on into the 1950s. But the Labour Government of 1945 had been elected on the promise that it would 'face the future'. And the electors – including returning troops – had no intention of allowing the country to slip back into a pre-war pattern of poverty, unemployment, and above all fear.

Britain's economic and social recovery depended upon a ready supply of manpower and raw materials, but neither was in sufficient supply to meet demand in the immediate post-war years.[8] Overall, recovery and output was painfully slow, and Labour's answer to Britain's endemic problems was to seek for nationalization as soon as possible, in order to recover Britain's place as a manufacturing and exporting nation. Many of these hopes were never realized. The Gross National Product figures were disappointing, even depressing. The growth rate between 1949 and 1967, rising by just 1.5 per cent to 2.5 per cent, was much slower than predicted. The closing year of Labour's rule proved difficult when the balance of payments showed a marked deficit. Between 1946 and 1951, imports rose to £2,022 million with exports at only £1,773 million, resulting in a balance of visible trade down at £249 million.[9] Productivity was poor and could only improve slowly when raw materials and manpower continued to be in short supply. The ongoing struggle to bolster an ailing economy and sometimes falling production could be costly. A decision to impose certain charges for spectacles and false teeth on the newly created National Health Service resulted in the resignation from cabinet of prominent Labour members, including Wilson, Bevan, and Freeman.

In 1951, at the age of seventy-six, Churchill was returned to power when the Labour Party were defeated in a September general election. With an improving economy and a new prevailing doctrine where 'the social morality of the means test had given way to the doctrine of universality',[10] some Conservatives sought consolidation in an attempt to maintain what they saw as the best in social welfare, though they did decide to dismantle some of Labour's nationalization schemes. Immigration began to grow from 1952, especially from the West Indies, leading to a restricting Immigration Act a decade later: a foreshadowing of racial problems and Race Relations Acts of the 1960s.

But that same year, following a stroke suffered by Churchill, it was Sir Antony Eden who emerged as the glamorous leader whose demeanour suggested confidence and competence. However, these early assessments proved misjudged when Eden effected the greatest debacle of his premiership in his mishandling of the Suez crisis in 1956, when British troops, with the support, indeed collusion, of the French, occupied Port Said to rescue the Canal from Colonel Nasser. Though many in church and state were bitterly divided over the action, the shock in Britain was profound. For once the country had not 'beaten the wogs'.

At home, and with stability in prices and the anxiety of the Conservatives to abolish controls, there was nevertheless a determination for expansionism and intervention on the part of Peter Thorneycroft and the new Prime Minister, Harold Macmillan. The earlier creation of the National Economic and Development Council (Neddy, 1951) fitted a period when stability in wages and prices, coupled with increased production and import of goods which appeared in shops, signalled a hitherto unknown affluence that heralded a shift from post-war austerity. Macmillan, declaring that 'badly-housed workers were unproductive workers', had presided over a greater expansion of new housing. No matter what social or domestic problems might ensue from such a growing affluent society, soon to have its new televisions and labour-saving domestic devices sought by housewives, the country was assured towards the end of the 1950s, in the immortal words of Macmillan, that it had 'never had it so good'.

1959 marked a climax for Conservative rule in Britain. The party was again returned to power following a general election, in which they gained 100 new seats, almost equalling Labour's victory in the aftermath of World War Two. The latest war, over recovery and stability, seemed for the moment to be close to victory; Britain now basked in its new-found affluence as the 1950s and early 1960s saw a marked increase in productivity. Yet despite these appearances of growth, British industry, 'the centrepiece of politics', remained inherently unhealthy. If 1959 marked a highpoint in manufacturing output and living standards, it also marked a slide in industrial relations. But the affluent society seemed to generate its own momentum, an inexorable rush towards even greater consumption without the safety net of good industrial relations and production. It seems an obvious equation, but it was nowhere near so obvious at the time.

The years following 1959 were marked by wage restrictions in the public sector and rising unemployment. And as Macmillan's premiership drew to a close, the age also began to produce, even in political circles, the moral casualties of what some saw as this growing decadent, never mind affluent, society. While Macmillan suggested that the troubled might take their moral direction and advice 'from their archbishops', one of his own ministers seemed morally untroubled. John Profumo, Minister of War, eventually resigned in the face not so much of a moral scandal – though there was that – as of the possible threat to national security coupled with the unforgivable revelation that 'he had, after all, lied to the House'.[11]

The Conservatives' long term in office faded when, in March 1963, Macmillan resigned in favour of Sir Alec Douglas Home who, though an able Foreign Secretary, inspired less confidence as the occupant of Downing Street. Politically 'something of an anachronism'. '. . . his aristocratic origins and education . . . served to emphasize his almost total lack of experience in British domestic politics. If the British knew little about him, he knew little more about them.'[12] His gifts in diplomacy could not save his 'faltering performance' at the dispatch box when Harold Wilson, on the opposition benches, turned question time into the 'socialist equivalent of a blood-sport'.[13]

(a) Inaugurating the welfare state

The inauguration of welfare provisions by the Labour Party at the end of the war and their maintenance by later Conservatives were significant features of the post-war settlements. The initial provisions for health and social care were to be major features of the new Labour Government in 1945, but for all their importance, they seemed to pale into insignificance before the awesome problem of housing, which Archbishop William Temple had recognized as one of the causes of 'varied forms of suffering', where in its worst manifestations it remained a 'wanton and callous cruelty'.[14] During the course of the war, and because of bombing raids in many centres including London, Coventry, Plymouth and Clydebank near Glasgow, 208,000 homes had been destroyed and another 250,000 made uninhabitable. 'Homes fit for heroes' had been a cry following the First World War, and even now, this was the issue about which most people felt most strongly – evident in the 'Great Sunday Squat' of September 1946, when empty and condemned properties all over the country were seized by homeless families, couples and individuals.

If the public had hoped for speedy results, the signs were not hopeful; indeed more slums had been cleared in the decade before 1939. Labour's attempt to embark on a new building programme involved the repair of damaged property, the start of a rebuilding programme, and, in an operation that would become a feature of the landscape for almost twenty-five years, the building of prefabricated housing. From Scotland, on open ground in Dundee's Mid-Craigie housing estate, alongside a little pre-war mission, to the green fields of Hainault – north-east of London – identical 'prefabs', as they would affectionately become known, proved remarkably popular, and because of excellent design, some 'mod cons', easy maintenance and enclosed gardens, were to be mourned in the passing when they were finally vacated in the late 1960s.[15] By the time Labour left office in the early 1950s, a million properties had been completed. The most significant increase in house building would not become evident till Harold Macmillan took responsibility in the new Conservative government. With the removal of some controls, builders doubled their activities, as the Conservatives attempted to alleviate the problems by encouraging private enterprise.

If housing was a priority in the rebuilding of Britain, post-war health and welfare, including unemployment benefit, came a close second. This no doubt was welcomed by many clergy including Donald Soper, president of the Methodist Conference, who in 1953, 'thanked God' for it.[16]

Bishop Wand at the Lambeth Conference in 1948 had also made it welcome. Welfare reform went back to proposed legislation that pre-dated World War I, and became the basis of Labour's assurances that there would be a deliberate attempt to create comprehensive care. On the statute book by 1948 was a National Assistance Act which abolished help based on Poor Laws, introduced a Family Allowance scheme financed from taxation and a National Health Service financed from National Insurance.

The National Health Service Act, first published in 1946, involved Aneurin Bevan in a long and sometimes bitter contest with the British Medical Association, which sought like other professional bodies to exercise hegemony over recruitment, training and remuneration. Sheer dogged effort, including financial inducements, eventually won the profession over, and Bevan, who had personally witnessed 'poverty, ill-health and squalor in abundance', had his way. The National Health Service began in 1948, and was to prove one of the lasting and most significant innovations of the post-war period. If some clergy welcomed these provisions, there were occasionally words of warning. Archbishop Garbett was concerned that it might 'weaken the sense of personal responsibility'.[17] Alec Vidler, writing in *Theology* in 1952, and looking at 'The Welfare State from a Christian Point of View', saw it as something Christians undoubtedly ought to welcome and approve, but cautioned against a possible future in which individuals could be 'exclusively occupied with material security and comfort . . . (a time) in which everyone will be comfortably off and have to work only moderately hard'.[18]

Labour's return to power in 1964 after the premiership of Home, was less watershed, less change of direction, than an attempt to work within existing industrial structures to ensure growth and development, though admittedly the party had just lost one of its most able leaders in Hugh Gaitskell. Labour's intention was to give Britain a cutting edge in an industrial world which, to use Harold Wilson's terminology, would be forged 'in the white heat of the (technological) revolution'. Labour's manifesto, *The New Britain*, concentrated on internal affairs. For Wilson, Britain had become a technological force to be reckoned with, a nation leading the way in the design and development of new industrial techniques and production. To do this, an incomes policy negotiated from workshop floor 'up' was intended to secure a basis for a national economic plan that would secure a growth rate of 3.8% per year.

This expected growth rate, however, was not achieved, and Labour again sought a salvage operation, this time with an explicit policy to meet rising wage demands and growing industrial action. Since 1954 the record of industrial stoppages had increased: no less than 2,524 stoppages in 1964 – one of the highest figures ever. By the mid-1960s strikes seemed endemic, as Wilson began to move against the unions. 1966 saw a dock strike, a Prices and Incomes Act – which the unions rejected – and serious strikes in steel, and in Fords. By 1967, the pound was devalued. Two years later, in a document entitled *In Place of Strife*, Labour outlined a new prices and incomes policy. But the document met with such opposition that Labour was faced with the not altogether unwarranted accusation that it could not govern. All the signs of a breakdown in consensus politics were now writ large. Twenty-four years of post-war struggle by both parties only served to demonstrate that British industry still lacked some of the inherent ingredients for sustained growth. Not only did Labour have to demonstrate that it could develop a credible opposition to Tory rule, but it also had to act as the vehicle for years of discontent in an economically divided country.

(ii) Cultural contexts

In the year that saw the end of World War Two, and Labour's sweep to power – aided not least by British squaddies voting in liberated Europe – almost half the population of Britain, some twenty million, visited the cinema. As one of the most popular instruments of mass media, providing entertainment, education and propaganda throughout the war years, it was to enjoy at least another full decade and a half of popularity before the sun would begin to set on its half-empty auditoriums. But before that, the cinema would share with the rest of the country a marked shift in cultural perspectives that would give the late 1950s and early 1960s their particular notoriety.

If so many queued for the cinema, as the political parties sought to bring some kind of normality to British life, they did so in the knowledge that they were just as likely to have to queue for everything else. Rationing, which remained into the mid-1950s, ensured that life changed little from the war years. What the people of Britain really wanted was an emergence from austerity as soon as possible. Perhaps a sad reflection on Labour's otherwise happy victory was that it fell to this party to begin the long, perhaps thankless, task of restoring the country to normality.

Before the 1940s turned into a new decade, however, plans were under way for an event deliberately engineered to mark a new beginning. The

South Bank of the Thames, like many other riverside areas reduced to rubble in the blitz, was to see the framework for new architectural structures which would mark the short-lived but highly popular Festival of Britain. Though the Beaverbrook press fell on it and Britain's Churches Advisory Committee was vigorously opposed to Sunday amusements in the adjoining Battersea funfair, the public loved it, extending its spirit so that throughout the country 'all that time we breathed, thought, imagined, willed, inhaled and exuded – Festival!'[19] It inspired a vision of a brighter future, hope against years of despair, and confirmation that reconstruction and innovation from architecture to fashion was not only possible, but had actually arrived.

In terms of mass culture, the written and spoken word still remained among the most popular forms. By the mid-1950s a small group of writers who would become known as the 'angry young men' aided and abetted a radical transfer in reading by shifting attention from traditional styles of writing and offering, through the novel, throughout the mid- to late-1950s, perspectives on a society altered, 'levelled' perhaps, by the experience of war.[20] Kingsley Amis's *Lucky Jim* (1954), and John Braine's *Room at the Top* (1957), set the scene for a very different and irreverent attempt to 'tell it like it is'. These contributions also found an echo in Alan Sillitoe's more popular novel, *Saturday Night and Sunday Morning* (1958), which according to *The Daily Telegraph* made *Room at the Top* 'look like a vicarage tea party', and suggested a new working-class literary tradition that, according to later critics, failed to materialize. It was in the theatre, however, that one of the most striking examples of contemporary commentary would emerge: John Osborne's *Look Back in Anger* (1956), which arrived as regional subsidized repertory began to flourish, upset for ever cherished ideas of the theatre as a reflection of the *status quo*.

But there were also causes for alarm. The social disruption of war and the continued austerity of the early 1950s were the setting for a significant rise in crime and 'delinquency' . The late 1950s and early 1960s saw the most rapid rise in convictions, and between 1950 and 1969 there was an increase of 11.9% for those between seventeen and twenty-one. A greater increase of 13% is evident for those between twenty-one and thirty. 'How Far are the Churches to Blame?' asked the photo magazine *Picture Post* in a 1954 article on crime and the lack of religious belief. But if the 1950s youth were being noted for their growing criminal activity, they quickly became the centre of attention for other reasons. As earnings rose, so did the opportunity to spend what was earned as the first vestiges of a 'youth culture' became apparent, with a growing interest in music, personalities and spending power, made explicit in the fashionable new 'Edwardian' dress of 'teddy boys'.

One of the most obvious manifestation of this culture was a musical style known as 'rock and roll', a phrase coined by Jerry Freed, a United States radio 'disc jockey', who, describing himself as 'moondog', invited listeners to share his choice of popular music. A combination of 'black blues' (sometimes known as 'race music') and 'white' country style, the musical cocktail that resulted quickly became the property of the young when a music group – Bill Haley and the Comets – cut 'Rock around the Clock'. Something of a nonsense song, but with instant appeal when backed by an incessant beat, it was taken very seriously by fans. The following year a film with the same title as the new song became a sensation, and was subsequently banned when riots broke out in several British cinemas in August and September 1956. The gravest suspicion of the establishment, particularly in the persons of schoolteachers, clergymen or the magistracy, 'told the fans,' suggests Sinfield, 'that their allegiance was significant'. Lonnie Donegan and his skiffle group said it all, when, in their popular song 'Puttin' on the Style', they claimed that

> Sweet sixteen goes to church just to see the boys.

By the early 1960s, when the pop culture had developed as a lucrative industry and come to dominate the lives of young people, the influences from America became even more apparent. The Beatles, attracted by 'rhythm and blues' influences from the United States, via Merseyside, became Britain's most successful pop group ever, with John Lennon, one of the group, claiming quite innocently – but in a remark that upset the more conservative – that they were now more famous than Jesus Christ.

If entertainment in the form of music became an almost religious obsession, another form of domestic entertainment was growing in popularity. While radio had provided wartime and post-war Britain with a major information and entertainment service, television, abandoned during the war, was to come into its own by the early 1950s, aided by the televised Coronation of Queen Elizabeth II (1953). It was soon appreciated that the system carried enormous potential as a commercial enterprise, and, after heated debate, commercial television (ITV) would be established in 1955. Within a few years, the figures for viewers had risen from 50% of the population to some 75%. The medium was now on a course that would change the way most of the Western world received news, information and entertainment. One of the BBC's first highly successful news feature programmes which ran into the 1960s was 'Tonight', and its arrival was significant; it was launched in the very year that *Picture Post* was forced to close – a poignant reminder that the habits of the public could change so quickly.

Print journalism was but one victim that fell to the popularity of television; the more obvious was the cinema. Its queues might stand in the mid-1950s just beyond another decade, but the signs of its decline were already evident; it had had its great day as the single most popular means of entertainment since before the war. Despite a range of exotic techniques to make the 'big' screen even bigger, it was too little too late. Instead, families clustered round the glowing tube in the corner of their living room, to watch on television (and on what was actually an inferior quality picture) everything from news and variety performances like Hughie Green's 'Double your Money' to the imported 'Highway Patrol' from America.

This is not to say the cinema had nothing to offer; the late 1950s and early 1960s were to see a significant British renaissance. Just as television was gaining hold, new comment, comic and serious, would deal with Britain's class structure. The most notable Boulting Brothers film, *I'm All Right Jack*, was 'a highly deliberate and historical sensitive social satire'[21] in which all the inherent problems of British industry were lampooned across the big screen. A harder-hitting example was undoubtedly the screen version of Sillitoe's *Saturday Night and Sunday Morning* directed by Karl Reisz to the rather haunting music of the jazz saxophonist Johnny Dankworth. It became nationally popular: when the trailer was shown in one of Dundee's cinemas in 1960, a working-class audience erupted in shrieks of sympathetic laughter at the hero's reactions and behaviour. Arthur Seaton's life in the factories of Nottingham compared well with the Dundonian's mills, factories and shipyards; his cynical and sometimes disenchanted voice south of the border was theirs too.

If a strengthening affluent society, epitomized by the enormous sales of new cars,[22] (and juxtaposed in the Church of England's statistics with a drop in Sunday School attendance) now entertained itself at home with its newly purchased means of making that entertainment, the moral fibre of the country seemed less secure. Sexual behaviour and 'sexual liberation', especially in the 1960s and because of the introduction of the contraceptive pill, found their way into the vernacular and the poetry of Philip Larkin, who reflected that:

Sexual intercourse began
In nineteen sixty-three
(Which was rather late for me) –
Between the end of the Chatterley ban
And the Beatles first LP.

Worse still, some believed this sexual behaviour was supported by an Anglican bishop, John A. T. Robinson, who not only defended the Penguin publication of *Lady Chatterley's Lover* in court, but who, one correspondent to the *Church Times* believed, shared in the responsibility for the decline in national moral standards. *Honest to God* had a whole chapter devoted to 'The New Morality', with Robinson admitting that there were those who believed that '. . . religious sanctions are losing their strength, the moral landmarks are disappearing beneath the flood, the nation is in danger'. And well they might have thought that as Robinson argued that 'love alone . . . can allow itself to be directed completely by the situation'.[23]

An affluent society enjoying near full employment amid a sharp and dazzling urban architecture – assisted by Hitler's bombing or the work of the municipal bulldozer – now replaced rubble and drab prefabs. Yet a rising and disturbing crime rate cautioned against the rather sanguine view that all was well in this age of advancement. In the 1950s, crime rates and the nature of crime were disturbing enough – Teddy boys had murdered a youth on Clapham Common in 1954 – the 1960s rates were positively alarming with an increase of 11% every year, and now including drug-related crime. There was the Great Train Robbery in 1963, the notorious Moors murders in 1964, the Shepherds Bush police murders in 1965, the decade ending with the Kray brothers being convicted of murder and sentenced to life in 1969.

For many social commentators, this ugly and rising crime rate was symptomatic of a rapidly changing society where class boundaries, and those between the 'haves' and the 'have nots', were becoming increasingly blurred. And it was against this general background that Britain's first worker-priests would emerge. The intention of this study, though not indifferent to how they engaged with this background, is chiefly concerned with the way in which they took a radical step 'down' to meet, at a shop-floor level, the men and women of Britain whose own lives were lived in that same context.

(iii) 'What about the workers?' Class and the working class

Any definition of class requires some awareness of at least two interpretative views. First the Marxist view, where social structure is seen as economically determined on the one hand by a capitalist minority who own the means of production, and on the other by those who contribute their labour. Secondly, a view which may be described as more functionalist argues – against the existence of 'class' – that there is simply a 'social stratification' where shared values contribute to different expectations and values. In post-war Britain there remained a view that there were indeed different long-standing groupings, divisions and social ties, economically determined, which had more to do with inherited wealth, value and culture, and which remained despite the devastation of war.

Britain's first worker-priests, wives and lay friends would eventually claim that they entered the working-class milieu because the issue was class. The institutional church, they would have argued, was supported and populated by generally middle-class, often professional men and women, who enjoyed a relatively comfortable life-style, while those in the working-class, however defined, were still subject to the economic and social forces which seemed to determine their present and future. For the first worker-priests and their families, understanding of the working class, let alone Christian mission – the business of trying to 'get over the gospel to the people of our time' – meant 'sharing fully the life of the working-class'.[24]

But the issue of what, precisely, constituted class, was far from clear. That class division continued after the First World War is evident, though Marwick in his studies on class quotes Vivien Hall, a Second World War ARP worker, who insisted on the outbreak of war that it was the 'instant and complete leveller of classes'.[25] Yet if, during the course of the conflict, the revelation to middle classes 'of some of the appalling circumstances of children reared in the country's slums' changed the minds of some, it might only confirm the prejudice of others. Civilian sentiments that this was a 'people's war' were 'remarkably widespread' according to Marwick. Yet in military service troops might react sharply to notions of hierarchy, though it was from the officers (often middle-class) that recruits into the Labour Party were later drawn.

By the end of the European hostilities there was clearly a general hope on the part of civilians and troops that divisions between classes might indeed be minimized. Marwick quotes a Methodist minister who argued that most soldiers 'are thinking of a world where there will be better opportunities for everyone, and more economic security than there has been since the early days of mankind'. Yet Antony Howard's judgment was that, far from bringing about a 'social revolution', the Labour victory of 1945 'brought about the greatest restoration of traditional social values since 1660'.[26] Sinfield's assessment, rather than tempered, is cynical; the post-war settlement was to be characterized not by some new fairness or social equality, let alone the 'revolution', but by an economic system 'which J. K. Galbraith likened to a squirrel wheel, as people chased endlessly round a self-defeating circle of production and consumption' and which, Sinfield goes on, 'still left many people out'. It was fear of the consequences of a socially unstable population which, he argues, was chiefly responsible for the post-war settlement.[27]

In France, by contrast, where worker-priests would first appear in any organized way, liberation involved a heavy blow to the upper class, who had generally sided with the Vichy government and who were 'fundamentally antagonistic to the organized working-class movement and the hard core of French industrial workers'. The church, however, often seen by the working class as siding with the upper class, now had its exceptions among individual Catholics who 'in the Resistance brought the church new credit and new strength', something occasionally highlighted in Britain.[28]

Despite C. V. Glass's classification of class in *Social Mobility in Britain*, which might help in an analysis of the definitions outlined at the beginning of this section, Marwick argued that such scales do not necessarily coincide with class as understood historically and colloquially. He highlights some of the post-war cultural revolution with its 'diffusion of relative prosperity' through an examination of British films which took cultural mores as their forms. He singles out *I'm All Right Jack*, with Ian Carmichael epitomizing the upper-class twit, whose family's uncertainty about his future means that he is reluctantly let loose on a factory floor. The sending-up of that class, contrasted with the working class, represented in particular by the naiveté of the shop steward (Peter Sellers), which 'outraged left-wing commentators', served to demonstrate the gap. Marwick also highlights the Bryanston/Woodfall film of Sillitoe's *Saturday Night and Sunday Morning* (noted earlier), with its contrast between the older generation of the working class, beaten down in total acceptance of its lot, and the rebellious younger generation personified in Arthur Seaton.[29] Here there is no identification of an 'enemy' other than what Seaton sees as 'organized society, with its demands, insurance contributions and military service . . .'

Though, as Marwick explains, an awareness of broad divisions between classes existed, there was less 'sensitivity', as he put it, among the working-class to the more subtle distinctions between occupations. He admits, however, that some studies, such as Goldthorpe's *Affluent Worker* in the late 1960s, only served to demonstrate that higher wages as monetary compensation for tedious work had little to do with promotion to a middle class. The skilled worker remained in a working-class context albeit better remunerated, but there was no real argument for *embourgeoisement* or 'status ascent'. Indeed, Goldthorpe attempted to show that, despite higher remuneration, there remained areas of common social experience which 'are still fairly distinctly working-class' and that 'affluence . . . and even residence in localities of a "middle-class" character do not lead on, in any automatic way, to the integration of manual workers and their families into middle-class society'; in short, 'powerful motivation to gain higher material standards of living did not in the main appear to be accompanied by status striving'.[30] Rather, there might be, as economic goals became achieved, a weakening of commitment to trade unionism and 'labour' objectives, indeed, 'the new worker, as a man who has been able to gain a good deal for himself within the existing system, will move towards a conservative and individualistic, rather than a radical and collectivist, outlook on economic and political issues'.[31] By the end of the 1970s, such judgment would prove prophetic, and by the beginning of the 1980s Goldthorpe suggested that hopes for an 'open society' were still far off, with little evidence of any progress being made towards it.[32]

Indeed, while the *Affluent Worker* was being published in the late 1960s, the Labour Party was actually being perceived as losing control of its working-class support as it struggled to manage an economy which, since the mid-1960s, had slipped from a Prices and Incomes Policy Act of 1966 to general unrest and the devaluation of the pound the following year. Labour, as has been shown, attempted to restore some industrial harmony with its publication *In Place of Strife*, but that policy was not to win popular support with unions and workers, and proved to be the precursor of Wilson's downfall and, perhaps, the end of consensus politics in Britain.

Towards the end of the 1960s that affluent society began to give cause for anxiety. To the cultural shifts, uncomfortable to some, shocking to others, not least to some churchmen and women, was now added evidence of a strained economic system where the expectations and frustrations of a relatively well-off society questioned the maintenance of such affluence. The 'real' value of liberal culture, which was to find popular extremes in the 1970s, found a different and radical reaction in the eventual construction of monetarist policy under Mrs Margaret Thatcher in the 1980s. That British class relationships were affected mainly by living standards did not, as Goldthorpe had shown, mean the inevitable shift to middle-class values and status, let alone a more open society. Yet the term working-class encompassed a broad range of occupations, and it was to the 'skilled', 'semi-skilled' and those at the lower end of these occupations, the unskilled, that a handful of Anglican clergy would gravitate in the 1950s and 1960s. The issue for them was that while living standards might indeed appear to have been improving, the position of working men and women in status, opportunities and work – which Marwick called 'arduous, uncongenial, or just plain boring'[33] – had changed little, and it was this life which had to be shared if there was to be any hope of demonstrating that the Christian gospel, and the kingdom of God, belonged to them – 'before it belonged to anyone else'.[34]

2. In the aftermath of war: church and people

(i) Churchgoers and the unchurched

Just as post-war political reconstruction in Britain became evident in a variety of new social and industrial ventures from welfare provision to nationalization, and in a change of cultural perspectives, so religious reconstruction would eventually involve at least a handful of clergy – including one or two senior clergy – in some radical new ventures in mission and ministry. Yet there was little evidence from the centre to suggest that from the institution's standpoint – and certainly 'from the top' – moves were afoot to listen to or engage in any radical way with a devastated country where belief and hope – as far as anyone knew – might have been destroyed, and where the churches in Britain faced hostility and marginalization. Historians of the post-war church have understandably tended to concentrate their analysis on the church's perception of itself – upon the broader issues and individuals who shaped the established denominations – and rarely (though Hastings is a major exception) on the political and social background. It has often remained a history of bishops and archbishops, of events and reports and decision-making, but reporting little of the church's contact with what is now known as the 'wider community'. There is some acknowledgment of changes in attitudes, but there is not always the same recognition of major shifts in society and culture and class,[35] though in what Edward Norman calls 'a rare example of the Church applying theological concepts to political behaviour', the Lambeth Conference of 1948 saw the emphasis on the nature of original sin in the doctrine of man as a serious challenge to what it understood as 'secular humanism'.[36]

If, after 1945, some of the population recognized that the world might never be the same again, the established church seemed to prove the general rule that its perception of society, as *Picture Post* suggested before the decade was out, went largely unaltered: 'The clergy do not recognise the great gulf fixed between them and the mass of the people' said one article.[37] There would be, it was hoped, a 'return to religion' at the end of the war, a religious revival to prove that the war had done nothing further to alienate non-churchgoers and shatter the faith of 'believers' in general, or the commitment of churchgoers in particular.

The war had, of course, produced surprises. Some of the population, scattered by evacuation, found themselves in the unaccustomed quietness of rural life. But if being bombed out of your home was an unpleasant shock, as Spinks acknowledges,[38] no less was the staggering experience of the sudden arrival of city dwellers in the 'clean and orderly houses of country districts' where one parson was astonished to find children who 'had no idea who was born on Christmas Day', while another found that city boys coming to him for Confirmation could not find the Acts of the Apostles when asked to look it up.

If the experiences of urban ignorance shocked some of the more sheltered during the course of the war, the post-war rise in marital infidelity served as a further reminder of the effects of the war and separation. Once a social blight, for Spinks this now '. . . came to be accepted as a social fact to which no social stigma was attached'. Some even saw it as at least one likely cause of delinquency, crime and irreligion.[39]

But one of the greatest shocks for the established church was less the recognition of what the war might have done, as to what could not now be done without the leadership of Archbishop William Temple. His sudden and unexpected death at the end of the war produced a kind of spiritual paralysis. Lloyd saw his death as marking the 'final end of Victorian Christianity'[40] . . . he more than any other churchman had summarized and crowned all that was best in it. It is not difficult to see Lloyd's comment as a shade premature; Geoffrey Fisher can be easily caricatured as another kind of Victorian. For Lloyd, Fisher's tenure was positive: that the church '. . . took little hurt from his hands, and gained much from his leadership'[41] is a kinder judgment than that of Hastings nearly thirty years later who described Fisher as lacking in '. . . charisma, theology and ideology', '. . . a man without doubts, without causes, without the slightest crisis of conscience' who exercised 'his considerable intellectual powers . . . chiefly on the *Times* crossword'.[42]

The immediate post-war years saw the established church having to deal with what Lloyd described as the 'malaise of deep discontent', where problems would have to be tackled without a real understanding of the nature of a war-torn society. At a local level, the established Church of England was chiefly concerned with its manpower and plant. Not only had many church buildings been damaged or destroyed,[43] but by 1945 many churches were without vicars, and clergymen, returning from duty as padres in the forces, were sometimes having their 'claims' to parishes either side-stepped or ignored.[44] Lloyd saw church members as 'benevolent beholders' rather than 'active participants', and he criticizes an apparent disregard for central theological issues of the gospel and man, such that the church could not see '. . . the point on which the whole weight of her thought, prayer and witness should have been brought to bear'.[45] But it was not to be.

> In the years following the war, ministers of religion of many denominations who had hoped for a 'Return to Religion' experienced periods of great depression . . . .The 'Return to Religion' did not come. People had attended the services for VE and VJ Day, as well as those arranged for the Sunday in November for the remembrance of those who had fallen in both World Wars, but there was no marked renewal of church life.[46]

Evangelism, however, was perceived by some as the best answer to society's problems at the end of the war. This would not be so much a sharing of theological questions of the time – there were few of them in the church anyway – as an attempt to present a clear and unambiguous gospel message to a population 'gone astray'. And some of the groundwork appeared to have been done. An evangelistic commission, appointed by William Temple before the end of the war, reported its findings in a document entitled *Towards the Conversion of England* (1945). It spoke of 'increasing urbanization', of a youth receiving its stimuli 'from the shop window', of a cinema 'almost totally devoid of any Christian background', and of industry which exercised 'a virtual tyranny over the lives of masses of men'.[47] Despite that last comment, a plan, comments Lloyd, is what it never was. A 'pretentiously entitled . . . ill starred document . . . [the Commission] contained many people of high distinction, who were gathered from all walks of life save one. The whole working-class area of life was left unrepresented.'[48] To this Alan Suggate has added: '. . . it spoke as if the church had little need to listen to the world and as if the gospel had only to be taught and understood to be effective'.[49]

If evangelism as a theory was thought of as one way of engaging with post-war Britain, then Bishop Wand's 'Mission to London' was its practical expression. Published in 1948, the Bishop's Charge, entitled *Our Day of Opportunity*, exuded hope and confidence as a preparation for a mission to his whole diocese – and possibly to the rest of the country. Though much effort was made, the results would prove to be as limited as many which followed.

> The already faithful members of the church were fortified and enheartened. On the general mass of the unconverted, living contentedly without God in the world, the mission had very little effect.[50]

This does not mean that churchmen and -women were any the less shocked by the devastation of war or that non-churchgoers were unfeeling or uncaring. Welsby saw the sense of desolation across Europe as something of particular concern to Christians who had seen 'isolation, spiritual desolation, and persecution of clergy and congregations of all communions during the previous six years'.[51] How these feelings and views were to be measured and assessed by the general population or churchmen he does not say, and it has always been easier for historians to assume that there was a widespread feeling of religious loss, than come up with evidence. But evidence there is; it comprises a rather extraordinary range of material, providing not only evidence of some downward churchgoing habits at the end of the war, but also, and in marked contrast, general expressions of belief and hope, which give testimony to a remarkable lack of hostility towards churches and churchmen. Yet much of it went largely unrecognized in the post-war years, as the churches remained inflexible in their institutionalized patterns of practice, and often unyielding in their demands for adherence.

(ii) Unchurched 'believers' in post-war Britain

Among more recent work Robin Gill talks about the period following the Second World War as seeing 'a continual overall decline in attendance'.[52] Of particular significance to this study were the religious attitudes of the British people in a post-war world where rebuilding programmes were as much about hope as they were about the physical repair of towns and cities. For some people, as Alan Sinfield has argued, the war years brought devastating loss. He reiterates the position of the poor, who during the blitz displayed a 'hopeless and indeed helpless capacity to appreciate the significance of their plight, and the reasons for the disaster', the plight of the bombed often adding to the social miseries they had known in peacetime. More important for Sinfield, it was the government's fear of losing control of a demoralized population which produced the post-war settlement.

After such a war, in which so many had suffered so much that 'the normal sensitivity of feeling had been overlaid (in sheer self-defence) by a sense of numbness against such horrors as those of Dachau and Buchenwald',[53] attitudes to religion, it might have been thought, would demonstrate less inclination to believe in anything at all, let alone try to live a religious life in face of past events. People were not always fooled by wartime euphoria or propaganda, and 'if people who had lost their homes,' Sinfield quotes Vera Brittain, 'had been blown up or injured, burned or buried were to be interviewed forty-eight hours later, the results would not always have been so useful to the Sunshine Press'.[54] Attitudes to what lay deepest in British breasts were openly sought in a number of post-war surveys which attempted to determine the levels of religious belief and practice in the population following six years of war. *News Review*, Mass Observation, the *British Weekly* (1949), and the BBC 's 1955 survey all show a degree of unanimity on questions of belief. David Martin has seen these researches, and others, suggesting 'a continuum of approval running from Christianity and religion on the positive side, to church and clergy in the negative'.[55]

In 1947 the *News Review*[56] took its own poll of the nation's church-going habits, raising the question 'HAS THE CHURCH OF ENGLAND HAD ITS DAY?' The paper took its measure from the war, 'a dividing line selected,' it said, 'because it altered so many people's routines and ideas'.[57] Thus the war was '. . . the biggest single factor contributing to decline of interest in religion'. 'The two world wars accounted for about one in three of those who had lost interest in religion.'

Among the more interesting of all post-war studies remains *Puzzled People, The Study of Popular Attitudes to Religion, Ethics, Progress and Politics in a London Borough* (1947). Perhaps the most significant study of religion made by Mass Observation, it appeared to many churchgoers at the time, and long after its publication, as a depressing revelation of 'an extraordinary state of ignorance', as one newspaper put it. The material, collected on behalf of the Ethical Union, was, according to the Union's preface, such that 'none of those who will look with interest . . . will find any reason for satisfaction unless (and there followed a now dated caveat) 'he is prepared to be satisfied with the triumph of Roman Catholic indoctrination, or the ignorance and confusion of those who call themselves Christians'.

Just one example helps our understanding. What Mass Observation called a sizeable number, one in five men and one in eleven women, responded to questions on the nature of religion with outright hostility. Though the reader is not told precisely to what questions the answers referred, and though those who dismissed religion as of no interest were few, the more frequent criticisms were not directed at the nature or content of religious belief but at those who practised it. 'A lot of bloody hypocrisy, if you ask me. Go to church and then tear your neighbour's character to tatters, that's all it is . . .' is close to a comment from the study's introduction that:

> There's a lot of good people in the world, but the people who call themselves Christian are the sort who go to church and put 'No hawkers, No circulars. Keep out' on their gate and wouldn't do a kindness to anyone under the sun. And that's why I'm not in favour of Christianity.[58]

Comments like this are not only about those who practise Christianity – and it is naive to think so. Here there is an underlying assumption that if Christianity were true, people who believed it would actually behave better; because they don't, or can't, means Christianity is not true. It was a rather simple but at the same time devastating logic.

The sense that there was a 'received orthodoxy' underpinned the survey's title. It remained a borough of bewildered people; not wicked, irreligious or irreverent, but puzzled, confused, it could be argued, by a range of credal beliefs not earthed in their common experience, hard to swallow before breakfast, and quite impossible to digest. Failure to meet 'ordinary people' – who sometimes did have incredibly 'crude' or 'odd' beliefs – with a credible story and expression of belief and practice would now haunt the established churches for the rest of the twentieth century.

In 1955 the BBC carried out its own survey, measuring attitudes to its religious broadcasts and religion generally. That part of the population classified as listeners to religious programmes, and towards religion, showed . . . 'an attitude of at least benevolent toleration . . .'[59] But churchgoing was no longer the 'accepted thing', and the survey concluded that it took no social courage to ask 'why one should go to church', but rather that the onus was now on those who though one should go 'to convince us'. Lack of attendance at church is put down to busy lives, loss of habit (a frequent reason given at the time) and indifference.[60]

But the question which dominated so many enquirers in those years was why some people regularly attended church while others did not. What made people persist in their 'belonging' while others gave up? What, precisely, had the war done – if anything – to sustain church decline? In a study of 'Religious Movements' in 1961, W. S. F. Pickering examined religion in two working-class towns, Heddington and Thornby.[61] He chose to consider a range of social factors: marriage, family, bereavements, moving house (which might account for more 'traditionalist behaviour'). By 1961 Pickering had also clearly recognized the arrival of a youth culture with its attractions and spending power.

Most striking of all his findings – supporting those of previous enquiries – was that the downturn in attendance did not seem to be affected by political events or religious perceptions. 'Few people,' he argues, 'appear to be swayed positively or negatively in their attitude towards churchgoing either through political happenings or through intellectual doubts or convictions about the truth of Christianity. No one said he or she had suddenly discovered religion either relevant or irrelevant to everyday life.'[62]

In the same year (1961), Tom Harrison of Mass Observation was still able to claim in his *Britain Revisited* that Christianity 'as an idea' is certainly not out of favour, so that 'I approve of religion but don't go to church myself' was by far the most common single reaction. He could comment that 'practically no one expresses any kind of hostility towards religion'. Even of the young, no real scorn or dislike of religion is openly expressed, 'and very seldom privately'. 'Neither,' he added in a later paper, '. . . did observers come across Worktown's (inhabitants) dismissing the whole concept of religion as irrelevant bunk.'[63] Harrison was asking the reader to compare these views on religion with those reported as what any half-dozen working-class people would be likely to answer, according to Richard Hoggart's *The Uses of Literacy*. Most of the phrases he quotes he believes to be typical of northern workers. While it is possible to see Hoggart's comments as dismissive, some of his pictures seem to bear out the very points Harrison wants to make. Hoggart's working-class simply don't go to church, and even when they were critical towards the parson '. . . it is usually a cheerful cynicism with no active hostility behind it. It's a good racket if you can get away with it,' they will say: 'Good luck to 'em.' Some of these comments seem to show some sympathy with 'religious ways' as interpreted as ethical values, 'being kind' or 'doing unto others'. Hoggart's investigation of working-class attitudes belies the notion of a view of Christian teaching as 'irrelevant bunk', as Harrison suggests. Because Mass Observation got different answers from respondents, it does not change the fact that the views often seem to be identical.[64]

(iii) Conclusions and consensus

Graves and Hodge in *The Long Weekend* (1941)[65] had charted a steady decline in the 1930s of regular communicants to a point where they claimed the Church of England's only just exceeded those of the Roman Catholic Church. But it was secularization which got the blame for the downfall of church attendance in K. B. Smellie's *The British Way of Life* published in 1955.[66] The Christian churches provided only confused teaching on marriage and family life, and in practice there had been little grasp of theology, so that the 'influence of Christian philosophy and doctrine has been receding since the influence of Darwin merely accelerated what Newton had begun'. By 1961 Nick Earle's appraisal of the Church of England – *What's Wrong with the Church?* – highlighted the points which the institution was quite unready to address: radical theology, liturgical revision, the parson's freehold, and ministry. Certainly none of these issues was the concern of the populace. And 'no one,' said Pickering in the same year, 'had abandoned religious practice because of an inability to believe in the trinity, the resurrection of Christ, or even life after death'. 'You can still go to church and not believe those things!'[67] was a reversal of another commonly held view. In *Anatomy of Britain* (1962),[68] Antony Sampson saw the church as a less 'discredited institution', but quoted Max Warren, who claimed that the church and the world were entering a new 'dark age'. 'We are now living in a society which has dropped Christianity and this challenges the Christians who are left to re-examine their basis of belief.' But then the church was theoretically ill equipped anyway. Indeed in Wand's *The Church Today*, the bishop showed little appreciation of modern culture and wrote in general terms of a 'political secularization' accompanied by a general decrease in religious observance, giving his own potted history of the church and closing on the theme of a distinctive apostolic body within society, so distinct – others might argue – that it made no contact with society at all.[69]

In a study published in 1977, Robert Currie, Alan Gilbert and Lee Horsley argued that the Christian churches' own records demonstrated overall decline in religious activity on the part of the general population. From 1900 to 1970 they showed gains across the main Protestant and Catholic denominations. In the case of 'Protestants' – and that included the Church of England – the gains peaked at over six million between 1920 and 1930, but suffered the most serious decline following 1940. The greatest gains, rising rapidly after 1950, were to the Roman Catholic Church, heading towards five million. The greatest part of post-war gains, insisted the authors, had 'disappeared' since 1961. But the most significant negative effect upon church growth, the authors believed, was 'secularization', 'simple disbelief in the supernatural'. They concluded: '. . . once such disbelief becomes widespread, individuals need unusual qualities to be sure of the utility of churches' religious functions'.[70]

Paul Johnson has recently argued that 'the impact of the two world wars on religious life was an ambivalent one'. He saw the post-war period on the one hand giving prominence to church leaders like Bishop Bell of Chichester, but at the same time challenging theological assumptions. In church membership he depicts a sharp fall in the 1940s but stabilization in the 1950s. He also argues for what he calls the limitations of statistics, where people might 'identify' with a Christian denomination. The widespread view that 'you do not need to go to church to be a Christian suggests that membership statistics may significantly underestimate popular religious belief'.[71] And Grace Davie has indicated, in a case of 'believing without belonging', that 'the discrepancy between believing and belonging, for example, is at its sharpest in urban working-class areas . . . Here belief persists . . . (albeit in a depressed form), but the expected reluctance to practise religion is compounded by a further factor, a mistrust of institutional life.'[72]

That latter point has been borne out here. The fact was that though numerical decline was in evidence almost everywhere by the end of the 1950s, there was far less hostility or antagonism towards the established churches. Attitudes to institutional religion and its teaching were often those of polite indifference, in an age when other 'distractions' – as Ted Wickham would suggest – were becoming popular.[73] While liturgists had their movements like 'Parish and People' and the theologians had a growing interest in continental theology, the general mass of clergy and committed laity carried on as before, with bishops and other leading churchmen bewailing a population which preferred to live – they supposed – 'contentedly without God'. Yet, as Norman (quoting Wand) emphasized, 'If you ask the average Englishman whether he was a religious man he would probably say No, but he would regard it as the greatest insult if you told him he was no Christian.'[74]

The institutional interpretation of what constituted a Christian life or 'believing' had less to do with 'being good' or 'believing in God and saying your prayers' than it did with denominational 'belonging'; in short, attending church, 'making your regular communion' and believing and accepting denominational confessions and creeds were what really counted. And there were no concessions. According to Tom Harrison, Henry Wilson, Bishop of Chelmsford, had claimed as early as 1944 that 'it was nonsense and wishful thinking to say that men and women in the services show deep underlying religious feeling, only waiting to be tapped'. It was never recognized or accepted that despite the evidence of a range of surveys, men and women, focussed as they had been on six years of war, had, despite it all, still maintained a level of belief and some understanding of Christian ethical standards, and still felt a need for prayer.

But the old perception of a population's 'apathy' lived on, and a church rooted in the territorial parish system dispensing the truth lived on with it. Indeed, Greenwood suggests that '. . . one of the chief strands of the Church of England's self-consciousness in this period was to identify the incumbent together with the parish church building itself not only as the representative focus, but as synonymous with the life and work of the church itself . . .'[75] Only slowly, as post-war Britain moved painfully towards social and industrial reconstruction, did it begin to emerge among a handful in the established church that the men and women of Britain might, after all, be met where they were; not in the *pews* of the established churches but somehow in the workplaces and streets of Harrison's Metrop and Worktown, or Pickering's Heddington and Thornby, where new ventures in mission and ministry would have to be tried and tested. In the event, only a handful of clergy would begin to explore new and radical patterns of engagement and ministry as Britain moved towards reconstruction in the urban and industrial centres. Yet the idea of the parish as the 'right' place for mission, ministry and even Christian life lived on, and a particular perception of clergymen with it.

3. Priests and people: some origins of radical ministry

(i) Developments in Anglican ministry

Before any consideration can be made of some of the more radical elements in Anglican ministerial practice and theology, from where it might be possible to find some of the 'roots' of Britain's worker-priests, some account of the historical development of ministry itself may be helpful. In the post-Reformation period, for example, it was George Herbert who contributed to the shaping of a distinctively Anglican ministry. By the middle of the nineteenth century, and following on the heels of more than a century of earnest evangelical ministry in which there was enthusiasm for 'high standards of clerical duty',[76] and in which the mid-nineteenth-century parson could later be described as a 'man without leisure',[77] the Oxford Movement's own insistence on the Christian ministry as a most sacred calling was epitomized in John Keble's life of personal holiness and piety;[78] his parish came to be regarded as a model by everyone, it seems, except Keble himself.[79] Though he cared for his people in a manner that became proverbial, 'it showed itself in ways quite at variance with the conventional portrait of him as a gentle milk-and-water saint'. The Oxford Movement emphasis on ministry as a sacred calling was further enhanced by R. C. Moberly's *Ministerial Priesthood* (1886), which, as Robin Greenwood has argued, furthered the view of the ordained ministry not as a social construct, but as something essentially 'given', stressing the separateness of a church which should confront rather than conform to the modern world. Yet in the post-war years, and certainly among French, and later a few British, worker-priests it would be precisely this interpretation of a ministry 'given' that was paramount: upheld not for its 'superiority over others', but *because* the whole notion of 'incarnational priesthood' should drive the priest not away from the world, but rather into its very heart.

Some of these sentiments might have been found earlier among one group whose ministry created something of a new tradition for Anglicanism, the slum ritualists. A decade or so beyond the beginnings of the Oxford Movement, young priests were found working in a variety of slum parishes and amid a working class who viewed the clergy as siding with the 'wealthy and the factory owners, and thus as having vested interests in social inequality'.[80] These priests took themselves to the worst that cities could offer: Charles Lowder and Alex Mackonochie to St George's-in-the-East, London, others to slum parishes in the North, St Saviour's in Leeds, or further south in Portsmouth or Plymouth. In general, as Antony Russell has shown, the period, with its developing theological colleges, saw the formation of a new kind of clerical professionalism.

There were, however, few direct criticisms levelled at the ills of society, and some early slum clergy could been seen as paternalistic. But the Christian Socialists – described by Edward Norman as producing '. . . a radical departure from the received attitudes of the church, both in their religious and social contentions',[81] and particularly in the person of F. D. Maurice – were already against the kind of society which had created such inequality.

Maurice's notion of a full unity in humanity, restored in Christ, underpinned his theology and gave impetus to his most lasting work, *The Kingdom of Christ*, a defence of the position of the Church of England, where some of the strands of later understandings of kingdom theology may already be in evidence. As Edward Norman has noted:

> Maurice's sense of human need, of the presence of Christ in all men, and of the reality of Christ's Kingdom as the end and purpose of human association, was the noble and sacrificial vision which underlay his involvement in Christian Socialism.[82]

While Maurice doctrinally upheld the Thirty-Nine Articles, along with J. M. Ludlow and Charles Kingsley he attempted to publicize the plight of the poor, and through their tracts and teaching identified among the root causes *laissez-faire* capitalism. A more committed socialist position would later be found with Stewart Headlam and the Guild of St Matthew (1877–1909), when Headlam combined his socialism with his tractarianism, leading the way, by the turn of the century, to a more general alignment of social concern with Anglo-Catholic theology, as he spoke of Jesus the carpenter who became 'a radical reformer both in social and religious matters'.[83] Headlam's newspaper the *Church Reformer* (1884–95) argued the cause: the Guild drew its readership almost exclusively from among Anglo-Catholics. The Christian Social Union, founded in 1889, was more representative of Oxford and 'centre' Anglicanism and was particularly influential before the First World War when Charles Gore, one of its leading supporters, was calling for a minimum wage and improvements in the living conditions of the working class. Many of the movements, however, lost much of their influence by the eve of the Great War. Nevertheless, the sum of the theological arguments by Maurice and others would influence men like Fr Kelly of SSM, and in turn this was passed on to staff and students at Kelham.

(ii) Padres and religious

If a handful of the Church of England's clergy and among them Christian socialists had begun to recognize the need for a ministry among the urban poor, the outbreak of the First World War would prove to be another opportunity for ministry to be tested and, in this case, to be found wanting. Alan Wilkinson's study of *The Church of England and the First World War* shows an institution and its clergy ill-equipped for such a context. This comes as a surprise when it is sometimes assumed that many padres were the image of Studdert Kennedy. They were not. In a chaplain, suggests Wilkinson, 'personality could count for everything; the fact a man was ordained counted for nothing'.[84]

There were, of course, exceptions like St John Groser, who would make his mark later in London's East End fighting fascism. In the front line, during the First World War, he kept close to men but refused to bear arms. Mentioned in dispatches, wounded and decorated with the MC, he was eventually sent back to England, But it was Studdert Kennedy who became a legend only twelve months after he had arrived in France. Unlike many a padre kept back from the front line, Kennedy often went where it was dangerous. In William Purcell's biography a rather traditional parson, Theodore Bayley, slightly over age for the battlefield at fifty, deliberately sought out Kennedy for advice on 'what to do'. It was unequivocal:

> Live with the men; go everywhere they go. Make up your mind you will share all their risks and more if you can do any good. The line is the key to the whole business. Work in the very front and they will listen to you; but if you stay behind, you're wasting your time. Men will forgive you anything but a lack of courage and devotion.[85]

Much later, in an autobiography, Father 'Joe' Williamson related his own days as a layman in the trenches searching out a 'padre' to hear his confession. There were few who came from the tractarian tradition of

Williamson's own 'slum parish', and when he did find a priest he had to teach the poor man what to do. 'He hadn't a clue,' remembers Williamson, 'I can still see his silly fat pompous face standing before me.' It was unkind, perhaps, but it was a common enough sentiment shared by other soldiers who saw clergy at best as well-meaning, but more often as useless and irrelevant.[86]

Between the wars lessons would be learnt. With the Report *The Army and Religion*, there came a new acknowledgement of a 'religion' unknown by people, and especially among the British 'Tommies', a recognition that if there was any drift from the churches, it must have begun before the war. In calling for a ministry able to engage with the world, and driven by a zeal for mission, both Roland Allen and F. R. Barry (himself engaged in the war), would begin to argue for different kinds of ministry that might engage men and women directly where they found themselves in life, though it would not be until after the Second World War, and at a time of serious clergy shortage, that these ideas would be heard afresh, and indeed in many respects brought to pass in the first worker-priests. By the end of World War Two, in which chaplains had been captured at Dunkirk (1940), lived alongside men in all theatres of battle, and had landed in Normandy (1944), or months later literally dropped into Arnhem, a rather different view emerged. Padres now often remained in the front line, and suffered with their men. Tom Harrison of Mass Observation was convinced that there were some servicemen at least who had benefited from a padre's ministry, and who had come to view the church and its clergy in a different and more favourable light. Interestingly, when the numbers of those seeking ordination began to rise in the 1950s candidates included ex-servicemen, and among them a high proportion of air crew.

But war experiences alone would be insufficient to shape the character of clergy who emerged in its aftermath. Greenwood considers the role of theological college staff as paramount, and highlights the lives of F. R. Barry, B. K. Cunningham and Eric Graham in particular. For Barry the primary task of the clergy was to train the laity for prophecy, and he earnestly believed there was a vocation for every person and not clergy alone, since it was 'an impoverished Christianity that concerns itself about the church rather than the entire order of creation'.[87] For college principals like Cunningham and particularly Graham (Cuddesdon), pastoral principles came first, so that 'Graham put doctrine second to pastoral work of a priest, though this was joined to the belief that the theological college as a kind of '"detached" permanent retreat centre' was the right place to train ordinands. As Greenwood adds, many of these colleges were subsequently closed, with the Church of England remaining '. . . ambivalent regarding how far it wished its ordinands in study, prayer, and life to embrace society, and how far to avoid contact with it'.[88] In short, the church was 'primarily concerned with demonstrating its historical credentials (and was) not in a position to communicate the gospel to the general public'.

Religious communities may also have had a significant place in the formation of a more radicalized Anglican priesthood. The Society of the Sacred Mission (SSM), best known perhaps for its base at Kelham, saw itself, especially under the guidance of Fr Kelly, as particularly concerned not only with industrial areas – like those around it in Nottingham – but with the training of boys from working- and middle-class backgrounds for a ministry in a church which according to 'Kelham theology' ought to be rooted in the everyday concerns of ordinary people. But even that was an early sentiment. Fr Bedale in 1922 saw that Christianity

> is not concerned with just one aspect of human life, but with the whole of it. The Church is, or ought to be, concerned not only with how men pray, but with how men make boots, and how men fight, make laws, fall in love, play football, and write sonnets.[89]

But it was Kelly earlier who had taken seriously the importance of ordinary human existence, that if God is not concerned with the ugly and the humdrum, there is no hope for most of us,[90] so that Kelham enjoyed the feeling that it could remain 'cheerful and worldly compared with Cowley'.[91] In the early 1960s, some young men who would not have to suffer the rigours of national service on its abolition were nevertheless to find themselves, at SSM's request, working in industry. Some would find themselves in Sheffield, under another of SSM's teachers, Roland Walls, influenced by Kelly, and already developing radical proposals for theological training.

Mirfield, by contrast, was academic, and drew many of its men from public schools. And though it also trained clergy, it had more in common perhaps with the Cowley Fathers in Oxford. But still its rigorous discipline, running in parallel with its theological teaching, was deliberately designed to 'rub off' on students, and Paul Ferris believed it to be a place where they had a 'knack, rarer among Anglicans than Roman Catholics, of combining the secular with the religious'.[92] Mirfield duly produced some radicalized clergy; its wartime padres, its outstanding pastor in South Africa, Trevor Huddleston, and indeed one of Britain's first worker-priests, Michael Gedge. It contained among its students a number with strong socialist sympathies, but it was never, like Kelham, a place where all that was ordinary seemed to be deliberately embraced in an 'earthy' theology.

Since the Church of England never developed communities for men in anything like sufficient strength compared with women's communities, there was a limit to what might rub off on ordinands. By the mid-1960s, however, a new Anglican foundation, The Community of the Glorious Ascension (in which some brothers and sisters worked in the community including industry, earning their own living), and the growing interest in the Roman Catholic order the Little Brothers of Jesus (and to some extent Taizé), both on the continent, began to suggest a rather different way of being a religious. Thus by the late 1950s and early 1960s, direct engagement with the world could be seen as a perfectly proper context for a contemplative life. However, there were few enough inclined to do this, though they can be seen as a part of that limited post-war attempt to engage directly with the world of work. What religious communities, whether Kelham or Mirfield, contributed to understandings of Christian ministry, as stories of worker-priests and other communities filtered into Britain, was a continuing emphasis on an incarnational priesthood as a sacred calling and a particular view of inner spirituality that came to be seen as something essentially adaptable to any worldly environment.

(iii) Popular parsons: Picture Post *and literature*

As Antony Russell has argued in *The Clerical Profession,* twentieth-century clergy could be characterized 'as the bearers of an old and respected cultural tradition, but one which has become increasingly irrelevant to contemporary social conditions'. The situation at the end of the Second World War may have been kinder. While the established church viewed itself and its clergy from a range of internal theological and ecclesiological perspectives, society might also reflect on the church, and in the person of its clergy in a benign, even flattering, way. Unlike the situation in France, where there was much anticlericalism, and a priest could be spat at in the street, many British had a 'soft spot' for the parson.

Thus the 'ideal' priest was sometimes the rural incumbent, and with that in mind, *Picture Post* in the autumn of 1948 presented a special feature on the Revd John Goodwin Wright, a typical country parson, shown on the cover lighting the oil lamps in one of his three country charges. In a double-page spread we see the caring cleric 'churching' a mum, visiting one of the local schools to teach 'scripture', scoring for a village game of bowls and, as the copy explained (though there was no picture), visiting a local army camp for the 'padre's hour'. The picture is of a man who is 'all things to all men', but it also reflects some of the cultural perspectives of the time, so that this 'typical' clergyman is shown in a sympathetic light, and perhaps as in need of a little sympathy himself.

> There are villages where (for clergy and families) second hand clothes are the rule, where holidays are impossible and where food is so plain that an invitation to supper is a highlight. Thoughtful people everywhere are beginning to feel uneasy about this situation.[93]

It would be more than a decade before such an 'uneasy' situation would be taken seriously, and more than a decade after that Ferris would argue that 'money worries many Anglican clergymen to the point of obsession'.[94]

By the mid-1950s *Picture Post's* depictions seemed wholly benign. In 1954, for example, we see clergy in a variety of rather different roles. In a feature on the present and future development of Birmingham (February 1954), two clergy, clad in cassocks, stand in the heart of the busy city about to be rebuilt, chatting to shoppers. Here, the reader is told, St Martin's in the Bullring, their church, is packed for Sunday evensong, and at least two to three hundred will attend a 'shoppers service' on Saturdays. Just a month before, however, the magazine raised one of its favourite topics when it asked whether the church was 'getting' anywhere, suggesting that the outlook was not good; this prompted one correspondent to claim that there were few clergy he'd met who were not convinced, for one reason or another, 'that a religious revival is taking place in their very own church'.[95] By the middle of the same year *Picture Post* featured Britain's two 'coalmining' priests, a rather extraordinary story of two parsons working beneath their parish. In the meantime, it demonstrated yet another example of the magazine's deliberate benevolence towards a calling it still believed was valued. At the end of 1954, for a Christmas feature the magazine went to the heart of the metropolis to show Fr Reindorp (later Bishop of Guildford) of St Stephen's, Rochester Row, where according to the story, there had been just eleven people when he arrived in 1946; now there were over a thousand attending services in his huge Victorian building. Surrounded by poor tenements, Reindorp is seen in his cassock towering over a little child; a priest among his people. And centre page, he lifts the host high at the altar as the community celebrates the birth of Christ. Yet even the priest himself appears to have had few illusions about the place in which he ministered. Reindorp believed he meant little or 'nothing' to the majority of his parishioners, in a place where 'the church is a minority movement (and) the parson is non-essential'. Ferris reiterated the popular view of the clergy who could be lampooned, as well as praised, and found little in Hoggart and Harrison's evaluations that could be described as positive.

If *Picture Post* remained at best benign, at worst ambivalent, like all magazines it liked a good story told, especially when dramatic pictures were possible; after all, that was what it was all about. Yet that country parson, living on the edge of poverty in 1948, was real enough, and if to some he may have been a rather remote figure, it was perhaps good to know that somehow or other he was still 'there', just as the city priest or the eccentric coalmining parson also remained somehow within reach, even if you were an ordinary reader still living 'contentedly without God'.

Another but limited picture of Christian ministry might be found in contemporary literature. Ferris believed Margery Allington's 'Canon Avril' in *The Tiger in the Smoke* (1952) was 'vague, happy, and devout' and it pleased many clergy. 'A grittier' parson was to be found in Pamela Hansford Johnson's *The Humbler Creation*, and she was subsequently invited to give talks to newly ordained clergy. While these writings reflected the Anglican position, a more generally considered assessment of Christian ministry in literature was presented in Horton Davies's book *A Mirror of the Ministry in Modern Novels* (1959).[96] Davies himself had been a Congregationalist minister, and although at the time of writing he was the Henry W. Putman Professor of Religion at Princeton in the United States, he had been educated in Edinburgh and had been a minister in London's 'flying bomb alley' during the war. The British scene may not have been so far from Davies' mind as he gave pictures of the way in which ministers of religion were depicted in contemporary writing. His assessments included Graham Green's *The Power and the Glory*, Georges Bernanos' *Diary of a Country Priest*, and others, including stories about north American revivalists in *Elmer Gantry*. Davies' conclusions were that on the whole it was Catholic clergy who ended up being depicted as those 'set apart', and whose lives presented greater 'dramatic possibilities' where the more exotic character of Catholic priesthood might stand in marked contrast to Protestant ministry. The latter could be seen as 'either a good Christian in the world or a bad Christian in the world but never a Christian withdrawn from the world'.[97] Davies does not of course mean that clergy who were somehow involved in the world and in the lives of men and women around them were dragged down, but that those who were wholly seduced by the *values* and 'blandishments' of the world could also become its victims. It might be true to say, as the adage went, and as *Picture Post* wanted to show, that clergy on the whole tried hard to be in the world, but not entirely of it.

(iv) Popular parsons: at 'the pictures'

If 1950s literature and the more popular press presented a benign picture, it was no less true in the cinema. Indeed, the post-war cinema continued to allude to religious belief, though the censor, according to Durgnat, 'maintained a policy of blandly and totally barring any serious critical portrayal of any Christian Church and its clerics'. Nevertheless, using a number of titles for illustration, Durgnat believes that 'though the film industry had a "contempt" for established Christianity that was unmistakable', yet it sought to raise problems of simple faith (illustrated by *Whistle Down the Wind*) in a complex and evil world.[98]

Those queueing for Britain's wartime cinema would have found clergy on the screen often submissive, a mouthpiece to be employed when morale was under threat. *Mrs Miniver* (1942) not only continued to depict the traditional English class structure of village life where the lady of the manor could affirm that 'we give the orders', but the proper place for the village parson as gentle, caring, ready with the necessary word of encouragement, so that at the end of the film and in a bombed-out church he could proclaim:

> This is a people's war. It is our war. We are the fighters. Fight it then. Fight it with all that is in us. And may God defend the right.[99]

Ealing's post-war comedy *Kind Hearts and Coronets* (1949), though set in an Edwardian era, is a comic attempt to depict a variety of characters, disposed of one by one as a future heir attempts to accelerate the arrival of an inherited fortune. In the process, clergy, especially a missionary bishop, are held up as harmlessly naive, and perhaps far from the world's concerns, including mammon. Another Ealing comedy, *The Titfield*

Thunderbolt (1952), depicts the local bishop not only among those determined to keep a branch line open, but as one of the few with the skills actually to operate the locomotive on the footplate – a skill not unknown among Anglican bishops.

Early 1960s productions in England found the clergy in generally humorous roles, and often in cameos. In *Crooks Anonymous* (Anglo-Amalgamated 1962), in which various crooks get rescued from a life of crime by 'guardian angels' and 'brothers', Stanley Baxter's (imitated) parson, perhaps a bishop, complete with top hat and gaiters is seen feeding the ducks in a London park. Baxter, in the film, as well as in real life, is an impersonator, and after some boys who have been playing football have knocked his top hat off, we suddenly find the otherwise jolly cleric in a foul temper. Clutching the ball with both hands, he responds to their polite request 'please can we have our ball back' by kicking it high – and with some skill – into the middle of the duckpond. We suspect he might not be a real bishop after all. But such was the picture of schoolmaster bishops, happy even perhaps in the company of schoolboys, that we cannot be sure until Baxter later appears in a number of other brilliant disguises. It may all seen rather overdone, but parsons, real and imaginary, were a source of fun.

There were other films in which clergy were depicted, but few actually centred on their character. One exception was *Heavens Above* (British Lion 1963), in which Peter Sellers is sentimentalized in a story of 'a northern parson with proletarian sympathies who is accidentally appointed to a shabby village where he converts the dowager aristocrat to works of absurd charity'.[100] Here once again was a story where the clergy were at worst naive, at best lovably eccentric, but the cinema simply reinforced pictures of clergy, Catholic or Protestant, with the perceptions of the time, that though their hearts were often in the world, delighting in its diversity, their minds might be elsewhere, their allegiance to orderliness and a 'higher authority', maintaining a detachment from its grimmer side. But it might also mean that, were a few of such clergy to enter the shop-floor, not as visitors but workers, there was every chance they might be made welcome.

4. Parishes and people: problems and solutions

(i) How do we engage with an industrial world?

How were the churches in Britain (or France for that matter) to minister to this industrialized society, where *Picture Post* believed there was a 'great gulf' between church and people, already supposed to be living 'contentedly without God in the world'?[101] Was Christian mission to be based in the parochial parish 'come to life', or was there to be a radically new approach which might take Christian mission right to the heart and heat of industrial life? A handful of figures within the establishment was seriously beginning to look at the nature of a society in which mechanization had not only contributed to two world wars but must now also contribute to peace. Discussion began, not least in the pages of some Christian periodicals like the *New Frontier* and the *Modern Churchman*. In the latter the rector of Christchurch, Bradford, was already acutely aware of Britain's special place in the context of industrial mission:

> . . . the church in this country has awakened to the problems which arise when she has to witness to her faith in the midst of industrial society. This is supremely an issue for the English Church, for although it is not our exclusive concern, we have a longer industrial history than any other country in the world, and our status as a nation depends almost entirely upon our industrial achievement.[102]

The focus, then, slowly shifted towards industrial society in which, as Leslie Hunter saw, individuals were shaped by their work; as much 'mass produced as mass producing'. And it is some studies which turn to Hunter of Sheffield – occasionally thought of as Temple's 'heir' – as one theorist who recognized the industrial setting, and especially in Sheffield a 'world' and its people as untouched by Christian churches. In 1939 Hunter, archdeacon of Newcastle, was elevated to the see of Sheffield, and would remain there till 1962. Aware of England as a new mission field, and concerned for working men and women, Hunter argued for recognition of industry as a major force in society, where the centre of power was often not in individual persons but in economic, social and organizational structures.

Among the discussions on industrial ministry in England and France generally is a suggestion that the French worker-priests and the missioners of Sheffield both worked within the context of a 'kingdom' theology that seemed to sit lightly to institutionalized churches. One Swedish commentator, Lillemore Erlander, who has made a comparative study of the French worker-priests and the Sheffield Industrial Mission, has identified 'Kingdom theology' as a single convergent focus in those radical missions which endeavoured to operate outside the traditional parochial structures.[103] In practice *and* theology, however, the two enterprises were more diffuse. Though they represented convergent attempts to challenge the territorial parish as the only focus for mission – and alarmed those parochially conservative – the theologies and practices remained different. In Britain, the eventual emergence of only a handful of worker-priests, as a parallel independent venture, and generally without the institution's full blessing, confirmed the overwhelming view that parochial ministry should remain the norm.

(ii) A proper place: the parish and its parson

If behind these attempts to experiment with a ministry to the workers of Britain and France was a recognition of the latter's estrangement from established religion, there would also emerge in both countries, and in their religious establishments, unease at the few unorthodox methods employed. In these institutional churches, it would be difficult to say that even *two* views existed on the church and its pastoral ministry. For on the one hand, in the course of the 1950s and 1960s, the accepted view of the church as community, as parochial, as 'the faithful' centred on an ecclesiastical parish remained virtually everywhere the normal expression of the church's mission and ministry. On the other hand (and as yet barely even a minority view), there began to emerge a radically different ecclesiology that suggested the church might emerge outside the parish structure altogether. Yet in 1950, when correspondence in *The Times* from a priest advocated a more radical approach to mission by a company of priests 'working in the professions, industry and trade', the heated debate that followed attempted to 'restate the basis of the territorial (parochial) system'[104] and the Revd Michael Brook, Industrial Chaplain in the Manchester diocese, in defining the work of an industrial chaplain, was emphatic:

> . . . he must not go into industry to recruit for the churches. He must have no truck with all the various activities which go under the heading of 'evangelism'. The proper place for recruiting for the church is in

the parishes and localities. There is no justification whatever for taking up men's time in the factories.[105]

Emphasis on the place of the territorial parish and ministry in Britain was constantly reiterated. Garbett argued that 'the work and influence of the Church of England depend more than anything else upon the character and efficiency of its parochial clergy . . . for in every parish they are the official leaders in religion', reminding everyone that the true pastor '. . . by his institution is given the spiritual care of all the people who reside within the geographical area of his parish'.[106] By 1951, Wand could be even more explicit about an authority given:

> One part of that universal Church is the Church of England which is the divinely authorized organization of Christ in this land. Inasmuch as the country is divided into different areas, in each of which an official representative of the church is placed, it should never be necessary for any enquirer to feel himself far from the guidance that he needs.[107]

So the parson was 'the channel by which the authorized grace of the Church and its authoritative teaching are made available to us'.[108] Some of the outworking of this would be marked by Joost de Blank in *The Parish in Action* (1954), Southcott's *The Parish Comes Alive* just two years later, where the writer saw Christianity beginning in the home, and the emerging accounts of Alan Ecclestone's 'parish meetings' in Darnell, Sheffield. All this had been highlighted earlier by Michonneau's *Revolution in a City Parish,* already known and applauded in Britain since its first publication in 1949.

Before some of the features of this concentration on the territorial parish are examined more closely, at least a brief mention deserves to be made of one enterprise which came to the attention of members of the Church Assembly, and which appeared at first sight as original. The Christian Commando Campaigns, as they were known, served as a reminder that even some 'odd' enterprises, apparently deliberately outgoing, were nevertheless ultimately aimed at filling the pews of established denominations. The Campaigns can be traced back to the Liverpool Methodist Conference of 1939 when a 'Forward Movement' had begun. Although almost immediately halted by the onset of war, they would get under way again in the war years as well as continue after the conflict, when *The Times* drew attention to the church's interest in the efforts.[109]

Consisting of groups of usually (though by no means always) interdenominational evangelicals, the 'Christian Commandos', using a combination of talks, Brains Trusts and general conversation, visited work sites, factories and entertainment centres such as dance halls, usually with the blessing of management, to set out the claims of the Christian faith.

> Commandos are usually called upon to capture a bridgehead . . . their work is temporary in its nature and limited in its scope. Its success is dependent upon speedy and sufficient supplies for the armies. If they are not forthcoming – then Arnhem![110]

Before a visit was set up Christians already on the 'shop-floor' were asked to identify themselves – even wear a badge – 'not easy in a modern factory, but a definite act of witness'. It is not clear how many were brave enough to do so. A general description of the visits, usually by clergy, records what was often a cool response: 'Your name is mud here' came from one shop steward, though the report continued: 'in less than an hour six hundred men were giving an emphatic request for another visit.' At a lonely bomber station the visitors were asked if all this was a 'stunt' to fill empty churches – no answer was recorded but presumably it was Yes. Discussing questions from the shop floor, the contributors to the 1945 book admitted a general respect for the Christian faith, but little love for the churches.

> The very distinction men draw between Christ and the Church is also full of encouragement. It shows that men realize what Christ stands for and how far short of that his church has fallen . . . this emphatic distinction they are always making between Christ and the church shows that they have not entirely abandoned Christ.[111]

But the CCC's, as they were known, made little impact (though it is difficult to know how that might have been judged) and were treated, at least by *Picture Post*, as little more than a well-meant but amusing venture. Though Lord Ingman is quoted in one copy of the magazine as saying that the drift from the churches 'must be stemmed' or there would be a 'pagan cataclysm that would send this country back to the dark ages', *Picture Post* reported, with tongue in cheek, on the 'invasion' of pubs, a 'strike' in the streets, 'raids' on dance halls and a commando 'fight' or 'love action with film stars'. And here, perhaps, *Picture Post* got nearer the truth of shop-floor visits when its reporter described a commando visit to a film studio where one 'well known and ill mannered actress made no attempt to hide her giggles and yawns while a long suffering commando did his hasty best'.[112]

Initially, where the territorial parish was the focus for most missions, some thinking on the revitalization of its life had come from Michonneau in Paris. His was a cry to do away with hypocrisy in Christian life and practice, and let the parish church live again on the strength of its laity and their sincerity. Although the Abbé commended the work of one of the first worker-priests, Father Loew in Marseilles, who had begun in his parish by purchasing an old pair of overalls and going to work in the docks, he still saw such action as 'extreme'. For Michonneau the parish could undertake its mission only if church organizations were transformed and the liturgy itself was harnessed to the upbuilding of parochial life and the real sense of corporate identity for all within its boundaries, especially those who knew nothing of religion. For a parish had, above all, 'official' recognition as the instrument of missionary work in a particular area:

> . . . the parish is like a mother cell, the source of all apostolic work. In the future – supposing the task of conquest is over and won – it is to the parish that all new cells must be joined in a common life.[113]

Joost de Blank in *The Parish in Action* (1954) also believed that the territorial parish in England had the primary responsibility for going outside 'to the countless thousands who had no first-hand experience of the Christian faith'. De Blank believed that the church was there so that God, through individuals, might also be at work in the world. He can be read as advocating what Southcott later put into practice: an active parish alive to the needs of the neighbourhood, not so much because God was somehow already there in the community at large, but certainly because he was present in the lives of faithful witnesses. One 'faithful priest' working in the 1950s East End was Father 'Joe' Williamson. The scourge of local authorities, and sometimes an embarrassment to the church's hierarchy (especially when he criticized the Church of England's bishops in a St Paul's sermon), he sought to be a faithful pastor and friend to 'down and outs', prostitutes and others who had fallen on hard times. Williamson had been born and bred in the East End, and his tirades, especially against bad housing, made him a legend – some suggested a self-made legend – in his own time.[114]

In the preface to Southcott's book *The Parish Comes Alive,* the Bishop of Ripon commended this different approach to mission, and compared the author's efforts with those of industrial missioners and 'priest workmen'. Southcott meanwhile declared an obvious interest in Michonneau's work in Paris, and threw himself body and soul into an enormous and exhausting project for the territory under his care.

His argument, like that of Michonneau before him, was that liturgy must stand at the heart of parish life, for 'we see the church most characteristically herself when she meets to break bread'. His parish eucharist, with innovations like lay participation, was mirrored in house celebrations across the parish where groups met in more simple surroundings. Some of these took place very early in the morning; that is, at the same time as a celebration might have taken place in church, with Roland Walls remembering stories of some poor husband having an early morning shave in the kitchen and wondering what on earth was going on in *his* house when *he* was trying to get ready for work.

Southcott's training of the congregation was an attempt to sharpen a faith that must become a reality in the work place, and not exclusively 'inside the church'; that was always a danger. It was in the work place that people must also be strengthened by mutual encouragement. He also believed that those outside or even on the edge of parish life should not be encouraged to 'come to church' until they were ready to understand its beliefs and practices. He may never have appreciated the problems of understanding a liturgy which, to some, would for ever remain foreign.

His passion for the home, hearth and work place at the heart of the Christian's life – when Christians must reckon with the importance of what was happening 'in the world' – was not always easy to 'make connections with' even in the context of a 'relevant liturgy'. Kenneth Mason, then a student at Wells Theological College, visited Halton for a conference and (because of a twisted ankle) watched the communion on an occasion when it was televised. He remembers Southcott's anxiety to 'bring them all in!' but, he continues, Southcott might just as easily have added 'chuck 'em all out'. 'For the final "shot" after dismissal' (which Mason assumed had been deliberately organized) '. . . the people poured out of the church – there was no hanging about'. 'Southcott clearly knew what he was doing,' added Mason, 'but his people might have been less clear-minded.'[115]

In Sheffield, and close by the Industrial Mission, Alan Ecclestone, who had been invited by Leslie Hunter to Darnell, in 1942, was critical of the institution's approach, and though he was dedicated to the parish ministry, was nevertheless determined to reform it. His particular contribution was the introduction of the 'parish meeting', a means of engaging his people with what really mattered in everyone's lives:

> ... week by week for nearly fourteen hundred meetings the parish in Sheffield sought to understand the implications of Christian discipleship in an industrial city and in a changing world ... (Ecclestone) told the parish meeting they were free to choose the night of the meeting, but that after that, they would continue to meet, and there would be no ending, no matter how small the numbers.[116]

Because '... the lack of connection between the world of daily life and the church meant that the great beauty of so many of the buildings ... served only to reinforce a sense of nostalgia ... where the need was rather to live in a more imaginative way in the outside world', Ecclestone's parish meeting brought all human issues to the fore and gave parochial life new meaning. It was, however, quite insufficient for his local colleague, Ted Wickham, whose own vision would prove very different from Alan's, so that 'there were suspicions, doubts, hesitancies on both sides ...'[117]

(iii) A frontier ministry: the council-house estate

If much post-war mission and renewal was to begin in the parishes as *Parish and People* believed, so that '... the parish as the total life of the pilgrim People of God in the locality is one which needs no elaboration among readers of this periodical',[118] this meant also that *new* parishes must therefore be established and extended in some of Britain's more isolating settings: the burgeoning post-war housing estates. These stretched from one end of the country to the other, and through Church Assembly, reports and papers like *The Times*, came to the public's notice.[119] These included, among the hundreds, Sheffield Manor, started before the war, Oxford's Blackbird Leys, and Scotland's Mid-Craigie estate in Dundee, where a pre-war 1930s scheme would be extended along the eastern edge of the city. An examination of some of the issues relating to urban housing estates was made by Ronald Frankenberg in his *Communities in Britain* (1966),[120] where he argued for two important features which affected life in them. First, they could be distanced from older communities; tenants moved out of the established areas and felt the disruption, while those on the edge of the new estates but in older sometimes private developments might resent incoming tenants. In addition, and with reference back to the pre-war estates, Frankenberg pointed out the age-old problem of housing developments built before – and sometimes long before – any amenities were provided. 'Separated from work and from play, from beer and from books, paved with good intentions, the social life of the housing estates seems as far as it is possible to get from the utopian dream of a village fellowship made urbane by town civilization.'[121] If this represented an accurate picture at the beginning of the 1960s it only served to demonstrate that in terms of social planning, little had been learnt.

In the 1950s and early 1960s this was another 'frontier' ministry, so that in Lloyd's words, 'the Christianity of England began to be decided in the new towns like Stevenage, or the housing estates which were already growing up on the fringes of all the cities where young married couples of the country with broods of children were being concentrated'. 'There if anywhere,' continued Lloyd, 'was the youth of the land living in great concentrations of immaturity with every box-like house entered by the family on the day the last window was filled with glass.'[122] Indeed, in the film version of *Saturday Night and Sunday Morning* (1958), Arthur Seaton's cynicism over the industrial world of Nottingham in which he sweats in a factory '. . . and nothing for it but money to drag you back there every Monday morning' is set in a scene near the end of the film, just above a bright new housing estate under construction, where, by implication, Arthur (Albert Finney) and his girlfriend Doreen (Shirley Anne Field), will find a home. As for ministry in these new towns or estates, 'the romance was plain' says Lloyd. 'Under his (a young clergyman's) hand he had the youth of England . . . the church could offer no man a job of greater importance, or even quite the same urgency, even if,' as Lloyd continues, '. . . like all other pioneers, he must be able to stand up to loneliness, for loneliness was all around him.' But even in 1957 Wickham was quite unromantic when he discussed the difficulties of ministering in the 'huge new estates and downtown wastes', and the Revd Colin Rushbridge, discussing new towns in the late 1960s, had to admit what many had known for years:

> . . . the church buildings are usually inadequate and are looked upon as the 'first stage', but ministers know from experience that all over the country there are 'temporary' buildings and halls that 'for the time being' are used for worship that have been like this for generations![123]

There were attempts at missions on new estates, like that by C. Morrison and Trevor Beeson in Stockton-on-Tees in the early 1960s. Although attendance at weekly meetings 'never fell below 200' and there was no 'revolution in parish policy', so that it continued to be based on offering 'Public Baptism, Parish Communion, parish meeting, House Church, etc.', the effects of the efforts could only be measured 'over a long period', though the authors of the effort believed there were 'already signs of a new awareness of what the twentieth-century church is trying to be and do and of a greater sense of obligation to share in the apostolic mission in which the church is now engaged'.[124]

But the problem with some of these 'heroic ministries', as some wanted to entitle them, was that the ministers themselves ended up being 'unsung heroes'; few people ever heard of them as they laboured, argues Simon Phipps, 'under guilt'. The Revd Rupert Mantle, chased by Teddy Boys past the local factories in Dundee's Mid-Craigie estate to shouts of 'Hi – father – how's mother!', or the priest reporting in *Parish and People* that he'd set up in an estate's butcher's shop because it 'was the only place that would have me' remained tragically isolated, even shunned by fellow clergy in town and shire.[125] Lloyd acknowledges these difficulties and says that ultimately 'the impact of the church upon the people in the myriads of council houses or flats built since the war is tragically less than might have been hoped'.[126]

(iv) Kingdom theology – new theological groundwork

An essential prerequisite for any radical mission had to be an underlying theology – even when parish ministry was still centre stage. F. D. Maurice has already been noted for his *Kingdom of Christ* and his insistence on 'Christ in every man', which more than alluded to a universalism. More than a century later, a theological ally for those who wanted to command mission in industrial areas, factory or housing estates, and even from the parish base, might have been found in John A. T. Robinson. In some of his early writings on 'kingdom theology', though, moving as he does in a different direction, he makes no reference to Maurice's work. Robinson visited Southcott in Halton, and praised his efforts. But direct references to some kind of 'engagement theology' are less easy to find. Anglican theology is sometimes done (and with justification) 'on the hoof', with 'theory following practice', and this may well be the case here where some radical theology, especially that on 'the Kingdom', does not appear so explicitly until the early 1960s and later.[127] Yet some of the more interesting things were being said by Robinson in the late 1940s and early 1950s, though not always heard or understood.

One of the best examples was his address to students at Wells Theological College as early as 1949 while chaplain there, and reprinted in 1950 and again a decade later. Robinson commends the idea of house churches, not as ways of getting people into larger more central parish churches, but in themselves as one way of 'being the church in the world'. A decade later he had moved further: '. . . the Christian society, the church, is the instrument of *the Kingdom* (Robinson's emphasis). And it is vital to keep this relationship clear. For the perennial temptation of the Church is to equate itself with the Kingdom of God on earth, and so regard itself as the only agent of God in this world.'[128] By 1959 Robinson was vigorously attacking the notion of 'two worlds' – that is, the world of 'the church' and the 'world outside'. '. . . it is no accident that the Bible never speaks of this as a distinction between two worlds. There is one world, God's world' and he goes on to contest the casual acceptance of 'other worldliness' where '. . . Jesus' words to Pilate, that "My kingship does not have its origins in this world order" are interpreted to mean "My Kingdom has nothing to do with this world".' But Robinson rarely endeared himself to everyone, and much later Edward Norman attacked him (1980), arguing that Robinson 'sought to reinterpret Christianity to show that its "other worldly" dimension was not really a part of its essential nature'.[129] Robinson was also to challenge the 1950s great rallying cry 'Let the church *be* the Church' which he believed perilous if the church were to turn in on itself and forget 'that it exists always and only as the instrument of the Kingdom'.[130]

Little did Robinson or anyone else know it, but these words would prove as prophetic as they would later be tragic. John de Satge, commending the *Mission de France,* believed that it was the present age which had brought about such theological thinking and that Robinson's work *On Being the Church in the World* 'would serve equally well as a summary of the French ideas of mission'.[131]

Before the decade was out, Robinson's themes would be pushed further, not only in his own *Honest to God* (1963), which many on the frontiers of ministry and theology, including early worker-priests, commended, but in the work of other theologians, which for the first time (and in a sense due to Robinson) were presented to the reading public.[132] There was little doubt: radicalized theology, from New Testament studies to systematic theology – some of it born from the horrors of the Second World War – was becoming a powerful ally to radical ministry including British worker-priests, evangelical and catholic. Nevertheless, others would remain anxious about this threat to orthodoxy. E. L. Mascall, in the May 1964 edition of *Theology*, would warn readers of Van Buren's 'Godless defeatism', and the 1968 Lambeth Conference warned of a world where 'the familiar teaching through which ordinary Christians learn their faith is being re-examined and in part rejected by some theologians'.[133]

But the importance here lies in some of the theological precedents being developed by individuals like Robinson in his reading of the New Testament, the previous work of Dom Gregory Dix in his liturgical work[134] or Michonneau in his parochial endeavours. Southcott, after all, saw these as support for his own parochial innovations. It might now be argued that some of the lines of theory and practice were beginning to converge. Excitement was in the air, and for the first time in a long while there were possibilities of radical change in ministry and mission; but the practical outworking would prove to be different. In a Britain now faced with rebuilding after the devastation of war, and in which a multitude of political, social and cultural changes were under way, there would emerge, as in France, a quite different view that would utterly shatter the received notion that the territorial parish was the *only* base for ministry and mission.

II

The Industrial Work-Site: A Focus for Radical Ministry

'The significance of the Bishop of Sheffield's Mission in our own country and of the *prêtres ouvriers* in France . . . is comparable to any great pioneering movement in Christian history, and those who undertake it must not be surprised if the whole of the church does not share their vision and concern.'

(T. L. G. Tyler, Rector of Christ Church Bradford, Manchester, in the *Modern Churchman*, September, 1954)

'I do not see how these parishes, as they stand, can ever gather in the unbelieving masses'

(Henri Perrin, French worker-priest, talking about the Michonneau kind of parish, 22 June 1946)

'Tha'll never be a f***ing vicar thee!'

(Sheffield steel worker to an ordinand gaining experience on the shop floor, 1966)

1. Location and strategy in mission: the industrial work-site – France and Britain

In Britain, where a complex range of influences had been brought to bear on the shaping of Anglican and even free-church ministry, it gradually became apparent to some that, given the broad range of ministries that already existed, the territorial parish might not, after all, be the only starting point for radical ministry. Varieties of ministry were already evident in, for example, schools, colleges, hospitals and the armed forces. But these were hardly radical; rather, they reflected the institution's traditional ministries elsewhere; they were almost a kind of 'holding ministry' while individual Christians were 'away' from their parishes. By February 1944, however, when the outcome of the war was by no means certain, the Revd Ted Wickham, then curate of Swynnerton and

Chaplain of the Royal Ordnance Factory No 5, was appointed by the Duke of Norfolk to be Chaplain and convenor of Shrewsbury Hospital. Two months later, Leslie Hunter, Bishop of Sheffield, appointed Wickham as an industrial chaplain in the diocese. A remarkable story of extra-parochial ministry and mission was about to unfold.

Meanwhile across the channel in northern France, events had begun which throughout the same decade would run in parallel to the enterprises in post-war industrial Sheffield. The problems in France were certainly not identical, and the contexts proved different, yet Wickham believed there to be 'real similarities'. In France there was a growing awareness, from the late nineteenth century to the early twentieth, of an 'alienation' of the working-class, far deeper than that ever experienced in Britain, that had been cause for concern in the French Church. In October 1942 a seminary for the Mission de France was established at Lisieux, where two young Christian workers' chaplains, Henri Godin and Yvan Daniel, embarked on an ambitious project which culminated in their publication, *France, Pays de Mission?*. Here, Grundy acknowledges that, even in translation, 'Godin's informed and forceful writing reads attractively and strongly and makes the writings of William Temple look like the speculations of an amateur, which in this league they were'.[135] The results of these and other efforts followed in 1943–44, when priests, with the blessing of the church, set out to join deported Frenchmen in the munitions factories of the Third Reich. The Nazis had refused the church the right to send chaplains; nevertheless, some priests went as workers. Perhaps the most celebrated was Henri Perrin, and the outline that follows highlights his singular contribution to theology and action. His autobiograpgical material became one of the only texts available to the English reader.

2. Non-parochial ministry in industrial France

(i) France and the prêtres ouvriers*: origins*

The origins of the *prêtres ouvriers* (worker-priests) movement in France have been documented and their place in the broader history of non-stipendiary ministries in Britain has been noted in recent studies.[136] Publications outlining the work of the movement often trace the beginnings back to the Abbé Godin's *France, Pays de Mission?*.[137] But a much broader background is given in Oscar Arnal's *Priests in Working Class*

Blue (1986), where the author argues that it was not simply some 'national crisis' alone which could have produced the worker-priests, but a range of ideas and endeavours 'rooted in a more distant past', since there was in France a concern for an urban and rural proletariat distanced from the church since the time of the Revolution.

But an urban proletariat already hostile to French Catholicism may have stood less chance of being met by liberal mission when Pope Pius IX's *Syllabus* of 1864 condemned liberal and modernist trends in the church, increasing, Siefer believed, anti-clericalism. The definition of papal infallibility six years later brought further anxiety in France, and not least from Archbishop Darboy of Paris, who saw it as 'inopportune'.[138] But there also appeared the following year what Siefer calls a 'new phenomenon':[139] 'social Catholicism', with the workers' study circles *Oeuvre de Cercles* founded by Counts de Mun and de la Tour du Pin in the Montparnasse quarter of Paris. Arnal described his efforts as the necessary groundwork for French social Catholicism and its subsequent evolution in more 'radical directions'. But efforts like these failed to win the support of workers, and the Abbé Henri de Torville, following Frédéric Le Play's *La Réforme sociale en France* and *Les ouvriers européens,* argued that the workers themselves should be given the opportunity to run the circles. De Mun had given his support to a bill that allowed for the establishment and recognition of trade unions which had previously been illegal, and this was vigorously challenged by Catholic conservatives. But it was the Papal Nuncio in Paris, Cardinal Ferrata, who recognized that only radical moves could begin to meet the proletarian anti-clericalism of France: 'One must go to these masses, root out their anti-religious prejudices, and let the beneficial influence of religion work on the lower classes of the population.'[140] The papal encyclical *Rerum Novarum* of 1891 called on the church in the face of conservative protest to recognize its need for mission and co-operation with the Republic, and Archbishop Ireland of St Louis (USA) the following year would urge French students: ' become one with the people yourselves'.[141]

The earlier founding of the Association Catholique de la Jeunesse Française (ACJF, 1886) and the first Catholic trade unions prepared the ground for proletarian evangelization, as did priests like Fr Charles Calippe who, in a serial novel published in the new *La Démocratié Chrétienne* (1902–1903), pictured a priestly worker, and Paul Naudet, a 'priest-editor' of a Breton Christian newspaper, who advocated a worker-priest ministry. Arnal also highlights the work of Marc Sangnier, founder of the militant organization Le Sillon (the Furrow) who advocated that workers should abandon the idea of separate Catholic trade unions and join in support of the Confédération Général du Travail (CGT), which would later be Communist-led, and which worker-priests, indeed, would eventually support. Thus

> ... by the dawn of the twentieth century, some catholic reformers were flirting with the idea of a priesthood which would identify fully with the working-class via manual labour.[142]

But while questions began to take shape about mission to the working people, other forces, monarchist and anti-republican, demonstrating the strong conservative elements in French Catholicism, were already at work shaping a reaction. Action Française, which began in 1899 'with the active goodwill of many Catholics', was a movement which '... regarded anti-clericalism as one of the proofs that France was ruled by foreigners, Jews, Protestants and Freemasons, (and) made it an energetic champion of the church'.[143] But even though the extremes of Action Française were met and condemned by Pope Pius XI, who ordered Catholics to leave it, it remained an example of that underlying suspicion of anything left-wing – the kind of suspicion that would eventually feed reaction against worker priests.

Four years after the First World War, in which many clergy and seminarians had been conscripted into the trenches, and Pius XI's encyclical *Ubi Arcano Dei* had challenged the church's ghetto mentality, further encouragement for 'Catholic action' came from Father Joseph (later Cardinal) Cardijn, who in 1926 founded the Jeunesse Ouvrière Chrétienne (Young Christian Workers, JOC), known as 'Jocists', beginning in Brussels but spreading to Paris only a year later, and shortly afterwards to the whole country. Despite the enthusiasm to 'penetrate' the workers' milieu it was, Siefer argues, becoming clear 'that there was no sense in beginning a mission among the proletariat as long as there was no missionary community behind it'. The ordinary parish was not and could never be that, [144] though Cardinal Verdier, between the wars (1920 – 1940), who had a special care for working-class families, erected churches and chapels in working-class Paris.[145]

Before the onset of the Second World War, certain factors were in place which would allow for a convergence of ideas on mission and ministry in some parts of industrial France. Quite apart from the social and theological theories of clergy and laity, there were those who had simply entered the world of workers: by 1939 Père Rutten had been working in a Belgium coal mine for several years and the Abbé Pesle in the Rhineland (he would later be sent to and released from Dachau); there was also the 'spiritual director' in the Resistance, the Abbé Bousquet.[146] At a formal level, in 1941 the French bishops and cardinals had founded the Mission de France seminary at Lisieux which would 'overlap' with the worker-priests and prepare the way for a more direct mission among the urban proletariat. Perhaps of particular importance was the account of Père Loew, the Dominican in Marseilles dockland who in 1941 went to work in the docks of his parish. 'I concluded it was no good wasting time on paper theories: the thing to do was to buy an overall on the old clothes market, get a job like everyone else, and then at the end of a day's work go off and live with the dregs of the population – the dockers on the ports.'[147]

(ii) A challenge to parochial mission: the Abbé Godin

The broad chorus raised in support of proletarian mission found a particular voice in the 1943 publication *France, Pays de Mission?* (1943) by two Jocist chaplains, Yvan Daniel and Henri Godin. Born into a poor family in the Jura foothills, Godin felt a particular calling to the working-class. Formerly a religious of the Fils de la Charité, he had later joined the Jocists. In their joint publication, the authors presented the reader with a France where in some areas Christianity still appeared to be practised and in others the faith was restricted to small groups, while yet others could only be described as pagan. In the latter, the tragedy was that '. . . from a Christian viewpoint nothing is left. There are vast rents in the map of France indicating entire lost areas . . .' The authors were at pains to highlight the differences between a rural proletariat and the urban, where the former 'becomes a pagan more slowly' and where 'the remains of old religious tradition always mean something for him, something deep, something usually solid' and the townsman for whom these things are 'almost without significance . . . merely conventional gestures'. 'Here we find nothing, sheer emptiness . . . with civilization superimposed . . .'[148]

France, seen by many as secular and with only pockets of Catholicism, seemed to suggest the existence of two worlds: on the one hand the workaday world, and on the other the one in which the institutional church drew aside and where believers 'have created for themselves Christian communities centred on their churches'.[149] This rather simple but explicit criticism, which might have shaken any Christian denomination in Europe at the time, would, within a decade, be echoed in Britain by Wickham, Robinson and one or two British worker-priests. It now became a kind of rallying cry for a more radical approach to urban mission that might enter this world instead of living 'apart', for, 'shut up upon itself, the great concern of the Christian community is to preserve its immunity and safeguard its existence'. Though the parish had been 'doing its best' it 'hardly touches the pagan world'. '[Christianity] must somehow get into the pagan world and bring the light of Christ there. Christians must become the leaven in that world.'[150] Here is no sophisticated theology 'of the kingdom', no certain acknowledgment of the presence of aspects or indices of a kingdom that must be identified; simply a raw determination to 'be there' because it had to be. Godin acknowledges the hard world of proletarian life in the 'blocks' (tenement dwellings) where drunks beat their wives; the family scenes, yelling and 'promiscuity in the courtyards' are hardly the kind of environment for a young Christian couple to start their life. He then slowly approaches the notion of a kingdom (though he never actually uses the term), somehow already present in his theological question 'Has Christ abandoned these young folk because they are caught up in the doubtful institutions of this era?' So Catholics must enter this world. Yet that, he recognized, will be far from easy: 'only very few,' he solemnly cautions, 'are called to this vocation,' for 'the parish and the proletarian worlds are not merely separate, they are also utterly different'.[151]

Godin's solution was that the gospel must be brought among these new pagans and that the good news must find its incarnation 'in their human actuality'. Missionaries must make departures for a mission field 'which offers no hope of return'. It would also mean entirely new methods in the proclamation of the gospel. And in a rather telling passage, he warns of the dangers of traditional parochial ministry, for,

> Both of us [Godin and Daniel] have experience of the parochial ministry: it gets hold of a man body and soul, it devours him, it possesses him to the point where he simply cannot think of anything else. We know all about it and we are anxious to set down in this book how great are the devotion and self-sacrifice called for by this ministry.[152]

The authors acknowledge the limitations of parish ministry. 'We do not blame it for failing to do what it could not possibly have accomplished.' Yet the good efforts of parishes and parish action, especially Catholic Action, were not to be underestimated. But there must be adaptation, and in a further challenge to the minutiae of parochial 'management', he concluded: 'surely the bishop did not ordain (priests) for such occupations . . .' Mgr Ancel, the coadjutor Bishop of Lyons, had argued that '. . . in certain circumstances it calls for a heroic faith to remain a Christian . . . Hence one may say that a Christian life can be impossible. *For many workers it is not possible to live a Christian life*' (his italics).[153]

What then was to be done? Godin advocates a Christian nucleus within human communities. 'In every mass of dough we must insert the leaven.' By all means multiply parishes, but he adds, in exasperation, 'this remains an integral problem of Catholicism; a mission is something that reaches out beyond', and he concludes:

> If we do not set missions on foot for our proletarians who lack religion and culture, others will do it. Soon they will have a culture and religion too. Please God that religion may not be unlike the religion of Christ.[154]

That the vision contained in *France, Pays de Mission?* was not to die was due largely to the Archbishop of Paris, Cardinal Emmanuel Suhard. This unlikely advocate, who as Arnal admits had welcomed Pétain's regime and had been accused of collaboration with the Germans, now sought to establish recognition for an urban proletarian mission. For a year following 1943 he strove with Daniel, Chenu, the Abbé Michonneau and others to outline such work, meeting first at Combes-la-Ville near Paris, then at Lisieux 'to create a concrete mission to the working class of the Parisian basin'.[155]

The premature and tragic death of Godin – due to fumes from a faulty stove – did not prevent the enterprise from continuing. Theological and ministerial groundwork had been laid, and Daniel's and Godin's ideas would remain a pivotal point for those who sought to uphold and extend radical urban mission in the following fifteen years. But for movements to develop there needs to be a catalyst if the theory is not to remain just that, and it was the deportation of Frenchmen to work in the Third Reich's munitions factories during the later part of the Second World War that led to priests being sent to Germany 'disguised' as workers. When the occupying powers refused to allow chaplains to go with workers, the Assembly of Cardinals and Archbishops allowed some twenty-five priests (out of an offer of over two hundred) to be taken on in secret. In time, many would be discovered, arrested by the Gestapo, and several would die in concentration camps. Although some clergy had already been arrested and forced to work for the Germans, it was this sudden and unexpected increase in forced deportations, including JOC members, that demanded radical and imaginative action.

(iii) Non-parochial mission: Henri Perrin – priest-worker in Germany

One of the most celebrated of the new 'disguised' workers was Fr Henri Perrin, whose diary *Priest-Worker in Germany*,[156] published immediately after the war, gives an account of his time spent as a deported worker. Because of its detail, and the fact it was published in Britain as early as 1947, the diary (followed in 1964 by a published account of his life as a worker-priest in France) deserves attention. This publication was one of the few sources English readers had to explain what was happening abroad, and the two publications help the reader to understand the theology and practice of French worker-priests in general.

He begins by relating his inner questioning on whether or not he should go to Germany as an official chaplain ('if such a thing exists') or as a volunteer workman. Although the English publishers Sheed and Ward maintained that this volume was 'not a book of Gestapo horrors', it nevertheless has its own underlying sense of dread. Perrin joined a group of apprentices in metallurgy, and enrolled at the offices at the Rue de Vaugirard with the 'painful impression that everyone was pointing at us as "those volunteers"'. From the Gare de l'Est on 16 August 1943, Perrin set off for Germany, arriving in Leipzig from where he would make a daily journey to Mockau. There, at a Junkers factory, and together with his fellow workers, he was enrolled.

Like some other deportees from France, Perrin was allowed reasonably comfortable surroundings, and was able to visit youth clubs, French and other churches, where occasionally he was provided with the opportunity to say mass. Working with other Catholics, he details a life in which, alongside Jocists, Rover Scouts, and a group d'Amitié,[157] he saw the importance of organized laity, and felt the need for constant fellowship and prayer, as he formed a particular friendship with a layman, Jacques. Yet life for Perrin and the others could sometimes be unpleasant, and though he had for the moment chosen this life, he was acutely aware that the others had not; 'we were simply deported like cattle, like slaves', he admits in a dark moment; though it would become darker still.

Late in 1943 Perrin's diary describes how he was taken into custody on suspicion of political activities. His visits out to a variety of groups made the authorities suspicious. Fortunately his locker at his accommodation was cleared just in time by Jacques, and incriminating evidence remained undiscovered. But in custody, facing frightening air-raids and cramped conditions, Perrin had to prepare for interrogation where he would eventually admit to being a priest. But he was 'grilled' not on that but on his lack of association with National Socialism and his failure to join the French Fascists. Perrin argued passionately that he had come to Germany simply as a worker, and only then with the permission of his superiors.

After a number of rather frightening delays,[158] and five months of imprisonment, he was liberated, and following a farewell to friends was soon on a train crossing the border into France 'which I feared never to see again'. All Perrin's experience was now brought to bear on a single resolution: that he must minister to the masses with whom he had spent the last year – much of it imprisoned with others. For a priest should realize, he commented, 'that our ceremonies have ceased to mean anything to these people . . .' 'For several years now a stream of priests have come along, who, with the full agreement of their bishops, wish to live as workmen in workmen's conditions, to continue the Incarnation of Christ in the very centre of human dough.'[159] With the end of the war one year away, Perrin resolved to be among them.

(iv) The worker-priests: wartime developments

In France itself, Mgr Rodhain, who had responsibility as a chaplain organizer for prisoners of war, had also found himself organizing the priests ready to serve in Germany. There were others like Fr Hadrien Bousquet, *Hors de Barbelés* (1945), a Dominican, Père Jean Doyen, and a secular priest, Joseph Gélin, who recorded their lives apart from Perrin. Some of these were singled out by Siefer, who also mentions Père Victor Dillard, a Jesuit discovered by the Gestapo who died in Dachau only five months before the war ended. In his posthumously published memoirs, *Suprêmes Témoignages* (1946), Dillard had found 'that there was an international class consciousness among these proletarians'. It was these discoveries which led him to believe that Christ's incarnation as a worker centuries before was a necessary part of God's plan.[160]Arnal reminds the reader that among those who embarked on this mission the majority were young men in their twenties, but a mixture: there were some from peasant surroundings, others from a urban proletarian background, others, though a smaller number, from higher sections of French society.

In July 1943 and within months of these clandestine activities beginning, moves were already under way for the establishment of a Mission de Paris, where a team of priests, relieved of all regular duties, would devote themselves to evangelizing the common people, manual and clerical workers of Paris. With the Liberation of Paris in 1944 came a new desire for the church to be 'neither bastion nor a ghetto'.[161] But before the year was out, the Holy See, alarmed by anonymous reports from French Catholics hostile to such experimental ministry, was already expressing misgivings. With worker-priests being installed in a number of peacetime work destinations, the Mission de Paris expressed its radical mission afresh 'to make the Church spring from the proletarian masses . . . it seemed clear that the priesthood would have to find new forms, the precise shape of which the future would determine'.[162] Now, heading for Paris, was Henri Perrin himself, determined to be a part of that future.

(v) Non-parochial ministry: Henri Perrin – priest-worker in Paris

In 1944, following his release, and just a few days before the allied armies landed on the Normandy beaches, Perrin went to stay at a Jesuit Action Populaire house in Vanves, a suburb of Paris. Hoping he would soon be able to join the ranks of the worker-priests, he corresponded with a number of close friends, and his sister, a Carmelite nun. Convinced that the church and its practices had alienated a whole people, Perrin confessed, 'You can't imagine how much I suffer almost every day at our ceremonies, our preaching, our bourgeois customs.' The publication of *Priest-Workman in Germany* would bring unexpected reactions from all quarters, and Perrin was growing in conviction that the parochial system was wholly inadequate to deal with urban mission. Despite his interest in the parochial work of the Abbé Michonneau, he confided some years later to his superiors, 'I do not see how these parishes, as they now stand, can ever gather in the unbelieving masses.' And later he confessed, 'I don't feel it tragic that I can't be incorporated right away into a team of the Michonneau type. I have great admiration for their work but I view it as only one among five or six possibilities for working in the missionary field.'[163]

By the end of 1946, and while on retreat at Enghien, Perrin expressed the hope that by the following year he might be a worker in Paris and was anxious at this point to train as an electrician.[164] Eventually he was able to begin work in a factory in the 13th arrondissement in 1947, on the eve of which he remarked to a fellow priest that, 'because our religion is unintelligible to people who chance to enter into contact with our institutions . . . we need to strip ourselves of a whole spirit of clericalism – a clericalism in opposition to the gospels'.[165] 'Yet I think the mass of our contemporaries are waiting for religion.'[166]

Even now, some of these passages may strike the reader as untypically radical even for French Catholicism in the post-war years. These were not, of course, public statements. Yet nothing quite like them was being heard even in 1940s Sheffield. Perrin, faced with what he saw as a de-Christianized population, was thinking the unthinkable; that a truly incarnational theology and ministry might take a priest into unknown territory, outside his own milieu, and certainly outside the parochial methods advocated by Michonneau.

Perrin was not, initially, to work as an electrician. He began in a factory making insulating materials, and the job had taken some time to find. 'In the factory itself, no one knows [I'm a priest] and I have said nothing to anyone. For various reasons I decided to keep it quiet.'[167] The day ran from 7.30a.m. to 5p.m. after which he spent his time in a local bistro, sometimes writing or making a few telephone calls. Slowly Perrin began a personal revolt against the capitalist system[168] and in a context where he met estranged workers whose understanding and belief amounted only to some nostalgia for the Gospels, '. . . yet no one accuses [the Gospels]'. Mass Observation had found almost exactly the same attitudes in 1940s Britain.

After resigning a later job in a radio parts factory where he had been accused of being a 'bad workman', Perrin was taken on by a Genevan firm 'engaged in automobile construction', where he sought a deliberate separation from the life of the local parish, though he remained in theory part of a team.[169] Confiding in his cousin (who often had to take the brunt of his accusing tone) he argued that the church had been in the process of betraying the working classes, pleading '. . . pray above all that the clergy and Christians should return to the gospel; so many, so often, are so far from it. That's really all the world reproaches us with.'[170] It all sounded quite simple, but quite devastating stuff.

Perrin found himself at the centre of a team composed of clergy and religious, including a nun, who were working among some 60,000 inhabitants. Among the more adventurous ventures was the establishment of a film club after they had purchased the 'Café La Musette'. Perrin admits that these efforts might seem 'very far from the kingdom of God', but then anything was worth attempting if it brought the team alongside ordinary men and women.

> . . . you must realize that what we are doing is spiritual witness in the

> sense that it is free from any sort of propaganda, and that we are working in brotherly spirit with all men, whatever opinion they hold . . . they feel that I am extremely respectful of their consciences and free from ulterior motive aimed at leading them to what they view as a Catholic bag of tricks.[171]

It was in 1949 that Ted Wickham came from Sheffield to meet Perrin at the 'poor little café' Chez Szeneck in the Rue Nationale: '. . . sawdust on the floor, workers propping up the bar, and the priest in overalls, a beret, two days' growth of beard, every inch an *ouvrier* from the local engineering works. He stood me a lunch and we talked and argued.'[172] Wickham was passionately interested in what was happening in France, and though hesitant about repeating the worker-priest experiment in Britain, nevertheless remained fascinated by what he heard.

Already in a variety of correspondence, Perrin was beginning to admit to contacts with Communists. By the beginning of the following year (1950) he was attending worker-priest conferences where the delegates had already determined that they should see themselves as a community set aside for a special mission, and one 'unattached to the ecclesiastical world of the church in a Christian country'. They were undoubtedly 'ready for rupture'. 'We must not be of the clergy, of the Catholic world or a religious order, but of a workers' world and its suffering . . .' Perhaps it was because of what he saw as some need to identify closely with others that he felt distanced by a friend, who, thinking of him still very much as a member of the clergy, wanted to address Henri as *vous* rather than the more familiar *tu* which had crept into their correspondence.[173]

Perrin took part in the 1950 strikes when employers refused necessary increases in wages. After some three years of working in the 13th arrondissement he left in September 1950, bound for a ten-month silent retreat as part of his Jesuit tertianship. Here, writing to friends in solitude, he began to express how he was tempted to 'independence'.[174] Returning to Paris in 1951 there seemed to be few opportunities for work or ecclesiastical support. There had been something of a proliferation of those who wanted to be worker-priests and a cooling, perhaps, among the authorities. By June 1951, in fact, although there were some eighty-five worker-priests in Paris alone, the Holy See was already anxious that the number should not be increased. Perrin began making contacts in Lyons and Marseilles, but was experiencing some difficulties with his own order, which tended to view its worker-priests as temporary; Perrin and others had taken Godin at his word – there could be no 'going back'.

Perrin was warned by a parish priest, for whom he had the highest regard, that it was his link with the Jesuits to which he really owed his 'achievement' so far.[175] Others, in good will, tried to deter him from his anxiety to be a worker-priest again, but Perrin defended what he understood as a calling, and would simply draw his critics back to the central theme of mission to the urban masses. Perrin eventually left the Society of Jesus at the end of 1951, and began the search for a bishop who would accept him as a secular priest. To continue with his chosen vocation was not going to be easy; conservative anxiety was already evident across France, and although they could not know it, the days of the first worker-priests were already numbered.

(vi) Voices of alarm: the fearful in France and Rome

Even by the later 1940s, Cardinal Suhard had been obliged to answer anxious questions from the Holy See concerning the nature of this new ministry now almost wholly detached from parochial life and the norms of clerical discipline. Couched in language that outlines the Holy See's understanding of what it means to be a priest, the authorities asked about religious life and exercises, the strange requests for evening mass, the nature of this apostleship. These had led Cardinal Suhard to attempt a variety of answers. The requests for evening mass for example, advocated by the worker-priests and supported by Suhard, had as much to do with the worker-priest's spiritual life as those to whom they ministered:

> We can prove by countless examples that young men and girls who communicated frequently before their marriage can no longer do so, hindered as they are by children, by the weekly shopping (which has to be done on Sunday morning), by fatigue, and by the impossibility of getting to morning mass in the week. The conditions of social life and of work deprive the greater part of our Christian militants of the eucharistic life.[176]

And Suhard went on to explain how several priests who worked in factories with his permission had been saying mass at 'half-past five in the morning before going to work'. This surely would be better done in the evening when the priest could go to the families of his workmates.[177] '. . . a mass said on jumping out of bed is scarcely prepared as it should be'.[178] Perrin himself had advocated evening mass, and with others looked forward to more use of the vernacular. Although these issues would be resolved, others still remained. It highlighted the fact that the worker-priests had, as it were, given themselves souls and bodies to a workaday world with all the implications for church and secular authority that that would entail. So it was, Siefer reminds the reader, 'that many bishops suddenly discovered that, almost without noticing it, they had suddenly surrendered to some managing director of a firm, or some trade union leader, or even some Communist party official, part of the jurisdiction over the individual priest which properly belonged to them alone'.[179] In Marseilles, according to Siefer, the ACO (Action Catholique Ouvrière) had asserted that a militant Catholic worker, 'of whom there were none too many, could very easily be led astray by a priest working beside him, who gave his allegiance neither to the ACO or the CFTC (Confédèration Française des Travailleurs Chrétiens), but to the Communists (CGT) of which he was possibly an official'.[180] In many districts, 'women, children and old people', perhaps the only ones who made up the regulars who attended church, were effectively part of the non-working population, and a priest's involvement outside this faithful group could have a detrimental affect on furthering the faith. Yet it was no accident that for worker-priests an 'absence of identification with this group might be a necessary condition for a successful ministry'.[181] If this was easy to understand, it was perhaps easier to misunderstand. Above all, Siefer believed it was the failure to get to grips with this problem early on that gave ammunition to those who would later accuse the worker-priests of stepping across the boundaries of what might be considered acceptable priestly practice and behaviour.

Even Suhard himself, the worker-priest's early champion, was on occasions concerned that the worker-priests might be unable to fulfil the obligations of simple prayer, '... how can they carry on, poor fellows, if they don't pray?' To this were added questions by some of the hierarchy about whether the soutane was still being worn – it had, of course, been abandoned early on. But perhaps a more alarming suggestion – repeated later in 1960s Sheffield – that they were 'founding a new church' separate from others, and not preparing these new Christians to enter 'normal parishes', highlighted the depth to which the mission had gone. There was an unexpected retort of course from Fr Deprierre at his community at Montreuil, 'If you think we are separating ourselves from the church, ask the three curates and the Dean of St Peter and St Paul at Montreuil how 250 of the real working-class *all* took part in the prayers of the mass at a recent wedding in *their parish* ...'[182] And there follows a list of events in which working-class people had participated in the life of the congregation. Deprierre added assurances that the saying of mass and his breviary 'were his daily happiness'. But it was not everywhere the case; and it was clearly not enough.

By November and December of 1947 a nation-wide strike began in which worker priests took part, and of which Suhard was aware. It was further evidence of the involvement of worker-priests in the Communist-led CGT in which a number had prominent roles. In May 1949, the worker-priests joined in their first national conference in which there was a common sharing of concerns: a solidarity that would eventually be necessary as the Vatican declared that Catholics should not associate with Communist organizations. Rooted in an anxiety over Italian Communism, the decree was interpreted as having 'only restricted' application in France. Yet it was a blow coming second only to the greater tragedy which befell the movement in May 1949 when Cardinal Suhard died. *Le Monde* would comment later in 1952, that it had needed 'all the saintly stubbornness of this aged man to ensure at Rome the success of a difficult cause'.[183]

In March 1950 another strike began in which worker-priests were again involved, and within a couple of months an order from the Holy See again forbade any increase in their number. By February the following year, the priests were forced to discuss a charge laid against them that they were no longer priests but 'ineffective'. The following month the worker-priests met their bishop amid growing anxiety, compounded when *Le Monde* warned of 'denunciation' and slander coming from certain quarters of the church and deliberately directed at the worker-priests. Following a peace demonstration in Paris that proved none too peaceful – and in which two worker-priests had been beaten by police – the Archbishop of Paris regretted the participation of his men but condemned the violent action taken against them. But if these issues were becoming at once blurred to the church, they were yet clearer to the worker-priests. Where the workers went, they would also go, and what the workers suffered, they too would endure.

(vii) Non-parochial mission: Henri Perrin at the Isère-Arc dam

Having difficulty finding some kind of 'sponsorship' for a fresh term as a worker-priest in Paris,[184] Perrin took the advice of a superior who questioned his attachment to the city and set out for a work site at Notre-Dame-de-Briancos (Savoy) where the building of the Isère-Arc dam was under way and where he could work with the blessing of the Archbishop of Sens.

Close to the site where he arrived at the end of 1951, Perrin made friends with a village priest, and because another worker at the dam had the same name, arranged for his letters to be posted to the curé's address. Within a short time, Henri had made friends with the priest's sister and mother, and was able to celebrate mass there in private. The physical work at the dam was demanding, with the accommodation in dormitories proving oppressive. 'One longs,' he wrote, 'for a room of one's own, a thing which seems a minimum requirement for living a man's life.' By 1952 a strike had broken out in demand for better wages and conditions. In an appeal statement produced by the strike committee, dangers, long hours, and a general lack of facilities culminated in a demand for a 20% increase. Within a short time, and not surprisingly, Perrin had become the committee's secretary, and it was his hand which produced many of the latter's communiqués. The strike soon became known throughout France, but after forty-two long days, it ended.

Within a year, February 1953, the completion of the dam was in sight, and though the work would have to go on for a further year, lay-offs were about to begin. By May, however, it became clear that another more serious dispute was on the horizon, caused by a number of different issues, one of them being Henri himself. When a workman had been crushed to death by a tractor, and not for the first time, Henri officiated at the funeral, and felt compelled to speak out about the lack of safety precautions.[185] When yet another roll of lay-offs followed a few days later in June, his own name was on the list. A dispute followed, and legal means were attempted to force the management to change course. This it stubbornly refused to do. Shorter in duration than its predecessor, the next strike was more bitter, with the issues keenly focussed on wage demands, bonuses, and the ever-present threat of further lay-offs. A CGT commentator in the *Journal de la Chute* commented on the affection for Henri: 'the best man among us – a man whom all the workers loved and respected for his uprightness and sincerity'.

When the management conceded a number of points and reinstated some of the men, with the exception, Perrin wrote, 'of two north Africans and me', he found himself in full-time work for the union, though by this time the management wanted him off the premises. But a collection had been taken realizing 80,000 francs, and Henri was made pay clerk at the social security office at Chambery. But the occasion of his dismissal and the subsequent wrangle had led to what the *Journal* called the *affaire Perrin.* The dismissal was eventually contested by the inspector of labour for hydroelectric works, and, in the end, the 'firm lost all the cases in which it was involved'.[186] Perrin, it seems, had won the hearts of his fellow workers but the hostility of employers. He may also have proved to many Catholics a good reason for ending such experimental ministries. After all, there had been too many strikes disrupting France, and too many worker-priests involved.

(viii) Victory for the alarmists

By 19 March 1953, a letter from Cardinal Pizzardo of the Curia demanded that seminarists should no longer be allowed to prepare for a ministry as worker-priests. By May, several bishops were seriously wondering whether the worker-priests' mission as conceived and willed by Cardinal Suhard had not been 'profoundly modified' by the worker-priests themselves. It was slowly becoming clear that suppression was only a matter of time. Mgr Delay, the archbishop of Marseilles, determined that at least three of his worker-priests should stop working, and by June, Cardinal Tisserant was reported to have in his possession an order from the Vatican which sought the 'utter suppression of the movement'.

In August 1953 worker-priests and militant laity were once again involved in the wave of strikes which had broken out nationally following a breakdown in wage negotiations, and the arrest of the CGT labour leaders Alain Le Léap and Benôit Franchon. Priests and laity had challenged the Catholic Union (CFTC), accusing it of betraying the interests of workers and 'monopolizing the faith'. The same month, and hardly surprisingly, *L'Observateur* claimed that the church was on the eve of important decision-making on the future of the worker-priests.

Siefer traced the initiation of restrictive measures against the mission of the worker-priests back to one fact: the replacement of Mgr Roncalli (later Pope John XXIII), who had been nuncio in France, by Mgr Marella.[187] Support for non-Christian unions and other groups by worker-priests was precisely the kind of activity which was bound to infuriate many Catholics and encourage the Vatican to keep up its pressure on the movement. Again in August, and for the first time, a confidential circular to the superiors of religious orders called on them to withdraw all religious working in industry. The following month Cardinal Liénart officially announced the closure of the Mission de France, planned to be reopened only when a newly constituted mission had been agreed. This was followed later by a meeting with Mgr Marella of no less that twenty-six bishops and superiors of religious orders to discuss the suppression of the entire movement on the grounds that it was first, jeopardizing traditional forms of church ministry, and secondly, collaborating with Communists. A key question was already emerging: was it possible to be a priest *and* a worker? Indeed was it possible to be anything other than a priest? A year or so later, with stories of the worker-priests crossing the channel, Britain's *Church Quarterly Review* would ask, '. . . how can there be priests who are teachers, doctors, lawyers, parliamentarians, and officers in the army? Is there not a difference being made between "proletarian" work and that of the "*bien-pensants*"?'[188]

Petrie presents a picture of acute anxiety on the part of the nuncio, Marella, and his desire that the hierarchy should begin with 'those readiest to submit' in an attempt to avoid public scandal, and perhaps because, as Siefer explains, 'he had no right under Canon Law to issue explicit commands to them without an express order from the Pope himself'.[189] But repercussions there were bound to be, and although the French bishops were split on the issue, they agreed to make no move.

Cardinal Feltin, aware of the advantages and dangers of this radical movement, was nevertheless astute enough to see its suppression as disastrous, and he was joined in support by Cardinal Liénart and Mgr Chappoulie, who had already confessed that priests should go to meet workers on their own ground in order to share their work and troubles, 'even as the Son of God by his incarnation made himself like unto his brethren'.

By now, the worker-priests, confessing themselves 'rejected as the working class is rejected by the established order . . .', hoped there might be support from the French Assembly of cardinals, archbishops and bishops. But support was never forthcoming. By autumn 1953, Liénart, Gerlier and Feltin had met the Holy Father, who maintained fearful anxiety at the experiment. The lull that followed seemed to indicate that a compromise might yet be reached, especially as press reports began to suggest that modifications of the worker-priests' role and not total suppression might be the outcome. This appeared to be confirmed when half-way through November Cardinal Feltin, in a meeting with worker-priests, informed them of the less than enthusiastic reception they had received at Rome. Yet there was to be accommodation. The experiment, it seemed, could continue after all under certain conditions; but these turned out to be conditions most worker-priests would never accept. First, they must be selected by their bishops; secondly, they should receive sound doctrinal training; thirdly, and hardest to bear, their time spent as manual labourers was to be drastically limited. Fourthly, and in a deliberate attempt to keep them on tight reins, they were to leave 'temporal' responsibilities to laymen. Finally, they should ensure they took part in the life of the parish church. It was much to ask; and for many it would prove too much.

The first religious order to withdraw its clergy was the Society of Jesus. The principle of papal obedience as a founding premise of the community may have made it difficult to ignore the ruling, though it is unlikely that the order, like one of their previous number, Henri Perrin, did other than agonize over the decision. By the beginning of 1954 the French bishops reiterated the general points made to worker-priests earlier, but introduced further particulars. They must not: work more than three hours a day, participate in secular organizations, or attempt to 'combine' nationally, and they should always be part of a community of priests. Finally, in an attempt to ensure there were no 'half-hearted' measures against their own worker-priests, the three provincials of the Dominican order were removed from office. By 1 March 1954 all worker-priests were expected to have left their full-time employment.

Worker-priests now faced a dilemma. They had sought all along to be obedient to what they believed was a calling, yet in the eyes of the bishops, acceptance of their consciences was interpreted as disobedience to Christ. More distressing was the warning that 'the priest who continues in a state of disobedience is in danger of punishment with the sanctions of Canon Law'. Arnal interprets this as a threat of excommunication. And the worker-priests of Limoges would write to Mgr Rastouil: 'without ceasing to love our Church, we prefer to suffer at her hands rather than destroy the hopes of our brothers'.[190]

On 20 February 1954 the worker-priests held their final meeting at the Café de la Paix in Villejuif south of Paris. The outcome of a two day meeting was a resolution to hang on or quit. There were to be no half measures. Two groups emerged: the *soumis* who would obey and return to the institutional church, and the *insoumis* (or *restés au travail*), who would remain at their place of work. There was never any question of accepting a three-hour day – for no worker enjoyed that. To Cardinal Feltin, in his letter of 24 February, what was at issue was not condemnation or even suppression but merely what he understood as a *modification* of practices. But if he hoped that worker-priests would all accept the Vatican's ruling he was mistaken. 'The meeting broke up,' relates Siefer, 'without any concerted action being agreed upon; each was left to decide for himself.'[191] A final and devastating blow had been levelled at the entire movement. The French liberal and left-wing press, particularly *Le Monde*, joined in an outpouring of scorn, with the hierarchy, irritated by the criticism, claiming for itself alone the right to decide what could and could not constitute priesthood.

At the time of this suppression there were about 100 worker-priests in France. In the event, only about one-third of that original number submitted in obedience, with many of the religious returning to their communities. The remainder carried on, and Siefer concludes, rather tragically, that many 'found themselves cast adrift, and gradually, all trace of them was lost'. 'From an official ecclesiastical point of view,' says Arnal, 'the worker-priests had passed into history . . .'[192]

There were some, of course, who had been able to maintain that fine balance between work and parochial life; Siefer explains that Père Loew avoided conflict between parish and mission, and Stanley Windass points to Loew as one of the 'original' worker-priests who, though he predated those who went to Germany, '. . . was all that Rome wanted a worker-priest to be'.[193] It was not the end of the story.

> The fact remains that the majority of the worker-priests have continued to live as workers, maintaining between themselves the same close contact as before and preserving as a group the same concern to be heard by the church.[194]

With some disobedient two-thirds of the priests still working and a few on 'three-hour days' hoping for a change of heart, Cardinal Feltin later sought clarification for a future for the movement. It was never forthcoming, and towards the end of the decade (1959) the Vatican reiterated its ban, through a letter from Cardinal Pizzaro which stressed the traditional understanding of priesthood as that constituted by the sacrifice of the mass, the public prayer of the church, and the administration of the sacraments to the faithful. It was very clear and very final. Work in a factory or workshop was deemed to be incompatible with the life of a priest,[195] and these views would not now change until after Vatican II.

(ix) French worker-priests: presence and theology

It is possible to view the French worker-priests as labouring without any precise or explicit theological consensus underpinning their efforts. To some extent they remained individuals left to reflect spiritually and theologically on a missionary enterprise that was very much an ongoing experiment. Yet there were some notable thinkers and theologians to whom they could offer the raw material of industrial experience for considered reflection. In daily contact with the working world, however, one overiding concern emerged which helped them shape a theology. As God had entered into the affairs of humankind in the life of Christ who was himself a worker, so too would they share in the full life of the proletariat. André Dupierre argued, '. . . we must work with new brothers, suffer, struggle, hope and love with them'.[196] It was 'being there' which really mattered, identification with all on the industrial site. When Ted Wickham, leader of the Sheffield Industrial Mission, met Fr Hollande he had asked the astonished superior, 'What did the worker-priests do? What happened as a result? An irrelevant question! *C'est la présence, c'est la présence!* And in twenty-five years' time the attitude of the French workers to the church will be different because of this presence.'[197]

The notion of this incarnational life lived among the poor and marginalized was to become a central theme, but spelt out in a variety of contexts. The Abbé Hollande's *équipe* had, within a year of the war, begun an attempt to develop a rationale which took the theme of incarnation seriously. There was the *imitatio Christi* position – not unlike that of the 'Little Brothers' – which concentrated on Christ's 'hidden' life as a worker in Nazareth. There was the 'virtue of work' idea, and the worker-priests' physical work as an extension of the sacramental life, especially that of the mass.

Rather in the way that early heresies sparked off determined attempts to give answers to complex matters of belief, it was often the demands for the cessation of the ministry of worker priests that gave rise to explicit theologies of incarnation. When the bishops of the French Church wrote to the worker-priests at the beginning of 1954, claiming that it was their duty to offer new 'guide-lines', and warning them against disobedience, one of the most striking responses came from the worker-priests of Limoges, and to Mgr Rastouil, when they reminded the hierarchy that as God 'was made flesh' so they would enter the working world under that compulsion alone. Perrin in his own notebook confesses, 'God himself, by making himself man, had to retrace the path in the opposite direction, reopen the passage towards God, make the sacrifice.'[198] Life in the working world was a life lived in the full spirit and inner dwelling of the incarnate God. 'Being there', 'being a presence', remained essential in the knowledge that they daily faced the reality of God's created world. 'Upheld by the love of God within us, we encountered the love of our brethren "made in his image and likeness".'[199]

And with this theology of incarnation went a broader understanding of priesthood; an implicit acceptance which again had created anxiety among the hierarchy. It was one thing for the worker priests to be living openly lives quite unlike those of a normal priest, of a sacerdotal nature, as one set aside to offer the sacrifice of men, quite another to make a case for it. But as Joseph Robert said, 'It is neither the clothes nor the lifestyle, nor the capacity for contemplation or intellectual work which defines priesthood, but rather the relationship of the priest to God and man . . .'[200] And some of Perrin's thinking was sometimes an example of that, implicitly warning the religiously conservative that worker-priests might be in as much danger of becoming 'Protestants' as 'Communists'. 'The Bible never speaks of priests,' Perrin writes, 'but often speaks of the holy people and its royal priesthood. In this lies a whole vein of theology and spirituality from which very few draw nourishment, in spite of the efforts made by some.' At the beginning of 1951 he writes to a friend Paul, 'The priesthood, far from belonging to us, is delegated to us by the body of Christ, which is the whole Christian community.'

Any argument that the worker-priests all engaged with a single developed theology for life and work is difficult to sustain. That they demonstrated a commitment to a new life in the presence of those outside the institutional church and began to work through various theologies is nearer the truth. 'How far can that which grows up outside the church be healthy for mankind, and how far should Christians be linked to it?', asked Abbé Richard in *L'Homme Nouveau* in November 1953. 'In every way,' the worker-priests might have answered. Yet not everything that grows up outside the institution is necessarily healthy. But they would not minister with a clearly defined notion of the Kingdom of God in or on the edge of industrial life. 'We know that the Catholic Church alone possesses the fullness of revelation and divine grace,' said the worker-priests of Limoges in their letter to their bishop in 1954, confirming fairly traditional notions of the concept of revelation and the position of the Catholic Church. There is sometimes the implication of a 'kingdom theology', but Erlander's suggestion that the worker priests had an understanding of the kingdom wider than the institutional church is less easy to demonstrate. The church remained a means of grace and it was the institutional church, in the person of its priests, that had to become incarnated into the world. Of the kingdom of God the worker-priests said little; it was not yet a central focus. They began with an incarnational theology because that was where the church began, and they took to heart the practical consequences of that fundamental doctrine:

We did not do it for fun, or because we were ordered. It was in very truth under the impulsion of the Spirit of God that, as we contemplated His countenance and His will, we repeated, 'He was made flesh', 'In all things like unto men'.[201]

(x) Henri Perrin: endnotes

By 1953 a majority within the church against the worker-priest movement had begun to eclipse even the labour problems faced by the priests themselves. For Perrin, limitations placed on worker-priests struck at the very heart of life and work: '. . . things like asking us to work for a few hours every day, or to keep out of the workers' movement – and leave the trade union movement – or to maintain a link with the parish, involve a basic misunderstanding of the conditions of our life as workers and of any genuine worker's life'.[202] Behind the scenes Perrin was sure that the hierarchy and other forces opposed to Communism were denouncing worker-priests to the Vatican 'either directly or through intermediaries'. Nor was he convinced by the bishop's solicitude for the priestly life behind which he felt there lurked a political anxiety about Communism. Yet there was a genuine fear, at times, even Perrin could see that.

Towards the end of February 1954 and facing his personal dilemma, he confessed that in the following week some fifty priests would remain at work (though the number was eventually much higher), preferring excommunication to what seemed to him to be 'a betrayal of the world of the poor'.[203] He makes no mention of where he stood himself, commenting only that those who decided to stay on deserved respect; 'God alone can judge,' he says, 'the Church has a right and duty to take the measures it deems necessary; no sincere Christian can make accusation.' Yet he would remind his friends that the Catholic ghetto, which he had spoken of years before, was not something to which he felt he could ever return. There was now a very clear breach between what Perrin saw as the institutional church, which had 'the right to adopt measures it thought fit' and what would inevitably be the outcome that would remain: 'the deep and tragic gulf that separates the church from the workers'. Perrin resolved to leave his own place of work by 1 March 1954, since the site itself was about to close.

On 25 October, on his way to a training centre where, with his bishop's permission, he was completing a course as a electrician, Perrin was killed when he was thrown from his motor-cycle. With no other traffic involved, a solitary cyclist was unable to give any explanation.

Perrin had in his possession an unposted letter requesting laicization: his ultimate intentions, like his death, were to remain a mystery.

For Arnal, 1954 marked the end of the pioneering phase of the worker-priests, and he closes his own study with that same year. But the story does not end there. Though condemnation was reiterated again in 1959, under Pope John XXIII, it was the Second Vatican Council and its breath of fresh air that allowed for new initiatives to be taken. Indeed Aral argues that there is nearly unanimous conviction that they were a leading impetus to the birth and success of the Second Vatican Council and the spirit which emerged in its wake. Since 1965 relaxation in the original rules meant an even greater influx of clergy into the movement, particularly in 1969, when some priests understood that they were part of a particularly 'high intake'.[204] At the time of his own writing there were 900, records Arnal, some 3% of the nation's clergy.

In his 1965 report in the United States, John Cogley gave an account of the first worker-priests, and their condemnation. Now, he says, it may all be revived, for under Pope Paul VI the experiment was to continue once again. 'This very special apostolate will no longer be known as *prêtres-ouvriers* (priest-workers) but as *prêtres au travail* (working-priests).'[205] Eventually, however, *prêtres-ouvriers* has simply stuck. More important, the worker-priests received support from the institution itself. With the establishment of their own non-territorial diocese and bishop, there came official recognition that their work should continue. That development had been possible only because of the witness of the first one hundred or so, even though many of them, as commentators have suggested, were lost to the institutional church for ever. Arnal concludes that despite much of their efforts to rebuild bridges, 'The demands of labour and struggles drew them further away from ecclesiastical life, but its mark upon them was there to stay. Some continued to write letters to their bishops; others met collectively to study social theology; and even those who later became atheists retained an interest in the church's proletarian apostolates.'[206]

2. Non-parochial mission in industrial Britain

(i) Britain and industrial mission – origins

The French Church, which through a number of individuals and groups recognized an estrangement from the working masses, had begun to consider ways of meeting that problem in the late-nineteenth century, particularly, as we have seen, by the post-war worker-priest movement. In Britain, influenced originally by Evangelicalism, the Oxford Movement, Christian Socialism and a range of wartime and post-war experiments, the Church of England too would consider new forms of urban mission.

Industrial mission proper in Britain had its origins in the late nineteenth century, and has been outlined in a number of studies including Lurkins (1981), Masumoto (1983) and, more recently, Erlander and Grundy (1991 and 1992).[207] The authors all trace this kind of mission back to nineteenth-century railway and canal building and the influx of men to areas where these new developments were under construction, and Grundy in particular notes the social and theological influences of the first Christian socialists on the thinking of later industrial missioners. Grundy argues, however, for there having been what he calls an 'unholy conspiracy', namely that, from very early on, businessmen and others 'excluded the churches from their affairs' and that the churches colluded with this, preferring, at best, to develop only a personal and private code of ethical behaviour. He also believes that up to the Second World War, the churches had had some influence, only to see it slip away.

Commentators rightly focus on William Temple's 'fostering' of the Church of England's social ethical conscience, theologically underpinning industrial mission. In his groundbreaking *Christianity and the Social Order* (1942),[208] which had the staying power Cyril Garbett's *Claims of the Church of England* never enjoyed, Temple opened with a clear condemnation of the view of religion as 'one department of life'. In a quite candid concern for the country, he concentrated on what he saw as the evils of bad housing and unemployment, 'the most hideous of our social evils', to argue that 'we are challenged to find a social order which provides employment steadily and generally, and our consciences should be restive till we succeed'. Temple strongly believed that Christians were bound to 'interfere' as he put it 'because [the church] is by vocation the great agent of God's purpose outside the scope of which no human interest or activity can fall', even though it was up to politicians to devise the means to these ends. Unlike Garbett, for Temple churchmanship was not the primary issue: '. . . the first necessity for progress is more and better Christians taking full responsibility as citizens for the political, social and economic systems under which they and their fellows live'.[209]

Between the World Wars the Industrial Christian Fellowship, formed from a merger between the older Navvy Mission and the Christian Social Union, engaged lay people in factory visiting, and their conferences, especially that of 1941, summarized by William Temple, began to sharpen the focus on an industrial society 'which made it hard (as that Malvern Conference concluded) for people to live fully Christian lives'. But the death of Temple, Grundy argues, was at least one of the factors which not only hindered further early developments, but helped bring about the 'conspiracy' which ensured that those 'specialists' involved in industrial mission would be 'marginalized' by the churches and their influence 'muted'.

(ii) The Sheffield Industrial Mission

In Britain, and in the post-war years in particular, where the majority of men and women earned a living in industry, there were, as in France, those who recognized that the church might make the 'world of work' a special focus of attention, perhaps initiating a mission beyond the bounds of the territorial parish. If Mass Observation's findings for the *British Weekly* (1949) could arrive at the unsurprising finding that 'industrial areas are less religious than the rural ones', most of the findings also indicated that there was often a decided lack of hostility to churches, parsons, and religious belief in general.[210] By the early 1950s, serious discussion on industrial mission was already beginning in the pages of a number of periodicals including *Theology, Frontier* and the *Modern Churchman.*

Between the end of the Second World War and the early 1960s, some attention came to be focussed on industrial areas, and a number of different enterprises developed. Among some of the pioneers would be the South London Industrial Mission (SLIM), based on the churches in Southwark, Blackfriars, Greenwich, Woolwich and Battersea, where Colin Cuttell had been appointed industrial chaplain in 1944. Later developments, following on from Sheffield, included Canon Ralph Stevens in Birmingham, 1954; H. M. Jenkins appointed a parish priest in Luton who became industrial adviser to the bishop from 1955; Simon Phipps in Coventry, who was based at the cathedral from 1958 and who has described himself as a kind of 'second wave' following on in the 'style of Sheffield';[211] and John Ragg in Bristol, whose base was local churches. Indeed, under the impetus given by the 1959 Report, *The Task of the Church in Relation to Industry*, there was '. . . an increase in appointments of industrial Chaplains by dioceses from about 20 in 1960 to nearer 60 by 1966'.[212] Some of these, when based parochially, could be described as independent ventures. Bill Gowland, a Methodist who founded the Luton Industrial College, had been a 'Christian Commando'. Much earlier, in the 1930s Church of Scotland under the independent leadership of the Revd George McLeod, ministers and working men, mainly from the west, and at a time of high unemployment, combined to rediscover Christian community while concentrating on the rebuilding of Iona Abbey, itself a symbol of mission in north-west Britain.[213] In the 1960s the Church of Scotland secured other developments under George Wilkie based in Edinburgh.

But the most striking and perhaps pioneering of all industrial missions in the post-war years would be that in Sheffield, where, in the late 1940s under Bishop Leslie Hunter and the direct leadership of 'Ted' Wickham, an enterprise emerged which would represent a radical departure in ministry and mission. Less dramatic, perhaps, than that of the French worker-priests which appeared almost simultaneously, it would nevertheless result in challenging experiences for the participants as fresh theological understanding changed the strategies and tactics 'on the ground'.

Leslie Hunter had been promoted to Sheffield before the outbreak of war in 1939. Formerly a Canon of Newcastle and Archdeacon in Northumberland, he was no stranger to the northern industrial areas, many of which were called out of depression and into the service of the nation as war approached.[214] Among the concerns occupying Hunter was mission to the working-class, which Atkinson believed had been placed in Hunter's mind long before with *The Army and Religion* report that followed the First World War. Yet, as he would later admit, he knew little about the daily workings of industry, '. . . where so large a part of the population earn their living, its working conditions and their pressures on human psychology, personal relations or the absence of them in works and offices, was unexplored territory . . .'[215] By 1954, on a visit to the United States, Hunter claimed that the church ought to identify with men '. . . from the base of the pyramid of industrial society . . .'[216]

The only comprehensive published study of the Sheffield Industrial Mission at the time of writing has been Paul Bagshaw's *The Church Beyond the Church*,[217] published to celebrate fifty years of industrial mission. Other studies, like Mary Walton's *History of the Diocese of Sheffield*, [218] may have done justice to Hunter's visions and Wickham's determination for mission, but perhaps do less to the unfolding drama that brought it to the verge of total collapse.

By 1961, when the Mission was well under way, and Michael

Atkinson was appraising efforts, the Diocese of Sheffield, some fifty miles long and twenty miles across, had a population of 1,134,169. Originally part of the Diocese of York, it had been created as a separate diocese when Wakefield had been formed. At its heart, and throughout the war years, the great steel and engineering works had provided for a country at war. By the mid-1960s, when the Mission was in full swing, the population and numbers at work give an indication of the task before the mission. There was a working population of 493,954, with local and nearby industries providing employment for vast numbers. One firm at Stocksbridge employed 7,500, two others in Rotherham 9,000 and 6,000. Along some twenty miles of the river Don the works spread, employing a total of 273,420,with at least 43,452 employed directly in steel-making, and thousands of others in related industries.

(iii) Ted Wickham

(a) Practice

'Ted' Wickham, who had already served as a chaplain to ordnance workers at Swynnerton in Lichfield (1941–44), was originally appointed by Hunter as Chaplain of Shrewsbury Hospital, after which he made a 'sideways step' into the world of industry, first with the supervision of a 'Bevin boys' hostel, and later in becoming Hunter's 'Industrial Chaplain' with a view to examining a role for the church in industry. For Wickham, the ultimate aim of the exercise '. . . to which clergy were strictly ancillary, was to disclose or induce a significant lay presence as the normative presence of the church in the world'.[219]

Wickham entered factories and works by arrangement with unions and management to visit men where they worked, to initiate conversation, questioning, and later debate. The 'snap-break' meetings – short engagements during morning break which 'became the hall-mark of the Sheffield model' are described in two later papers: Michael Atkinson's *The Sheffield Industrial Mission*,[220] written in the 1960s, and Philip Bloy's published paper, which describes a return visit he made to Sheffield in the 1980s.[221] These show the way meetings were conducted in the mission's heyday, with up to eight chaplains visiting some twenty local works, including parts of British Rail. 'It was Ted Wickham's device . . . a brilliant exponent of "between man and man" . . . adept at pressing theological points in straightforward and stimulating language.' 'This example inspired the missioners who joined him' so that 'in a space around someone's job or in a "snap cabin" the men met the chaplain'.

These informal sessions enabled anyone passing to join in. Men 'got into the habit' of attending these and sometimes encouraged fellow workers. Though many were 'cagey' about being confronted by 'the vicar', 'those who let their arms be twisted found they enjoyed themselves'.[222] It is easy – as subsequently occurred – to question the depth of what was going on, indeed Clive Everett-Allen, who participated as a 'working ordinand' on the shop floor, recognized their initial superficiality.[223] But Atkinson himself describes a common experience of the chaplains, 'that underneath a flinty exterior of indifference to and mistrust of "religion" in any shape or form, people are wrestling with some of the most baffling of the problems that man faces when he asks the basic religious questions: What is life really about?' Some early groups would also meet Wickham at his home, and it was becoming clear that the 'gulf' between 'church and industry' was all that Wickham had feared. 'People assumed,' remarks Bagshaw, 'that a churchmen would simply want to recruit them, or take their money, or stop them drinking or swearing and enjoying sex.' The 'Christian Commandos' of the late 1940s were finding exactly the same, and in a discovery, already well known to Mass Observation and Henri Perrin in Paris, 'men distinguished the Church from Christianity and both criticism of the Church, and respect for Christianity were starting points for discussion'.[224]

Wickham's early entries into the work place were already an open criticism of the parish structure which he believed woefully inadequate as a starting point for mission. He agreed with Hunter that new strategies must be attempted; 'workers associated with the mission were to be formed into groups which would remain outside the parish structure . . .' Indeed Wickham, as Roland Walls remembers, could be utterly scathing about the territorial parish, and his efforts, Walls believed, could sometimes be viewed as a deliberate attempt to 'prod' the church into more radical outreach.[225]

After five years of experimentation and innovation, Wickham became permanent Chaplain of the Industrial Mission, and what in hindsight must be seen as significant, workers began in financial terms to contribute to the work. In 1950, an agreed document was been published, which declared that those interested could make a further step forward and 'come over' to join 'God's union' – the church. Many accepted this 'offer' and thus formalized their part in the life of the church. It stressed that for the workers 'the church' was not some 'other institution' on the outside, but was represented *in* the mission itself. 'By making this step in the Industrial Mission you belong to the church'; there was apparently no need actually to 'go to church'. The idea was unambiguous: it was the Mission itself which rooted the church in the work place. By now, the most committed of lay leaders met regularly on Thursday nights, and to join in the worship and attend discussion was to 'cross the line'.

A range of conferences and training programmes also proved instructive for those hoping to become a part of the mission who were then in theological training. There were inter-works conferences – held several times a year – for lay leaders who set up and took part in shop floor discussion. Some works sent men to a seventy-two-hour conference which proved useful and illuminating. A Steel Peach and Tozer Works Councillor who went became the first of regular delegates, as the company sent further individuals to each of the three conferences each year.

In another major development in the mission, 'lay projects' were developed much more significant than 'snap-break' meetings; these were (as the title suggested) lay led, and formed the means of maintaining interest between meetings and chaplains. They were later described as the most audacious and creative mission experiment 'in recent years'. These methods, tried and tested in the steel works and catalogued by Bagshaw, were the outward testimony to Wickham's understanding of a church rooted in the faith, but now emerging and lived in a new industrial context. By 1957 Wickham was already down a track few others would follow. That 'Christianity must be stretched to apprehend the totality of human life and history' begged questions which perhaps only Wickham would attempt to answer; the problem was, there were very few in the established church even asking such questions.

(b) Theology

Wickham's *Church and People in an Industrial City*, published in 1957, was the declaration of the theological and sociological perspectives which he had researched and within which he was operating. Within a short time it would become a classic analysis of the Church of England in the context of industrial society, with the now well-known conclusion that the church had never lost the working-class – it had never had them. Today, argues Grundy, these '. . . conclusions seem commonplace but in the 1960s they were seen to give a historical/sociological perspective not to say explanation about the dramatic decline in church attendance in the twentieth century', though Wickham's thesis has been challenged more recently as taking less account of flourishing non-conformity at the height of the industrial revolution.[226]

Satisfied that in the past the nineteenth-century Marxist critique of religion as 'ideological and epiphenomenal' had validity, Wickham argued for self-examination of the present.[227] Wickham had no illusion about the task ahead, '. . . a radical self criticism is demanded by the Protestant principle of the Bible itself. A knowledge of history is the beginning of such purgation.' It was the kind of language which made Edward Norman suggest that Wickham was familiarizing younger clergy with '. . . the interests of the Christian Social Union's critique of society' in a work that 'breathed' the spirit of Temple.[228] Wickham went on to analyse the relationship between the church and the world using terminology borrowed from Paul Tillich. First, the church might be a reflection of the secular. For while the church can indeed reflect the total life of the Christian community, yet it can degenerate into a debased condition of 'mere conformity'. Secondly, there can be 'heterogamous' relations when the church refuses to adapt to the society in which it is set, and sees itself over against society – something Wickham believed was the norm for Western Christendom. Thirdly, the church could find itself belonging to a world it sought neither to manipulate nor dominate, but to understand, prophesy in, and interpret. For Wickham, echoing what John Robinson had already expressed, the church remained subservient to the kingdom of God, that 'primary theological truth that is imprisoned in the textbooks'.[229]

Wickham concluded that there must be a new 'machinery of engagement'. He quotes Gore that at present the church was asking too much of the development of the outward exhibition of worship. It trusted too much in church building 'and the organizational plant'. Then, in an extremely telling but simple line, he added, '. . . we try too much to get people to come to church'. But it was ever so, even for Hunter, de Blank, Southcott, Ecclestone and Michonneau, all thought of as enterprising and original. Even if they all recognized needs for new initiatives – and occasionally took them – they were yet further from Wickham, who engaged a radically new dimension in actually *being* the church.

But there was, as yet, no consensus on a theology of the kingdom, and Wickham had become passionately concerned for the development of a 'new structure of engagement' if there was to be any dialogue, influence and impact. He was calling for nothing less than a 'supplementary non-parochial structure', since the church, whose organization was charted in territorial and geographical forms, could never hope to make a mark upon an urban industrialized society. Wickham believed that men's lives were shaped not necessarily by where they lived, but by where they worked and found their leisure interests. (Though it was a view already esposed in *Frontier's* editorial on Industry in its November edition of 1951.) Thus he argues that some special agency of the church must be developed, an agency with 'planned machinery' whose role and influence would fall outside the parishes. Atkinson was able to spell out some of the theory in claiming that:

> Parish boundaries in Sheffield have little sociological relevance, nor perhaps have they ever had since the old extensive parish of Sheffield underwent fragmentation in the eighteen hundreds. From that time on, people have increasingly found themselves working and recreating themselves without deference to ecclesiastical planning.[230]

Thus Wickham had his close disciples, and he and they were echoing the words of Perrin and other worker-priests who, acknowledging the important practical work of men like Michonneau in Paris, were nevertheless determined, when necessary, to abandon parochial structures. Wickham suggests real engagement with those who shaped the world of industry, but believed this could happen only where a trained specialist agency, 'continuing and permanent' (and that was to be a key), would be able to create what he described as a 'web of relationships' . . . and so, presumably, over a very long period, enable an indigenous church to emerge.

This 'web of relationships' upon which ministry and engagement were to develop was not, hopefully, about some formally developed structure for an alternative institutionalization, but, much more simply, where what he called 'single-minded and long-term work' had engendered mutual confidence and a common understanding and language had removed suspicion, inhibition and a cautionary fear about 'religion'.[231] Wickham then describes in his own words the methods needed to engage with men on the shop floor in Sheffield, and openly confessed that such meeting was not about education or church membership, but rather about genuine encounter through which the church is engaged in a project which the bulk of men concede to be its most popular function, 'coming among us' and 'going into the highways and hedges'. Nevertheless he called for a thorough-going training of the laity to equip them for active theologically-based encounter with fellow workers, and the lay projects perhaps in infancy were seen as something which might become commonplace up and down the life of the nation, even 'within Caesar's household'.

For Wickham, nothing less than national co-ordination, and the planned deployment and continuity of staff, would enable this work to begin in earnest across the country, and he went on to outline a range of measures. Like Robinson before him, he explicitly challenged the church – which he believed lacked coherent theological perspectives – to an understanding of the kingdom. He could already see that the church had organized itself not to respond to the existence of such a kingdom, but for its own worship and institutional well-being.

> The church has no real policy except that of maintenance; there is no attempt to work out the required shape of the local church if it is to be a missionary instrument, as distinct from a centre of public worship . . . there will be those who regard all attempts to produce a new shape of the church as new-fangled nonsense . . . they may be able to do this in more favourable districts but not in the industrial areas . . . [232]

By the time *Church and People* had been published, the Sheffield Industrial Mission had already been shaped to engage with the working world, as lay projects produced committed groups who now began to gather for eucharist in Sheffield Cathedral. Bagshaw gives an ironic illustration, however, of a persistent divide between middle-class office and managerial laity sharing in this worship while men from the shop floor 'hung back'. The reader is left to imagine the setting of a cathedral service and all that might involve, standing in marked contrast to a worker's more familiar ground, works canteen or corner pub.

(iv) Leslie Hunter: extending theological enterprise

Alongside Wickham's continuing efforts on the shop floor, one or two theological enterprises began at Hunter's initiative – though he did not always confide in Wickham if they did not directly concern him. There were conferences for students, including ordinands, from the beginning of the 1950s, increasing the numbers who eventually came to work on the shop floors. The Society of the Sacred Mission (with its House at Kelham), and King's College, London, both sent ordinands to work in the heat of Sheffield.[233]

As early as 1958, and already fascinated by the French worker-priest movement,[234] Hunter gained support for an experiment in which ordinands, during the course of their training, might spend the second of three years living and working in Sheffield. This would be followed by a residential period at Ranmoor Grange. Hunter had visited Cambridge to meet deans and chaplains, hoping that potential ordinands might be encouraged further north. Roland Walls, then Dean of Corpus Christi College,[235] who had been encouraged by Fr Kelly to study F. D. Maurice, took up the challenge. After visiting the Mission de France, where he found himself up against 'French realism as opposed to an Anglo-Saxon romanticism',[236] Walls returned to Sheffield, and serious theological reflection began with the ordinands working on shop-floors, where under Walls, 'kingdom faith in the light of gospel study became central'.[237] These experiments were not isolated: in other separate schemes like one in Birmingham in 1959, candidates who had been employed in factory work completed training in a college.

After three years work at Hunter's invitation, Walls prepared a report for CACTM arguing for a radical shift in theological education. Its committee, however, engrossed in discussion on the establishment of a new ecumenical Queen's College in Birmingham, only received this, and in a loss which has never been calculated, it was never heard of again. Walls, disappointed and alarmed, abandoned Sheffield in 1962, and visited George McLeod's venture on Iona and Brother Roger in Taizé before moving to a location south of Edinburgh where he founded his own community with one of his Sheffield 'students', John Halsey. They took their inspiration from a number of sources including the Little Brothers and Sisters of Jesus, and from there in the mid-1960s new ventures in teaching and industrial mission began.

In 1958, the British Council of Churches published *The Church and Industry*,[238] an assessment of the issues that faced the Christian churches in Britain and an appraisal of some of the current ventures. It acknowledged a God concerned with all human beings and creation, and commended the work which the churches were doing, and it called for new and specialized ministries in the work place, but these were not spelt out in detail and it frowned on those 'who go it alone'. By 1959 the Church Assembly's own report, *The Task of The Churches in Relation to Industry*, with Wickham as secretary, seemed to vindicate all the experiments that had gone before. It 'outlined a strategy for the development of industrial mission across England . . .'[239] and presented for the first time since the narrow calls of *Towards the Conversion of England* the recognition that the Christian church was concerned with 'the quality of human life, both of men individually and of their society, and that industry was responsible for determining the quality of human life in society'. Although Bagshaw claims that 'it looked to a future with co-operation and integrated learning in order that the church might have a place in industrial society' (a place already won by Wickham), he also believes it still saw mission as essentially parish-based. Wickham, Bagshaw suggests, won the battle but lost the war. Had such sentiments evolved into a successful industrial secretariat, its head would have been *de facto* a non-territorial bishop (as indeed the French worker-priests would later have) and it would have had to be Wickham. But he remained 'politically and ecclesiastically unacceptable'. His subsequent elevation to the episcopate was to gag his effective voice in industrial mission, and his consecration, rather than being some great beginning, marked the ending of a brief but major chapter in the life and witness of the Church of England.

(v) 'Dismantling' the mission

Michael Jackson replaced Ted Wickham as senior chaplain in 1959. Trained at Ridley Hall in Cambridge, Jackson had taken an intense interest in the French worker-priests, and for a time had worked on the shop floor himself. With the dynamic 1960s just around the corner and a new senior chaplain at the helm, the team at first worked well together, though changes were in process which would have a crucial bearing on the tragedy that would shortly unfold. Three years before he retired, says Bagshaw, Hunter began to demand of Jackson what he had not demanded of Wickham. No doubt he yearned to see things 'happening'; perhaps an essentially conservative man, he may have expected to see pews filling, and an appreciable movement of workers 'across the bridge' and somehow 'into' the establishment. Wickham's '. . . creation was an alternative church, I believe (Hunter) understood this but never accepted it'. [240] Yet it was not so much Hunter's departure after twenty years that would prove the decisive factor, but the appointment of Francis (John) Taylor as the new bishop: he was to prove himself 'a conceptual world away from that of the Chaplains'. Not only could his style be described as hierarchical, but he appeared to relate only to Michael Jackson, with whom a bond developed, making the rest of the team feel like 'curates'.[241]

Jackson would now call for a recognition of changes in industry itself, and a need for fundamental research, rather than assume there were clearly agreed principles from which the mission could move forward. Despite all the years he had spent working in industry, says Bagshaw, Jackson now 'stood theologically, as it were, outside looking in'. There began a shift in direction, so that by the time the broader questions about the nature of Christian belief had begun to emerge through publications like Robinson's *Honest to God*, Jackson was already alarmed at the theological climate. By 1963, it was becoming clear that he was no longer in sympathy with the original aims of SIM, and a growing and protracted debate began. Jackson is then understood to have had a 'change of heart' and was apparently converted to a thorough going orthodox authoritarianism. The change is described in a variety of ways. John Halsey remembers the reaction of those left in Sheffield that Jackson had 'gone all evangelical': 'like a convert', Roland Walls has added.[242] From a position where he had once argued for a non-professional ministry where the priest's concern 'is his place of work and organizations connected with it like trade unions', and where he could say 'today it is impossible for the church to serve that nation adequately through the parishes . . . it must find other ways of "being parochial" ', Jackson now seemed to be arguing a different viewpoint, and clearly wanted to implement his own vision. Yet Walls argues that industrial mission is essentially 'an ambivalent thing . . .' and that Jackson earnestly believed that it should be more than simply 'politics and social concern'.[243] But Walls also admits that all this had much to do with the change of bishop and a bishop's theology.

In late 1965, during an annual two-day conference for the Mission, Jackson set out an entirely new position 'utterly at variance with what Wickham had taught and the position they [chaplains] had held since joining the mission'.[244] In the ensuing arguments, Jackson gave two chaplains, Parker and Mackey, twelve months' notice to quit their jobs, arguing that they had as it were 'gone native' by crossing the gulf, so that Christian distinctiveness had been lost in a deliberate identification with industry. Roland Walls echoes some of this, believing that Jackson may have had some sympathy with the rejection of the French worker-priests in 1954 and 1959, in which he had originally so much interest.

Jackson's determination not to discuss the issues but relentlessly to pursue the dismissals he had made did little for the image of the Mission and much for an approaching breakdown. Every offer to Jackson or the bishop of assistance or intervention was dismissed. In a letter to an industrial body the bishop made it clear that it was for the church to 'exercise authority about where and how its ministers should serve'.

An ensuing 'Barker' enquiry, set up by Donald Coggan, Archbishop of York, blamed Wickham for what had now befallen the mission. The chaplains were criticized for 'interfering' in the day-to-day running of industry, but worse, the report gave the impression that the direction and style of the mission had evolved 'over against' the church, 'developing a distinct orthodox sectarianism',[245] an argument close to that levelled against the French worker-priests. Bagshaw details what was virtually the end of the original mission by September 1966 when nearly all the chaplains had gone. But the most serious aspect was the collapse of the lay projects, which focussed their disappointment in the institution, and in Jackson in particular.

> The Thursday Evening group declared itself separate from Jackson, and, with one or two discussion groups, continued a separate existence. After a while, however, it all petered out. Most people simply voted with their feet, disillusioned with the church. Some recalled years later that they never again received Holy Communion. That the groups continued was a tribute to Wickham's success in establishing a para-church; that they were unsustainable revealed the shallow roots of the enterprise.[246]

Wickham himself might have admitted such shallowness – after all he had argued as early as 1957 that the venture had to be permanent, sustained, there was to be no going back. Even the Abbé Godin had said as much. But Jackson's position was set out in a 1966 article in *Theology*, where he claimed that the task of industrial mission 'was to preach the gospel and to bring men to acknowledge (the) love and vision of God as revealed in Jesus Christ . . .':

> It preaches the gospel of the kingdom of God who is King. There is no Kingdom without naming the King. The task of proclamation is to say this and of teaching to work out its implications for men in industry. There is no new gospel for them, nor is there a special theology of the Church's mission and ministry in Industry.[247]

In May 1967 a report on the past history and future prospects of the Mission was published under the Chairman of H. P. Forder, of United Steel Company Ltd, and himself from an evangelical background. Here is an attempt to tidy up theory and practice by asking whether the Mission as they thought recently constituted and operating, had been able to fulfil its 'original' mission. A key element was the question of whether the Mission had achieved its aim of building a 'bridge' between the church and industry. Was progress made to 'change the attitude of men and women *towards* the churches'? (my emphasis). The argument became more explicit. Concern ought to be expressed that the 'bridge' ought to connect with 'the recognized church, and not with "industrial mission" as being a destination in itself'.[248] But Wickham would have none of that, and was all for confirming that those attached to the mission were already a full part of the life of the church, which had emerged in the working lives of those who had joined. However, Forder's 'nevertheless' was that 'vital Christian belief must always be the goal in view . . .' and that had clearly been downplayed since 'the mission has had the not uncommon experience of finding the right path to follow difficult to find, and a loss of confidence over this seems sometimes to have diverted attention in favour of other easier objectives'. This was hardly surprising when in Forder's view the mission had attracted into its ranks '. . . some men out of sympathy with traditional church ideas'.[249] This devastating halt to progress, shocking even in its reading now, was reported in some quarters as the 'failure of a mission' rather than an event which was the result of a complete change of tactics and theology, which then led to breakdown. Mary's Walton's *History* (1981) glosses over these events, but admits to various important records being unavailable for use; with much of the material 'strangely biased and some of it bad tempered'.[250]

Although it was not the end of the story – for the Mission with a 'new' constitution continued – it was certainly the end of a chapter, not only in Sheffield but, as Grundy says, in the world of industrial mission itself. Ranged against a committed group which sought to allow an indigenous church to emerge in the context of everyday life and work, was a deliberately based strategy, an institutional strategy, which sought through its own understanding of apostleship to dispense 'the truth' to that industrial world. That was certainly the view of the Forder Report. Even though he had modified his views, and had grown increasingly uneasy about the very few that seemed to be carried 'over' by a bridge, Leslie Hunter was able to respond, when asked if the original aims of the Mission had been clearly presented in the Report, that they were *not* accurate, indeed:

> They ignored the utter irrelevance of the Church to industrial society. The Mission's aims had never been articulated in this way and the Mission would not have succeeded if they had been.

But Hunter's perspective was too far from that of the Forder enquiry for them to accommodate it. They assumed that the nature of the mission was indeed to fish in a muddy pool, and to draw people out of it into the uncontaminated waters of the church.[251]

The work of visiting began again with a newly constituted team, and a new purpose. But the damage had been done, says Margaret Kane, '... to individuals who had found meaning in their lives and some glimmer of faith through industrial mission. Trust was destroyed, lasting damage to everyone ...' Factory visiting, thought of in the 1950s and 1960s as lacking roots and ending in a cul-de-sac, could not now be described as even that. One man talked about '... the vacuity of the subsequent meetings'. 'The padre came in, exchanged plenty of greeting certainty, but tended to flit through rather than stay. When this happens we as missioners ourselves feel the emptiness.'[252] A manager later recalled that though the mission originally took people as they were, later meetings 'began with prayer; that turned us off; and there was a kind of sermon talk from the minister. One didn't want that.'[253] Those with little impulse to join the established churches had less inclination to do so after 1966. Philip Bloy mentions some as having taken a part in their local parishes, while others claimed that these local parishioners were still not ready for people who belonged to industrial mission. One remarked: 'The local church wants me to do chores ... (while) industrial mission has done far more to help me grow.'[254]

Saddest of all, the mission's eucharists[255] were brought to a halt by episcopal closure in the first half of the 1960s, and many members of the mission never received Holy Communion again. As Roland Walls put it (and whether significant numbers or not ever attended or received): 'To Jackson, the Holy Communion was a kind of club for the redeemed; for Wickham it was about the healing of humanity.'[256] It made Wickham's words in 1964 sadly prophetic:

> All too easily it has been assumed, and still is assumed, that on the one hand was the church, possessing and embodying the gospel, and on the other hand the 'world' without it, and the evangelistic task was to preach it from one to the other, and so to win the world into the church.[257]

Wickham talked much later in the early 1970s about the 'institutionalization' of industrial mission, commenting sadly that: 'we have even seen the dismantling of [Industrial Mission's] largest and most radical expression in this country by diocesan action and without the intervention from wider church authority'. At the time, *New Christian*, a radicalized paper in the style of *New Society*, in its leader for 28 July 1966 commented that the unhappy story of the crisis had moved from the 'tragic to the incredible', adding that though it was easy enough to dismiss chaplains, 'unfortunately it is not possible to dismiss Bishops as easily . . . and that therefore resignation remains the only honourable course open to those who have failed'. The implication was crystal clear: 'failure' there had indeed been; but it was not the Mission that had failed.

4. Conclusion: introducing Britain's first worker-priests

That the 'world of work' focussed the attention of some institutional churchmen in England and France in the post-war years goes without saying. That the mission had to begin in the industrial areas went without question. But was it to be parish-based or work-site based? Were clergy theologically, pastorally and spiritually prepared to meet these challenges, and how would laity respond? Strategies would be different in both countries, yet both would be attacked from within, as the startled and nervous saw in these new endeavours a direct threat to their traditional theological perspectives and practices.

What France and Sheffield shared was an attempt to articulate the problem – albeit provisionally – and to act in consequence. In France, Godin's *France, Pays de Mission?* set a scene and raised tantalizing questions which Temple was not yet asking. In Britain by 1962, A. J. Drewett, Rector of St Margaret's Lothbury, could describe England as a 'mission field' where the churches had failed, so that now 'The industrial mission faces the fact that the place where a man works is likely to be a greater influence in his life than the place where he lives.'[258] Wickham 'conceded' a case for the worker-priests in France, where the estranged working classes were different from those in Britain where less hostility warranted a less radical approach. So while France's worker-priests slid anonymously into factories and working-class tenements to maintain *la presence* among the industrial poor and marginalized, Wickham and his chaplains went forth on to the shop floors of Sheffield as visitors to engage and debate, usually with the blessings of management and unions. Perhaps only in England could there have been such 'even-handedness'.

In common, however, and perhaps before there was time for reflection and further long-term planning, tragic loss of leadership befell both enterprises. The death of Godin in 1946 and Suhard in 1949 deprived the worker-priests in 1953–1954 of vital patronage and the spiritual dimension they were so often accused of lacking. In Sheffield, the fatal appointment of Wickham to Middleton and the retirement of Hunter robbed the Mission of a vision, if not always shared, then at least convergent. Wickham had piloted the Mission into uncharted waters; Michael Jackson believed it had been driven on the rocks of heresy: Gnostic, pantheist, anything but a reflection of a faith rooted in the saving work of Christ.

And there were always strong voices showing real anxiety. In a leader in the *Modern Churchman* in March 1960, the author, looking at the 'Signs of the Times', alluded to the 'error' of the French worker-priests and asked if the Church Assembly, in voting funds to extend the work of industrial mission, was not jumping 'on a bandwagon just as it grinds to a halt'? He believed that it was wrong for priests to 'identify' with workers or management, and right for Britain's industrial chaplains to draw their keep 'from independent sources'. Then, raising again the territorial parish as 'the nub', he suggested that in a second 'error of divorcing evangelism in industry from the mission, life and worship of the parish . . . we have not been so blameless'. In a direct allusion to Wickham the leader continues: 'The first and best known of our industrial chaplains, who is one no longer, has been very vocal in denigrating the parish and its clergyman as out of date, out of touch, and out of luck.'

If there was any common understanding of the needs for industrial mission in France and Britain, there was, by contrast, some difference not only in the methods but in the theology. The French worker-priests, in time, and through experience, though determined not to be clericalized, nevertheless maintained a sacerdotal understanding of priesthood which marked them off from the laity, and in the early stages, at least, made them think of themselves as the 'real' representatives of the church. It was, after all, Godin's intention that believers should 'bring the light of Christ' into an industrial world. And later, in arguing that Christ had not 'abandoned young folk in the ghettos', he might have been implying that Christ was only present in these same believers. Yet there was also, perhaps, a deeper understanding of an 'incarnational ministry' in responding to a God who had 'made himself like unto us in all things . . .'

But the 'gulf' and the hoped-for 'bridge' also existed in Britain. Industrial chaplains were already well aware of a Britain where class divisions remained, yet where a growing affluence in parallel with crime, youth culture and other developing social changes might be making any 'gulf' even wider. In centres like Sheffield, where Wickham's novel methods produced, in the eyes of Hunter and his successors, no 'obvious results', the new leaders could ultimately question the methods employed. Yet the converging points in these attempts at mission have been the subject of Erlander's study, which has highlighted a theological dividing line between the 'church and the world'; between the forces for parochial ministry and the territorial parish on the one hand, and the radicalism of 'worldly pioneers' on the other. Although Erlander admits to great differences in the social and economic background to the missions, that 'the Kingdom was a notion that should be seen in common' may be less obvious. It is true that John Robinson and Ted Wickham, both as early as 1957, had talked about the kingdom standing in question, even in judgment, over the institutional church, but the idea of kingdom is less stressed among the French worker-priests, though Emile Poulat begins to explore the theme, and Catholic theory explained by Cardijn claimed 'No kingdom of God without work'. But the worker-priests themselves were quieter on the subject of kingdom, though Perrin, on at least one occasion, makes mention of it. It was not that they might have disagreed, but their early perspectives were different; an incarnational presence was their starting point. Simon Phipps' *God on Monday* does not stress kingdom where we might expect it, and Margaret Kane, who has written much on the subject, admits that this kind of thinking is not developed till the 1960s.

Of the two enterprises, however divergent in theory and practice, convergent perhaps in unconventional determination and optimism, the radicalism of the worker-priests, albeit in a nervous, autocratic and highly clericalized institution, was the more remarkable, so that David Edwards in an introductory discussion could say that it was

> . . . the most courageous and extensive experiment undertaken by any Christian church anywhere in the world to bridge the gulf fixed since the nineteenth century between organized religion and the working class.[259]

And it was perhaps for this reason that Ted Wickham himself was willing to admit:

> . . . whenever the question of the church and the poor or the church and the workers is raised, the worker-priests of France will trouble the conscience of a comfortable church just as the Poor Man of Nazareth does himself.[260]

And because he admired them, those who chose to be like them in Britain were always a threat to Wickham's own radical missionaries' endeavours on the shop floor. For in the early 1950s, and just as the French were being condemned for the first time, a small group of Anglican clergy embarked on this most radical mission of all, entering factory and mine as workers, and thus occupying a place alongside the French. Bagshaw singles out this small band of British worker-priests as the 'one influence (which) threatened Wickham's vision, not by dilution but by its strength'. Later, in the 1960s, John Rowe, one of Britain's first worker-priests, would write to a friend:

> Our complaint against industrial chaplaincy and all other kinds of approach to the working people except our own was precisely that it was an attempt to love from one level *downwards* to another. We have said that this has been enormously significant . . . characteristic of so much of the churches' love for centuries. We want to witness to a way of loving which is we think more genuine, more *Christian.*[261]

But Wickham need not have worried, though discussion for a brief time highlighted Britain's first worker-priests, and *Crockford's Preface* gave them space and credence. As a critique of Wickham's methods they could not be ignored. In a changing Britain, where modern industrialization and a new welfare economy developed alongside significant cultural and social changes, it was they alone who pushed out furthest, taking the church at its word that it must come to terms with the world of industry, they alone who pushed out to a more radical expression of non-parochial ministry and mission, taking even Stanley Booth-Clibborn and Michael Jackson at their word, 'that the traditional Anglican conception of the established church ministering to the whole nation . . . should be carried over into a field where so many members of our society spend so much of their lives'.[262] However, Britain's first worker-priests – a most radical expression of post-war ministry – would for ever remain a handful, as an institutional church and the majority of its clergy, rooted in the territorial parish, found it hard to comprehend this vocation.

III

Among the First Worker-Priests: Origins and Collisions 1943–1962

'. . . I have always wanted to work with my hands . . . I felt half consciously that I was not a man, because I have never done what the world calls "useful" work. I suppose only a celibate would feel this – not a man with children; certainly I felt it, and was glad at last to be a man among men at work. Something of the same joy was being felt almost at the same time by my opposite numbers (if I may call them so) in France.'

(The Rev Michael Gedge beginning manual labour in an armaments factory, 1943)

'Those who seek to speak to people in this situation (factory life) must understand it . . . in order to understand it one must also live in it.'

(John Strong, writing about his experience as a worker-priest in the *Oxford Diocesan Magazine*, Vol. 8, No 7, 1975)

Introduction

Stories of clergy[263] in Britain who sought a means to earn their own living outside the constraints of the institutional churches out of a sense of necessity (they could not live on the stipend alone), missionary zeal, or other calling, are not necessarily new, and certainly pre-date the efforts of those who followed the French and might be described as Britain's first worker-priests.

The most comprehensive study of the slow but significant development of clergy who might earn their own living in secular employment has been undertaken in Patrick Vaughan's *Non-Stipendiary Ministry in the Church of England*,[264] in which he traces the history of that later ministry which evolved in the 1960s, but whose tortuous gestation is given much detailed attention. In examining the developing interests of Thomas Arnold, Roland Allen and F. R. Barry, who all argued for different kinds of 'non-stipendiary ministries' – as Barry would name the practice –

Vaughan describes the long history of different working clergy, from those who toiled on a small piece of land or 'glebe' in mediaeval times, to those who earned their living teaching. He highlights important theologies of the protagonists who argued for a variety of 'supplementary ministries', and how these slowly became acceptable on the more pragmatic grounds of shoring up the parochial system, especially at times in the twentieth century – and between the wars – when there was a chronic shortage of manpower.

Outlining 'early experiences of priests in industry' he notes those like Wickham who had had some experience of factory life, but highlights first Hugh Lister, an engineering graduate from Cambridge, who, in 1929, following ordination, held 'no ecclesiastical office . . . but devoted himself to Trade Union and WEA work among factory workers in Hackney Wick where he lived at his own expense'. Lister lost his life after becoming a combatant in 1944. An article in *Theology*, 1947, comparing Lister with the Abbé Godin, and a later biography, were seen by Vaughan as '. . . written testimony to this Anglican priest's actual life (which) appeared at the very moment that the notion of priests in industry was prominently under discussion'.[265]

There may have been many more 'working clergy' who for a variety of reasons took to secular employment before Lambeth officially withdrew objections in 1958, though it is difficult to track them down, and efforts for this study have often drawn a complete blank.[266] One example, however, is William Simpkiss who, in 1955, gave up his 'full-time' employment as a clergyman and began working in a woodwork shop. Simpkiss, who had been a combatant, suffered badly during the war, particularly in hostilities in the later stages in Holland. Finding it very hard to settle down, he left his wife and child for a while, and sought work outside the church. A devout man, and devoted to his family, who in turn understood his suffering, Simpkiss began work in Reading in March 1955. With little knowledge of other worker-priests – and the story from France was barely known – there is some evidence he was aware of Perrin's *Priest-Workman in Germany*, and may have felt that 'the church was out of touch'.[267] An Oriel College scholar who was trained at Wescott House, Cambridge, Simpkiss was ordained deacon in 1949, serving originally in the Portsmouth diocese. There is also some evidence that he discussed his proposal for manual work with a bishop at the time he was serving in a parish, for the latter's reaction is remembered as one of 'total incomprehension', but Simpkiss nevertheless went to work, and decided to keep a diary for the first three months.

The carpentry in which he was engaged gave him some time for mental prayer, and he admits to saying the offices while at the bench. There is some reflection on the camaraderie at work, and he clearly enjoyed much of it. He comments on the work that men do, on swearing, which he believed a simple way of expressing oneself, and wondered why so often others took offence. He found the work place 'not unlike the army' – there were very few churchmen on the staff – even though church furnishings were made at the place.[268] He took a close interest in the workings of the union, was aware of Ted Wickham's work in Sheffield, and listened to a radio broadcast service from there, uncertain of some of the things Wickham was driving at but generally sympathetic. He realized that Rogation Sunday might be renamed Industrial Sunday, and shared the concerns of many others that the institutional church remained out of touch. But the reader is also struck by the total lack of support from anyone who thinks like the diarist; he is entirely on his own. Simpkiss later served in other parishes before an early death.

Whenever ministries like those of Lister, Simpkiss or others appeared, they were marked by individual effort alone, and rarely by the support of an institution 'from the top'. For the early protagonists like Arnold and Allen, there were very real underlying theological issues about the true nature of Christian ministry, but these were lost as the clerical and professional were maintained. In England, the church continued to draw men from the middle and upper classes, and generally only for the parochial ministry. But it was from these clergy, interested in the industrial settings within the context of a new social and cultural post-war Britain, that some would seek a means to engage with that working world either as chaplains or some kind of worker-priests. The motivation for this would prove to be mixed, and had something to do with a fearful curiosity and respect for an 'industrial world'. It was this 'other world' that made the Revd John Bickersteth (who would later enter it for just a fortnight in 1959) realize just how '. . . appallingly difficult Christian witness, positive outspoken Christian witness, must be for the ordinary layman in that sort of job'.[269] If that was the case in 1959, by which time industrial mission had already won a place in the church's mission it must have been more so some sixteen years earlier, when the first Anglican clergyman who deliberately identified himself with the French, and who would document his life among workers, began to consider another way of being a priest.

1. Michael Gedge: priest-workman in England

(i) Theological and pastoral background

In 1943, and without knowledge of what was about to happen in occupied France, the Revd Michael Gedge began seriously to consider a role outside the territorial parish, though he later admitted that '. . . the inner process by which one makes up one's mind is a long and complicated business of which one knows less than all oneself'.[270] Gedge had studied classics at Leeds University (1923–25) and spent a further two years at the Community of the Resurrection, Mirfield, before he was ordained at the end of 1927. He began his ministry as an assistant curate at St Mary – Extra, Pear Tree Green, Southampton, under the then incumbent William Mowat, and remained there from 1927 to 1931.[271] This was an area where he recalls some 3,500 people 'and a group of large, almost entirely pagan (youth) clubs'[272] and a 'long history of anti-clericalism among the workers, and sometimes open hostility – sometimes rather distant courtesy – between church and clubs'.[273]

Gedge later became a parish-based Charterhouse missioner and remained so for more than a decade, with thoughts of moving from a parochially-based life far from his mind till he met what he describes as a worker-priest on a 1943 visit to the Cowley Fathers in Oxford.[274] Later, and through a friend, Gedge made contact with the manager of Benham and Sons Ltd (Heating and Ventilation Engineers), at Garret Lane, Wandsworth in SW 18, where he would work from 1943 to the end of the war. This would later be followed by six months at Hoe-Crabtree, manufacturers of printing equipment. The main result of these two jobs was the publication of a book by SPCK in 1951, which, following the translation of Perrin's diary, *Priest-Workman in Germany*, Gedge would entitle *Priest-Workman in England – A Study in Life*. For the first time, the title priest-worker is used, as Gedge deliberately places himself at the beginning of what he hoped might be a new tradition.

The introduction to Gedge's story gives his own reflection on the priest-worker movement in France – then in full swing. Their stories now filtering through from France must have come to Gedge as a total vindication of all he had attempted during the war and immediate post-war years. He leaves the 1951 reader in no doubt as to the importance of what was happening across the Channel, politically, liturgically and theologically. For Gedge, however, there had been a personal motivation as he had asked himself in 1943, 'How is it that our most faithful church people, more than that, our most faithful Christians so often frankly admit, and sometimes firmly claim, that one cannot be a real Christian at work?'[275]

(ii) Into work 1943 – timetable and tasks

Michael Gedge confesses that it was dark when he first made his way to 'Mannings', the pseudonym he used for Benham and Sons, to begin work a little after 8 a.m. on a late autumn morning in 1943. When the vicar with whom he worked asked him if he was afraid, 'I told him no – and meant it'. 'I felt strongly,' he wrote, 'that I did not look much like a priest in my rather old boiler suit and open-necked shirt.' Father Loew in Marseilles had done precisely the same in 1941 when he had set out to find the true nature of his parish by purchasing an old pair of overalls and beginning work as a docker.[276] Now Gedge suddenly felt a sense of fulfilment, even solidarity: '. . . glad at last to be a man among men at work'.

Gedge describes his day beginning at 8 a.m., with a clock-in that 'had to be at 7.59 a.m. Alf is reading his paper; Paul, opposite me, is at his tool cupboard, where he cherishes a valuable set of tools which he has built up for years.'[277] With everyone else in place the day begins 'mechanically'. 'I mean I am almost as mechanical as the job.' Gedge found himself keeping an occasional eye on the time, because if he 'got off to a good start' before the 9.50 a.m. 'lunch' break, it seemed to help the passage of time for the rest of the day.

Within the first hour, and by at least 9.15 a.m., he already confesses to feeling bored. He describes in detail the 'race' with himself as he attempted to get through as many jobs as possible, without looking at the clock before tea came round; and when the break did arrive, it was down tools for everyone, as Gedge admits:

> My eye catches the clock as I talk to Tom, and I can see that I can get one or more of these brackets done; for it is a serious offence to go on working after the break comes – that would be to sabotage the time which generations of workers have wrung, or negotiated, from the management.[278]

With the break, machines are switched off, and the chatter begins. At first, Gedge did not always join his work mates at the snap-break meeting, sometimes leaving time for reflection, even meditation in mentally saying one of the monastic offices. His training at Mirfield had impressed a discipline upon him, and he wondered, later, what the French would be doing in similar circumstances. But Gedge also used the time to talk to work mates, and anticipated, from the 'inside' as it were, what would evolve only a few years later in Sheffield when Ted Wickham would 'walk into' this closely-knit community. Gedge, even at the beginning, felt uncertain about 'what to do' and how to react to 'dirty jokes' or the general camaraderie, but was at least able to listen and learn from his work mates as they talked and joked openly about their life and times.[279]

After the break Gedge began his drilling again, 'the real morning's run'. After thirty minutes a welcomed 'music while you work' from the radio came over the shop-floor loudspeakers till 11a.m., when the tannoy resumed its more mundane task of summoning individuals to the general office. But Gedge, like other workers, enjoyed that musical interlude, even though he quickly felt at home in a context that gave him satisfaction at the press on a red button, '. . . in time I came to love my machine in a way which everyone in the shop noticed'. Before the midday break, however, Gedge would long for some kind of contact that would break up the monotony of what he was doing. Indeed the foreman had admitted to him that 'every man needed to get away and have a break from time to time: to walk around the firm and have a smoke, to chat to friends and so on'.[280] But this mid-morning period was the worst of all for the men, and Gedge began to consider how he could use the time mentally and spiritually. Sometimes towards the end of a morning it would be Gedge's turn to take the bucket of hot water around in order that hands might be washed and spirits raised a little before it was time for the canteen and dinner at 12.58 p.m.

Gedge details his work under 'Paul', 'the best engineer in the firm', when he began operating a massive drilling machine (later used in the cover design of *Priest-Workman in England*) and working on sections which would eventually become parts of 20 mm. anti-aircraft guns. Relishing its power, Gedge describes how it would bore into jobs at speeds from 16 to 830 revolutions per minute. And it could be heavy work, fixing the job in place to be drilled with lifting tackle which only the men and not the women were allowed to handle. Nevertheless, the tasks required skilled setting on a jig by Paul before Gedge could begin drilling. The mysteries of precision engineering with patterns and jigs were slowly becoming clear. 'The art of modern engineering, therefore, is mostly a matter of jig design . . . the skill required of the individual man is almost nil . . . How sick a good engineer gets at this sort of work!'[281]

On pressing the red button which started the machine, the bit was sent into the job, throwing off 'swarf' and liquid as the job was constantly kept cool, with clothing, as Gedge found out soon, torn to shreds. But the drilling gave him the pleasure of what he described as 'a small boy with a model railway engine'. On a good day he was able to get four of the gun-carriages drilled and tapped (the fixing of screw threads), learning essentially by watching others, especially 'old George', just how to get maximum leverage on the job.

(iii) Of social and spiritual reflection

Gedge soon began to appreciate just how inglorious work could be, and he remarks that he would never again listen without impatience to those who, without experience of manual labour, saw it only as 'an offering to God' . . . 'as a means of making it glorious'. 'Such people,' he suggests, 'have more experience of liturgy than life.' In his reflection now upon what the industrial revolution had done to working men, Gedge recognizes how: 'The overseas capital on which we have lived for two great wars, was the direct fruit of the exploitation, through slum, factory and mine, of millions of human beings in the nineteenth century.'[282]

> Thus machinery produces the seeds of human destruction: not only through atom bombs, aeroplanes, and the like, but through mechanizing man himself, through tying man to the machine . . .[283]

Wartime work went on day and night, and the opportunity soon came for Gedge to do night shifts. He never really got used to this. The difference in time-pattern was such that he had some difficulty adjusting to 8 p.m. to 7.30 a.m. Monday to Friday, with just three breaks in the course of the night. In the middle of the shift, possibly in the 9.30 p.m to 10 p.m. break, like others, he found it particularly trying when his strength 'seemed to ebb'. It was often the case, he admits, that if he sat down at any time between 3–5 a.m., he might simply fall asleep. He was already feeling the strain of worship in the early morning for which he still had some responsibility. When it came to more theological and spiritual reflection, and by the end of the first year, it was already clear to Gedge that it was none too easy to be a Christian – in the sense that he understood it – at work. He had, at times, hung back from some conversation, or continued to work when others had stopped, determined not to cheat the system, claiming on more than one occasion that he was putting the effort in 'for the boys' (those fighting on the front).

When it came to spiritual disciplines themselves, Gedge saw it as a challenge to maintain a number of practices in the context of this new life. Some were imposed; he still had responsibility for a daughter church in his parish, which stood – as it happened – opposite the gates of the factory. But it was in his daily routine that he attempted to interlock work and prayer, not easy when one was building weapons; Perrin was able to admit to deliberate sabotage of German products.[284] Gedge, by contrast, saw himself a part of the war effort.

On the day shift, Gedge's day began with a 6.45 a.m. eucharist, after which he said Prime (one of the monastic offices).[285] This was followed throughout the day by other offices which he said by heart as he worked – perhaps a Mirfield man was well suited to this routine. Terce he said in the lunch break, though not always, and he wondered as he later reflected in writing, what the French might do. On other occasions he would keep the hours of the cross, rosary, or simply have a book. Seeing the machine as a possible cross for man, and the often wretched nature of labour, he had more chance than most clergy of coming to terms with what he felt was the reality of life and prayer. Indeed, in his second job in 1948, Gedge found that his round of prayer fitted more easily into the daily routine, where he would pray seated on the floor.

Thus, like others after him, Gedge had had to begin to learn to use that 'slow-motion' time that can envelop the worker. Mentally and constructively, while still attentive to the job in hand, he was to learn to pray his labour. Perhaps it was essentially the business of using that endless time. About a decade later, in Alan Sillitoe's novel, Arthur Seaton, hunched over his lathe, admits:

> That now whole days could be given up to wool-gathering. Hour after hour quickly disappeared when once you started thinking, and before you knew where you were, a flashing light from the foreman's office signalled ten o'clock, time for white overalled women to wheel in the tea urns . . . [286]

Gedge, too, was thinking; but the same expanse of time was being put to different use. In his inner searching, through the discipline of office or meditation, he admits to getting '. . . through the next hour till about 12 noon'.[287] Even in the writing of his narrative, the reality of those long days is brought home to him again, days which he sometimes thought would never come to an end.

Later, in 1948, while Gedge was in his second job, but very much at home in a new working environment, one man had remarked that he could not see how Gedge could actually feel God's presence 'in a loathsome place like this'. But Gedge was quite clear, '. . . that was just the joy of it. It pierced through me with an indescribable sweetness to be with God.'[288]

(iv) Of men and morals

Moral and ethical issues played a large part in Gedge's reflection, though the occasions which came to hand were often difficult to deal with, and raised questions about his very reason for being on the shop floor. Early on he openly admitted to the fact he was a priest, and was then faced with a combination of reserve and indifference. 'Religion was your affair,' he reflected, 'and provided you were prepared to speak up for it in your daily argument, as I was, then that was that.' The daily lunch break, as Ted Wickham was to find out later, was the general occasion of such interchange. Gedge could sometimes find himself involved in heated arguments, only to discover unexpectedly thoughtful and kindly replies from men; '[it] . . . made me realize that we can seldom judge what is the real value of a man's soul, or what goes on in it'. Yet Gedge felt compelled to take a moral stance on a number of issues, including the use of time, effort for the war, and price-fixing for jobs, where he stubbornly attempted to see fair rates agreed. On one occasion, on admitting to being perhaps too candid and honest resulting in the price of a job actually being cut, he adds:

> I never discovered whether the other workers knew that I have been guilty of what they would have considered sabotage of their interests . . . a priest had a considerable advantage over the lay Christian. They expect me to be an odd person doing mad things, and they were not always disappointed.[289]

This contrasts with Perrin's feelings in 1950s Paris that he shared low wages, which were certainly in evidence after the demands of war. There were other 'oddities' too. Gedge admits to howls of protest from work mates when he handed back a bottle of whisky he had won in a draw, a bottle which his workmates considered theirs too!

Confronting individuals with moral decision-making was no easier than sharing what he felt was the natural expression of his faith lived in the context of a working community. 'Bob' Turner, with whom he spent many hours on fire-watch duty,[290] was clearly a welcoming individual, who made a considerable impact on Gedge. Here he was confronted with an engaging humanity. Yet 'success' with Turner (by which Gedge implied some kind of conversion) there never was: that, 'He and his wife welcomed me' can be read with a warmth inherent in the admission, but is followed by a kind of disappointment that there '. . . was a time when I very nearly got Bob to church during Lent'. But Bob was not going to come to church for Lent or anything else, leaving Gedge decidedly ill-at-ease. For Hunter and Wickham a little later in Sheffield, there would be a different approach for the likes of Bob, meeting him in discussion at a 'snap break' meeting as the industrial mission sought its own way of moving beyond the territorial parish. For now, Gedge reflects almost with bewildering hurt: 'What are we to say of these people whose friendship warms our lives, whose conduct may well be as good as ours, who say prayers from time to time, and perhaps turn up at church once or twice a year?'[291] What indeed? Mass Observation's enquiries just a couple of years later showed there might be lots like the Turners, who, despite what Gedge had to offer, felt they could not make a 'move' into the institution. For Gedge, the territorial parish, and allegiance to it, remained the hallmark of committed Christian life. He was not yet able to contemplate another form, though he admitted that for the laity there were long hours of work, a family life, and that they too deserved rest and recreation.

In his second year (1944) Gedge began a youth club in the parish; something with which he had had much experience. Gedge saw here, and now with the hindsight and knowledge brought from the shop floor, the shocking reality of what the war had done. He could see for himself a 'dislocated' community, as pressure came to bear upon families where husbands and fathers remained overseas. Sinfield's quotation, 'He was away for five years – Now can you imagine that', could have been echoed by Gedge at any time.[292] When VE day finally came, the works manager took up Gedge's suggestion for a thanksgiving service in the church. 'I . . . was truly astonished to find the church packed with men standing in the aisles and at the door.' Some – though not all – might have come if it was simply the local vicar making the invitation. But it was a fellow worker here; this, above all, was precisely the right moment – and the right thing to do.

With the war ended, and munitions factories turning to peacetime production, Gedge left his secular employment and returned to his former ministry as a parish priest. What he later describes as an unsympathetic vicar in Wandsworth, and a surprising lack of parochial posts elsewhere, led him to seek a second 'term' as a worker-priest in 1948, with his bishop 'slightly peeved' that he had got himself the job, 'though he couldn't deny that he hadn't one for me at the time'.[293] In his autobiographical work, Gedge describes his role as a labourer at an engineering works which he names 'Blands'. He explains that, at the time, it might only take two hours from entering a labour exchange for an individual to find work; such was the demand for skilled men.

Once again Gedge gives an account of his working day, which this time began with a 7.30 a.m. 'clock in' only after he had celebrated a 6.30 eucharist followed by breakfast. In this second job, there is no let-up by Gedge on his self-appraisal of attitudes and responses to his workmates. He again tried to engage with men who had become 'lapsed' in their religious practice, and for a second time attempted to start a prayer group – without any great success. Worried less about continual swearing (which some others seemed to think difficult for a clergyman),[294] he was more concerned with 'illicit tea drinking', something disallowed by the management. But because he believed men worked better for a 'cuppa' he took one when offered.

(v) The process of reflection

In the third part of his *Priest-Workman in England*, and following some reflection, Gedge sets out a deliberate 'So what?' to his factory life. Somewhat hardened by several years on the shop floor, he attempts to analyse the encounters he had had with working men and begins to make generalized remarks about their ability to shape and shift their own mental processes. He thought young men in their twenties already fixed in their thinking, and men over forty positively 'ossified'. They could not be 'changed' (which he had felt was his mission), but they might trust a priest, and consequently be willing to listen and learn. In fact, throughout his story we do not hear of a single 'conversion'. He comes close to men, and they to him, but it is at a human level, an encounter warm, accepting: it does not lead to a commitment, explicit spiritual life, or churchgoing, for which Gedge might have wished. Gedge's solution was not that clergy should suddenly drop everything and enter industrial life; rather, there is the clear conclusion that the parochial role remains normative for a priest, who should be prepared to stay in his parish 'not less than ten years'. A priest's essential duty, therefore, is the nurturing of the young. If the young could be encouraged, then they might grow into faithful believing adults. He remained a passionate believer in youth organizations which should help to develop a youngster's life.

But what about the very question with which he began, the question John Bickersteth would ask some nine years later: was it possible to be a Christian at work? In one sense the simple answer was Yes. But it would not be easy. The Christian at work must not aim to make 'as much money as possible', and should not be afraid to be seen as 'a rather peculiar person'. It was a tall order, when achieving self-esteem in a place of work had something to do with being accepted by others. But for Gedge, the Christian, marching off to war, must put up with the constraints of the battlefield and the disciplines of the spiritual life.

Gedge returned to his main theme – that a large majority were left 'fixed' in their ways – so that the youth club or general work with the young remained essential. Parish missions, with their door-to-door visiting, are valuable, often received with warmth. 'Many people are glad enough to have the church come to them, or to do anything for them, or to argue with them. It is quite another matter when they are faced with the challenge to do something for God.' To 'do something for God' has always been a kind of code which refers the believing Christian back to responsibilities of regular church commitment.[295] In short, going to church and making one's communion were the outward and visible signs of adherence to Christian teaching about the visible body of Christ, the institutional church, embodied in the local territorial parish.

There appeared, from time to time, and understandably, some contradictions in Gedge's thinking. He admits to the high probability of the difficult if not impossible task of 'changing' twenty- to thirty-year-olds set in their ways, yet he also wants to allow for 'the slow growth of the human soul':

> . . . and ask ourselves if it is fair or sufficient, to give a man one invitation in these pagan days (when his knowledge of God may be much less than a Jewish villager in our Lord's time) and then pass him by if it is not accepted the first time.[296]

Mission should be in theory (what it had so often been in practice) an enterprise to 'build up the Christianity of a congregation' – encouraging disciplining ventures.

Gedge firmly believed in this role for the local Christian congregation, and less in what might be described as the outreach, through industrial chaplains, in factories. In the latter there may be positive disadvantages. (a) Any chaplain may be viewed as a governor's man; (b) to visit workers *in situ* (as Gedge well knew) could prove to be an interference with production. But Gedge would never condemn the experiment of industrial chaplains, but would watch with interest and sympathy, though he remained convinced that 'in depth' contact could only be made on the shop floor and over a long period of time. Despite the importance of, perhaps even because of the existence of, the territorial parish there was still a place for the worker-priest

Essentially, Gedge wanted to see Christians in the work place 'owning up' to who they were, and at one point advocates the wearing of a badge, by which common recognition might be made. But he extends this, suggesting a permanent diaconate (possibly leading later to priesthood) in which he fairly accurately anticipated the later development of non-stipendiary ministries, with part-time training which, he then added, should 'not include any ancient language'.

In a sense, Gedge considered these possibilities from a position of almost complete isolation. He is not at this stage in touch with any others who share his thinking, and there is never any mention of episcopal initiative or encouragement, only a sometimes reluctant toleration. He advocates another possibility for engagement with the industrial work in the establishment of a religious order, an idea to which he is able to give considerable thought. Like his ideas for 'non-stipendiary' ministry and training, Gedge anticipated what emerged in Europe under Fr René Voillaume and Sister Madeleine of Jesus, when following the example of Fr Charles de Foucauld, religious communities known as the Little Brothers and Sisters of Jesus would immerse themselves and their communities in everyday life among the working-class poor in the 'deserts' of industrialized Western Europe.[297] Indeed Gedge saw life in a factory as having certain 'monastic' qualities about it, and could see no reason why a religious life could not be lived there. Some of this would later be recognized by Chadwick when in 1951, in an article in *Theology*, he suggested that: 'The disciplines of Br Lawrence (in meditation) argue that a monotonous job affords a heaven-sent opportunity for the practice of continual recollection . . . [but he does add] . . . not everyone is Br Lawrence . . . the practice of continual recollection is not something that can just be picked up at the conveyor belt . . .'[298]

But Gedge remained deeply opposed to the kind of para-church which would later evolve in Sheffield, and thought it unwise to copy the French method of forming 'special groups' of working Christians who might 'celebrate mass at the kitchen table in the evenings'. This 'is precisely what led in England to the Wesleyan schism: the French church would be wise to beware . . .'. Priest-workmen should therefore be part of a normal parish staff, for those who become Christian had to be integrated into, not separate from, the body of Christ.

Yet Gedge certainly favoured liturgical reform and passionately criticized the settings of Holy Communion in the establishment. Like others later, he was concerned that the celebration should become 'as far as possible an act of the whole people of God'. In this Gedge once again anticipates many of the changes which would later become almost commonplace to Parish and People and Southcott's admirers. These reflections were followed by calls for a revision of baptism and confirmation so that a greater sense of responsibility might be felt by those who brought children forward for these rites.

Thus an active participation in the sacramental life of the parish was a key element in the living of the Christian life. To be a Christian, for Gedge, was to live this corporate life in communion with God, with an understanding of its importance for the inner nurture of the soul. It is not something that can ever be done in isolation, and he commends in a section 'cells of witness and prayer' a kind of corporate life which the reader may feel he often missed in his factory work, though he had tried, through several groups, to initiate them.

In the context of the economy, he was clearly aware of the class system, and calls for a 'truly co-operative approach in industry and a social system where reasonable equality of education and opportunity is provided for every child of God', [299] and as decent housing for the family 'as will make decent and moral family life possible'.

He ends his 'So what?' by advocating young militants in factories and possibly on an ecumenical basis with their own 'rule of life'. At the end, however, Gedge leaves till last – revealing perhaps the greatest hurt of all – a rather damning remark about the place of the hierarchy in what he calls 'reforms'. He already recognized at least one negative feature in the ministry and mission to the industrial areas of Britain; a lamentable lack of support 'from above'. He found that

> . . . an atmosphere of uneasy suspicion, not to say hostility, seems to prevail between those who attempt reforming movements and practices, and the bishops, who, often kind and charming to (clergy) in their personal affairs, are reluctant to give them the official support. I beg the bishops to remember that a good many English priests have

fought, perhaps died for principles without official support; but we all alike accept the fruit of their struggles.[300]

(vi) Presence and theology

For its time, Gedge's narrative remains intriguing if pedestrian. From a later perspective he can appear rigorously conservative, but from an earlier perspective, a man anxious to live prophetically. His story lurches between a straight narrative of everyday working life and one where suddenly there is a flash of theological insight and recognition, that God, after all, breaks into the workaday world and into the lives of those around him. At one level Gedge was not as radical as his counterparts in France with whom he sometimes aligned himself. The worker-priests in France embraced manual labour and all its constrictions and desired to share all that came their way because of an incarnational doctrine that took them deliberately out of the parochial setting and into new and uncharted territory. Gedge, by contrast, and unsurprisingly, had difficulty letting go of the institution's framework and ministrations. He only became critical of the church towards the end – and essentially where he saw a lack of understanding and support for the kind of ministry in which he was engaged. Perrin, for example, is continually asking how, without sharing the lives of ordinary people, we can come to know how the gospel can impinge on everyday life. There is a deep and passionate concern to meet men and women where they were, to eschew some of the conventions and practices of catholicism, and to allow the estranged working class to speak for themselves. For by its life, liturgy and historical complexities, Perrin knew the institutional church had contributed to this alienation.

Gedge would not have known the early stories of worker priests; Perrin's post-war biography – compiled by friends – was not published till the 1960s. By contrast, Gedge worked within a different framework. He was a passionate believer in the teaching of the established church, the need to 'work out' one's spirituality in life, and to accept almost without reservation the spiritual practices and disciplines that came with the institution. Initially at least, he is not concerned to speak of mission as such, but to discover whether it is possible to be a Christian in the workplace at all. His answer in the end is that though it is possible to be a Christian it is very difficult, and he warns those who try to be on their guard against problems and pitfalls. Gedge falls back on the notion of the individual being a part of a 'living, believing community'. In one sense,

Gedge goes to work in a factory in order to determine the right way for the territorial parish to understand the working man. Manual labour was a means of discovering how such an engagement could take place, in the context of the parish which he still saw as the right context in which mission and ministry should continue.

There are, from time to time, difficulties in facing everyday factory life. He is sensitive over issues relating to honesty and responsibility at work, sensitive to the home lives of his workmates, yet sometimes less than fully aware of what must have been involved in bringing up a family at a time of conflict and austerity. Sometimes he is clearly less than sympathetic to the 'factory culture' around him which Perrin mentioned only infrequently, and with a rather different tone. But then Gedge is writing publicly if anonymously, while Perrin's feelings emerged from private correspondence. Sometimes Gedge seems to have something of a 'hidden agenda'. He speaks of himself as a 'crusader for Christ'. He never preaches or bullies, but nevertheless ensures that the course of his own life is directed by what he clearly understands to be firm Christian principles of compassion and honesty. Yet Gedge was constantly bewildered by those who continuously maintained that 'they never did anyone any harm'. It reflected Mass Observation's moral findings that 'doing good' was what essentially mattered. For Gedge, it was not enough. Being a Christian was about commitment to the identifiable body, the local Christian community.

But to argue that here was a warm-hearted Christian priest with conservative values meeting head-on all the vagaries and ambiguities of life in the work place, who in the end never, apparently, made a single convert, is to miss some important asides. Gedge himself came from a background where learning and community life, not to mention considerable time in the parish, had contributed to his spiritual perspectives. If it was true, as he himself believed, that men over forty were 'ossified' in their thinking, was he among them? It is difficult to avoid the conclusion that in talking about men with their set ways and practices, Gedge was unwittingly also describing himself. Rigorous, and sometimes appearing unmoved in his moral and spiritual outlook, he was faced not only with changing times, but also the unchanging, even unnerving, courtesy of the British working man.

But there was also a theology of ministry. Gedge may have admitted to entering the factory to discover whether or not one could really 'be' a Christian, but he may also have entered from deeper motives. His reflection on his very first morning, that he was '. . . glad at last to be a man among men at work. Something of the joy was being felt almost at the same time by my opposite numbers (if I may call them so) in France', reveals an inner longing to incarnate his faith in the working place, to earth it in the reality of everyday life, and in that, he shared fully the feelings and expression of France's worker-priests.

Gedge may not have been Britain's 'first' worker-priest, though that begs the question how such a person is to be defined.[301] But he was one of the first to be working in a period when the experiment was taking place elsewhere, consciously and in earnest, and the first to record in detail his reflection on events, and place himself in an entirely new tradition. What he commends for the institutional church is in many ways prophetic. In the end he did engage with working men at every level, visiting them in their homes, discovering sometimes that couples were not, after all, married, but living together. He listened and learnt, yet none of these things would have been possible unless he had had the advantage of becoming their friend on the shop floor. Rarely admitting shock or surprise, his astute judgment of others never deterred him from living his Christian life with discipline. Perhaps that was only possible because he was Michael Gedge with a Mirfield background. But he advocated for the established church all manner of practices which came to pass with astonishing accuracy.

And if there was sometimes ambiguity about what he might do at any moment of the day, and if he could not rejoice in converts, it is nevertheless the case that in terms of 'Christian mission' Gedge was forced to work in isolation. In this sense the contrast with Perrin could not have been greater. When Perrin was alone, it was never for long. In Germany he had made contact with the local churches and militant groups, he knew himself a member of a wide religious order, and he had close friends and relatives in whom he could confide. Later in Paris he was part of a growing movement, even community. It is not possible to say precisely where Gedge found his support and he says little about relationships outside the factory. We hear little of his fellow clergy, or the parochial structure which he advocates as the norm for the Christian community. Above all, Gedge's final remarks about the lack of support 'from the top' revealed the painful reality of a life and witness that deserved the blessing and encouragement for which he yearned, yet which he never received.

Gedge's was a radical step in a changing world where controversy and lengthy debate about the role of the ordained in ministry and mission was about to begin. 1948, the end of his second period in a factory, would not be the end of his story. Gedge's labouring life had yet another chapter to run, and on this next occasion he would not work alone. Yet by the time that Leslie Hunter was beginning to contemplate a new and radical mission in Sheffield, and Perrin was beginning in Germany, Michael Gedge had already clocked into the workshop to discover for himself the human realities of day to day life in a factory. So much a part of Anglican Catholic tradition, he never wished to work other than with the full sanction and support of those above him; often it seemed, he had to work without both.

2. Michael Gedge and John Strong – miners and ministers: 1951–1955

(i) Together – 'By the pure guidance of God'

Towards the end of *Priest-Workman in England*, Gedge, advocating a community of clergy and religious, perhaps lay-brothers, working together in an industrial setting, and reflecting what was happening elsewhere, ends with an invitation for others to join him in such a venture to see what 'by the grace of God we can do together'.[302] Whatever reservations he may have had, now in the light of the French experiment, he must have felt vindicated, even if he could not as yet feel the support of the episcopate.

It was an old but 'inexperienced' colleague of Gedge's, W. P. Baddeley, who was unexpectedly made vicar of St Pancras in 1949, who asked Gedge to assist him, though this spell in the Southwark diocese was to be short-lived.[303] Before two years were up, Canterbury's Diocesan Missioner Tom Savage invited Gedge to conduct a mission in the largely working-class village of Eyethorne in Kent, where the incumbent, who had developed unhappy relationships within the parish, was ill and in decline.[304] In an attempt to keep things going, Gedge was already thinking of taking up work at the local coal mine.

Kent's small coalfield bore little comparison to the great fields in Yorkshire, Nottingham, Wales or Scotland. There was only a handful of pitheads and the quality of coal 'like dust', only suitable for burning commercially. Gedge had already visited the local working men's club, and had made himself known to the NUM branch leader. The stage was set for Gedge's third period as a worker-priest, but still with a commitment to the life of the territorial parish.

Gedge's informal account reveals a man now perfectly at ease in the company of other working men. He had been able to walk – quite uninhibited – into the working men's club, establish who he was – and be accepted. And this time, though more closely involved with his working parishioners than before, he would not work alone. For the first time he would have a fellow priest by his side; a community of at least two would be established.

The Revd John Strong, a younger priest, with nearly eight years behind him amid the rubble and austerity of late-1940s London, who was growing increasingly interested in the way symbolism could play a part in conveying the faith through the liturgy, enjoyed the colourful worship of St Paul's Deptford where the 'Western rite' was celebrated in what he described as 'an unfussy and intelligent manner'.[305] But he was even more interested in the nature of priesthood itself, and the way in which the life of an ordinary person might be held up to God. Perhaps because of these reflections Strong confessed to feeling himself 'a little inadequate, if not a fake'. Although initially he showed no interest in the secular role of clergy hinted at in Temple's *Towards the Conversion of England*, and the story of France's worker-priests had not yet filtered through, he confesses to remembering the phrase from Michonneau's *Revolution in a City Parish* about the clink of money 'around the altar'. John Bickersteth admitted the same a decade later: 'I realize afresh how much non-churchgoers hate the clink of money . . .'[306] Later, however, Strong remembered helping to put up a pre-fab church and 'running a wheelbarrow up and down' when one man working alongside remarked, 'I've never seen a parson doing that sort of work before'.[307]

Strong, an Associate of King's College, London (AKC), had studied at Lichfield Theological College and was ordained deacon in 1938 and priested the following year.[308] Between 1938 and 1943 he served as a curate at St Philip's, Cheam Common, and from 1943–45 at St Stephen's, Battersea. At the end of the war he took charge of Holy Cross Mission, under St Saviour's, Raynes Park, before later going on to Streatham and Deptford (1949–51). Despite all his experience, Strong clearly needed advice and support; there had been 'nothing in King's BD syllabus' to guide him. There was in England, as yet, no articulated conviction that ministry to the working-class should be a priority, in the way it had become for some in France, even though Wand had sought to meet 'ordinary man' in his London mission, and Temple had already offered some theory. If Strong wanted a ministry in a working-class context he was on his own. 'I decided,' Strong said later, 'to invent a new kind of parish priest, which was, as I discovered later, the kind of phrase used by French worker-priests.' The Bishop of Southwark proved sympathetic and offered a licence and some nominal stipend of a few shillings a year if Strong found something suitable.[309] But the Bishop did remember Gedge, though in a rather dismissive remark he suggested that the latter had given up factory work 'as a waste of time'. Although unfair to Gedge, who was already looking for another priest to share his chosen ministry, the simple mention of the name was enough to set Strong off on a search.

Gedge and Strong agreed to meet at Charing Cross station and thereafter at Gedge's flat, where they 'got on remarkably well'. Gedge explained the situation in Eyethorne where he had conducted his mission, and that the local bishop was sympathetic to his working at the local mine, Tilmanstone. But the omens looked gloomy; this was the diocese of Geoffrey Fisher.

There is something extraordinary about the meeting that then took place between the two priests and their archbishop. The latter's conservative nature belied a surprising readiness to support what would be an unusual enterprise, providing that those who undertook it knew what they were about.[310] This was no sanction for a movement; Gedge and Strong could collaborate in an experimental venture together, suggested Fisher, and because he would field any complaints (and 'He would no doubt get complaints') '. . . they need not bother about that'. All Fisher asked for was an annual report; he would let his men do what they thought best. Despite all the criticism of Fisher which would later emerge, there was a mark of generosity here. 'One knew,' reflected Gedge, 'where one was with him.' At the time, however (and of considerable significance later), no one thought to ask about the precise nature of this 'experiment' nor by what 'criteria' it might be judged a 'success' or 'failure'.

Already Gedge had been in touch with the local branch of the NUM which made it clear the mine was short of conveyor belt cleaners, a new but essential job following a disastrous fire at Gresford Colliery in 1950. Suddenly to have the prospect of two parsons working underground demanded discussion at NUM and PCC level.[311] The NUM meeting were in general agreement by a small majority, but the Church Council were divided on this, with two ladies most unhappy at the prospect of not having a young man with a wife to look after the Mothers' Union. Although Gedge believed it was the casting vote of the local bishop, Rose, in favour of the two that enabled them to apply for underground jobs, five laity are actually recorded as voting in favour, with four against.[312] Strong, only a few years later, commented that not all miners were happy about their parish priests working in the pit.

> Their reasons were various: 'Religion has nothing to do with this; keep to your own class.' 'What must your father think after all that money spent on your education? I'd disown my son if he did that!' Other comments were revealing: 'You must be at rather a loose end when you get home.'[313]

And more than twenty years later he described a 'lot of local opposition' with one miner's wife commenting 'with unconscious humour' that she could 'never look up to a vicar who worked below ground'.[314]

Meanwhile the incumbent of Eyethorne, who had remained in hospital 'like a gentleman, died', says Gedge,[315] though another priest, brought in during the absence of the incumbent and before Gedge returned with Strong in tow, 'took the opportunity in the last parish magazine before our arrival of writing a distinctly unhelpful letter about how ghastly it was going to be for the parish under the forthcoming arrangement'.[316]

Although the principle of the two working below ground had now been established, there remained obstacles. A medical examination proved Gedge strong and stocky, well built for the job. But the same doctor refused to pass Strong – 'long, lean and light-boned' – as fit. 'Most depressing,' Strong reflected, 'everything else in order, and now to fall at the last fence.' Friendly persuasion, however, and a joke with the man at the office saw Strong's medical report binned. But in time the doctor would be proved right.

There would be no quiet start to this enterprise. Where else in England could two established clergymen be seen donning helmets to work in a mine beneath their own parish? When asked questions of the press, Gedge and Strong would admit to no fixed blueprint for the enterprise; for a variety of reasons they had resolved to meet local men where they were in daily work. Strong was already trying to justify his actions theologically, Gedge, now with more experience and caution, was simply anxious to get on with the work. None of this made much sense to the newsmen, and Strong records that:

> They went off round the village for garbled information and made stories out of that. Some of it looked very odd. 'The little church is now going to be kept warm with local coal.' They did not know the local

coal was only suitable for power-station boilers; as we ourselves soon discovered.[317]

(ii) Going underground

Because of a shortage of workers, Gedge and Strong now faced a training programme which, though it would normally take six months, had to be compressed into three weeks. Rather like Gedge's early description of life on the factory floor, Strong lists the training: making up the coal train, using props, girders and lamps properly. A local man, a teenager at the time, remembers with surprise the 'two parsons' training alongside him. He was most impressed. The two worked full-time on opposite shifts: 6a.m. to 2 p.m. and 2 p.m. to 10 p.m., though not night shifts; Gedge had had enough of that during the war. On the first morning underground, no sooner had Gedge taken his seat on the crowded trucks to the main working area, than the man behind him, blissfully unaware of his presence, 'effed and blinded' about a football match the previous night. Roars of laughter greeted the question from the man sitting next to him, that, 'did he not know the "new" parson was sitting behind him?' Gedge grinned, but did not turn a hair; he had heard it all before.[318] Three and a half years underground had just begun.

The first few days proved 'exhausting in the extreme', especially for Strong. Like others who had never previously been underground, Gedge and Strong found, on a tour with the safety officer, and to their astonishment, that miners had at various places to crawl on hands and knees, the roof being so low. The safety officer '. . . scampered along on all fours like a large puppy under miles of roof, seldom more than three feet high with a six inch girder every yard' reducing the height of the roof to sometimes a mere two feet.

Strong gives a brief but detailed description of the pit with its 'gob' or waste area, 'an eerie place full of creaking noises'. At Tilmanstone the roof was weaker than other mines, and large areas of coal were left in support. With right-angled tunnels driving out from the main roadway, the complex passageways proved wet or dry depending on position and angle. Ventilation was poor, and although fans were in operation, the 'return air' could prove unspeakably foul. 'One often thought one could never endure it. There was no sanitation, decaying food, evil smelling fungi, etc., all made their contribution.'[319] Both men were responsible for looking after the main conveyor belt which took up half the tunnel, complete with haulage cable and no fixed lights save those on their helmets.

Occasionally, when the need arose, they would send messages to each other on the belt. But it would prove to be lonely work. Even the nearest worked seams could be half a mile away, and it could be over an hour before anyone appeared.

After the initial training period pay was increased to £7/10/ – (£7.50) a week, but it included 'danger money'. The wage structure was such that with the completion of five full days one got paid for six. But if a man missed a shift or part of a shift – for whatever reason – he lost his day plus the 'bonus'. Timing was vital, and in a sympathetic understanding of what his parishioners had to endure, Strong adds, '. . . one might have had a bad night with the children, or forgotten to wind the alarm, but unless one could persuade the doctor that one was unwell, one lost one third of the week's wages . . . it was a draconian way of keeping people at work'.

Like worker-priests before and since, Gedge and Strong had to face the almost inevitable strike. Strong remembered one occasion when working equipment, dumped by the night shift upon roadways, was causing aggravation. They both supported this strike, and it proved to be the first time that they were to feel a degree of opposition from local clergy.[320] Already such events were a contentious issue within the church and *Frontier* in a leading article on 'Work, Welfare and "Differential" Reward' (November 1950) had discussed disputes and stoppages but had concluded that those who suddenly withheld their labour 'are our near neighbours; and a closer view of the causes of their exasperation would show us how human it is . . .'[321] Already Strong and Gedge were down a path about which few clergy, if any, knew anything. But they had pushed to get the jobs, they had established themselves underground, and would now have to face the responsibilities that were theirs too, on the surface.

(iii) Parochial and domestic life

At the point when they began work, John Strong was already courting his wife-to-be, Veronica. Because of this he took up residence in the vicarage while Gedge moved into digs. Gedge, the senior of the two, was priest-in-charge, while Strong was simply licensed. 'John had a little feeling about that,' Gedge remembers, but they worked as a team to fulfil all parochial duties that came the way of any village parson. There were three services on a Sunday, and these were shared, with weekday responsibilities like funerals, as Strong wryly put it, 'Done (if one may be forgiven the black humour) by whichever of us was above ground at the time'.[322]

General reaction of parishioners to two parsons working underground slowly turned from apprehension to surprise and favour. Gedge and Strong undertook traditional parochial roles, visiting people regularly in their homes. Strong related that eventually there came from the parish unanimous approval of what they were doing. But he admitted that the previous incumbent had been so unhappy and was so sufficiently disliked that it began to look as if 'they could do no wrong'. Gedge had dug his way into the parish in that early mission and had been clearly liked, especially by working men. In such a setting, both men felt themselves fulfilled and wholly in touch with their community. 'If you were not in the mine,' Gedge remembers, 'you were out of things.' In their own way the miners were 'tickled pink' to have two parsons alongside them. When sickness came, Gedge and Strong visited their work mates in hospitals and their families at home, even though they never came to church.

The working-class community remained resolutely at a distance from the institutional church. Though later some miners formed a choir at the church and turned out on Sundays, weekday practices, interrupted by shifts, left it less than successful. And the reactions of local clergy varied. Gedge and Strong had little opportunity to attend local clergy meetings (there would be no concessions to their chosen way of life). Some clergy, at a time when parsons were scarce, complained about this waste of manpower, with two priests spending all their time on secular tasks. As Strong observed, 'numbers doing things like teaching; administration, etc. . . . were seen as "proper" – but ours as highly improper'.

In 1954, Gedge and Strong were visited by one of the most popular media channels of the time when *Picture Post* paid a summer call. Three years into the 'experiment' Gedge and Strong were happier to speak about their work, and found themselves depicted as 'Britain's Coal Mining Priests'.[323] The writer casts the two in the same mould as the 'priest-workmen' movement in France, 'recently restricted by the Vatican' and suggested that the Church of England's bishops were watching in the wings with guarded interest. Some indeed may have been curious; but they remained cautious men.

The writer found a good rapport between miners and ministers, 'an unforced intimacy, free-and-easy yet based obviously on mutual respect'. 'That,' said one man of Gedge after a joke about clerical collars, 'is the best man in the pit. He's the most conscientious worker we've got.' Gedge's efforts underground remained what they had been in the factory, honest, committed, even legendary.[324] Whenever there was disapproval, it came neither from pitmen nor parishioners. After a small article in *Time* magazine, a vicar in the north of England had sent a copy of his parish magazine with 'verses of insulting doggerel of which he was clearly proud . . .'[325] The austere 1950s favoured few, though there were some among the clergy who believed the Strongs to be better off than themselves. The same question would be raised later by *Crockford's* 1961 Preface over potential worker-priests in steel works whose earnings might be above stipends.[326] But in early-1950s Eyethorne, Strong had to fight off notions that he was on two incomes (miner's wages plus a stipend), and that he was consequently enjoying a higher standard of living. 'The truth was that never in the first fifteen years of our marriage did we reach even 70% (including such matters as housing) of the going statutory minimum stipend of an incumbent.' Indeed Strong insisted that not only did his wife have insufficient to pay for groceries when she reached a shop's till, but she acquired clothing at jumble sales and followed road menders – once they had packed up – looking for coke for the fire.[327] And that was ironic; like all mining couples, the Strongs were entitled to free coal, but the local pit's was of such poor quality that on Strong's first day at work after their wedding, he returned home to an exhausted wife who had got the fire going only after eight attempts. Yet Strong and his new wife Veronica were perfectly at home in people's kitchens 'without the least suggestion of any formality, and just as one miner's wife to another . . .'

By 1954 Strong was again having health problems and was in pain. The medical officer back in 1951 had been quite correct, and a surgeon in Dover confirmed that though Strong's earlier rupture 'repair' was 'still holding' he must cease to work underground. At the same time Gedge began to suffer blackouts. Both men concluded that their days at Tilmanstone were numbered. A farmer in Sandwich offered Strong farm work, and he took this up three days a week while he sought something more permanent. This time, however, the assumption by Strong that he could, as it were, move casually around seeking employment, displeased the local bishop. Strong visited John Ragg's industrial mission in Bristol but got nowhere. Ragg saw factory visiting from a parish base as the only right method. But Strong remained resolutely committed to the shopfloor itself and would have none of such half measures. Indeed Ragg had added, to Strong's astonishment, that he and the Industrial Mission had the whole of Bristol's industry cared for as far as the church was concerned, 'and that he could not afford to have someone like me on the loose'.[328] Before going to work on the farm for a few months, John Strong had announced his resignation from the NCB to the PCC. The minutes then simply record that they moved on from this to discuss the proposal by a member that they should build a lych-gate; the minutes show no response or reaction, but since they were recorded by Strong himself, it is always possible that humility prevented him from reporting any.[329] Michael Gedge left Eyethorne first on 30 November 1954, and John Strong and his family on 3 January 1955. After nearly three and a half years, the 'experiment' was over; the new incumbent, the Revd A. E. S. Karney, from Croydon, then a part of the diocese of Canterbury, would remain in Eyethorne for twenty years.[330]

(iv) Presence and theology

Michael Gedge and John Strong were two remarkable men who shared an equally remarkable ministry. In physical build, character and temperament, they were quite different. Yet Gedge had always been convinced that it was the 'pure guidance of God' that had brought them together. They had clearly met with a common concern: to engage with their parishioners' daily life in a way few clergy had ever attempted.

But in the 1950s, when everyone still saw the territorial parish as the focal point of ministry and mission, many might have been both alarmed and heartened by Gedge and Strong's efforts. To hearten the establishment, it was from the point of the territorial parish that they essentially began. Just four years later Michael Jackson would highlight the persistence of the territorial parish as an important starting point for reorganization, mission and the question of any 'auxiliary' ministry.[331] But for Gedge and Strong the reason for being in Eyethorne (and they could, theoretically, have been anywhere) was that the very existence of the village church in this mining village afforded them a place in the institution that they might otherwise have been denied. There was, as the French (who learnt of this experiment) would later comment, a 'domestic flavour about it', meaning that Strong's marriage in the context of the community was 'nearer the majority of people' than the French, who were celibate and might have had an easier time finding work.

On the other hand there would be the inevitable questions from fellow clergy (though none are recorded in detail) about what they thought they were 'doing', and what the results in the pews might be. Strong suggested that though for some time people sat 'on the fence', 'more people began to be seen at church services'.[332] In his capacity as Secretary of the PCC, Strong recorded an increase in congregation on at least two occasions, and though numbers are not given, some of the increase may have been children. But the whole tenor of Strong's stories belies the suggestion that he and Gedge were preoccupied with what was happening on a Sunday. The PCC were chiefly concerned with the good order of church building and services, and Gedge and Strong's efforts showed a marked respect for these. Holy Communion (in favour at the time) replaced matins, servers and choir were introduced, and a certain 'beautifying' of the church went on.

Politically too they were close, but it was commitment by Gedge to Labour politics and hesitancy on the part of Strong. At one union meeting in Eyethorne, Gedge had so impressed his fellow miners that they invited him to become an official. But he refused; only too aware of what had happened in France, especially with the CGT Union. Nevertheless he remained a member of the Labour party, though he rarely 'talked politics' underground.

A common theological focus for both men is less easy to identify and analyse. They were, undoubtedly, dedicated priests in parochial terms, undertaking their parish duties with a real sense of responsibility. In the chair of the PCC, Gedge fully accepted his responsibility for the care and upkeep of the church, and his ministry to parishioners. But they rarely distinguished, for pastoral purposes, those 'inside' or 'outside' the congregation when real need arose, and were aware of how alien church life was to the men with whom they worked on a daily basis. When there was sickness, miners in hospital, or bereavement, Gedge and Strong went directly to them. Any priest, it is true, might have done as much; but Gedge and Strong had more of it.

Neither attempted to articulate an explicit theology of their involvement or presence in the community. In a sense the work had only just begun, was still all 'in process', and they might easily have thought it presumptuous to start making statements for the theologically astute. Gedge's fellow miner Goff Hares sometimes asked Gedge why he, a parson, was doing all this, and received from Gedge the answers: first, if he were told, Goff might not understand, and secondly, anyway, Gedge was none too sure himself.

But John Strong was already willing to confess to identification and presence. Twenty years after they had gone, a local man commented that though he knew they (the miners) did not all come to church, yet 'there was quite a different feel about the whole village when you were here'.[333]

For Strong it was the community pit-head bath-house which was the ultimate leveller.[334] 'We felt no need for title like reverend "rector", "vicar".' Strong eschews any special dress which would have suggested a quite artificial division between life below ground and that above. They were fundamentally the same. It was one life in which they shared, and a full life with other mining families; Veronica Strong was happiest to be thought of simply as a miner's wife.

If there was a slight difference in emphasis it may have been that Gedge, despite his previous experience as a worker-priest, was more conscious of the place of the parochial or territorial parish, whereas Strong, according to Gedge, might have been content to work without a parish structure, living and working perhaps independently with some opportunity to celebrate the sacraments yet without any necessary attachment to a church. Gedge had less sympathy with any idea of being the church outside the territorial parish, while he believed that John Strong, labouring at almost anything, would have felt it was a sufficient expression of his priesthood and ministry, and he would have been happy to have somehow remained 'on the move'; the loose cannon that alarmed John Ragg of Bristol. Essentially, Gedge and Strong had recognized a real need to engage with the men and their wives wherever they were to be found – mine or kitchen – and they were unequivocal in that.

Historical analysis cannot always hope to make meaning out of muddle – though we may try to bring some coherence. The search for a neat theological appraisal of Gedge and Strong would remain as difficult as it would be to give an account of the handful who would shortly follow them. Strong left few theological notes, and put less reflection into writing compared with Gedge earlier. Although a debate was about to begin in the church on the subject of 'part-time' priests, it would prove to be driven by support for the institutional structures, and less with an 'incarnational mission and ministry' of the kind that was lived for a short time in Eyethorne.

In seeking work in Bristol, Strong was hurt by the lack of interest in his personal vocation. There was indifference from some, perhaps alarm from Ragge: 'I meet this outlook on other occasions,' reflected Strong. 'What is it? Delusions of grandeur? No corner left for someone like me to work something out? What a nonsense.' Given the then unadventurous range of thinking on ministry, mission and the role of the church in industry, Strong had reasons to sound disillusioned. His explanation of trying to 'work something out' was clearly insufficient; and his earlier belief in the importance of liturgical symbols reflected in sharing connections 'at the bottom end' was ill understood. England was lukewarm on this; there was no anxiety, just the careful conservatism of moves 'towards the conversion of England', which for ever seemed all talk and no action. Travel and participation at conferences, the support of an archbishop here and a bishop there, were clearly not enough. There was, it seemed, and in the south at least, nothing of the northern episcopal leadership's support then given for the albeit different strategy of the Sheffield Mission. There was no essential theological debate, no kingdom theology, and little on 'life and work'. Rather 'let the church be the church' was the cry that went up, though few understood what it meant except that it had something to do with keeping the church focussed on itself.

Three years after Gedge and Strong left Eyethorne, and Strong had continued as a worker-priest, the BCC published a paper *The Church and Industry*. Here their efforts either went unknown or were deemed unworthy of mention. In the publication, which highlighted, in detail, the story of the French worker-priests, all manner of experiments in Britain are mentioned from George McLeod's efforts on Iona to Ted Wickham in Sheffield and John Ragg in Bristol. Of Eyethorne the reader hears absolutely nothing; there is only a kind of veiled reprimand against 'independent' experiments. In fact, the lack of any recognition suggests that in terms of the Church of England's overall ministry, what had happened in Eyethorne was without significance. Then, the following year (1959), the Church Assembly's working party on Industry published Th*e Task of the Church in Relation to Industry*, which, as Patrick Vaughan notes,

> . . . was utterly silent about worker-priests (whether French or English) despite purporting to offer a survey and appraisal of 'the present State of the Church's Work in Industry'.[335]

What then of that 'experiment'? Gedge and Strong, towards the end of their time in Eyethorne, would be judged by the institution's own values of the territorial parish. Twenty years on, Strong admitted that when he and Gedge had finished, 'the general opinion outside the community was that they had failed' (presumably to fill their church with miners!) yet the criteria for success or failure had not been explicitly determined, and though Fisher supported their ministry and was one of the few Bishops in support of experiment generally, he declared at a meeting of convocation that he would vote against any resolution drafted for the setting up of regulations for a non-parochial ministry;[336] experiments, open-ended and ambivalent, were one thing, regulations – leading to possible sanctioning and possible encouragement of practice – quite another.

Yet even if they were to be judged by the institution's value on ministry and people in the pews,[337] Gedge and Strong had manifestly succeeded – for numbers *had* been raised. But to both, that fact might have been less important than the comment Strong remembered from one miner: 'What you did appealed to my imagination like nothing else the church ever did – and that goes for every man in the pit.' [338] In their hearts Gedge and Strong were not naive enough to believe they could 'convert' the entire working population to Church of England religion, and made no attempt to do so. While Ted Wickham's men donned boiler suits and walked into the work place to meet men and then left the works, Gedge and Strong, stripped to the waist, and working sometimes alone in stifling darkness for the sake of the safety of other men underground, cleaned the conveyor belts that carried the coal to the surface. When Gedge sat down at his 'snap break' to join in the day's chatter and banter ('When did you last have a woman, Michael?!'),[339] he gave and took with a sense of humour that lasted a lifetime for the men who remembered it. Despite Gedge's anxiety to 'witness' in his earlier days there was now, perhaps, more maturity, a simple love of remaining with the rest of humanity – a 'man amongst men' – as he had discovered himself in 1943. He did not talk much about religion or politics underground, claimed ex-miner Goff Hares, who never himself darkened the door of a church, and who confessed to not really knowing 'what Gedge was all about', save one simple theory which had stayed with him all his life, and that was that 'Michael,' above all things, '. . . was trying to live . . . like Jesus Christ'.[340]

3. John Strong – collision course at Harlington

(i) Working vicar, 1956–1962

John Strong's lack of fitness for work on a farm found him seeking a job elsewhere. Later, he was invited to join the staff of Christ Church, Luton, where the vicar had been an industrial adviser. The Strongs left Eyethorne at the beginning of 1955, a few months after Michael Gedge, who later became a Roman Catholic, and who would try to interest the English hierarchy in worker-priests.[341] Strong began working as an oil meter calibrator at George Kent's in Luton. This was not physically demanding, and gave Strong the chance of a rest after three and a half gruelling years underground.

It was early in 1956 that the Strongs first heard of Harlington, a small village with a working-class element some seven miles north of Luton. The population according to the 1951 census had been 634 with little more than an increase of 100 by 1956. Despite its location, there was a good train service to Luton – taking only ten minutes – and many of the locals were already working in that area. Strong began to feel that there might be the possibility of a ministry here with the waiting and the journey itself providing him with a good opportunity to meet parishioners and 'for periods of up to half an hour'; a time he believed far better than many home visits.

Some doubts had been expressed at diocesan level as to whether Harlington could survive as an independent parish. Strong also knew that at least one man had turned the parish down on the grounds of the vicarage accommodation alone. But the Bishop of St Albans, Michael Gresford-Jones, wrote to Strong asking whether he considered Harlington a possibility, though in the same letter he expressed doubts about Strong's desire to remain a worker-priest and 'visit' at least some of his parishioners on the train, '. . . but then,' confessed the bishop, 'I prefer to travel in silence.' The bishop wanted Strong as a full-time incumbent, asking him to give up his factory work after eighteen months or so. But the bishop's statements were none too clear. Like many episcopal offhand remarks to hapless clergy (who then take them as definitive future intentions), the remarks remained ambivalent, and Strong lacked sufficient experience to demand episcopal clarification. Nevertheless he visited the bishop, having no intention of giving up his work. Supporting the general appraisal by Michael Gedge in Eyethorne that he was a man who would have been content to be without the full responsibilities of a parish, Strong reflects that he had actually no wish to become 'full-time' incumbent of Harlington;[342] commenting later like the Abbé Godin that, 'The parochial system can easily swallow the lot and still be hungry, having devoured many of its own vital roots and shoots put forth to explore.'[343] Precisely that, it must be said, would partly contribute to Strong's later downfall. Nevertheless it was agreed that Strong would take on the role of priest-in-charge, and report to the bishop after six months. If all was well, the 'experiment' could continue. The management at Kent's proved accommodating, and would allow Strong time off work for what they would consider 'civic duties', in his case, certain weekday services and funerals.

In 'A Worker Priest's Day', a contribution to the *Oxford Diocesan Magazine* in the 1980s, and 'Impressions of a Factory', in George Kent's own house magazine, Strong's accounts, both written in the 1960s, describe how his day began on the train, where he would often say the office. These records are brief, and remain, sadly, the only accounts of Strong's work. His task at Kents, calibrating meters, took place in a test-shop at the far end of the works. It was messy, and though he might have to wait some time for tests to be completed he could easily end up being sprayed by chemicals. During some of these waits, he would jot down in a notebook (since lost), 'comments and observations, and any idea that might arise from the Psalms, lessons or anything else . . .'

In encounters with work mates, Strong found many of their problems could be described as 'basically religious', '. . . involving one's view of the world, of one's life and of people. There was often surprise, and no little interest, when I pointed this out!' After a while, Strong, like almost all the worker-priests after him, was invited to be shop steward in the area where he worked. 'I cannot,' he remarks in his account, 'claim to have been a great success, but no one else seemed to want the job.' But there were disputes from time to time, and Strong had a way with the management and says he seldom if ever 'found his way blocked'. Strong's foreman, Jim Oliver, found Strong a 'good and steady worker, a worker – just like the rest of the people', but a man with a real concern for his fellow men and women.[344] Strong's brief account of life in the factory ends:

> No doubt there are still some who wonder why I ever went to work in George Kents. One answer is that it enabled me to serve the parish of Harlington without charge to anyone – 'free of charge' as St Paul said. Yet, more important than that was that I and my wife had our economic roots in the factory. Also, the job there involved no superiority of social status. All this had an effect on the way we thought and acted.

Thus work began in the parish with Strong determined to live on the same income as any other parishioner. But he and his family were expected to live in the vicarage, now revealing – in its unpleasant dampness – the very reason why others had rejected the living. The Strongs had difficulty finding the money to pay the heating bills, and even when they did, visitors would still remark on how 'chilly' the house could be. Forced by the church to live in this ageing and ugly accommodation, like others clergy across the country the Strongs were simply expected to grin and bear it.[345]

John Strong began by maintaining Sunday School and services (up to five every Sunday) though the figures for attendance were low with never more than thirty, and that would be at Evensong. The church itself was in poor repair, and what capital existed was being used by the PCC to 'balance the books'. Strong's agreed visit to the bishop took place after six months and was cordial. After a further six months and a visit by the archdeacon and diocesan secretary to Harlington's PCC (at which Strong was not present), all was reported 'well'. During 1958 the church organ was repaired, a new air heater installed, and the timber treated. For the latter, Strong had been able to raise a band of willing volunteers, many of whom were not churchgoers, despite the fact that regulars assured Strong that he could not expect village support. On one evening when work was expected to be done, Lawrence Beasley, a railwayman, recalls that on his way home by motorbike, he found a dejected Strong leaning over the church wall peering anxiously up the street for his willing parishioners. But most had made an excuse not to come. Beasley, a local Methodist, helped to rally the support of non-churchgoers, and the work got done, much, it would later appear, to the displeasure of more conservative parishioners.[346]

All the while, however, Strong was aware that there must have been some who still hankered after a 'real vicar'. Sometimes unknowingly working against age-old practices and prejudices, he appeared up against the things that might have plagued any village incumbent. Like the Church of England in the 1950s generally, when hopes of a post-war revival had been dashed in ineffective mission, and when liturgical revision and engaging theology were still in the future, Strong was left to cope with a poorly heated church, not in the best condition, where parishioners wanted an ageless diet of staid worship. Harlington, if the truth be told, was straight out of a Giles cartoon: a village church 'there' where it had always been, with the nightmare of an enthusiastic priest, 'supported' by a handful of sometimes indifferent parishioners.

(ii) Of pastoral principles

John Strong proved to be a dedicated priest who visited '. . . the hospital during his lunch break and his parishioners in the evening'.[347] It would not be enough. There was clearly an 'old guard' in Harlington who viewed the territorial parish and traditional role of 'full-time' parish-focussed clergy as the only right one, and who found the presence of the worker-priest something of a nonsense. From the beginning, with few in church anyway, Strong had an uphill struggle to bring life amid the pews. As at Eyethorne, numbers were beginning to rise a bit; by 1958 weekly attendance at Holy Communion was improving,[348] with a discussion group starting in the vicarage. As much was later admitted by the parish council; indeed by 1962 Strong claimed numbers were three times greater and rising.[349] Most of his parish duties were done in the evenings, after a hard day's work, and when a funeral came along, he took time off work with loss of pay. Visiting the sick in the local Luton hospitals was often done in the lunch hour, and the more distant institutions he visited on a Saturday. Peter Young, contributing later to a brief account of Strong's work in *Prism*, commented that from the parishioners came the claim that Strong was 'a most industrious parish priest . . . and they all testified to his hard work in visiting and conducting parish affairs in general. I have been told that every evening he was to be seen calling on his flock; the church was enjoying more services; the morning congregations had considerably increased . . .'[350] A parishioner, writing later in the *Luton News*, and with almost fearful anonymity in the face of conservative reaction growing against Strong, retold how:

> A sick visit from him after a walk of several miles in roughest weather, up hill, and on top of a day's work in the factory . . . will live in the grateful memory of – A parishioner.[351]

But it was the 1950s, and from the establishment's point of view in a darkling period when there was so much to attract the young in Luton or London, the institutional church was fading in the twilight. Harlington, poorly supplied in the past with able clergy (though Strong's immediate predecessor was well loved), turned down by the few who 'looked it over', now had a man – as the civil council would later affirm – totally committed to his community. But he could not see that, in the eyes of some parishioners at least, not only was he acting too vigorously to initiate change, but was simply not the 'real' vicar for which they longed. There had been no tradition of progressive let alone 'working' vicars in Harlington; Strong was about to pay a price for being one.

(iii) Of 'unspecified complaints'

In 1958, not long after Strong had managed a first round of repairs to the church, he was visited by the suffragan bishop to inform him that 'complaints had been received by the Bishop of St Albans about the state of parish life'.[352] The suffragan agreed to meet the PCC and, at a subsequent meeting, a 'resolution' was passed stating that Harlington would prefer to have an ordinary full-time incumbent. But this was not news to Strong – he was well aware of the general feeling and of the ongoing possibility that Harlington could still be linked with another parish. As early as 1959 Strong had made it public at least in the church press and in a rather alarming paragraph that a worker-priest might be:

> . . . classed, by those who fancy themselves, as a crypto-Communist and as somehow letting them down. His very existence is an affront to snobbery and class-consciousness. He needs to say nothing in those respects. (In a village these things still count for a lot and, alas, in few places more than the parish church.)[353]

The suffragan evidently decided that more evidence was needed about parish life, and Strong set about a written update. It took him time to complete this, and one is left to imagine the value he placed in giving what he understood as the most favourable blow by blow account of all he had tried to achieve. The diocesan bishop appeared duly impressed, and in December of 1958 he wrote to the PCC 'to the effect that there did not, after all, appear to be an urgent need' for the Strongs to go.

But Strong had not reckoned with those weighty middle-class forces which would now be levelled against him. At the centre of a disaffected group, anxious for a traditional vicar, was the Lady of the Manor, later reported by the *Daily Herald's* Jack Lucas as Mrs Gertrude Tabor, who now became the focus of all discontent.[354] A 'Harlington Women's Guild' now began to raise funds 'for the church'. Strong argues that subsequent money-raising ventures never specified how monies raised might be used, though there was the explicit claim that they aimed to obey the bishop's injunction by raising funds for a 'future incumbent's stipend' as well as 'beautifying the church'. But there was confusion – it was never very clear just how the funds might be divided. Events to raise the funds were centred at the Manor, and without any reference to Strong.

There now followed a rather tragic series of moves which began with the bishop suggesting that Strong 'take time' to 'consider' his next move. In a PS, the bishop, clearly feeling somewhat guilty at the decidedly ominous tone of his missive, added:

> I do appreciate the devoted work you have put in as priest-in-charge and I know that you have given yourself to the limit of your strength.[355]

It would not be the first time that a bishop, aware of major personal efforts on the part of an individual, was nevertheless unable or unwilling to demonstrate support. Clearly the bishop had decided to bow to the traditional forces in Harlington. Strong raged. For the second time in a year these conservative voices (and the bishop refused to admit who they were) had been raised effectively against him. And how had a 'reorganization committee' come to agree to a 'full-time' priest'? To the best of Strong's knowledge this committee had never visited Harlington, and had they done so they would have discovered the best argument for a full-time man; a new estate was about to be built. It was a cruel and ironic omission.

Strong's fury was vented in a letter to the bishop in which he admits to the possibility of a 'lack of proper respect' (towards the bishop). He then made a rather gloomy journey to St Albans where little was achieved. Mindful of the respect and obedience he was supposed to show, he now bitterly regretted that he had not, in the first instance, insisted on seeing the complaints. Later, the bishop simply gave him eighteen months to quit, and Strong, occupied in ordinary parish affairs, and unable to write for some time, eventually penned a lengthy communication which cries out for justice, but which, in the end, effectively threatens:

> Clearly both you and the committee think there are real grounds for criticism, and I can only assume that these are based on information gained directly or indirectly, from local people. I am not ideally too proud to ignore the stated opinions of experienced persons, even if they do not always choose to give reasons. At the same time I am not entirely a greenhorn either in parish affairs or in the world of industry. On Advent Sunday I shall have been a parish priest for exactly 20 years, including 3.5 in a coalmine, 3 months on land, and 4.5 in a factory, in several widely different kinds of parish. Should not that experience count for something? But if I am denied the opportunity to hear, discuss, and answer clearly stated comments and criticism, I fail to see how it can.
>
> The purpose of an experiment is to test something. I am still without a clue as to what it is you meant to test, or what I was expected to accomplish (and in so short a time!). All I myself expected to show in that time was whether this was a workable proposition for Harlington.[356]

And the bishop could have answered that it was not; but he did not. He simply states that the decision had been taken on pastoral grounds and that:

> . . . there is no need to read into it criticism by individuals of what you may or may not have done at Harlington. The fact is that after 5 years with a part-time clergyman, during which the church has grown in strength as your figures indicate, by midsummer 1961 the time will have come for a full-time vicar of Harlington. I am afraid I cannot continue to argue this point with you by correspondence.[357]

At this point something of a low note enters the correspondence as an embittered Strong paints himself as the aggrieved party treated with scorn by an institution and its upper-class support which neither understood nor cared for what he was about. He turns to veiled threats: he is known abroad, he feels, like Jeremiah, that he stands at a sensitive point between church and industry, 'anything that looks like the expression of political prejudice or . . . vested interests . . . is likely to come in for some very rough handling'. In the final remarks in the section, he aligned himself with the French:

> the people I live and work with have not forgotten the Vatican. It has been said to me, 'Now I suppose the Pope will be writing to the Archbishop to suggest how he deals with you!' It was only partly meant as a joke. You may find it difficult to believe, but there is a widely held belief in these circles that, though they profess to be at loggerheads, the Romans will always act with Anglicans to preserve the status quo. Not even the Romans swallow whole the 'reasons' given for the suppression of the worker-priests. They have a strong stink. [358]

It remains the bitter correspondence of a man for whom a sizable majority would not speak up. Bishops, when faced with this kind of difficulty, know only too well that to become embroiled in a correspondence does them no favours. The bishop then sought to bring matters to a swift conclusion. He claimed that the PCC had agreed that Harlington should be a sole parish. The PCC replied that they had agreed to no such thing. But it was too late; Mrs Gertrude Tabor and her supporters had done their job well. Suddenly, with the offer of a council house that had to be taken up almost immediately, the Strongs prepared to leave for Blackburn in Lancashire, following an announcement in the church, and a pinned note to the vicarage door, alarming a couple who turned up to arrange a wedding.[359]

It was not quite the end of the story. The national press enjoyed a few days of lively news coverage, with varying reports all favourable to Strong. It was, after all, the nearest thing to the Anglican suppression of a worker-priest. The strongest support came from the local press, the *Luton News*. It was the parish council who wrote to affirm Strong's ministry, to say that he had played 'an active and useful part in local affairs, that the leaders of various groups and associations greatly admired and respected him and appreciated his work'. It added:

> The bishop may take the view that the selection of a vicar is only to be considered in relation to active church members; we respectfully suggest that in this, and perhaps other parishes, the selection of a vicar ought to be related to village life as a whole. A priest respected and admired, outside his own flock, for his personal qualities and activities might be well on the way, in the long term view, towards increasing the size of the flock.[360]

It is relatively easy to cast the bishop as the true villain of the piece: a middle-class Oxbridge-educated prelate, rather than a caring father in God, or – as a later correspondent argued – one who was anxious above all, to make clergy acceptable to 'the "old ladies" of the church'.[361] The traditionalists at Harlington were not prepared to support Strong – and why should they? For generations the right place for a clergyman had been the parish; how could they be expected to understand the 'queerness' – as Strong himself put it – of his perceived role? The conservative forces, here no doubt as anywhere, and supported by their bishop, understood ministry, even mission, exclusively in terms of the territorial parish. The bishop, of course, need never have taken Strong on, and while in the initial stages Strong actually hesitated, he himself remained insufficiently astute to recognize the problems that might evolve. In the end, the bishop decided to support the view of the 'Manor House'[362] against any other, and the lady in charge by implication later admitted to a part in Strong's removal.

In the *Daily Herald* Jack Lucas took a more sombre note, commenting that '. . . the events in Harlington are disturbing to those who want a living experimental church'. For those who did not, and who alone had the bishop's ear, however, things might perhaps return to some kind of normality.

(iv) Presence and theology

John Strong appeared the victim of a contest between an overwhelming consensus in favour of a traditional interpretation of parochial ministry and his own understanding of his vocation to a new and as yet unspecified parish and working ministry of total identification with working men and women.[363] To place a man of Strong's convictions in an English village (and for Strong to accept this) where the more traditional patterns of ministry had long been the norm was to court disaster. Yet with so many working people in that neighbourhood, Strong had a care to love them and stand alongside them in the changing world which they occupied, and at the very least, the experiment deserved a more careful monitoring and appraisal than it ever received. Strong later recalled, as has been noted, the monotony and challenges of manual work, and would have been well aware of the growing aspirations of the men and women of a changing post-war Britain who lived in and around a growing Luton. But Strong, also devoted to his parish, was effectively left unsupported by his bishop, and then forced to pay the penalty for an experience which he thought successful, but which others thought undesirable. A crucial and determining factor in the sorry story was that once again, as at Eyethorne nine years before, the term 'experiment', and its criteria for 'success' or 'failure' had never been determined.

It is a sad feature of the experiment that the turn in events did much to obscure Strong's factory life at Kent's, and his theological analysis. The reader hears little of his perceived role (though Strong might have wished to keep it hidden) or his theological reflection. Instead, Strong could be accused of deliberately creating his own myth. Here is the picture of a committed socialist, viewing himself as a victimized worker-priest in the French tradition, who, having identified himself with the working-class at work, and having visited them on their new estate alongside his church,[364] is now vilified for that role by the powers of ecclesiastical conservatism. Peter Young raised the obvious question: 'Can it be that by some people it is considered a trifle undignified for a priest to soil his hands in a factory?'[365]

Strong, whose own understanding of his role in both parish and factory was no doubt in a state of constant evolution, made some attempt to explain himself in a 1959 *Church Times* article, one of his very few efforts to give a theological analysis and appraisal of his chosen life. First, he went on to the shop floor to preach the gospel free of charge (meaning he cost the institutional church nothing).[366] Secondly, it assisted in a different kind of relationship 'whose nature is not at once obvious, and after perhaps resisted by those who think along traditional lines'.[367] It was indeed, 'not obvious'. Strong, like other worker-priests beginning to emerge, was in the process of trying to analyse his own thinking at a time when the church itself had little understanding of the need for any kind of 'identification', certainly not that chosen and lived by Gedge and Strong. But if Strong and his emerging companions in this ministry proved unable to articulate their chosen vocation, what hope was there for a theological appraisal in the context of mission and ministry? The truth was that any articulation would take time. With a knowledge of the French before him, Strong had already sufficient experience to appreciate that this was an entirely different way of thinking about mission and ministry in general and priesthood in particular.

> . . . like their French counterparts, the worker-priests in this country entirely reject the notion, promulgated by the Vatican, that their manner of life is out of keeping with the priestly vocation. They hold it pious nonsense to affirm that the priestly soul is more in peril in factories than in Paris salons or in some church congregations.[368]

Strong argued that clergy with freehold (though he enjoyed none) had the kind of security many working people were denied. And for him, to stand alongside ordinary working people – whom he did nor regard, as others did, as 'benighted and pagan' – was to be 'in full accord with the spirit of Christian priesthood'.

John Strong's story is about a priest with a high doctrine of priesthood who was anxious for the institution's blessing and backing for a singularly individual role. The hesitant institution, however, despite the lip service it might pay to Assembly or ecumenical reports on industry, had nothing to offer. As yet, there was barely any recognition of what Strong was trying to do, no hurry to admit to or assess the ambivalent nature of this work, no time to engage with this 'modern ministry'. From day one, the bishop could not have been expected fully to understand Strong's motives, when Strong himself admitted to only 'working them out'. The two were caught up in a conflict of interests where for Strong, the realities of mission and ministry were bound up with a gospel and a priesthood that had to take incarnational risks in theory and practice, and where for the bishop, for the sake of the survival of the institutional church and the territorial parish, it was chiefly about avoiding them.

(v) Getting organized: beginning the Worker Church Group – 1957

Sharing the lives and wagepackets of miners, and sharing perhaps some of the perceptions about the post-war Britain around them, Gedge and Strong never doubted the vocations they had chosen. While in their singular attempts at ministry and mission they were among the first to experiment with this radical identification with the working world,[369] it was while he was in Harlington that Strong became a founder member of the Worker Church Group, the only organization that would speak for the first worker-priests and laity committed to radical identification. Within eight or nine years a small group would begin to develop a rationale for their total involvement in working life, and would challenge Ted Wickham's methods. Despite beginning with only a handful, this group would attract nearly thirty, effectively challenge the church's assumptions on mission and ministry, and would survive, albeit changed, for over thirty years.

By now, with the story of the French worker-priests becoming known, and a growing interest developing in Britain's home-grown 'representatives', the time looked right for expansion. It was during their time in Kent that, unknown to Gedge and Strong, a handful of other clergy, who would eventually become part of the Worker Church Group, began to explore ministry among the working class. They would all come from different backgrounds, some inspired by accounts of the French, some by contacts with men like Gedge. But for them all, the initial problem was to find sympathetic support from the church at large. Of this there was almost none. The institution, despite its 1959 rhetoric in the *Task of the Church in Relation to Industry*, was fearful of the kind of experimentation that might threaten the parochial system, even when a man like Strong demonstrated that he firmly believed in it. With the exception of a handful, the institution's bishops, fearful of loose cannons, and generally unsympathetic to these kinds of ministerial experiments, gave neither encouragement nor support. To a large extent, the worker-priests were on their own.

IV

Among The Next Worker-Priests, Wives and Laity: From 1956 – Evolution to Organization

'What's brought you down to this . . . ?'

(Personnel officer, enquiring of the Revd John Rowe as he began labouring work in an East End brewery)

'Here's another . . . now don't bugger that one up for Christ's sake'

(Factory foreman handing the Revd Ken Ramsay a new drilling bit)

1. In London: John Rowe and Martyn Grubb

(i) John Rowe: into work – the East End

By the late 1950s, and with little knowledge of the events in Eyethorne or Harlington, one or two other individuals were deliberately seeking a vocation as worker-priests in post-war Britain. Unlike Gedge, not all would relate their story in lengthy autobiographical material. One of the most distinctive features of the next worker-priests would be the way that some, like John Rowe, would deliberately avoid publicity or the prying eyes of the curious. Sources for this study, then, have been drawn from personal oral reminiscences and the limited amount of documentary material that exists.[370] They support the story of a vocation where a keynote is about being alongside a class viewed as estranged from institutional religion.

Born in British Guiana in August 1923, John Rowe had left the police force in which he had served (1942–45) to study Philosophy and English at McGill (1945–48) and theology at the Montreal Diocesan Theological College and McGill University (1948–51).[371] At first, Rowe had no intention of becoming a worker-priest, and was destined for a parochial ministry in Canada. But he spent only three months as a deacon in 1951, before coming to England where he was able to take up an exchange scholarship with Selwyn College Cambridge, while serving a curacy at the same time. After two years, Rowe decided not to return to Canada but make his home in England, moving to London to serve a further period as curate in Bow Common, in the depths of London's East End, between 1953 and 1956. It was during this period that Rowe began to feel what he describes as a growing sense of contradiction between the status of parochial curate and the people in his parish. Inspired by a fellow Anglo-Catholic in Canada, Rowe, who already had some knowledge of the worker-priests in France, began to take a strong interest in the works of Suhard, Mounier and René Voillaume.

With conventional training and curacy behind him like Gedge and Strong, Rowe was effectively free to do as he pleased in terms of his ministry, always provided he could find support. He found this initially not only in the Bishop of Stepney, Joost de Blank,[372] but also in Father R. G. Kirkby of St Paul's, Bow Common, who would become his 'sympathetic vicar'.[373]

Rowe found work in the East End at Truman's Brewery in Brick Lane, where he would remain for almost thirty years;[374] by any standards, a measure of commitment. As regards his peculiar status as a priest, he found his employers' attitude 'impeccable'. He had made it clear that despite the fact he was a priest he wanted no publicity at a time when his role was already the subject of interest. At first the press knew nothing; later, when they realized there was a story, the firm duly kept the press at bay, and Rowe was able to make a quiet start, with the puzzled personnel officer enquiring rather sadly, 'What's brought you down to this?'[375] It was the kind of question worker-priests were to become used to, as workers and managers sought to understand what sometimes appeared a 'waste' of good brains and education. At first John Rowe laboured with gangs whose job it was to clean out the gigantic vessels which held the liquid for brewing, and later the yeast presses. The jobs themselves, according to Rowe, were 'filthy', but the cleaning of these areas was a vital part in ensuring the kind of cleanliness necessary.

After two years, Rowe became an electrician's mate and remained one for eleven years. In keeping with times of fairly high employment, Rowe was able, as others were, to seek a better role within the workplace and to move into more interesting work. This was in no way an attempt to 'move up the firm', but simply a way of changing from labouring duties to more skilled and better-paid work on the shop floor. This was a pattern that would involve worker-priests in France and in England, who became sufficiently engaged with their work, that they sometimes naturally gravitated to, or took responsibility for work, that inevitably meant that they became skilled. Rowe, for example, had become particularly interested and aware of the range of tasks necessary to keep the brewery operating, since the electrical applications employed for brewing included a whole range of motors, pumps, lighting and bottling applications which all demanded regular maintenance. But it was the 'time-served' electricians he remembers who got the 'interesting jobs', though he quickly learned and began to 'make up little devices on the bench'. But being an electrician's mate was not enough for Rowe, and he began to consider another job in a laboratory and in a quite different setting. However, the job he hoped might eventually emerge at Hackney College never did, though he decided to remain at night classes, in the City and Guilds electrical course he had started.

Rowe was to find it none too easy to be accepted as a qualified electrician in a shop where those working as skilled men were all 'time-served'.[376] The fact that Rowe had not done this in the traditional way meant that his fellow electricians were less than happy to accept him at first. But his own union (TGWU) was to prove supportive and quite adamant: Rowe had completed his studies and had worked as a mate for many years; he was to be accepted as a skilled electrician even if he was obliged to join the Electricians' Union, as he did. Rowe remained in this trade until the end of his working days at the brewery, in the late 1980s.[377]

In a rare disclosure of what he was about on the 'shop-floor', Rowe disclaimed any idea of 'converting' fellow workers, 'which they tell me is impossible anyway. I wish simply to share in their way of life as much as I can, for they are no less God's people than those who go to church.' As for the reaction of his fellow workers, he 'mucked in' with them, while they simply called him John; it seemed all there was to say; for John Rowe it was probably quite enough to be going on with.[378]

There was no overt liturgical role in the work place despite the day-dreams of 'places of worship', nor any 'gathering up of Christians' – 'though I did sign a lot of passports'. The primary objective, in the context of priesthood, was simply to participate and share the conditions of workers' lives as wage earners.[379] If John Rowe's papers leave a limited account of his time on the 'shop floor', it must be borne in mind that he was deliberately quiet, though he proved to be one of the most articulate of worker-priests, particularly active in the Worker Church Group, was responsible for the publication of his Rejoinder, and helped to edit their original joint Statement.

(ii) Martyn and Anne Grubb: before ordination – into work, Southall

In contrast to John Rowe, Martyn Grubb and his wife Anne left something of a full account of their life, particularly through the publication of newsletters to friends, as the Grubbs' chosen entry into working life began long before ordination.

Martyn Grubb was son of Sir Kenneth Grubb, Chairman of the Church Assembly's House of Laity, and a later sympathizer, because of his son, with worker-priests. Originally students together in Cambridge, Grubb and his wife came fom a sheltered background. Born in 1927, Grubb did his obligatory National Service in the Royal Navy as an able seaman, 1945–47, before going to work as a trouser-presser for six months, and after university, a general labourer 1951–52, a capstan operator 1952–53, a gramophone record presser 1953–55 and a driller 1955–56. Grubb had a desire to live among the working class, following his experience in the navy. Even from the context of evangelical Christianity, he had long had doubts about the existence of God, and later wrote an autobiographical booklet *Truth and God*, published by the Quakers in 1989. He believed it possible to live 'for Jesus' even if one could not understand 'the doctrine', for he felt that '... truth is something you do, you live, rather than merely talk about – a total relationship to existence – and that the only way I would ever find truth would be by getting on with the practical business of living'.[380]

Grubb intended to become a personnel manager, but his experience working in a railway yard one summer vacation convinced him that he could never have the kind of relationship he wanted in a managerial or professional role. 'The experience that class divisions were such that I could never have the kind of relationship with people I wanted ... I must become a worker, not temporarily, but for life.'[381]

> My desire was to preach the gospel but I felt deeply that I could not and should not do this except by sharing the life of the workers. Only by sharing the situation of being the oppressed people in a capitalist society would I be able to demonstrate the love of Christ and relate to them without hypocrisy; and only in that situation would I be able to face up to reality and to learn. [382]

Back at university after this experience he met another student, Michael Jackson, who would later (as this study has shown) become involved in the Sheffield Industrial Mission.[383] Grubb learnt of the French worker-priests first from Jackson, and together they paid a visit to Bishop Leslie Hunter in Sheffield inviting him to visit Cambridge to talk to students from university colleges.[384] About forty to fifty people attended a subsequent gathering which Hunter chaired and at which Grubb and Jackson both spoke. But Grubb, determined not to become a clergymen, intended to get a manual job in a working-class setting after university. It was a commitment, which at the time made a great impression upon the theologian Professor 'Charlie' Moule.[385] Grubb's fiancée Anne, a student at Girton, shared similar sentiments. In may be difficult for a reader in the twenty-first century to grasp the genuine youthful enthusiasm of those who sincerely looked at a life among the working class as a vocation. Anne Grubb, aware of the promises of employment in a post-war world, had grown up with the 1930s in her background. 'We had not suffered personally . . . but had seen and heard of the thirties . . .' Anne's understanding of suffering and class division made her equally determined to live among workers.

After university, but about five years before Martyn contemplated ordination, he and Anne sought advice in the heart of London's East End. They paid a visit to St John Groser, 'already an old man' at St Katherine's, where Groser had been well known as a radical. He was a protester they remembered, beaten by police in 1930s riots, and still living in the same setting. Martyn Grubb's own suggestion was that he should work in the docks. But the older and wiser Groser – wholly sympathetic with Grubb – knew this to be an impossibility. One effectively had to be 'born into' the docks, and anyway it was a 'closed shop'. Groser then volunteered that if he were in Grubb's shoes and starting out all over again, he would look to the west of London, and the Great West Road where whole new industries were growing up. So it was that, following their marriage and honeymoon, Martyn and Anne Grubb began a life together in Southall, where with a break for ordination training and curacy they would remain for the rest of their lives, and from where they would make a substantial contribution to the story of those who committed their lives to workers and racial justice and harmony.

In 1951, then, the Grubbs came into Southall looking for rooms like any other young couple, and found some in St Peter's Road. They immediately followed this with a search for jobs, not difficult at a time of high employment. Anne felt motivated in what she calls a Christian and social sense; there were good things happening in the church which they both felt workers knew nothing about. But for Anne, that social conscience and simply a desire to be among the working class meant that she would work happily anywhere, and she quickly found herself at Bachelor's pea factory 'picking out the bad ones' on a production line.

In a series of letters to friends that lasted most of their working lives, Martyn and Anne gave vivid accounts of their life and times in Southall. Anne describes her part-time work of five hours a day beginning at 7.30 a.m. and ending at 12.30 p.m., though in this first letter she reports her work had stopped.[386] They were expecting their first baby, and she found the work and the company interesting, confessing to 'looking young' . . . 'like a student still' – so she did not 'stand out'. She wanted to earn cash 'and the rest of the women didn't see me as any different'.[387] But Anne was not to be inactive in terms of welfare, and having to sit for up to five hours in the draught, and in low temperatures, led her to attempt to improve conditions for her fellow workers.

Martyn meanwhile found work in Abbot Brothers' furniture works (employing about 150 men) in a 49 hours a week job, 7.30 a.m. to 5.30 p.m. Monday to Friday and further hours on Saturday morning. Here Martyn laboured at the rip saw pulling planks being cut to size. The work was hard, and, like his young wife, he was forced to work in inadequately heated premises where in winter the snow on the wood when it arrived in the workshop refused to melt, and was still there at the end of the day.

Like others before him (Perrin, Gedge, and even Alan Sillitoe's Arthur Seaton) Grubb found time, above all, to think. And he felt the educated man better equipped to deal with this time than the 'uneducated'. For he thought the educated mind '. . . better trained to think and he has more to think about, so that he has more chance of keeping his mind occupied while doing work which in itself cannot possibly occupy the mind of anyone fully. I am especially lucky in this respect, and can do this work with unusually little frustration, because I have a great capacity for entertaining myself with my own thoughts.'[388]

But how was the gospel to be spoken of? Grubb later confessed that it was there as he and others were 'moved around' that he learnt he '. . . ought to keep quiet: . . . I am as yet incapable of talking about the Christian faith . . .'[389] But Grubb soon found work at Abbot Bros tedious, and after a year sought, as a natural progression (like John Rowe in the East End), more skilled work, this time at the Chiswick Engineering Company in Montague Road. Here at CEC, a 'low pay sweat-shop' Grubb began as a capstan operator working a small lathe

> . . . on which I made the bolt part of nuts and bolts at the rate of some 500 to 1,000 a day. It is classed as a semi-skilled job but it was a very simple job to learn. We worked a 47 hour week, 5 days a week, 8.00 a.m. to 6.00 p.m. with half an hour break for lunch from 2.00 to 2.30 p.m. and a quarter-hour tea break in the morning but none in the afternoon. The pay was £7 a week, and more interesting than most . . . [390]

After dismissal from the Chiswick Engineering Company because he had helped form the union and become a shop-steward in secret (this is explained later in full), Grubb was unable to find another job as a capstan operator. In 1953 he was at EMI, 'pressing out' individual gramophone records. This factory was 'the largest around here employing about 10,000 people . . .' and where His Master's Voice, Columbia, and other record labels were manufactured.

> I operate a press making the gramophone records: I put two labels into the press, followed by a lump of hot, soft, black material, close the press, prepare the next two labels and the next piece of material, open the press, take out the gramophone record (which is finished ready to play) – and then repeat the operation . . . there is no variation in the work . . . It was not an easy job to learn and was interesting at first, but now I do it entirely automatically and I find it very monotonous at times. The attraction of the job for an unskilled man such as I am is the pay . . . [391]

'I love to go a wandering', a song that was one of Martyn's favourites, like other records, was repeatedly played over the tannoy for the workers; 'I must have made thousands of that one', he claims.[392]

But after two years Grubb sought an opportunity to develop his skills and for a relatively short period in Spring 1955 moved to Hoover:

> I got a job as a capstan (lathe) operator at Hoovers, on the strength of my earlier experience as a capstan operator at the Chiswick Engineering Co. But at Hoovers capstan operating was very different – it was all mass production work, and very fast. Hoovers has the reputation around here of being the best factory in the west of London, and I was indeed fortunate to get there . . . it was good clean conditions . . . But these things cannot make up for the drab monotony of the work, nor do they necessarily mean good relationships between management and men . . . [393]

In a newsletter of 1956 Grubb admits that under a bonus system he could make up to thirteen pounds a week here – good pay at the time. Alan Sillitoe's fictional Arthur in his Nottingham bicycle factory, and on piece work,[394] had calculated that if he worked like a madman, 'his calculations' – on the *Daily Mirror* margins – 'gave an answer of thirty six pounds'. '"Which would never do," he swore to himself, "because they'd be down on me like a ton of bricks . . ." So he settled for a comfortable wage of fourteen pounds . . .'

But the snag was night work, and a fortnight on – 9.30 p.m. to 7.00 a.m. 'It is the wives and families who dislike nightwork even more than the men, and we found it was such a strain and had such a detrimental effect on family life that in the end we decided that it was worth sacrificing all the other advantages of working at Hoovers in order to get out of night work . . .'[395] By the following year, the factory life was beginning to take a toll upon family life anyway:

> Family life is a tremendous joy, but all the same we find having two small children a very full-time and exhausting business. This coupled with the fact that a full week's work in the factory leaves Martyn with very little time, means that our energies are completely taken up with the basic things of existence – namely, eating, sleeping and washing, looking after the children, and keeping sensitive to each other – that we seem to have hardly any left over for taking an interest in other people.[396]

It was during his period at Hoovers in the previous year (1955) that Grubb was to note fellow workers 'more interested in life and (more) intelligent than most of those with whom I have worked'. During this period he was able to build strong relationships with two men in particular, both of whom he felt encouraged his thinking in the direction of ordination. Bob was a Roman Catholic, and Jock, originally from Glasgow, an atheist. It was through a deep relationship with these two that Grubb was persuaded to seek ordination. For though he claims both men understood his vocation to be a worker, 'both felt that my work would be more effective if I were also ordained'.[397] In a later document, the basis for a talk to the Southwark Diocesan Synod in 1961, Martyn remembers:

> Some of my workmates said to me, 'Look here Martyn – we believe in what you are doing – it is the only thing that is ever likely to convert us

– but why don't you get the official backing of the church?' I think the thought they were trying to express was this: 'You could do so much more for us if you were able to have more say in the church: if you were able to preach: to be in charge of a congregation: to build the church in new ways.' Eventually I became convinced that I could not escape this responsibility . . . [398]

In 1955 Martyn was on the move again, seeking a change from night work. He found work at the Cramic Engineering Company, which employed about 250 men making high-quality parts.

I am employed there as a driller; although the work is only classed as semi-skilled it needs a lot more skill than any of the other jobs I have done . . . We are paid by the hour instead of on piece work, so one can work at one's own speed without being rushed. The pay (£9.11.6d gross [£9.57p] for a 44 hour week, since increased by 10/- [50p] a week due to the Engineering national increase in the spring of this year) is good for this kind of work . . . [399]

The 'more skill' which Grubb mentions as being required related to the fact that when not all the work was drilled through a 'jig' or pattern, some work had to be 'marked off', that is, specifically measured and marked by hand – skilled work. Within a short time, Grubb and one or two other men were being asked to work a radial drill (skilled work) which they point-blank refused to do unless given the skilled rates. Although there was no union representative on this section, the men there eventually won their skilled rate and Grubb found himself duly elected as shop steward in the Amalgamated Engineering Union.

As shop steward my main task has been to 'get the section organized' which means in effect to make Trade Union members, and a thankless task it is with many of the men apathetic.[400]

(iii) Ordination, curacy and the return to Southall

In their 1956 letter to friends, the Grubbs declare that the decision for ordination was taken the year before when Martyn 'was put in touch with the Bishop of Kensington, '. . . who is the suffragan Bishop in charge of this area'. During a friendly interview, the bishop threw cold water on the suggestion that Martyn could become a worker priest, commenting:

'It can't be done: it has never been done before.' For a time (and with some relief) ideas on ordination were dropped. Later, however, the Bishop of Stepney, Joost de Blank, who was to prove very supportive,[401] sent for Grubb and said that the London bishops had discussed his vocation, and had decided that they would support him if he were approved in the normal way. Following a CACTM selection conference Grubb was recommended for training, and would start the same autumn at Westcott House, Cambridge.

Grubb was resident for one full year at Westcott (he already held a degree in theology) chosen, though he came from an evangelical background, in favour to Ridley Hall (the evangelical college), because Westcott was more 'open' and 'sociologically aware' than Ridley. A further one and a half years were to be spent in a parish – Grubb didn't want to be out of a factory long.

It was while Grubb was preparing for ordination that he was able to visit Paris with another Westcott student, where they spent a week with a worker-priest. Here, Grubb discovered that the experiment had not, after all, been halted; there were some 150 worker-priests, though many were most unhappy with the restrictions that had been placed on them. Indeed he believed there to be some 70 who would not observe the restrictions, and who were prevented from exercising their priesthood, though they had not been excommunicated (which had always been a threat). There was certainly no rift of fellowship between what would later become known as the 'old wave' and the number which had obeyed the Vatican's ruling and were now under its 'control'.[402]

The one and a half years spent in a curacy in parish ministry will be examined in due course. The leadership of an enlightened incumbent had not deterred Grubb from his intention to remain a worker, and this time to join the small ranks of worker-priests. In March 1959 the Grubbs wanted to return to work, and indicated an interest in the new towns. But it was skilled workers only who were finding work in the latter, and, not yet accepted as part of their ranks (for Martyn lacked some of the necessary paperwork that proved him a skilled worker), the Grubbs returned to Southall. They had remained on the housing list, and now, in April 1959, moved into two small rooms owned by West Indians, sharing one cooker with three other families. Martyn began work as a capstan operator with P. W. Dilloway, agricultural engineers, three years after John Rowe had started work in London's East End.

Working what was sometimes a sixty-hour week, with three children, and Anne working at night washing-up in a cafe from six till after midnight, the Grubbs had a hard time of it, though a little later they were able to put down a deposit on a house. But by 1959, with barely a year in Dilloway's, Martyn, even though he had begun some skilled work in a 'hardening shop', once again found himself sacked.

(iv) Presence and theology

Rowe and Grubb, starting from what initially appeared as rather different positions, and quite unknown to each other, felt deeply the enormous gulf between working people and the institutional church. In the growing post-war economy, when at times employment could be relatively high, but housing and all other manner of material things were still in short supply, they sought a means to challenge the 'contradictions of the time' by living and working with their families in the same conditions as millions of other ordinary men and women. Now in a different sense from Gedge and Strong before, Rowe sat lightly to the territorial parish, with Grubb more committed to its structure. They both received, however, through diocesan and area bishops, a sanction and blessing for their work, though the rest of the church, in this early period, knew very little of their commitment.

Any analysis of *la présence* in their case presents the reader with difficulties. Perhaps deliberately, neither recorded precise details of encounters with work mates, though Grubb's newsletters highlighted one or two instances, the immediate problems that often arose between union representatives and management. Anecdotal references are to specific encounters when moments of tension or relief were etched on the memory. In both cases, however, many of these moments are about risk-taking in the context of difficult or dangerous work practices (enforced by management), the attitudes of the work-force, which could be racist, or the failure of their fellow workers to act in solidarity with one another, all of which they could easily have ignored.

For both, job satisfaction clearly had some importance. Rowe sought further training as a qualified electrician, meeting some opposition from his own work mates, who even after eleven years of Rowe as a 'mate', still felt him insufficiently 'in the know' to join their ranks. Only the intervention of his union in acknowledging Rowe's experience and qualifications allowed him to take on the role for which he was clearly qualified. Grubb also sought opportunities to develop the skills of which he was clearly capable, and as he found out he could soon be taken advantage of.

There is little recorded in Rowe's case of direct encounters with fellow workers. Typical of a worker-priest, these encounters had something of the 'seal of the confessional' about them, though they may also reveal a simple understanding of others. Like Gedge, or Strong before him, Rowe simply accepted the day to day encounters which came his way in the context of his labour, and saw these as normal, unexceptional, certainly not to be recorded. To be a worker-priest meant being in solidarity and having the respect and confidence of those around you, without any Christian proselytizing. It remained a 'secret ministry', and to have made it more public would surely have destroyed the very thing it was.

In one of their first letters from Southall, describing the environment in which they found themselves, the middle-class Anne and Martyn Grubb told of what they saw as the 'appalling aimlessness of people's lives', and they catalogued attitudes to family life as 'poisonous'; 'divorces are so common one doesn't notice them', and if it came to a choice between a child and a television set – the television won. Abortion was commonplace in the community, and their landlady was 'utterly amazed' to discover not only that Anne was pregnant, but also that she intended to keep her baby. 'Gin and Epsom salts will get rid of it for you' was the only advice she could offer to the mum-to-be.[403] But Anne and Martyn were beginning to find the sheer drudgery that everyday labour could be:

> Although we have not been here long, we have already experienced for ourselves what a deadening effect this kind of work can have. . . . Work has always involved pain and drudgery, and we do not say that in this respect factory work is necessarily worse than other kinds. But we all know how it is possible for the most uneducated countryman to be a man of culture, in its fundamental sense of the development of the soul, and we feel that this is very difficult, if not impossible, for these factory workers.[404]

In a note of some anxiety that at first seemed almost in sympathy with F. R. Leavis and Denys Thompson's pre-war anxiety about a culture in danger of being destroyed, the Grubbs contrast what was possible in terms of the countryman – with some residual culture – and the townsman[405] with little feeling, as had already been observed by the Abbé Godin. Here too in 1950s Southall, an alienation seemed to have been in place, and the Grubbs were already beginning to understand some of the driving forces: 'This effect of factory work helps to explain why, in his leisure hours, the working man usually turns to recreations which many people deplore.'

Please do not blame him when you see him queuing up for the pictures; we should rather blame ourselves, for our culture is only possible because he supports us by work which makes culture, even in its fundamental sense, for him well nigh impossible.

We are destroying these people's lives in order to save our own souls . . . If Christians had the faith to renounce the influential jobs . . . and to take upon themselves the soul destroying work, which in our present civilization has to be done by someone, they would be dealing with the problem in God's way. This is the way God works to save the world . . . [406]

It may indeed have been 'God's way', his incarnate way, as Christian readers would soon hear Bonhoeffer arguing in his *Letters and Papers from Prison* (1953) that '. . . God is weak and powerless in the world, and that is exactly the way, the only way, in which he can be with us and help us . . .'[407]

Grubb's desire to progress to more skilled work has already been highlighted. Thus, when working in the furniture factory's wood yard became tedious, it was natural for him, like any other worker, to seek something more interesting. Chiswick Engineering began to offer that, EMI did not. Hoover and Cramic Engineering were better again. Gradually, proven ability on the shop floor brought him skilled work – and trouble – as he fought for recognition with a management all too frequently ready to allow able individuals to do the 'odd bit' of skilled work on lower wages.

More than Rowe, Grubb kept memories of specific encounters, but tells his story almost 'as it happens' and more specifically when the story relates to his union work. His costly involvement and subsequent sackings neither discouraged nor disabled him from continuing, like Rowe, to support the workers by taking on the role of shop steward, something which became a hall-mark of early worker-priests who found in this responsibility a real – but undisclosed – ministry.

Rowe and Grubb represented a different starting position from Gedge and Strong before them, as both sought a presence first among workers, without 'running parishes' at the same time. In this sense, they had more in common with the French. Rowe admits perhaps only with reluctance that he had a 'ministry' of any sort at work. That was not essentially what it was all about, and 'ministry' could be viewed in secular terms anyway. Thus: 'I grew into a limited pastoral role, which later emerged into that of a shop-steward.' In a rare contribution, when Rowe described his work in *Trade Union Affairs*[408] he took the opportunity to talk about the paternal attitudes of his employers, who thought themselves to be acting with 'loyalty and responsibility', about attitudes to 'materialism' and union apathy among workers, and to express his certainty that:

> . . . I for one, have found no less Christianity in the behaviour of workers towards one another than I find among churchgoers . . . But when I talk about the recovery of the Christian faith I mean a faith in a God who does not want people merely to believe that He is 'there', or to behave considerately towards one another, but in a God Who is always moving to change the human situation . . . This God requires love among men not merely because it makes life pleasanter but because such love is the only successful means for human well-being, both of the individual and of society. It is a revolutionary principle and it calls men into the association of the church because only together can men change the face of human society.[409]

Rowe was accepted as a very ordinary member of the work force, and when 'religious' events or issues arose, they still stand out in memory. When some twenty-five fellow workers attended the tenth anniversary of his ordination, the sting in the tail was that '. . . they never let me forget it!'. Just one visit to a church service, it seems, was an effort, yet Rowe could appreciate the largeness of the gesture.

Rowe would make himself 'useful' in a religious sense only if necessary: 'I talked to them (on religious matters) if asked . . . sometimes I could talk about their problems in an intelligent way.' Many of the assumptions about religion he found 'crass'; '. . . they'd want to talk about Sunday School or church . . .' But Rowe didn't want to talk about 'religion', got impatient, and would sometimes say so. 'One carpenter was a cynic . . .' telling Rowe he was the only clergyman he knew who wasn't fat . . . 'assuming none of them did any work'. When it came to major criticisms of the church, Rowe could only agree, sometimes pointing out that the class system operated in the church too, and that the institution could certainly be on the 'right wing' politically.

Rowe's anxiety simply to have a presence and to share fully in the lives of ordinary men could only be described theologically as incarnational. The sense that priesthood might be focussed 'on the altar' brings to mind the notion that Perrin would have embraced: that all could be 'offered up' there. The fact his fellow workers did not share that understanding was of no matter; he shared their humanity, and that was the essence of the thing.

Martyn Grubb described himself and his wife as politically conscious, alive to the gulf separating workers and the church, and to where the services appeared irrelevant. In their earliest days at Southall, 1951–54, they saw the place as a 'depressing community . . . much more depressing than the slums of Bristol'. Several years later, by the time Grubb had decided on ordination it was nevertheless to be as a worker-priest: 'I could not preach the gospel in any other way than sharing the life of the people: and not only of the people, but of the least privileged class among the people . . .', and he continued:

> . . . I would rather die than give way about this. I do not mean to condemn the full-time ministry, in which a man receives his support from his fellow Christians for the Christian work he does. To do so would be contrary both to common sense and to scripture. But if I were to attempt to preach the gospel in any other way I should feel that I was a hypocrite.[410]

The apparent contrast with Rowe was clearly that 'preaching the gospel' was a kind of 'evangelical code'. But Grubb was no typical evangelical, and already there was a strong sacramental awareness driving him towards the outward expressions of 'inward and invisible grace'. Sharing totally in the life of work drove Martyn and his wife deeper, where they discovered the 'deadening effect of work' which sometimes offered only 'pain and drudgery' and which '. . . seems to be destroying that for which God made man . . .,'[411] thoughts long since shared by Michael Gedge during the war, and now by Leslie Hunter in 1950s Sheffield.[412] Thus, like other early worker-priests' wives, Anne Grubb was involved in this sharing of working life, most noticeably in the domestic backdrop where the business of sharing a house, even though by this time it was their own – which they had opened to a homeless couple Sheila and Peter – now resulted in tension: 'My main problem at the moment is that it gets on my nerves terribly sharing the house, as it is very unsettling for David (their son) now he's older and also when I am feeding the baby etc., . . . to have Sheila and her son in and out of our living room all day (the only access to the kitchen) . . . it would be unthinkable to turn them out . . . isn't it just too easy to stop caring about things when they get difficult?'[413]

Martyn Grubb's presence on the shop floor, however, is also related in incarnational terms, for although at an early stage he admitted to 'doing this' work, 'to convert people to Christ' – a very clear evangelical sentiment – the explanation before a Southwark diocesan conference was more explicitly incarnational:

> Christ died to save the world. In the last resort he saved the world not by his teaching, nor by his wonderful deeds, but by his love expressed in action – namely, in his incarnation and death. He came alongside men and bore their burdens. That love was the creative principle which brought new life into the world. We are called to love our fellow men with the same love with which he first loved us . . . [414]

Grubb's presence was lived in these terms. His encounters, related in terms of his personal working problems or those of his fellow workers, were often about unhappy experiences, especially sackings. He found Christian solidarity not among fellow evangelicals but elsewhere:

> It is noticeable that nearly all the Christian fellowship I have had on the shop floor has been with Roman Catholics . . . Their Christianity seems to me to be more real when applied to everyday life than that of non-Roman Catholic Christians I have met; and the latter are very much fewer. [415]

By this time, it was possible to begin an exploration of kingdom theology. In responding to a remark by the Bishop of Southwark in 1961, Grubb admits when talking at the Southwark Conference to siding with the bishop, who had said that the whole weight of theology 'bears witness to the fact that the church is not an end in itself, but the means to an end . . .' That end was the kingdom of God, and such remarks indicate that this was already emerging as working theology, explicitly undeveloped, but implicitly in use.

Separated on either side of London, Grubb and Rowe were soon to engage in a new and more purposeful community as a new group developed with the encouragement of John Strong in Harlington. The common bond of working life would bring these worker-priests, wives and some laity together, as a new body – the Worker Church Group – would give more explicit expression to what they believed they were about.

2. In Oxford: Tony Williamson

(i) Into work – Cowley

Tony Williamson's background would be partly responsible for encouraging him into a life of manual labour, but a developed theological and social outlook would make him one of the most articulate and forthright of the first worker-priests. The scope of his life, from student to shop-floor worker, Trade Union and Labour party leader (including becoming the Lord Mayor of Oxford), shows the outworking of principles to which, as one of the youngest worker-priests, he dedicated more than thirty years.

Born in 1933 the son of Father Joe Williamson, vicar of St Paul's, Dock Street, Stepney, whose efforts as a devoted parish priest made him something of a legend,[416] Tony Williamson found himself at the receiving end of a father's determination to give his children what he had never himself enjoyed. '. . . [M]y father was determined we should have the education he never had and I went to boarding school and University (Marlborough and Oxford).' From there he claims to have 'drifted' towards ordination.[417]

It was while he was a student at Trinity that Williamson met David Wood, 'a sort of industrial chaplain' in Wolverhampton, where a group had gone from the College to experience factory work in the north. 'The church and industry' as general topics were already being debated in Oxford Christian circles – with the encouragement of men like Kenneth Woollcombe[418] – as indeed they were in Cambridge at the time Martyn Grubb took an interest. After taking a degree in geography Williamson began at Cuddesdon under the Principal, Knapp Fisher, in 1956, with the full intention of becoming a parish priest, hopefully in some industrial setting. Factory visits while at college, he believed, would prove one of the best ways of preparing him for such a role.

While at Cuddesdon, however, a number of different influences came to bear on him. Williamson and others paid a visit to London's East End, and, to avoid ending up as a one of a number of the curious peering in on his father's parish, he went elsewhere; later he met John Rowe. This, together with his discovery of some of the Grubbs' circular letters and a general knowledge of the French and English worker-priests, some of whom he had already met, convinced him that there was an alternative to conventional ministry in the territorial parish. He determined, therefore, before ordination, and with the encouragement of Knapp-Fisher, to seek full-time employment on a shop-floor before beginning a parish ministry. At this stage, however, he had not considered becoming a worker-priest himself.

Knapp-Fisher had already had contact with the Vicar of Cowley, John Betton, in whose parish the major car manufacturing was based. It was arranged that here Tony Williamson would spend a year in the Pressed Steel works before ordination. Betton had already found it difficult to get into the Morris works, even as a visitor, and at Pressed Steel there remained hostility. The Transport and General Workers' Union (TGWU) were unhappy with the idea of a visiting chaplain when, at the time, they already had problems with management. Then Betton changed tack altogether and simply suggested an ordinand on the shop-floor. Unions and management eventually agreed to something that might do a young man 'a world of good'. Tony Williamson would be that young man, and he would remain at the Pressed Steel complex for virtually thirty years.

In April 1958 Williamson began work as a 'trucker', moving scrap metal and steel plates to a press shop where they would be pressed into car bodies. This was essentially a labouring job, and, throughout his career, and unlike other worker-priests, Williamson would remain unskilled.

When he began, Williamson was guarded with work mates about who he was or what he was 'trying to do'. 'I kept my mouth shut,' he recalls. And it was to be during this early period, just prior to ordination, that he found out about (possibly from John Rowe) and was able to visit the little group which had just been formed around John Strong. This was just at the point at which they were discussing the compilation of a 'Statement' which they hoped would spell out their commitment and aims.[419]

Williamson soon became convinced that he wanted to stay at Pressed Steel, be ordained, but, if at all possible, forego any kind of conventional curacy. The Bishop of Oxford, Harry Carpenter, faced with this most unusual request, was at first reluctant to sanction such an unconventional practice, and 'would not agree to ordain me while in the factory'.[420] Williamson then had to do battle with historic precedent in order to survive intact with his ideas, and sought the help and support of Knapp-Fisher, his former Principal. Although they had often clashed in the past, there was still mutual respect, and Knapp-Fisher believed that if Williamson could survive Pressed Steel, then perhaps he would indeed be ready for ordination.[421] But Williamson was not automatically expected to remain at Pressed Steel and now had to seek the support of the personnel manager, whom he had agreed to meet after an initial year. The manager was extremely wary of Williamson's intentions, believing that the latter's obvious intellectual gifts might result in frustration if he remained at a labouring job.

Williamson stayed at Pressed Steel into 1959, with his local vicar John Betton quite convinced of the rightness of what he saw as Williamson's vocation. He secured digs for the young man in the home of a union official, a move which took Williamson into the Labour Party, and for which he would stand in local elections in 1961.

In March, the Bishop of Oxford was prepared to license Williamson as a Lay Reader, believing that this was one way at least in which Williamson could have some recognized standing in the work of the church while at Pressed Steel[422] and . . . 'pending the final decision about your ordination'.

By early summer, the bishop, while congratulating Williamson on his recent engagement, replies to a letter in which the latter had clearly expressed anxiety about a future ordination directly 'to the work place'. The bishop replied, however, that he had been misunderstood:

> I certainly did not intend to convey that impression. On the contrary everything seems to be moving and developing as I hoped and expected it would. I have consistently said that I thought you ought to be a workman for two years before being ordained to the double vocation . . . it is important for your own sake that you should thoroughly establish yourself as a workman before being ordained. If I had thought . . . that your ordination was unlikely, I should certainly have told you plainly.[423]

The bishop added that Williamson should reflect on how much more difficult his position would be after ordination (presumably because he would then be a clergyman on the shop-floor), but that he understood Williamson's impatience arising out of his conviction on the 'rightness of your purpose', 'but,' he added, 'I should not be acting responsibly if I allowed your impatience to outweigh other considerations.' This would surely not be wasted time in Christian witness, 'unless,' he added, 'you take the impossible view that only a priest-workman can give that witness'. In reply, Williamson admitted that his immediate anxieties had been allayed, though he goes on to reveal what he sees as some kind of episcopal obstruction, and with the nagging fear that at any moment the bishop might change his mind. Here Williamson admits no exclusivity for the priest. It is the layman who remains the chief witness in industrial life. Yet establishing himself as a layman would not be easy for, 'However long I work with them, my mates cannot accept me as an ordinary worker, because clearly I come from a different background . . . on the other hand if I have come from outside for a purpose, ordination seems the only concrete way of the church showing its support.'[424]

Within a few days the bishop replied again to reassure Williamson that he would ordain him at Trinity the following year (1960), 'unless any obstacle occurs between now and then which I neither foresee nor expect'.[425] By letting slip this cautionary aside, the bishop then threw Williamson into a state of further anxiety. He now pressed the bishop to ordain him at Advent 1959 (that was within just four months), when he would have already been at Pressed Steel one and three quarter years. Williamson reminded his bishop that he had in the past sought the advice of others, 'but apparently you have completely disregarded what they have said . . .' [426]

It was the commonplace frustration of a young man clear in mind and impatient at the caution of his elders. He already knew he must go where the church had refused to go. In an essay (possibly 1959) in which he reiterates his feelings, he looks at the ordinal, showing the difficulties posed in a service which clearly does not envisage 'worker-priests':

> Finally there is the question of whether the church as a whole means to face up to the challenge of the world with action, or only with words. The Lambeth Report (1958) had said that there is no reason to prevent a Bishop ordaining a man while in full-time secular work; but no Bishop in England has yet done this, without demanding a period of full-time pastoral work. Other priests in this work have acted on their own, and received some sort of episcopal support once they were established in manual work. This, as well as the employment situation in Oxford, is why I asked, almost from the start, for the bishop to take the initiative in ordaining me to do this particular work.[427]

(ii) Ordination – to the shop-floor

Though the correspondence reveals a cautious man, Bishop Harry Carpenter took the then radical step of ordaining Tony Williamson (as indeed the essay later confirms) at a service at Christ Church Cathedral, Oxford, at the end of June 1960, amid much publicity. This publicity revealed some of the initial reasons given for this chosen vocation on the shop floor. The local paper, the *Oxford Mail*, gave full coverage of the events, quoting from the statements of bishop and ordinand, all of which was taken up by the national press the following day.[428]

The Daily Telegraph, which described Williamson as a tractor driver, repeated the young man's left-wing remarks that 'the Church has given the impression that it was on the side of the middle classes and the bosses. It has failed to appeal to the workers. We have now got to make good that deficiency.'[429] And the views of Bishop Carpenter were added in the *Daily Mail* and *The Guardian*'s articles following a 'DEACON CLOCKS ON' headline that: '. . . only rarely can this kind of worker-priest arrangement be properly made, but the conditions seem favourable in this case'.[430]

At the time, neither the bishop, nor Williamson, nor anyone else for that matter, would be aware just how 'rare' this 'arrangement' would prove to be, as Williamson now joined the handful of worker-priests in England. The *Christian Herald* and the *Church of England Newspaper* provided some mission and pastoral reasoning, the former commenting that the Bishop had explained that 'Mr Williamson had taken the unusual step, partly to provide a link between the Church and Industry, and partly as a witness to the dignity of manual labour . . .' but there was the added caution that while this was a valuable and useful experiment, it was 'unlikely' to become a general practice, adding the words of the bishop (as if in some dreaded anticipation of a future gone mad) that: 'The work of the Ministry, both from a preaching and pastoral standpoint, is of such a strenuous character, that the average man would break under such a strain.'[431]

As for relations with his work mates of two years, Tony Williamson was described in a variety of ways, all very favourable, and his presence was touched on in a *Daily Mail* cartoon.[432] He was 'one of the best of them', and the *Oxford Mail* quoted the comment, 'he's a good lad . . . the sentiment simply expressed, was echoed by dozens of others in the press shop'.[433]

If responses from the shop floor proved warm, these were no less than those Williamson received from other sources on the occasion of this unusual ordination. The 'Ecumenical Orthodox Church Travelling Mission Byzantine Rite's' bishop, the Rt Revd Imre, 'appointed titular bishop of Murkacs acting Ethnarch of the Hungarian Church in Exile' (and from the Priory, Leatherhead, Surrey), congratulated Williamson and welcomed him into '. . . the small band of monks, deakons [sic] and sacrificing priests of various nationalities who are living in exile in this country and earning their living in secular employment'.[434] These sentiments were repeated in a letter from the Revd Fr Francis of the Ancient Catholic Church in Exeter.[435]

And at a time when many clergy still appeared in cassock or at least in a clerical collar, the story would be front-page headlines in the church's own press: 'Tony Williamson in his blue works overalls opened the door to a *Church Times* reporter. He had just come home from work and was having tea with his wife in the small dining room at the back of the house.'[436] It was here that Williamson briefly outlined his position for readers, explaining his 'departure' from a conventional curacy but much more significantly from the now growing popularity of industrial mission. 'There is a tremendous lot of good work done by industrial chaplains but their contacts have to be with the leaders and the articulate.' By contrast, it was a union official who had remarked to Williamson that: '. . . there are 13,000 heathen in this factory, and if that was not enough for one man . . .' then he didn't know what was.

If up and down the country parish priests were reading these headlines with some apprehension, Williamson was more than ready to give an explanation for his chosen vocation. 'The ordinary parish priest has so much time taken up with the pastoral and priestly that he has little time for the prophetic . . .' 'I shall fulfil the function [from the Ordination Service] but I shall concentrate on the parts the parish clergy cannot do.'[437]

When he had started work at Cowley, initially for only one year, few of his workmates had taken special notice of Tony Williamson, and as he himself later confessed, he had kept generally quiet about who he was or what his intentions might have been. He later described[438] how for the first ten months at Pressed Steel Co. he had worked with a gang of six 'loading and unloading roofs, doors, wings and other parts of car bodies, after they had been pressed into shape from sheet steel, and before they were trimmed, flanged and pierced ready for assembly. Being in the press-shop where this work was done I met the noise and dirt from the first day, as well as the danger from handling steel.'[439]

It was in this early period that Williamson had become convinced from contacts with industrial chaplains and worker-priests that he should remain in industry, 'both as a manual worker and as a priest'.[440] Shortly afterwards he moved from loading and unloading to driving a tractor delivering the pressed steel to the appropriate locations in the press shop. But even earlier, in fact within only a few weeks of starting at Pressed Steel, he had taken on a role on the union's factory canteen committee, of which he later became secretary. This would be the start of a long and important role in the union, and one which would bring him into conflict with management and a warm relationship with the men around him as he sought to devote time to the one organization which gave the workers an effective voice in the work place.

At work and in his local community Williamson found 'pastoral opportunities', and used the phrase as a heading for one of his short essays. He noted again what Gedge, Southcott, Wickham had all noticed before: the church so often spoke to the women in a family context (though Williamson mentions men and women) but confessed that we '. . . have only provided generalizations about how men should live their individual lives in the secular world of everyday work – generalizations which often sound better in the pulpit than on the shop-floor on Monday morning. Our aim . . . [and then talking about his own home life] is to live in a normal house, work in a large factory, take our full part in secular life and try to do what seems right in these circumstances rather than to tell others what they ought to do.'[441] At the end of 1960 the 'redundancy story', when Williamson faced the sack and went to work as a van driver, gave the local and national press another opportunity to highlight the nature of Williamson's work before Trinity 1961, when he was ordained priest. By spring, and with buoyancy again in the car market, Williamson's hopes were realized and he had 'clocked on' again at Pressed Steel.[442] This time 'mates' came to his ordination, with 'Bill', father of four children, happy to admit that the measure of 'Tony's success' was that he '. . . had persuaded hard cases like me to come here today'.[443] And as the account of his priesting reached France, Jean Canninade, a worker-priest from Noisy le Grand, who had already met members of the little (barely three years old) Worker Church Group, wrote '. . . I am praying very hard that God will assist you to help you in this presence in the world of work'.[444] Williamson's ordination and subsequent return to the shop floor resulted in more publicity and exposure for a worker-priest since the time Gedge or Strong prepared to go underground at Eyethorne almost a decade before. Reporters were often relatively faithful to the story lines supplied, and Pressed Steel were happy enough to allow photographers in. No doubt it looked good for a major manufacturing industry to be demonstrating an interest in its own worker-priest, but unlike John Rowe, who had requested a total clamp-down on publicity, Williamson was happy to tell his own story, though there was a least one attempt to manipulate its drift. Just before an ATV religious programme 'Eye Level' was to be recorded, Williamson was summoned to Pressed Steel's PR department and reminded that those who watched such programmes only wanted to hear about 'things spiritual . . . they would not be interested in what goes on in a factory'.[445]

Unlike any other worker-priest before him, Tony Williamson had been ordained directly to the shop floor without first being required to serve a full-time parish curacy. This was not because he eschewed the parochial ministry (he had been brought up in a vicarage), though he had certainly established the principle that that was no vocation for him. Rather, his setting for ministry was to be on the industrial site. The bishop, accepting this 'double vocation', as he called it, and the subsequent ordination, was recognizing that Tony Williamson's life as a priest would take an entirely different path from that of the hundreds of other clergy in the Oxford diocese. At the same time, however, like John Rowe but unlike John Strong, Williamson recognized that there was a radical alternative to parochial ministry, in that his chief vocation lay outside the territorial parish, in the world of industry and local politics.

(iii) Helping John Strong

It was while at Cowley that Williamson was able to assist John Strong in what would prove to be the latter's last period as a worker-priest. Williamson became aware that the Strongs were less than happy in Blackburn. Despite the sympathetic invitation to go there from the bishop – rescuing them from the turmoil in Harlington – their spell in the north began with unemployment for Strong. He became depressed, and his wife Veronica discovered for the first time how unemployment could make a man feel useless.[446] Later he got a job with an earth-moving equipment firm, where the work was heavy, and he began again to suffer physically. This was only relieved when he got the chance to move to the work's stores.

But life proved hard for the Strongs. There was culture shock; the northerners were different, and, Veronica thought, '. . . fifty years behind the times . . . the women going to work with curlers in their hair'. The climate was colder, and in the terrible winter of 1962–63 they never saw their back garden till the end of May.[447] Most depressing for Veronica, her son was being bullied by a gang who lay in wait on his way to school. This might have happened anywhere, but the boy's southern accent and a new pair of prescribed glasses didn't help! But he wouldn't tell, '. . . and was trying to be strong about it'.

The church the Strongs attended (since demolished) was a considerable walking journey from the house. It was evangelical, and though the clergy were sympathetic, there was still a lack of understanding about Strong's role and he was clearly liturgically not at home, though he remained insistent that being a worker-priest and a parish priest was his vocation. John Strong saw the shop floor as only one of his foci for ministry. 'His feeling,' said Williamson, '. . . was that he needed to be running a parish – or at least helping to. He couldn't do it in Blackburn, and he was thrown out of Harlington for doing it.'[448]

Williamson now set to work to secure a place in Oxford for John and Veronica Strong. First a job was found for Strong at the Morris plant and on the assembly line, and secondly, a new council house was secured on the Blackbird Leys housing estate. Here a large wooden shed served as a place of worship till a new and rather extraordinary concrete edifice was built in the early 1960s.

John Strong remained content with his role as a 'team' priest at Blackbird Leys alongside Peter Malton, the parish priest already so well established on the estate that he couldn't bear the thought of moving into a newly constructed vicarage.[449] All along, however, Williamson's feeling was that, ironically, Strong was never quite as happy as he'd been in Harlington. Nevertheless, in Oxford, Strong again shared the working life of his parishioners – for the Blackbird Leys estate had been built for Oxford's car workers – till the return of his old physical problems forced him to give up manual labour altogether. In the late 1960s John Strong and Veronica settled in 'the Baldons', a small group of Oxfordshire country charges; after nearly twenty years of manual labour, his days as a worker-priest had come to an end. 'John never really settled in to this . . . and I felt guilty at having such a big house.'[450] But they remained unorthodox, with Veronica taking up a paper round.

(iv) Presence and theology

Unlike John Rowe before him, because he was already a public figure in Oxford politics and had to face the press, Tony Williamson's profile appears openly colourful. He was the youngest of all the early worker-priests and, perhaps enjoying some of the spotlight, was resilient enough to take the knocks that might come from conservative church circles,[451] including some from his own parish when he was found to be supporting car workers on strike or in dispute, or fighting issues on the city council. He fitted rather well into an Oxford where the ancient university, of which he was a graduate and ordinand, remained in what might be described as its 'Latin quarter' in sharp contrast to the industrial areas on the south-eastern side of which he was also a part. Williamson did not waver in the role he had set himself when, after some fourteen years in the car industry, he still had to defend his vocation. 'These decisions (made by unions) are vital to the life of everyone. A Christian should be involved with politics and trade unions. I am a mixture of priest, trade union official and city councillor. The three can't be separated.'[452]

But like the other worker-priests, and especially Rowe, Williamson's engagement with work mates, at the very heart of what he was about as a tractor driver, remained essentially 'sealed', if clearly warm. At his ordination, one of his fellow workers from the early days, arriving a little late for the ceremony, was approached by a sidesman who had asked if he had arrived for the 'ordination'. The workmate responded in some bewilderment, confessing he knew not what all that was about but that he had simply come 'to see Tony done'. As for special pastoral moments, Williamson numbers them simply as things which happened 'often'.[453] In his short and early paper on 'Pastoral Opportunities'[454] Williamson mentions dealings with neighbours on the estate where he lived, and then adds, '. . . several people from the Labour party have asked me to take services for their children or themselves . . .' He dealt with misunderstandings (on weddings and baptism) '. . . marriage and sex are subjects that I have been able to talk about deeply and clearly with a few men whose marriages have broken down, and with others who have read Lady Chatterley. During my time in the laundry I have had several casual conversations with three men whose marriages are on the rocks, and another young man about to be married . . .' (and he adds in the same vein as Martyn Grubb earlier) '. . . the ignorance and narrow outlook of them all is sad'.[455] But the detailed 'specifics' of pastoral encounters, where and when they occur, are, after all, no one else's business, though the very fact that workers readily approached him with all manner of personal problems speaks for itself. There were of course the more general encounters, problems with marriages, the business of getting married in the parish church, . . . and tombstones.[456] And there were the lighter moments. If he could be called upon at a dispute rally to give them 'a hymn', he was also considered knowledgeable enough to assist in the daily business of crosswords, where he was expected to know the answers to all the religious questions.

In the early days there was mention of 'religious talk' when at his priesting (1961) a fellow worker had made the somewhat unlikely admission that, 'Until three years ago we talked about just the ordinary things you know, about football, women and so on. But now religion, God and life after death are our main talking points.'[457] If it is hard to believe that such conversation was now commonplace, what the statement may confirm is that Williamson, like others, knew that only some kind of permanence in the work place made for the kind of trust and understanding that enabled such talk even to begin. For Williamson, later in reflection, there was 'not much' encounter on the real questions of faith, or Jesus or God. 'People don't challenge the professional in his area of confidence.' There was the occasional funeral . . . in one case of a trade union colleague whose line had been that he always put 'C of E' on forms 'because there might be something in it . . . but I buried him', says Williamson.[458] Essentially, Williamson has explained, as John Rowe, Gedge or Strong might have said, that he 'shared working conditions, lived near the factory, with children in the local schools[459] . . . and I used my abilities with and for the benefit of fellow workers and others'.[460]

And when the first worker-priests produced their Statement in 1959 – which will be examined later – Williamson would receive warm comments revealing relationships from his early days in the work place, encounters which had obviously been something of a 'success'. Vera, 'a working woman with children', whom Tony Williamson had met while a student, hints at life in the work place in response to a copy of the Statement which Williamson had sent her:

> George the labourer – I don't know if you remember him but he said there was no God and that we are all daft. So you could do with packing your bags and coming back to Bradleys . . . [adding]
>
> . . . I think what you are doing is good . . . working side by side with working people getting to know them their ways to share their troubles . . . [461]

Those who would seek for a cogent theological or ideological rationale of the worker-priest's chosen role in the work place will continue to be disappointed. What is said often emerges as a kind of 'religious apologetic'; just as the worker-priests in France in the 1950s tried to defend their position against the Vatican or their own bishops who often felt compelled to side with the institution. But statements were made by Williamson regarding his own theological position, and appear in talks and sermons, many from his first decade as a worker-priest, when the role was still something of a novelty. At the time he was invited by conferences, theological colleges and later courses[462] to explain his life when concerns surrounding the church and industry were still relatively high on the agenda. This would change in the late 1960s and early 1970s, when synodical and liturgical changes tended to sweep 'industry' from the church's agenda, ironically at a time when a range of highly contentious issues about the future of industry and its inherent unrest came to dominate the social and political agenda.

Close to his ordination, questions emerged on a theology of priesthood. If it was true, as many seemed to think, that the laity were at the forefront of the church's action 'in the world of work' (and the arguments persisted for different reasons into the 1990s)[463] and it was therefore essentially the task of the Christian laity to be the 'presence' in the world – why the need for ordained men, deacons or priests?

Two articles addressed perhaps to two different groups give explicit expression to Williamson's thinking. In an undated paper (possibly 1960)[464] he extols the laity as the prime witnesses in secular life. Indeed he agrees with one of the contributors in Denniston's book, *Part-Time Priests?*, that laymen should be living lives of integrity in the world, through the practice of 'moral righteousness'. Perhaps the question in Williamson's mind was – is this possible? It was after all the very question that Michael Gedge had asked back in 1944 as he set out to work on the shop-floor. On the contrary, says Williamson, leading laymen are often encouraged to find their 'vocation' by leaving the cut and thrust of the secular world and becoming full-time agents of the church as parish priests and so

> . . . some priests who are the acknowledged spiritual leaders should be involved in this great task and thus show that the church as a whole recognizes the need to take the secular world seriously.[465]

In the *Cowley Chronicle*, 1960, Williamson reiterates these points. 'I am here (on the shop floor) to bridge the gap between the church and the rest of life in this country; because the clergy are too busy to meet the problems adequately; and because the lay people need some help in understanding and tackling their task.'

'Bridging the gap', or 'the gulf', remained a favourite description of a task to be fulfilled by clergy or laity. Why be a priest then? Williamson adds the practical element that those with 'theological know-how' should also be involved on the shop-floor. At that time of writing, with less opportunity for laity to undertake any serious study, this emerges as a strong point. But there was another attempt to provide an answer, immediately before he was ordained, less pragmatic, more ontological perhaps in that the '. . . answer is that I feel that this is the right course for me . . . no verbal explanations can be completely satisfactory, and this inner feeling must be borne in mind with the reasons that follow'. It is at this point that he highlights his understanding of priesthood:

> 'In the priest and his action is focussed the corporate relation of God and man.' In this phrase is the nearest I can get to explain the function and purpose of the priesthood.[466]

There is more than a hint here of belief in ontological change through ordination, and his earlier emphasis on 'inner feeling' suggests that Williamson believed that there was a place for a priest on the shop-floor precisely because it had something to do with 'God and man'. It may not appear quite as explicit as the kind of incarnational 'apologetic' one finds among the French worker-priests, but it is the nearest Williamson gets to a direct reason.

Another explicit focus of Williamson's theology relates to his understanding of God in creation. For the faith proclaimed that creation was good, though sin had damaged it, and that redemption involved the restoration of a relationship between man and his environment, 'between man and man', and between the whole creation and God. 'Thus Christianity claims the whole of life.' Men and women were to witness to that redemptive power in their everyday lives and in some cases to do so with the help perhaps of leadership and example which in some cases should come from those in whom God and man were focussed – the priest. This involvement would be called forth from some and is highlighted by Williamson's illustration (in his own *Priest-Workman Why?)* of a drowning man – a rather crude little illustration but one which he admits himself should be taken as a 'cynical analogy':

> . . . a man is drowning in a river; on the bank a priest kneels in fervent prayer for him, mentally identifying himself with the man's suffering in the water and with Christ's suffering on the cross; from the other bank a communist, or even a layman, dives in and rescues the man.

The worker-priests were constantly questioned as to why there was the necessity for one of them to 'jump in' when surely the faith and action of a competent layman was sufficient. Apart from the fact that some outside the worker-priest circle would actually retort that laymen had been 'there', too few had achieved anything visible (something of which worker-priests too were accused). Williamson could have responded that the onus was on those who argued that the worker-priest should not be present in the world of work. Like other worker-priests he clearly believed that being a priest was not a 'job' at all; it was part of the very nature of his being, of what it meant to be Tony Williamson; and where he was and where he placed himself – or God had placed him – in his relations with other men and women.

Time and again, however, the answer to the question 'Why I am ordained?'[467] was answered in pragmatic terms. It was about 'breaking down the barriers caused by the past actions or inactions of the church and present misunderstanding'. And again it was so often reiterated in newspaper articles at the time of ordination: '. . . I am here then because of the gap between the rest of life in this country; because the clergy are too busy to meet these problems adequately . . .'

There is little admission here, apart from a very few oblique remarks, of what may have been an overriding anxiety of worker-priests – and Tony Williamson among them – to stand apart from the horrors of anything approaching 'churchianity'. In an ecclesiastical sense, they were part of the human race first. Some, like John Strong, with reservations, acknowledged the importance and value of parochial ministry; others, like John Rowe, deliberately gave it second place. John Strong had admitted in his early days to 'feeling a bit of a fake', Michael Gedge before him 'glad to be a man amongst men'. John Rowe refused point blank to talk 'church and religion' in the work place, and Ken Ramsay, who never denied his evangelical roots, knew 'it was not about bums on pews'. The worker-priests had a morbid fear of being aligned not with the good and the faithful, but with those who revelled in membership of what was almost a caste; they found this a twisted interpretation of priesthood that sucked the humanity from a man, setting him apart from his fellow human beings. For some, to be a priest might indeed involve ontological change, something indelible perhaps. But it was essentially also about being human. There were no two ways about it; worker-priests, above all things, held clericalism in utter contempt.

3. In Battersea and Portsmouth: Ken Ramsay

(i) Into work – South Bank and South Coast

Another and slightly later participant in the little worker-priest 'circle' was Ken Ramsay, who, while a curate in Southall, had decided to spend a month working in a local factory. In his own words it 'blew his mind'.[468] Ramsay, like the others, was essentially from a middle-class background, and, not unlike other worker-priests, had attended a major public school. But it had been while he was in the Regular Army (1940–48), indeed while in South Africa, that with the help of a friend he had sought some understanding of God. But there was little comprehension – right through the war – and it was only after a later visit to Lee Abbey, and a return journey from there in the company of Jack Winslow's book *When I Awake*, that Ramsay came to a conscious conversion experience, the sense of which he never lost, when 'everything dropped into place'. 'I must have broken some records,' he admits; 'my initial conversion was at Easter; I went back to Lee Abbey, and by September (1948) I was in theological college.'

Following his training at the London College of Divinity and his ordination in September 1952,[469] Ramsay entered the ministry as a curate at St John's Southall under Prebendary Desmond Money. In his subsequent newsletters, Ramsay described the Southall already known to the Grubbs (whom he would soon meet). The area in which he went to live was over eighty years old and one where: 'Most of the houses are joined together and have no bathrooms, one street looks the same as the next. It is not unlike the East End I suppose.'[470] He describes the usual round of parish visiting, the primary task of many a curate, and a role conscientiously undertaken by the committed evangelical clergy of Southall. It was the non-churchgoers who struck Ramsay. Though these families might have children in the church choir, many mums and dads did not themselves attend. Most were factory workers or labourers. By the end of the first year Ramsay had become acutely aware of the 'gulf' between them and his busy church (where attendances, by the standards of later years, were enormous). Yet there was no sense of any 'spiritual superiority', rather one of frustration at the role of the institutional church. It is at this point that Ramsay, unaware of the working relationships he would later share with the Grubbs, describes the witness of this local layman:

> We have an interesting person in our parish who feels this problem so

> strongly that he has given his life to unskilled factory work in an attempt to bridge the 'gulf' . . . He is Martyn Grubb son of Sir Kenneth Grubb.[471]

Ramsay clearly enjoyed parish life – and there was much to do. When Billy Graham's Harringay Crusade was on, St John's, Southall, and other local churches went *en masse*, all 1000 people in 18 double-decker London buses. But as the years passed, Ramsay's frustration at the divide between the institutional church and the working world grew stronger. He spent hours talking to Martyn Grubb, and eventually decided to spend a month in a factory to find out for himself what it was like. Grubb, who at the time was contemplating ordination, had admitted to 'giving up trying to do anything evangelistic': the shop floor was effectively the only place to be. At Siemens on the Great West Road, Ramsay spent his 'mind-blowing' month learning for the first time the reality of life for the poor.

> The trolley work saved me from being in the degreasing plant, a smelly headachy job as well as an extremely heavy one. I realized how important it is for a man to know how to do something. Three of my mates were completely incapable of doing anything demanding skill. They are the POOR of this generation, and they can sink to the bottom and stay there like sediment.[472]

After five years as a curate, Ramsay took on a chaplaincy role at Lee Abbey – a second home for him. Happy in its community life, his newsletters share with his reader friends his evangelical enthusiasm for the experience of conversion he had known himself. There was the account of the man who came to install the diesel generator, and who, one evening, 'committed his life to Christ'. 'He came,' Ramsay relates, 'to bring us power, and he went away with a new power himself.'[473]

A further spell in this kind of role – this time at Scargill House in the north – came just before his decision to rejoin the Army as a chaplain. But despite Britain's attempts to keep squaddies abroad, guarding 'British interests', the costs were clearly rising. With delinquent youth on the streets as well as the barrack squares, the Army changed its rules. It clearly decided on fewer chaplains and dropped the age limit from forty-five years to a mere twenty-eight; he was out – and for good.

With his new fiancée Valerie, Ramsay now had no hesitation in joining the ranks of the few clergy on the shop floor: '. . . we decided that I would try my hand as a worker-priest in a factory for two months . . .' Although this was to be a 'trial period only', his working life would in fact last more than thirteen years. With the enthusiastic support of Mervyn Stockwood, Bishop of Southwark, who had already demonstrated an interest in the role of worker-priests, and had just founded the first part-time ordination training course in Southwark,[474] Ramsay set out on his bike to find lodgings and work in the Southwark area. The job he found was at the Langdon Precision Engineering Company in Battersea. In a room at the local YMCA, over the next year or so, he compiled notes of his life as a worker-priest. Ramsay was effectively 'in' with Strong, Grubb, Rowe and Williamson, had read and endorsed their Statement, and had also read about the French worker-priests; he knew precisely what he was doing.

Through the Log he kept as a worker-priest, there is a unique and remarkable record of Ramsay's early days and encounters with his fellow workmates. His very first experiences, like others, were well remembered. An insurance card without any stamps on it at the time alarmed him – he could he thought be taken for an ex-prisoner – or worse:

> At first I thought they had rumbled that I was a parson but I don't think that is so, because today (second day) the nice woman at the press next to my bench winked at me and smiled, also the sweeper said about six words . . .[475]

There was tension, even anxiety, in these first few days – something he'd felt during the war, '. . . like we did in Italy when everything was quiet before a big offensive, no noise yet lots brewing . . .'

Like Michael Gedge before him, Ramsay was put on a drilling machine, drilling bases for Roneo franking machines. He describes the details of the work: of beginning slowly and gradually working up a speed on the job. It was a case (just at it had been for Gedge) of setting the 'job' on the 'jig'. But the jig itself wasn't clamped, and as the half-inch bit cut in, it threatened to spin dangerously. The foreman came to show how it could be done but Ramsay quickly sensed that he was being asked to do something that was not strictly legal, but rather 'well beyond the safety thing'.

As he grew accustomed to the drilling – and as boredom might set in – again like others, Ramsay used the time to think . . . or do some of Arthur Seaton's 'woolgathering'. He went for 'mental walks' around Lee Abbey (something he had loved to do) and also tried 'meditating and praying'.[476] Just how to keep some kind of accurate log became a problem. Scraps of papers or mental jottings were inadequate, so he took to writing notes around the margins of the newspaper's racing pages, so that anyone observing him might only think he was studying the form. Only one week into the work, the monotony of it hit Ramsay for the first time.[477] Yet he was also suddenly aware of the enormous contrast between this and the occasional baptism visits he did for the local parish – they were so discouraging, so unreal, and unlike the work where he now earned a living. Even industrial chaplains, he thought, break little more than the topsoil.

Ramsay, like most of the worker-priests, kept questions about his past life at bay, saying that he had been working in Yorkshire and Devon at places rather like holiday camps 'but with a difference'. For all his background, Ramsay was a far from typical conservative evangelical anxious to 'witness' to anything that moved. 'I was a rebel,' he admits, and part of the nature of that rebellion was to 'incarnate' himself in a very catholic sense in the work place, preferring to let relationships begin slowly, and to go simply where they would take him: 'One man has never spoken a word to anyone as far as I know. He is now on the next drill to me and I intend to offer him a sweet tomorrow as a Christian gesture of peace and good will; I feel so sorry for him, he looks very unhappy and drawn.'

With an obvious aptitude for the work, Ramsay nevertheless might find himself at the wrong end of the firm's anger if the work he produced was poor, incomplete, or resulted in damaged tools. On one occasion, when drilling bits were breaking with monotonous regularity, the foreman brought him another with the words, 'Now don't bugger that one up for Christ's sake.' Again like others before him, Ramsay found that he was able to progress to semi-skilled work, and the foreman assured him that he could be taught to sharpen drills, remarking that after fifteen years of drilling '. . . the best thing (about) engineering was that there was always something new to learn'.[478] And Ramsay found the satisfaction that might come from others who in turn benefited from his efforts. 'Alf stopped me on the way back from the lavatory today and said, "You made a bloody good job of those castings you drilled, it's a real pleasure to do the finishing, you get the holes exactly right . . . "'

If he was developing skills after a year, and growing accustomed to the environment, he was nevertheless sorry for those who found the labour hard. When two lads had arrived at the works, he recognized that they became quickly exhausted, and reflected that 'first days at work must resemble training in the forces; shock tactics I think'.[479] Living now in a flat above the vicarage, Ramsay became more aware of the area in which he had found himself. He made friends with the newspaper seller 'at the traffic lights' from whom he would purchase his *Church of England Newspaper* (the favourite of evangelicals). 'He knows I am a "Rev" because I gave him my address on a printed postcard. He showed no surprise . . .'

The slow, almost painful, process of getting to know work mates continued on the shop floor. There was the Indian lad, Ray, who began to talk to Ramsay, gradually opening up and sharing equipment and time. He gave Ken the loan of a precious file and 'said I needed it more than he did'. The 'ownership' of tools, as Michael Gedge had found out in the mid-1940s, could be a contentious issue, especially when these were not supplied to workers.[480] Ray also helped Ramsay to carry boxes across the shop floor. This was a slight, apparently irrelevant gesture, but of such were the makings of relationships. And as Ramsay reflected, 'some weeks ago he would have done neither of these things'.[481] This was not peculiar to Ramsay – it was simply what every worker learnt. His relationship with others reminded him of his month in Southall, that there are always those with no real skill to offer the market, '"beggars can't be choosers" has hard hitting truth about (it) for such people. They live in perpetual insecurity. No wonder they look to the football pools, or go to the dog track.'[482] And in the same month he noted and recorded: 'poker dice is now all the rage. Chris started, Peggy joins with him and Paddy', adding with resignation, 'who can blame them?'

Gradually Ramsay allowed it to become known who he was. There was no note of a sudden revelation that he was a priest, or of any dramatic response, though for a relatively short time mention of and discussion about the church began. Ray, the Indian youngster, admitted to attending a church, and was wondering how you could tell if it was C of E; then, 'Norman . . . said he actually came (to church) last Sunday at 6.15 p.m.- saw just a few folk and went away again.' As for himself, Ramsay jots down how he went to Communion on Ash Wednesday, only to find 'three people present apart from vicarage families'. He could not only see, but was now forced to feel, the strangeness of what seemed like two different worlds.

In August of 1962, intending to stay in work, Ramsay moved from Battersea to live in Earlsfield, in an attempt to help the vicar, Dennis Bratt. After leaving Langdon Engineering, like Tony Williamson he became a van driver for about five months. This was for Unichem,[483] and, like Tony Williamson, he found out what it was like to have to deliver materials over a wide area. Driving between Kensington and Southall (where he met some of his old parishioners) he also undertook some warehouse work. This brief interlude was followed by a new job at Redifon, where he became an electronic 'wireman' soldering electrical wiring on ships' radio systems '. . . good quality stuff'. This was a rewarding job, where the working relationships also proved more interesting. It was piece-work, and again like Gedge in the 1940s, Ramsay admitted that a game had to be played with those who fixed the rate. 'If you worked too fast they alter the rate . . . so I learnt this skill' (in working at a manageable pace, a pace that did not exhaust the individual). But here Ramsay now learned something else, because relationships were better – perhaps freer. 'I learnt about this barrier where people won't let you into their lives beyond a certain point . . . I reached that point quite quickly.' There were just a few, however, where conversation went deeper, and Ramsay was even able to take two individuals, one a Salvation Army lad, to Ashburnham. But though general relationships were warm, there was never any question of directing individuals to the institutional church. 'There were no bums on pews . . . not a single one . . . that's not what it was all about,' he reflected. 'It wouldn't help them . . .' People approached Ramsay with all manner of 'religious' questions, such as 'I was at this baptism and . . .' 'But it wasn't a question but a statement . . .' For Ramsay, reflection on some of these encounters has been painful, as he pondered in later life why he didn't 'do better'. For on the one hand there was always the evangelical in him, anxious, perhaps, to see changed lives, redemption at work, while on the other hand the worker-priest in him knew that 'being there' essentially came first.

By 1963 Ramsay was able to describe himself as three years in factory life, and though many encounters seemed superficial, the work at Redifon proved among the happiest years. Indeed he became convinced that people were often at their happiest when working hard and enjoying good relationships, if often in not ideal conditions. As for industrial unrest, he was sure that people worked better when there was work to do, though he remained convinced that any blame for Britain's industrial troubles also had to be shared with the management.[484]

Politically, while other worker-priests were generally left wing, Ramsay appears to have had no firm convictions. He had no illusions about the way labour was treated, and recognized the importance of the unions. Although he never held office (and indeed was the only one of the first worker-priests not to do so) he was a firm member of the ETU and attended its meetings. By 1968 Ramsay was already fascinated by changing times, and though describing himself later as a 'laid back liberal' was not unsympathetic to the workers and students then challenging the French Government where French worker-priests had taken part in demonstrations. He went off to a student demonstration in the centre of London close to Grosvenor Square, and though he questions the actions of the young, added, 'I nevertheless add the "students" to my list of priority topics, the others being: (i) world poverty (ii) nuclear war (iii) race relations and human rights (iv) housing and family.' Here was someone with the same concerns as his fellow worker-priests, putting as (v) and last, 'revival and unity in the church'. Though he was taking on a new vision of the church influenced by charismatic renewal.[485]

In 1969 a major change took place. Ramsay moved with his wife and family to Gosport to begin what he hoped would be a new experiment in community life. His evangelical background led him to feel somewhat uneasy at the attention given to a 'presence' alone, though he never despised his fellow worker-priests who felt this way. Although Ramsay was happy with most evangelicals, he sought an opportunity to work with Roman Catholic worker-priests in the Portsmouth area, who were already engaged in the docks. One was Michael Butler, an English Capuchin who had actually worked in a French factory alongside two worker-priests, but who had returned to Portsmouth area to start a community. Indeed it was the Roman Catholic friends of the Worker Church Group who led Ramsay to new work alongside '. . . others in the same vocation, and it so happens that there is a small group of worker-priests in the Gosport/Portsmouth area who are in touch with the local social and industrial outreach . . .'[486]

Ramsay took up work at Plessey's in Havant, once again working in electronics, but this time, although the work was pleasant, it proved a long journey to work, and he soon changed to C&N Camper Nicholson boatbuilders, who had an electronics division. From what he found poor and unpleasant working conditions, he made a third change in 1969, when he found work at Marconi's; here he worked happily in a small workshop for two years.

It was while he was at Marconi's that Ramsay soon identified with a Christian group in the work place. 'There,' he admits, 'we had the "God Squad". Lunchtime get-togethers at the canteen table were one of the few ways in which the group might be observed . . .' But Ramsay was clearly uneasy about this, and 'despite the fact one part of me said it wasn't a good idea to meet together like this . . . yet I was all for it . . . we were a diverse group . . . but I was the only person at the bench'.[487]

After a period in a Gosport rented house, the Ramsays moved next door to a worker-priest who had joined the Worker Church Group – Bill Millard, a postal worker and leading member of the Post-Office Workers Union. The intention here (since the Roman Catholics had now left the scene) was to set up a small community of like-minded individuals. Besides this, Lee Abbey, with which the Ramsays had long had an association, were encouraging community life outside the Devon centre, and the Ramsays saw this as a golden opportunity to share their own building with another family. They established just such a community, though, unfortunately, because of differences in temperament it did not last.

The combination of a holiday in Dorset, a visit to the Post-Green Community, and the impact of the house-sharing experience led Ken Ramsay to an entirely new direction. While he had understood and shared in a conversion experience in his early life, he was now to experience charismatic renewal. He returned to his job calmer and happier than he had been for some time. Nevertheless, he now believed it was time to leave the factory environment, and set up a painting and decorating business with a friend, a little enterprise they called the Home Care Team. Eventually, however, Ramsay was drawn deeper into the charismatic movement, left his business, and, after a spell as religious instructor in the RN, together with his family moved to the Post-Green community itself. The Gosport experiment may not have appeared a success, yet he was far from thinking such enterprises a failure, any more than that of the worker-priests in the Group who had been an inspiration as well as his friends. He was simply placing greater emphasis on some of the areas he had long felt important. But his life as a worker-priest, which had lasted some thirteen years, was nevertheless coming to an end. However, it was not to be forgotten or denied. Rather, more than twenty years later, in the late 1990s, it would lead to a radical motorway work site ministry on the M25 widening.

(ii) Presence and theology

Like the few he followed as a worker-priest, Ramsay was influenced not only by individuals like Martyn Grubb and John Rowe, but by French worker-priests whom he and his wife had visited in the 1960s. He was also affected by simple parochial encounters on Sunday afternoons in Southall, where superstitious mums asked for baptism ('it improves your luck', he remembers one saying). For it was meetings like these that had brought home to him the enormous divide that existed between the life of the church and its understanding of the faith, and the lives of most working men and women. Then there was his reading and meetings with the French worker-priests: 'I read one of them – this got under my skin – I said, "This is how to do it!"'[488]

In particular, Ramsay was interested in those arguments that called for a greater understanding of the tactics needed if any headway were to be made in industrial post-war Britain. Indeed, like Martyn Grubb, he had always felt a strong affinity with Roman Catholics with their theology of redemption. This appealed to his evangelical commitment, and stayed with him all his life. But he also had a ready ear for the radical. Early on, at an induction service, he had heard John A. T. Robinson speak, and though it is not known what Robinson said, Ramsay found him a '. . . progressive and stimulating speaker . . . easily the best sermon at any induction I have attended'. He also kept notes from a sermon by Mervyn Stockwood preached at Great St Mary's, the University Church in Cambridge, in May 1960, when he commended the 'priest-workers'.

Ramsay, like Stockwood, was optimistic about people, especially those in the parish who had asked him in for a cup of tea over Christmas time, '. . . factory watchman, lorry driver, and builder handyman'.[489] Like many an ordinary parish priest and worker-priest, Ramsay had a simple inner warmth for ordinary folk that gave him his optimism and, perhaps in a sense that set him slightly apart from other evangelicals, was ready to admit to a notion of God, even grace amongst them. But he could also see that the institutional church, no matter how outgoing (and he was happy enough with the Billy Graham Harringay Mission), was simply unable to communicate. Regular parishioners might be content, but:

> . . . the fact is we seem to make little impact on the other 22,000 souls who live here. We see them only in the event of a birth or a death or a wedding. This is a problem common to most industrial parishes I gather; the great 'gulf' fixed between the masses and the church. Going into their homes makes one feel there is something wrong at our end for many of these folk are not Godless, they just don't want to get mixed up with the Church 'set'.[490]

It was indeed a 'common problem to most industrial parishes', the difference here was that Ramsay wanted to do something about it, and would eventually spend part of his curacy locally on the shop floor before he won the approval and backing of Mervyn Stockwood in becoming a worker-priest himself.

By the late 1950s, Ramsay felt inspired by Grubb and Rowe, and though he had no direct part in the production of their 1959 Statement, he was nevertheless fully in sympathy with its contents[491] and later reflected: 'I re-read the Statement . . . it (was) packed with important principles . . . I agree with it all but doubt if I could ever live up to it.'[492] In his *Newsletter* of August 1963 Ramsay was able to say:

> We feel that the church has a duty to carry the gospel to all people and that it is at present out of touch with factory workers and others like them. Participation in their situation with all its frustrations and insecurity may be the one way of building a 'bridge' across which there may be communication. Nobody can say where this approach is likely to lead us, but neither could Abraham know when he set out in response to God's call . . . [493]

By Easter 1966, Ramsay had replied to those who from time to time seemed to have questioned or even criticized his approach. This was not, after all, an essentially evangelical way, and he may have had to take different criticism from that his more Catholic brothers endured. There were, for example, those who asked him if he would not have been better off in a parish. He remained resolute. 'Contact is the first objective. The Church has been out of contact with working people ever since the industrial revolution . . . Christians at shop floor level number 1 or 2 per 100. It is not surprising that they feel bewildered and discouraged. It is now urgent for men and women to enter this situation by vocation . . .'[494]

In the same *Newsletter* Ramsay admits – as he was always ready to admit – that contacts (with working people) were essentially superficial with '. . . only the occasional thrust into the supernatural'. And of these 'deeper' encounters – in common with other worker-priests – we hear very little, but contact there was, and the possibility that some new structure such as house churches, where ordinary men and women might be made welcome ('and not flummox them with handshakes or freeze them with splendid isolation'),[495] gave the Ramsays a reason to declare that they intended to 'hang on' where they were in industrial life 'until retiring age'.

Ramsay proved to be very much alive to the culture of the 1950s – especially a growing youth culture – and to attempts to deal with difficult 'teenagers' new on the scene. He was well aware of 'teds', and so was particularly captivated by a BBC programme on 'Carnegie Groups' working with Teddy boys and girls in Bristol. 'They recommend the use of street workers, to get to know the young . . . with no strings attached.'[496] But listening to the radio was not enough. 'George [a work mate in 1961] asked me several times if I had seen programmes.' Ramsay concluded that he must at some point purchase a telly if he was to have any hope of engaging at this level. But he visited the cinema and was clearly appreciative of Sillitoe's reflection on industrial life in the 1950s, voting *Saturday Night and Sunday Morning* 'best of new films' for 1960. Indeed he was later aware that 'Stan', one of the lads in his shop, who had seen the film, proved 'strangely quiet the next day': Ramsay was convinced the film had made an impact on the youngster.

As for actual contact with young and old outside factory circles, there is occasionally a note of almost despair in his realization that institutional religion in its formal setting was 'keeping churchgoers shut in a box'. Writing to his bishop on one occasion he added at the end of a letter: 'I preached here at evensong yesterday, to five giggling "teddy girls" and four other people! I can't say I felt the prayer-book service was exactly relevant!'[497] Day by day encounters threw up all kinds of questions. When working as a van driver for Unichem and having to go through a packing department, he encountered language worse than anything he had experienced in the army. But if there was any shock or surprise, there was also a recognition, even resignation, that for the packers this was something essentially natural, and just as natural as the ethical standards demonstrated on and off the shop floor. In a log dated January 1962, he records – without any judgment – something said 'confidentially' by a mate, Chris, on his own floor: 'Ron has had his cycle stolen; two wrongs don't make a right, but he is going to pinch another one.'

By 1962 and still fairly early on in his life as a worker-priest, Ramsay was enthusiastic about the 1962 publication *Priests and Workers*, the Anglo-French discussion edited by David Edwards. Ramsay clearly saw not only that he and his fellow worker-priests were at one with the French[498] but also how very different were the views of those outside their 'movement', a movement still, essentially, in process of evolution. In the same year (1962) Ramsay was also clear that in some corners of the institution, despite it being generally 'out of touch', there were attempts to deal with the industrial world. He felt that Southwark at least was attempting to address these questions. In a magazine article from *Over the Bridge* (Southwark's Newsletter) for March 1962, Ramsay highlights and annotates the new Wychcroft Centre, where one of the main functions was to '. . . train the laity' to make their impact on the workaday world more effective, for '. . . to be the church where we are in factory, office or docks is not easy'. In a note scribbled in the margin Ramsay reflects that the priest-workers could actually give leadership to the laity in that very work situation, a sentiment that would later be echoed by John Rowe in making his defence of worker-priests.

It was at least that greater sense of the need for visible unity with others which led Ramsay into the 'God squad', at Marconi's in Portsmouth. He was, in the late 1970s, at the beginning of a time of some frustration with the worker-priest scene which he knew so well. He felt, perhaps, there was yet more to be done in 'awakening the church'. His taking up of a period of self-employment as painter and decorator was the first in a series of steps that would slowly begin to distance him from the factory life where he had been a worker-priest for over a decade. The departure of the RC worker-priests – with what he saw as their emphasis on redemption – from Portsmouth just as he arrived disappointed him, and the subsequent failure of his little community at Gosport led to a time of further searching which ended in his charismatic experience, which like his early conversion was never to be denied. He later wrote to David Wilson, priest-worker in Southwark: 'I must let you into a secret! My theological centre of gravity has shifted quite a lot.'

Any notion that Ramsay, in moving out of the factory, had abandoned the original perspectives of the worker-priests, would be to misunderstand him. He had originally made a life-long commitment to the shop floor, and for thirteen years laboured alongside ordinary men and women in a life that was clearly a vocation. He knew, and confessed, that in the context of this chosen life there would be no dramatic changes, no sudden experiences of conversion. Unlike some parochial catholics who might expect from potential believers a measure of commitment to the institution and its sacraments on the one hand, and evangelicals who might seek evidence of inner conversion on the other, Ramsay remained resolutely his own man. In the end, his departure from the shop floor was not out of any sense of failure – or any estrangement from worker-priests who remained lifelong friends – but was essentially about his own 'inner' or psychological journey.

In a sense, however, Ramsay never felt fully at one with his fellow worker-priests' understanding that a presence alone might be sufficient. Though he always believed in that presence – 'I say Amen to that' – he also believed in a change that could be wrought in the lives of men and women, believing that the time had come when he could no longer live up to the ideals of the Worker Church Group. 'I've got no record of "success",' he has confessed, any more than his fellow worker-priests, but of the original handful of worker priests – of which he had been one – he could only say 'they had love you see . . . real love-in-action . . . they did it . . . they actually lived it . . . but I was not sufficiently sanctified'.[499] 'Yes,' people had to find Jesus in their hearts, 'yes eventually there comes conversion', '. . . but we've got to keep our feet on the ground and that's why we have to get into the factory'.[500] Later life found Ramsay picking up from his experience on the shop floor. With the blessing of the Southwark diocese, he made his own way to the massive road works where the M25 London orbital was being widened in the mid-1990s, wandering about where few parish priests had time or perhaps inclination to venture, to talk to men in canteen and work sites.

4. More worker-priests and working laity

(i) John Wilcox, Tom Quigley, Tom Waldon: common themes, common callings

There remains a yet smaller group of interested individuals, clerical and lay, who were part of the story of the first worker-priests and their group. One was John Wilcox, who for a time became a member of the Worker Church Group. Wilcox (born in 1928) had studied theology at Kings College and Warminster, but took a break of two years before his final term in college.[501]

At the end of the war, Wilcox had begun work as what was then called an 'improver' with Precision Models, Northampton, and later, between 1945 and 1952, a student apprentice with W. H. Allen production engineering in Bedford, though the period coincided with his national service (1947–49, when he worked in the RAF as a marine fitter). At first, Wilcox had no intention of becoming a worker-priest (though his brother had gone into the ministry). Initially, like Gedge, he had never heard of such a thing. But during theological training under the Dean of Kings, Eric Abbott, Wilcox learnt that there were other ministries such as worker-priests besides those in the territorial parish.[502]

And so Wilcox returned to industry as a maintenance-fitter at a wire works in Warrington. Like Tony Williamson after him, Wilcox was actually ordained to the shop floor as a deacon, though he simultaneously served his title in the parish of St Margaret and All Hallows, Orford, Warrington, where the Revd Norman Carter, a sympathetic man, was his vicar. His was not the only sympathetic voice. Dr Clifford Martin, Bishop of Liverpool, sent Wilcox off to Carter, admitting he was the only vicar in the area 'who will understand what you are doing'. There was, however, a condition attached to the role: Wilcox had to promise to undertake a full-time curacy, and eventually did so in Liverpool.

On the shop floor Wilcox's confessed aim was to 'merge'. Wilcox believed that some knew he had been studying theology, but he also gained the impression that a few thought that for some reason he might have been chucked out of college! Brought up in a family that was generally conservative, Wilcox rapidly moved to the left, became an active union member, and while a worker-priest went on strike for a week with the AEU, taking months to make up the loss of wages.

Wilcox quickly learnt that there was little point in doing anything specifically religious on the shop floor. An early communion in a store room was quickly abandoned and never attempted again, without any sense of loss. There was the occasional visit to a sick work mate, or attendance (in the pews) at a funeral, but for most of the time he engaged as his fellow worker-priests had done in the south. When he returned to parish life as a curate and began contemplating a role as a worker-priest, he heeded a trade union official who said 'don't go taking a works job from someone else if you can get a paid job in the church'. Then with the offer of an industrial chaplain's job in another diocese, Wilcox set out for a different ministry. At the point these decisions were in the making, he confided with his fellow worker-priests that he could not yet sign the Statement (though he fully endorsed it) because he was not yet sure whether he would end up a worker-priest. When he chose not to be, he nevertheless valued their later contribution, and found himself very much at odds with new developing 'auxiliary ministries' when they claimed to be doing what worker-priests had done.

Two other important names feature in the Statement, effectively making up the earliest members of the Worker-Church Group (see Appendix 1), namely Tom Quigley and Tom Waldon. Quigley's name first comes to light while he was working in Carlisle. Quigley took a London University BD in 1945, but had been ordained a deacon three years before to serve a title at Herne Hill, 1942–45. He became a chaplain to the forces, serving between 1945 and 1958, including a time in Malaya. But Quigley began to feel a sense of belonging to a privileged class. This was quite acceptable in the officers' mess, but he often felt distanced from the men. Later, when asked why be a manual labourer, his answer was:

> I spent a total of five years of my army service as chaplain to operational troops in the Far East. When I got the chance I used to accompany the patrols, usually ones out for about five days. Going through the jungle with heavy loads was very strenuous, and the camping out, particularly in wet weather, uncomfortable. But it was then that I felt closest to officers and men. In civilian life one obviously gets nearer to that sort of thing when doing manual work with others, than, say, office work.[503]

When cuts came in the military ranks, Quigley decided to leave. It was in industry where he determined to begin a new ministry, and '. . . where he thought he could get alongside those who are less privileged, many of whom think that non-manual workers, including clergy, have a soft time'.[504] Quigley became a labourer in a Metal Box Company factory in Carlisle between 1958 and 1962, before moving to Accrington where he continued as a labourer. Tom was unmarried, and, perhaps with more time on his hands than the others, gave hours out of his factory jobs to help the local vicar.

The records of the Worker Church Group indicate that he attended meetings from as early as 1959, and was a signatory to the Statement, though at the time he had been unable to participate fully in the drafting of the document. By the mid-1960s, Quigley had emigrated to Australia, at which point some contact was lost.

Among the most faithful founding members of the Worker Church Group were Tom and Sherry Waldon. Their full part in the WCG as laity, and their chosen vocation and subsequent commitment to being Christians in the workplace, demands mention, for from time to time there were other laity and religious who visited or joined the WCG, though few stayed. The WCG would always maintain that they were entirely open to lay or ordained, men or women. The Waldons anyway were already a part of John Rowe's little community in Piggot Street. Tom, married to John Rowe's sister Sherry, had graduated from the University of British Columbia in 1949, and had worked in a construction camp on the Canadian Pacific Railway, following this with a number of labouring and factory jobs in Montreal from 1950 to 1953, when he moved to the British Isles.

Waldon's self-confessed impetus came from an anxiety – as a Christian layman – to do something about the 'gap' between the church and the manual wage-earner, and for him it was a case of 'trying to live conscientiously as a Christian layman in this particular sphere. The longer one stays at it, the more natural it seems.'[505]

In England, Waldon worked in an oil warehouse for a year, followed by six years in a tobacco factory, where he became a shop steward, before taking an outdoor job in London County Council's Parks Department for three years. In a later move to Swindon, he continued this work, while his wife Sherry took up secretarial work. Tom and Sherry remained absolutely committed to the Worker Church Group and to the Campaign for Nuclear Disarmament, something strongly felt in the Piggot Street Community.

5. Industrial sites: institutional church

(i) Of unions, strife and strikes: worker-priests and industrial relations

In addition to their life on the shop floor and the day-to-day encounters with the people in the streets, the worker-priests had at least two other groups with whom they had a specific relationship and engagement. The first was those with whom they shared trade union membership and the second the clergy and churchgoers of local churches with whom they were often placed.

At one point or another, Michael Gedge, John Strong, John Rowe, Martyn Grubb and Tony Williamson all played a role in trade-union activity, usually as shop stewards, and many had to face industrial action and stoppages, on the increase in this period. Of John Strong's activity as a shop steward at George Kent's very little is known save the fact that it was on receipt of the information that he held this post that the 'lady of the manor' sought his removal from the parish. At a time when strikes were endemic, the thought that the local vicar could call men out proved too horrifying.

In the East End, John Rowe was a member of the Transport and General Workers (TGW), until 1979 when he joined the Electricians Union (ETU). He was committed to union work, but in the publication *Trade Union Affairs* for Spring 1960 he tells, not of the support and activity of fellow workers, but of the apathy that is everywhere. On the other hand, the same article 'Faith on the Shop Floor'[506] describes the dutiful 'parade before the directors . . . combined with a handout of . . .

miserable proportions. It must be a relic of feudal times.' The only union recognized by the employers was at the level of the officials who negotiated with the Court of London Brewers: 'The Branch does not exist' and 'At meetings of the brewery council (works committee) the union in fact is never referred to'. The local leaders of the union he applauds. 'The political mind is Labour – though frustrated, rather angry, and very disappointed Labour'; at shop-floor level it was worse:

> The signs of rot appear at the level of, for example, the problem of the replacement of shop stewards who retire or leave the firm. There is little confidence in the youth . . . We suffer of course from the bugbear of 'apathy'. Branch meetings are very poorly attended and there is precious little interest in trade union work between crises.
>
> . . . the worker . . . can be counted on for support, they say, only when his pocket is immediately threatened . . . [507]

Rowe went on to criticize the lack of co-operation between different unions who clung 'jealously to agreements negotiated by their own unions'. For Rowe it all added up to a failure of faith – of men's faith in one another. Later, in the 1970s, relationships were much improved, and Rowe confesses that he would not have written in the same terms in the 1970s and 1980s.

For the Grubbs, accounts of trade union activity were mentioned in their newsletters – outlined previously – and their subsequent oral contributions. In his first job at Abbot Brothers, Martyn Grubb became a member of the Furniture Trades Union. Later, while working in engineering, he joined the Amalgamated Engineering Union (AEU). At the Chiswick Engineering Company in 1953, he found the place filthy and the conditions generally bad, yet when he attempted to suggest that others might join him in the AEU there was opposition and even the suggestion that he was a 'Tory' for saying that the Unions had improved the lot of working men! Grubb made his first tentative steps to encourage men into the union as well as to attempt some improvement in conditions, holding clandestine meetings with a union official in a local cafe. Grubb was elected a shop-steward at the Chiswick Engineering Co, but was immediately dismissed. His fellow workers stood up for him, and for this, they were all summarily dismissed. Although some compensation was awarded through union efforts, none received their jobs back. Grubb adds:

> In spite of their original opposition to the Union the others were very loyal when it came to the point, which was a great relief to me, and there was not a word of resentment at losing their jobs . . . My duties as shop Steward have taken me into each of their homes since we were dismissed, and I think they really feel I am a friend and someone they can trust.[508]

Grubb again became a shop steward at the Cramic Engineering Company where he had begun in 1955, and where he later became a branch delegate to the local Labour Party. In 1959, after his ordination, he had been at Dilloways agricultural engineers barely a year when, together with another engineer and union member, he worked in secret with an AEU official to improve conditions. The rest of the workers then elected them both shop stewards. The management's response was to summon all the workers to a meeting, where Grubb and his fellow union representative were publicly and summarily dismissed with the warning that the same would happen to anyone else; the firm would not tolerate trade unionism. But the members insisted that the shop stewards be reinstated, and the firm eventually recognized the union. However, a few months later Martyn was 'made redundant' and began to suspect he was on a 'black list'.

For Grubb, it was bad conditions at work which led him to engage with management from a trade-union base.

> I have come to see Trade Unionism as the only power which gives to the industrial worker his basic human rights of freedom, justice, and the opportunity to have a say in the running of his own life. And so I have come to see Trade Union activity as a very practical expression of the gospel in the lives of the workers.[509]

It was not necessarily an expression of the gospel which other evangelicals might share, but it was already in keeping with John Rowe's understanding of a gospel about a God who cared and where the 'revolutionary principle' was about men 'changing the face of human society'. But the union looked after its own, and Grubb was soon working again, this time at AEC Ltd, building London buses. This was the biggest firm in Southall, employing over 4,000 men,[510] and he would work there for the next six years as radial driller and, once again, shop steward.

What Grubb remembers were the difficult encounters, the challenges set up by frustration and division on the part of men. When on an earlier occasion at Cramic Engineering a national dispute arose, and some men in his shop refused to take part, a shop-floor meeting exposed the frustrations of those who sought solidarity. The thing to do with a blackleg, claimed one worker, was to 'drop a spanner' on his head . . . Grubb's shock at such attitudes resulted in his own outburst that this was no way to behave or carry on a campaign. The atmosphere in the shop, he remembers, changed instantly to a more positive note. 'That was one of the more pleasing memories, for there was a recognition that we need to make a stand on moral human issues.'[511] Grubb was no stranger to the problems of dealing with the management, though he also acknowledged – as John Rowe too had found out – that getting men organized 'was a thankless task . . . with many of the men apathetic'.[512]

In Oxford, at the end of 1960 – to be precise on New Year's Eve – and after just two years at Pressed Steel, Tony Williamson, already a TGW union member, became the victim of a union agreement that when redundancies became necessary the 'last in' would be 'first out'.

> The recession in the car industry had caused the sacking of 1500 workers in my factory, including all those manual unskilled and semi-skilled workers who had been with the firm for less than two and three quarter years.[513]

Williamson was lucky to find a job driving a laundry van, reckoning himself 'well-off' compared with others at a time when jobs were 'sticky'. Now he was forced to work longer hours for less pay (£4 a week less) but he clearly also felt a solidarity with the many others forced from work.[514] This job-change may have been the occasion of a telegram from Jack Pleasant of *Reveille* newspaper who was after a good story and wanted an interview.[515] Taking on an entirely new job, and having to explain himself all over again, may have seemed too much to Williamson, but he went for the laundry job when the company advertised for new drivers over the Christmas period.

> I did not give them any information about myself, except what was directly relevant to my working hours – i.e. my previous job. The firm is non-union, has disgusting toilets, a dirty canteen, and a laundry building that lets in the rain; from the start I felt that the firm did not respect their employees, and this became clearer as time went on . . .[516]

But there was worse to come, as without warning Williamson found that at short notice he could be asked to drive up to 240-mile round trips across country. 'The drivers never know quite what is happening; the rounds are changed with little consultation . . .', and, Williamson adds, 'In all this I have tried to point out to management ways in which the system could be improved and by which the employees could be treated better. Neither has been well received, and I will not be sorry to return, I hope soon, to the greater security of Pressed Steel.'[517]

An election to a seat on the City Council as a Labour candidate in May 1961 alarmed a number in the parish where Williamson had a place on a 'team' under John Betton. But for the next six years Williamson remained on the shop-floor (returning there after redundancy) as a fork-lift driver, but now taking a keen interest in the TGW union, and on the council, chairing the housing committee. He then lost his seat in an anti-government swing, giving him a chance to rethink his position in terms of his role as a city councillor.

Of those six years there is no detail, though Williamson drew on his experiences when he gave talks. By 1967, however, he had so established himself at Cowley that he was already recognized as a possible leader in the union. In same year the chief shop steward, Josh Murphy, clearly a capable man, had died of cancer. The funeral in the local crematorium, officiated over by the duty priest, shocked Williamson, since no mention was make to a packed house of the man's name or contribution to the union.[518] The new shop steward proved to be a dogmatic character, something 'of a disaster',[519] and in an internal battle that then ensued, Williamson was asked to stand as a junior member of a team of three. Coming third in the ballot heartened Williamson, who then took on the task of minute secretary. Now driving a fork-lift, Williamson became immersed in union work, so that by 1969/70 he had become involved in the fraught negotiations over 'piece work' which the company planned to scrap in its planned production of the new 'Maxi'. Gedge had pointed out over twenty years before that he found piece work had a destructive quality about it;[520] now Tony Williamson found he was having to try to defend it.

When the trade union's chairman died of appendicitis ('he had known he was ill and had done nothing about it') Williamson became chairman, and was present when matters became difficult. The company management were quite determined that piece-work had to go, and wanted all on timed work or they would be out of a job. It was at one of the workers' rallies that Williamson climbed the platform to be met by the humorous cry, 'Give us a hymn, padre!'[521] Despite his position on the union and the seriousness of the occasion, they had not forgotten he was also a priest.

In the end, after lengthy negotiations, a compromise was reached which satisfied both sides, but which was neither piece-work nor, strictly speaking, time rates. It would do. At this point Williamson himself was elected branch chairman (1971), although the next year he would be back on the City Council, and in harness as housing chairman again. Meanwhile at Cowley he became a full-time union official and deputy shop steward till 1987. At the time the *Oxford Mail* had calmly reported Williamson responsible for some 5,000 union members, with the Sun exclaiming 'OH BROTHER! PARSON TONY TAKES OVER AS UNION BOSS' . . . who had helped win a massive new pay deal . . . and where one of the bosses commented: 'That man is more a politician than a priest. He's always very polite but completely dedicated to his men. It takes a box of gelignite to move him.'[522]

Details of trade union activity by the first worker-priests are few, though they did on more than one occasion choose to discuss these issues in their Group. But limited details suggest that, like their work itself, it was a matter of day-to-day activity. It was part of what it meant to be a working man, but for them, also, of what it meant to be a priest. On the factory floor, it was simply the way you cared for others.

(ii) Of parishes and people: worker-priests and parochial relations

In order to receive some kind of recognition or 'blessing' for their work within the institutional church, all worker-priests sought out a relationship with the local bishop and diocese and, more immediately, a parish, where a number like John Strong and Martyn Grubb at first felt very much at home. Those were days when this was the only way to maintain a ministry and remain within the establishment. Michael Gedge and John Strong had successfully sought a double role in Eyethorne, just as Strong unhappily failed to continue in Harlington later. Soon, however, other worker-priests saw their priesthood more in terms of their secular place of work and the responsibilities that went with it. Ken Ramsay was ever aware that this business was not about 'bums on pews'. Tony Williamson saw his role essentially at his place of work, and in time John Rowe would begin to distance himself from the territorial parish.

Thus in the East End, John Rowe sat lightly to responsibilities in the territorial parish (Bow Common). On Sundays there was a parish celebration of the eucharist – the vicar played the organ, 'trusting no one else' to the keyboard, while John would often preside. As this was his only parochial function it meant that the whole of Rowe's life as a priest was centred on the work place itself, though he felt that his vicar's view was that he had 'stifled' a real ministry: if he had talked about 'focus' of priesthood then 'I might have said altar', but,

> My primary objective was simply to participate in order to have a horizontal relationship with the people one wished to serve . . . the work was the means by which you placed yourself in a certain position in society.[523]

In 1956, and most important for the Rowes, they took a house in Pigot Street with Tom and Sherry Waldon, John's sister. All four were members of the 'Society for the Catholic Commonwealth',[524] and were able to sustain an significant community life quite separate from the parish. 'We wanted to be a Eucharistic community which lived in industry', and so they 'undertook a daily mass, and went together to the parish church on Sundays'. It was a common commitment which would continue for some eight years, with Sherry and Isabel bringing up the children

> . . . in a street where the kids played out in the street as well as in our garden . . . It was a house to which the world came and also the neighbours when they needed something. It was very much a part of *la presence*, in a way no vicarage could be.[525]

Martyn and Anne Grubb in Southall, long before any real thoughts of ordination arose in his mind, had found a home in one of the local churches in Southall, St John's. Here was a fairly traditional evangelical church, with matins and evensong as the staple diet in worship. Martyn and Anne were made warmly welcome and were happy to have the friendship of vicar and curate. Although they did not go 'out of their way' to join in everything, Martyn was elected to the PCC. But in the context of this congregation, the Grubbs felt they 'were getting nowhere'. The church could be glaringly 'irrelevant' to local workers. Martyn perceived an acute need to build a community, and wondered whether this might be possible through a parish communion, advocated by the Parish and People movement.

> . . . we have always felt that the Communion ought to be the central

> congregational service in any church, and we are finding it rather difficult from our own personal point of view to fit in with the 8.00 a.m. Communion 11.00 a.m. Matins set-up. Both from the spiritual and from the practical family angle we would prefer a Parish Communion.[526]

It was not to be; the local clergy were not enthusiastic. 'I began to feel,' he suggests nearer the time, 'that the church wouldn't listen to me unless I became a priest . . .'[527] But the Grubbs were able to develop a most important house group on Sunday evenings for 'Christian fellowship' shortly before the decision to seek ordination.

> It consists of two men apart from ourselves whom Martyn got to know at our local church. Neither of them has been a Christian very long: both are working men, one a window cleaner, and the other a semi-skilled worker at the AEC Service Station. It seems to be meeting a real need in their lives . . . The Fellowship has flourished beyond our expectations and now, as the time for our move is drawing near . . . others outside the church, including one man at my work at the Cramic Engineering Co, are taking an interest.[528]

Grubb's first curacy after ordination, and between factory jobs, was served at the Anglo-Catholic church which they describe as 'St Peter's, de Beauvoir Town (Hackney)'.[529] On a reconnoitre – a weekend spent at the vicarage under the vicar John Perry – Martyn and Anne were taken with 'family life in the parish' as much as they were with the personality of Perry and his creativity. Grubb had clearly been taken with mass in Paris, facing the people and celebrated 'as a family meal',[530] and perhaps here, in Hackney, and for the first time at home, he felt something of that.

Their own accommodation, 'a great falling down place with broken windows',[531] which would be their home for the next year and a half, was made up for by the enthusiasm they felt for all that was happening in the parish. Most noticeable was the Sunday evening 'People's Service' packed out chiefly because it was designed 'for the outsider'. 'It draws mainly Teddy boys and girls, who come very largely for the Rock 'n' Roll dancing which we have afterwards for those who have been to the service.'[532] This was something Grubb admits would have 'horrified' his mother – though it would have horrified many more at the time had they known the use to which St Peter's Crypt was being put on Sunday nights.

Once back in Southall, the Grubbs found factory work again, and returned to parish involvement including a house group. By 1962 they report the existence of a weekly discussion and Bible study group which included 'a young man from the factory brought into the church and baptized through the group'. Meeting people in this kind of context was important for the Grubbs, and such encounters meant that friendships stayed with them for the rest of their lives.

Life in the context of the parish church was favourable until, on an occasion when the vicar was away on holiday, Martyn wrote and spoke openly on the issue of race relations[533] in what might be interpreted as a prejudiced church. It all came back at him. Although the horrified vicar allowed Martyn to continue to preach, relations were never to be the same again. By 1965 Martyn and his wife reported that they had moved on to a 'different type of parish' because he felt the 'set-up' of St John's was not one 'with which he felt able to work'. After this, and for a variety of reasons, Martyn took no further part in the formal life of any church. He hoped that their new chosen church, Christ the Redeemer, consecrated in 1964, would provide opportunities. However, their new vicar did not intend to let Martyn's licensing make any 'practical difference' and was not prepared to let him preside or preach.

By this time, their letter also reports that Martyn was already on the local International Friendship Committee, and this was a hint of what would follow. In May 1966, Martyn left his work as a skilled man and took a full-time job as Community Relations Officer of the Ealing Community Relations Council in what he understood as a progression of his work alongside people in his community. But, now no longer a 'worker' in the strict sense that worker-priests and others had come to understand the term, Martyn felt he had to leave the WCG. He continued in race-relations work well into the 1970s, though the strongest links were maintained with all members of the Group.

In Oxford, Tony Williamson, who was essentially ordained to the shop floor, would have his parochial relations determined before he began in the factory. All this was agreed by Bishop Carpenter: 'It was clear,' says Williamson, '. . . that I was not ordained to help the parish clergy with their work.'[534] With such a radical move, yet within the context of the established church, Williamson had been and was wholly dependent upon the ongoing goodwill of his bishop and incumbent. Fortunately, from the beginning, he had both. Soon after ordination, Williamson's sole weekly liturgical responsibility was an early morning eucharist on a Wednesday (6 a.m. and later 6.30 a.m.) attended by a mere handful, and presided over by Williamson for the next twenty years.

John Betton, whose considerable sympathy and energy had long supported Williamson, was followed in turn by the Revd Patrick Parry Okeden, a rather 'different man' but still supportive of the worker-priest and one 'who wouldn't dream of interfering'.[535] But by 1980 the Cowley parish had became a formally constituted team ministry, where a later strong Anglo-Catholic incumbent proved less than sympathetic to having a worker-priest on the team. For this man the territorial parish was the only context for ministry, and he began to disregard Williamson because he would not participate in the pastoral roles within the context of the parish.

Ken Ramsay enjoyed reasonable co-operation with his parishes, and close relations with Mervyn Stockwood, yet the strain of ministering to inward-looking congregations indicated a rising frustration over the irrelevance of parochial life to those among whom he worked. More and more he saw the way the establishment failed time and again to reach people, even those who came for baptisms, weddings and funerals. He began to seek ecumenical fellowships and larger communities, away from conventional church circles.

Worker-priests recognized that they owed a debt towards sympathetic parochial clergy, who, by the very nature of their chosen role, were more concerned with the daily needs of supporting the faithful. Had the worker-priests not been accepted by those parish clergy – who went without support in their parish chores of visiting and administration – the worker-priests would have had little part in the life of the national church. The establishment was in no mood to 'let them loose', and while the French worker-priests would enjoy the fellowship and support of their own non-territorial bishop, the Church of England offered no other framework to support its own worker-priests, of whom anyway it knew precious little.

6. Organization and Recognition

(i) The Worker Church Group: the early years

While Gedge and Strong in their singular attempts at ministry and mission were among the first to experiment with this radical identification with the working world,[536] it was during his time in Harlington that Strong became a founder member of the only organization that would speak for the first worker-priests and laity committed to radical identification. Within a year or so a small group would begin to develop a rationale for their total involvement in working life, and would challenge Ted Wickham's methods. Despite beginning and indeed continuing with only a handful, some thirty or so 'members' would come and go over the years, effectively challenge the church's assumptions on mission and ministry, and survive, with a changed name, for just over thirty years.

A variety of sources suggest that the Worker Church Group (the papers of which remain fragmentary) was founded in 1957.[537] The subjects of their meetings, and the particular interests, theological, political and ideological, which they shared, must be examined separately, particularly when a consideration is made of how the 'worker-priest' might be actually defined.

As for the times and venues of these early meetings, surviving members have admitted to unreliable memories about who knew whom and precisely how they all got together. But John Strong and John Rowe were known to each other, as was Martyn Grubb, and Tony Williamson had already visited Rowe on a college visit to the East End. In an *Evening Standard* edition of 1959 an article appeared on the existence of the country's first worker-priest group. The meetings took place annually in May at Harlington Vicarage till Strong left in 1962. The *Standard* mentions the names of the participants: John Rowe from the East End, Martyn Grubb in Southall – a 'mutual friend' – and two other clergymen (unnamed in the article), one from Warrington (John Wilcox) and one from Carlisle (Tom Quigley). By 1959 John Strong spoke of a

> handful of worker-priests in this country [who] claim that theirs is a religious vocation in the true sense. Whatever the future brings forth for it, they feel bound to obey the spirit that is in them. So do their wives and other lay associates. For all are one in this, and all alike have a voice in their conferences.[538]

Because it was a group that included the laity from the beginning – and this is vital in understanding the group – Strong declined the title 'worker-priest movement', though the ordained members were initially content to be known as worker-priests. '. . . Rather [the Group] is conceived as a cross section of the church united in a common cause. Between its clergy and laity there is no sense at all of any difference in status . . .'[539]This remained one of the hallmarks of the group from its very beginning. In membership and internal structure there was absolutely no difference between individuals. If you were a worker – you were in.

It was newspaper publicity, which the group must have sanctioned, that gave rise to a request from the television company Associated Rediffusion to make a programme about them. Indeed, the end of the 1950s and the beginning of the 1960s was to prove a period of maximum publicity. But clearly, even at this early stage, such publicity tended to be kept at a distance. The Group remained hesitant about going on 'telly' and declined the offer of a programme about them, much to the disappointment of Alexander Jacobs, a Rediffusion editor who, while he 'appreciated' their point of view, defended his programme against their caution.

> This is understandable after seeing the press cuttings perhaps, but in our own defence I would say it is definitely possible to have presented you on television as you wish without casting aspersions on your group's work but at the same time showing the important enterprise it certainly represents.[540]

Jacobs' letter, if intended as a last bid to soften reaction, failed. There would be no programme, but Jacobs' intentions demonstrated a genuine and growing interest in what they were about.

The WCG met for its first six years at the Strong's Harlington Vicarage until 1963, when it was forced to meet at a variety of other venues. Some seven months after they had published a Statement (February 1959), the *Church Times* reported that this group of worker-priests and laymen were 'discussing their problems'. Precisely what these were was not made clear, but it is possible to read the tone of the article as slightly suspicious. The headline alluded to 'problems', evoking perhaps the feeling of the institutional church at the time that a group like the WCG was something of a curiosity; they were described as an 'unusual group', with John Strong admitting that they were 'in no way an organized movement'.[541] The article went on to list the participants and their various jobs, and after several column inches a paragraph heading assured nervous readers – if there were any – that 'all have the full support of their bishops'. The article concluded that the basic reason for living in this way was that 'each feels this to be his way to perform his part in reducing the gap between industrial wage earners and the church but none feels this is the only way, or that this is the only task facing the church today'.[542] Thus were the worker-priests categorized by the *Church Times* as a feature of industrial mission – in no way challenging the territorial parish. And indeed in a sense it was true. In the same month another article, on this occasion in *Time* magazine, described 'England's worker-priests' and opened with a rather glamorous picture of John Strong: '. . . tough square-jawed . . . for years he has lived in slums [a not altogether accurate account of his recent past] and worked in factories . . .' But it made good copy: 'To most Church of England clerics,' the article went on, 'he is an odd fellow, honest but peculiar. Reason: worker Strong is also a full-time minister.'

The magazine, which had had its part in reflecting the French experience previously, now directed its readers to a Church of England already 'wary' and, remembering the ill-fated worker-priests in France, quoted Leslie Hunter that '. . . this was a waste of skilled manpower'. It is none too clear what precisely Hunter meant, and it seems a pity for *Time* to have picked on the one man, no arch-enemy of worker-priests (and even Ted Wickham could not be accused of that), who had done more than any other bishop to support the extension of industrial mission into the heart of the work place. But then there was a conservative streak to Hunter, and perhaps, after all, he meant precisely what he said.

The few magazine and newspaper articles that remain in collected papers, sometimes without title or date, and probably collected around 1959, often raise questions about how and why the group, in its initial stages or as individuals, allowed publicity to go forward. Perhaps they were simply a little naive; they could surely be allowed that; yet the refusal of participation in a Rediffusion programme, and their later discussions on publicity, may indicate increasing disquiet at where publicity might lead: misunderstanding and marginalization.

Dates and locations of the WCG's meetings are shown in Appendix 2, though at this juncture only the first decade is considered. Each year, members were treated to the latest instalment in the saga of John Strong's difficult relations with the 'Lady of the Manor' and her supporter, the Bishop of St Albans. In 1963 the Group met for the first time at St Katharine's Foundation in London, and by 1964, with the Strongs moving to Blackburn, the group met at St Peter de Beauvoir Town in Hackney (though there is separate evidence that they may have remained at St Katharine's). The Strongs, with John unemployed, had their travel paid for by the rest of the Group.[543] In 1966 they met at Bobbingworth in Essex, and then the following year, and until 1979 they remained as they had originally done with the Strongs, but this time at Marsh Baldon, near Cowley in Oxford, where, for virtually the first time in his life, John

Strong worked as a 'full-time' stipendiary parish priest. He had become physically incapable of further labour; his years underground, and on shop floors, had finally taken their toll. But the WCG and his association with it would continue at the 'Baldons'; Strong's parish would become a later venue for meetings.

Surviving reports indicate that at these meetings, trade union affairs, strikes and stoppages, general political and social problems were all discussed at length and in great detail. Theologians like Edward Carpenter, David Jenkins, John Robinson, Ted Wickham and others all came to talk and listen, and Len Murray, General Secretary of the TUC, also paid them a working visit. From the continent came Belgian and French worker-priests, and the records of these particular meetings (possibly taken down in shorthand) indicate detailed conversations on ministry and mission in a working world. When there were no visitors, and especially in the early years, the Group worked hard on their Statement, and other means by which they could better articulate their chosen vocation.

(ii) References and recognition: from Frontier *to* Crockford's Clerical Directory

In that industrial setting, and in a fast-growing consumer society in which factory life was commonplace, those first worker-priests, very often through conviction and self-motivation, decided on an individual basis to seek a role in industry, but always with the formal request for recognition and support by the established church to which they all subscribed. As these individuals represented what others saw as 'odd states of thinking', so the church at large nervously began to be made aware of what it saw as 'experimentation', though their efforts were rarely admitted publicly by the establishment. When in 1959 the Church Assembly received the report *The Task of the Church in Relation to Industry*, it was, says Patrick Vaughan, extraordinary that:

> . . . from beginning to end, the report was utterly silent about worker-priests (whether French or English), despite purporting to offer a survey and appraisal of 'The Present State of the Church's Work in Industry'. In view of the fact that (on a small scale) some priests were continuing to work in industry, it seems a high-handed approach to have excluded their experience altogether.

And Vaughan continued that, perhaps because Leslie Hunter sensed this, he added in introducing the report:

> It must be a layman's movement, but also with a place for the priest-workman and the workman-priest, for the whole-time padres and the parish clergy part-time – a total ministry of the whole church.

Indeed Sir Kenneth Grubb (father of Martyn Grubb, worker-priest in Southall), in a deliberate intervention during the debate, had been a lone voice drawing attention to the example of French and English worker-priests.[544] But it was all beside the point. *The Task of the Church in Relation to Industry* took note of industrial chaplains, but still saw the 'task' as parish based, even parish led.

> Undoubtedly one of the soundest convictions of the Church of England, however ideal and difficult it may be to realize to-day, or however it may have been exercised in the past, is the belief that the parish parson has a proper concern with the total life of the parish, with its spiritual and its material side, with those who are close to the church and with those estranged from it, with homes and families but also with the public life of the community and with its varied social institutions.

And to support this, the report gave over the next three full pages to a passage commissioned from a parish priest whose account exemplified what the report saw as 'the ideal relationship' of a parish priest 'to the works, factories and offices of the parish'.

But it was their decision to form the Worker Church Group that gave the worker-priests their first chance to articulate their efforts. The considered results of their first deliberations appeared in 1959, a couple of years after their initial formation. In the 'provisional' Statement, which the group had prepared primarily for its own use (though that must be taken with some caution), and only secondarily, they claimed, for distribution, was a summary of where they placed their own life and work. Thus they declared themselves '. . . priests and lay who have chosen to be wage-earners in industry as an expression of their faith'.[545]

In 1959, within a twelve-month period of the Church Assembly and The British Council of Churches' Reports on Industry, the *Church Times* offered its own leader on worker-priests, reacting to an article by John Strong in the same edition, and reflecting the seriousness with which it viewed the issue. Repeatedly maintaining that nothing could take the place of the parochial ministry, it described worker-priests' efforts as a 'bold venture' where 'the indelible mark of the priesthood is not obscured by dirty hands or the sweat of the brow'.[546]

The following year (1960) the publication *Part-Time Priests?*, edited by Robin Denniston (the managing editor of Faith Press), first appeared. This was a most important book, an attempt to engage the wider church in a considered discussion prompted by a related but rather different issue – how to fill parochial gaps or broaden concepts of ministry – at a time when there was a chronic shortage of clergy. The Revd John Bickersteth, in a chapter entitled 'Not Workmen turned Priests but Priests turned Workmen', explains how he had gone into a local factory for a fortnight actually to work there, though he had visited the place for three years previously and reported his experiences in an early 1959 edition of *Theology*, where he confessed, 'I wanted to see whether it would be possible at all to be a part-time parson'[547] (which it must be said was precisely not what the worker-priests were trying to 'find out'). Bickersteth tells how the men on the shop floor opened up to him as a priest and he believed therefore, '. . . that we need, in this supplementary ministry, discussion to concentrate on the priest turned workman rather than on the workman turned priest'.[548] But why choose Bickersteth to make this contribution when men like Strong or Gedge had been at this years before? In fact there was little discussion on what was already in place: even John Porter in a chapter entitled 'Deacons, Priests and Minor Orders' mentions the French briefly, and only in passing, 'the few we have had in this country'. What Denniston's book illustrates is the lack of recognition of a group already in existence and of any attempt to analyse their theology and practice, which might, after all, have contributed something to this discussion. But the Worker Church Group, newly formed, had sought little publicity or recognition, and ironically, even as they were now granted that, were 'sidestepped', as Denniston's published debate, 'from the top down', began to move in an altogether different direction and away from ministerial enterprises that might 'weaken' the very nature of priesthood. Something of that possible dread came from E. G. Knapp Fisher in *Theology*'s 1959 debate on training for ministry, when in answer to an article by John A. T. Robinson on preparing ordinands he reacted:

> I sympathize with and share his desire that the church militant shall be staffed by an informed ministry which will make an effective prophetic impact upon contemporary secularism. If this is to be achieved our ministers must in a deep degree be involved in the world and identified with the men and women they are called to convert and serve . . .

How that 'deep degree' of 'involvement' and 'identification' was to be achieved he did not say, only that:

> it is possible for involvement to be *overdone* [my emphasis] and Christians who overdo it will, despite their sincerity, destroy precisely the quality of holiness, that capacity to leaven the lump, which the Lord requires of them as the necessary condition of effective apostleship.[549]

No doubt it would have come hard to the likes of Gedge or Strong, or the few including Tony Williamson whom Knapp-Fisher was supposed to be supporting, to discover that they might have been in the process of destroying 'the quality of holiness' (however that might be interpreted), when they believed it was precisely what they wished to bring to the workplace.

Two years later (1962) a publication *Priests and Workers*, edited by David L. Edwards, opened a broader discussion on the worker-priest movement, and for the first time gave the Worker Church Group an opportunity to make a contribution, though it largely consisted of a reprint of a *Frontier* article by Anne Grubb, in which she described the English worker-priests. Nevertheless, for the first time there would be a broader distribution of the ideas. Edwards outlined the achievements of the French, raised questions about the nature of ministry and priesthood, and offered a penultimate chapter by Ted Wickham. The latter argued, however, that because of the great differences between industrial society in France and England there was no need for worker-priests in England (though he may well have felt that such a movement might threaten his industrial chaplains – Bagshaw 1994).[550]

An assessment of Wickham and Grubb's articles will be made in the next chapter, when underlying theologies of worker-priests and the Worker Church Group are considered. Nevertheless it is important to recognize here that the version of Anne Grubb's article in *Priests and Workers* was included to balance Ted Wickham's unhappiness with worker-priests, and to outline what was already taking place. The brief chapter by Grubb had of course enjoyed only a limited circulation in *Frontier*, and now its appearance once again could be seen as the first and only appraisal of what was happening in Britain.[551] Alongside the title and implications of Michael Gedge's early book, the inclusion of Grubb's article here was the latest explicit claim that there were those deliberately trying to follow in the French experiment that had gone before.

In the same year as *Priests and Workers*, Nick Earle's *What's Wrong with the Church?*, questioning why clergy should not earn their living in manual labour, highlighted the fact that 'There exists already a handful of such men working in industry, most of them doing only Sunday duty in church . . .'[552] Earle remains cautious, but agrees that there should be an opportunity for a worker-priest movement to develop if that was the direction younger priests wanted their discipleship to take, though he concludes that there is always a danger with 'identification':

> There are always dangers in individual initiative and no priest should normally be excused the discipline of Daily Offices, a weekly celebration of Holy Communion and canonical obedience in some form. But even a Church which attaches great importance to a common discipline must allow the voice of God, particularly in a matter of lifelong vocation, to be heard by the individual priest.[553]

And it was precisely this lifelong vocation that most of the Worker Church Group were seeking, not some temporary 'experiment' which a bishop might prefer. Experiments (even where, as has been shown, there were often little criteria for success or failure) can be halted; vocations ought to be lived and tested. The 1961 profile was further enhanced when the church's handful of worker-priests received recognition from *Crockford*'s Preface (1961–62) in which the anonymous author, who exhibited, according to *Prism*'s reviewer Timothy Beaumont, a 'far-reaching and courageous mind', highlighted the existence of 'priest-workmen' about whom, in a previous edition, there had been only 'depressing' evidence.[554] Now they are commended for 'more encouraging' experiments where young men were 'combining the priesthood with full-time manual work'. 'And we may be thankful,' the author continued – in keeping with the *Church Times* sentiments two years before[555] – that today there are bishops wise enough to let them try, and, we hope, to give them guidance.' But Michael Gedge (1951) and Michael Jackson (1955)[556] had pointed to precisely a lack of encouragement years before, and as John Strong and others had found out now, there was to be no rush of episcopal support.

In one sense, John Strong and Michael Gedge's departure from the parish and mine at Eyethorne marked the end of the initial phase of Britain's first post-war worker-priest ministry. Gedge and Strong had been among the first pioneers; they had established a practice strong in expression if perhaps a little weak in theory. But Strong, once in

Harlington, had begun to formulate thinking, and shared in the formation of a group that he hoped might begin to develop a rationale. By the time he left Harlington others, namely Rowe, Grubb, Ramsay and Williamson, had entered the 'movement' – committed to a life alongside the working class.

But the questions were now about support and encouragement from a middle-class church which knew little of all this and was at best diffident, at worst ill-at-ease with what was evolving. The established church had its own agenda on ministry, and though it spoke of demonstrating through experimentation, 'the relevance of the Gospel to the twentieth-century human situation, and [of working to] re-Christianize the life of England' (F. R. Barry, Bishop of Southwell),[557] in reality, its concerns had rather more to do with maintaining the territorial parish and satisfying the committed, the traditional focus of concern.

For the first time, and largely due to *Priests and Workers*, and a scattering of other rather minor references discussed here, the Church of England was slowly becoming aware of worker-priests making a radical departure. This might be conveniently 'located' in the context of 'industrial mission', though they remained an insignificant minority. But with the anxiety over insufficient numbers of ordination candidates coming forward for training in the late 1950s, and a continual shortfall of clergy to man parochial posts, the church was suddenly faced with the prospect of discussing the introduction of some kind of 'part-time' priesthood. The fact was that the issues were about to become blurred. As the Worker-Church Group hoped for some expansion, and sought to develop a theology of mission and ministry, the church at large now decided it was time to address the problem of the shortage of clergy. For the consequent and more pressing problems were those of manning and maintaining the territorial parish.

For the first worker-priests, and for their developing theology and ministry, it was not that the signs were less than encouraging; in one sense, but unknown to them, the worker-priests had had their day. Very few would now join their ranks, though a number of the curious would visit their group; only an original core would remain totally committed to working class areas for much of their lives and their like would never be seen again.

V

Worker-Priests and Non-Stipendiary Clergy: New Agendas – New Interpretations

'. . . just as there was a day when God had called tentmakers and fishermen and tramps as well as physicians and more academic types so today he might call dockies and insurance agents and school masters – butchers, bakers or who you will.'

(Sermon preached by Stanley Evans to the Southwark Ordination candidates on the eve of their ordination)

'This little book . . . is about priests in working-class jobs . . . The reader must not confuse the case that is advanced here with the case that is being made for the ordination of men in all kinds of professions and avocations . . . the book is primarily about the vocation to share the working-class life.'

(John Rowe, *Priests and Workers – A Rejoinder*, SCM Press 1965, Preface)

1. British worker-priests and the shifting agenda

(i) Church of England clergy: the post-war shortage

At the point where Michael Gedge and John Strong had parted company in Eyethorne and Strong had shared in the formation of a 'worker church group' with a handful of others who had opted to be worker-priests, one of the issues facing the Church of England was the shortage of 'men and money'. Among the solutions, social, theological and economic, a range of new 'part-time' and non-stipendiary ministries would eventually emerge.

Alarming figures for serving clergy showed that from a 1901 peak of 23,670 the total number of serving clergy had fallen by 1951 to 18,196.[558] Of greatest concern, however, was the serious loss of clergy through retirement, and the statistics provided in 1961 pointed to a peak loss of 681 (which overtook the intake) in 1958, 'caused by the increased numbers of retirements'.[559] But after the Second World War, and before statistics were compiled, the anomalies were already well known, when, to put it – as it was so often crudely put – the people lived in the industrial towns and the majority of clergy seemed to live in the country. Apart from the general shortfalls in the supply of ordinands, it was not difficult to see that in a church which by custom and practice had dedicated itself to serve the traditional territorial parish, ordinands were unsurprisingly drawn to a particularly attractive location – the sunny south. Here a generally more manageable parochial population with a middle-class appreciation of the clergyman's role was there to be served, and in due time would produce yet more candidates for the church; little wonder that Leslie Hunter had journeyed south to speak to deans of Cambridge colleges about a north 'bled white'.

A few years after the end of the Second World War a debate, with elements of it reported in *The Times*, began on just how this problem might be alleviated.[560] Part of that debate would be aired in the pages of *Theology*. As early as 1948, George F. Townley (Archdeacon of Cleveland in 1947 and later Suffragan Bishop of Hull[561]) in an article entitled 'The Supply and Distribution of Assistant Curates',[562] warned that there was severe pressure on incumbents, with an adequate replacement of manpower 'not in sight'.

While the Archdeacon of Nottingham in 1950 called for the provision of more full-time priests just as Townley had done two years before, other voices were now raised in support of an alternative strategy. Among these was that of W. O. Chadwick, Dean of Trinity Hall, Cambridge, who wrote on the subject of 'tentmakers', an allusion to St Paul who had earned his own living, initially for pragmatic reasons. He also drew attention to the hardship of clergy and the need for mission, and looked at the two possible remedies that most obviously presented themselves. First, the extended use of trained laymen, though he immediately asks, 'What then is the place of Readers?' Secondly, there is the question of deacons, and here he revives this issue raised by Thomas Arnold the century before, though he goes on to reject the idea. Rather, he is all for men drawn from the ranks of everyday life, though he remains fearful of night school training degenerating 'into a series of not very efficient confirmation classes'. Little of this was new, but perhaps it needed to be said again, and more importantly, it was Chadwick who was saying it.[563]

There then followed some discussion on Chadwick's article. In support, the Revd F. Bennett from Wigan[564] argued that the church was obsessed with a myth about the 'type' of English clergymen who existed. 'Is not (God) calling us to something bolder and more imaginative than mere maintenance?' R. C. Barsley, from Heywood in Lancashire,[565] suggested for the first time that the real issue could be narrowed down to a question of 'massing priests'. The overtones were derogatory. But at least someone was trying to define priesthood, and perhaps the readers of *Theology* were thankful. One year on (1952), John A. T. Robinson (then Dean of Clare College, Cambridge) entered the fray, and argued that because the church now had had theological colleges for a century, a certain 'standardization' had emerged, resulting also in 'the ministry becoming from a class point of view almost solidly bourgeoisie'; 'if anyone enters it from a working-class background he is effectively declassed'. Robinson went on to challenge the notion of ministry as a profession. Like Chadwick before him he wanted to see men drawn from secular jobs, and he advocated part-time training, but also a stepping-up of academic work if any chose to become full-time clergy.[566] The debate in *Theology* went on. In September 1954 James Collins of Chippenham, Wiltshire, admitted to the problems raised by this shortage of clergy and drew attention to the work and ideas of Roland Allen, already noted, which he clearly felt were not being considered. When the numbers of those seeking ordination began to rise again, reaching a peak in 1961, it would be true to say that the concentration on the subject of 'supplementary ministries' began to focus more on the theological issues surrounding mission and ministry. *The Modern Churchman* also attracted contributors to the theme of ministry. Aware of the French worker-priests, and in generally sympathetic tones, it noted the French events of 1954 and 1959 (when the worker-priests were denounced a second time). Pushing the arguments into the theological context, Canon R. Stevens, Vicar of St Paul's, Birmingham, and Bishop's Industrial Chaplain, talked about being 'continually faced with the alarming consequences of the church's withdrawal into itself'. Openly following Bonhoeffer, he asserted that man had 'come of age', yet the faith asserted 'the doctrine of the incarnation, that God and his world are made one'.[567] This at least could have been taken as a hopeful sign that the agenda had begun to shift from how numbers of ordinands might be increased to what kind of ministry ought to be exercised anyway. A contributor in *Theology*, January 1960, argued that '. . . ninety per cent of the population remained untouched, do what we will we just cannot get at them'. Yet having been invited to visit a factory work site, the contributor hailed the invitation as a breakthrough, 'for you see the men and on their own ground'.

In 1961, to Parish and People's delight, the Church Assembly passed a resolution asking CACTM to consider the deployment and payment of clergy, though Parish and People wanted another question addressed: 'whether or not the proper functions of the ministry might be obtained by methods of deployment radically different'.[568] The Church Assembly debate came just at a time when the figures for ordination candidates were rising. Although a certain amount of pressure was off, the Paul Report duly appeared in 1963, a detailed but (as it would turn out) misleading picture of exactly where the numbers of ordinands were going.[569]

Among the most interesting figures in the Paul Report were its wildly inaccurate forecast of the numbers of men who would come forward for ordination in the near future. Predicted numbers for ordination by the Church of England 1963–1971, based on the rising figures at the time he published, suggested that of all ages the numbers ordained in the church would rise from 642 in 1963 to 831 in 1971. But Paul was way out in his calculations. The figures peaked in 1963, so in 1964 the predicted figure of 662 was actually 636. By 1966 the prediction of 713 had dropped to 576 and in 1971 the predicted 831 had plummeted to 393.

Between the late 1940s and early 1950s alternative views emerged in published correspondence about the nature of Christian ministry and who might exercise that office. On the broadest front the church exercised a ministry to the territorial parish through a professional priesthood which believed in the specialist training and preparation for that role within the institution. There were, it is true, a few who believed in some kind of supplementary ministry drawn from the Christian community and exercising a ministry in the context of the work place and territorial parish, and who believed this to be not some 'expediency', but integral to the nature of Christian ministry itself.

(ii) Theories, strategies and solutions: non-stipendiary ministry

If the problems of insufficient funds and clergy to man parishes in the post-war years drew forth a range of arguments and apparent solutions from the contributors to periodicals, some, as indicated, were not new. Indeed calls and arguments for a variety of non-stipendiary ministries had a long history, and recent studies of that by P. Vaughan and J. Fuller (1986), Hacking (1990) and P. Vaughan (1990)[570] have traced the arguments for what would become known as non-stipendiary ministry

(NSM). Despite a pragmatic driving force, many of the arguments had their origins in a considered theological position that could have been shared by worker-priests.

With reminders that in New Testament times the apostolic ministry was largely dependent upon itself for a living, or that in the Middle Ages at least, clergy might live alongside their people, working on the land, went the view that now in the twentieth century there might be a case for simple and godly men being ordained to the ministry while they remained at their occupations. Vaughan describes the Anglican 'prophets' who from the nineteenth century onwards sought to enlarge the scope of the ministry by the restoration of certain early orders. Thomas Arnold (1795–1842), headmaster of Rugby, because of his very deep concern for working-class communities, called for the restoration of the order of deacons and sought the means to break down that 'pestilent distinction' between clergy and laity. While he confidently believed that no alteration in the law was required, he was able to recognize the power of traditional practice. The problem, as the church had painfully found out in terms of its ministry and liturgy, is that practice and custom carries with it a great deal of authority. In this case it was custom acquired over time and pressed home in the establishment of theological colleges in the nineteenth century. It was Anglican ministry seen essentially as a profession in its own right that prevented Arnold's ideas developing beyond discussion with laity, Convocation of Clergy, and even the House of Commons.

The second major figure in favour of a new kind of ministry that might bridge the 'church' and the 'world' was Roland Allen (1866–1947), whose singular contribution put the theological issues of work-based ministry to the fore.

> He wrote with such single-minded conviction and with such systematic reasoned argument that anyone concerned with the missionary structure of the church and its ordained ministry was obliged to listen.[571]

Roland Allen had served as a missionary in China, but returned to England to serve in the parochial ministry in the 1920s. Vaughan makes the case that the reason Allen's 1923 publication *Voluntary Clergy* (1923) gained a hearing was the 'drastic falling off' in numbers of ordinands coming forward after the First World War.[572] A reduction in congregations and ordinands had perhaps less to do with the effects of the First World War itself than general decline (Gill, 1993),[573] though it focussed minds on an assumed reason for such decline. Allen believed that a great barrier existed between 'church' and 'world', since a professional ministry 'bound' by contract inhibited an understanding of the church's true nature.

Allen's prophetic argument, born in the Far East mission field, was that when a man came to exercise his vocation in full-time participation in the life of the institution and with the total abandonment of any other means of support, it proved a clear and effective demonstration of his commitment '. . . [F]or a man to abandon all other means of livelihood and to live on the alms of the faithful was a most powerful and effective method of revealing the spirit which moved him to minister in holy things . . .' But Allen then added, '. . . we need today a kind of counter-poverty . . . which says, I will not receive anything from my fellows for ministering to them in spiritual things'.[574] These sentiments would certainly come to pass in the lives of worker-priests.

But Allen had a second argument, pertinent to this study. He argued that a 'great gulf' existed between the people and clergy of the country and that it was the clergy who must cross it. Again in almost the exact words which were echoed by Michael Gedge some twenty years later, Allen argued that such clergy should be in the world but not of it.

> They must live as men amongst men. They must bring their religion into the daily life of men. They must share the toils and labours and common hopes and fears of those they would draw to Christ and his church. They must work beside men in the office and at the bench.[575]

Vaughan shows how Allen's banner was taken up by F. R. Barry, who coined the phrase 'non-stipendiary ministry', and who again, and in keeping with Allen's original ideas, 'attempted to re-present the case for voluntary clergy not simply on grounds of expediency but of ultimate Christian and sacramental principle'. This ministry may thus not have been seen as essentially about the staffing and support of the territorial parish, yet that is precisely how it would sometimes later evolve.

In the decade following the Second World War, the question of the possibility of voluntary clergy would slowly emerge again as the church began to face a chronic shortage of funds, and candidates to man its parishes. Sir Kenneth Grubb would complain at Church Assembly that 'the expense of everything is so much higher'. As Vaughan argues, debate thrived in an atmosphere of clerical shortage but tended to wane when the numbers of men in training for ministry were buoyant. In the mid- to late-1950s, a consensus emerged admitting not only to a shortage of manpower, but also to a great numerical imbalance between north and south. In 1955, Michael Jackson and Stanley Booth-Clibborn, in an article quoted by Vaughan, argued passionately for new ministries: 'the provisions of chaplaincies (e.g. armed forces, prisons, hospitals, etc.) should be carried over into a field where so many members of our community spend so much of their lives'.

But if Britain's first worker-priests were aware of the shortages, they nevertheless saw their place in industrial society from a different perspective. For them it was not that working priests should somehow supplement the parochial ministry or that 'men might be drawn into the church from other occupations', but that the church itself, in the person and presence of its clergy, must make the first step into that 'other world', the 'workaday world', where by all accounts it was difficult, if not 'impossible', as Michael Gedge had heard, to be a Christian. Indeed, it was about doing what Allen and Jackson and Booth-Clibborn had all suggested. For the first worker-priests, talk of a non-stipendiary ministry which might support the status quo was simply not the issue. 'For us the issue was class,'[576] claimed John Rowe, who was happiest on the edge of traditional parochial structures. It was surely to do as the French had done and 'be I suppose a presence among others', argued Simon Phipps.[577] For them the real issue was not exclusively turning 'workers into priests' (though John Strong certainly once suggested that)[578] but, as a contributor to Denniston's *Part-Time Priests?* had argued, turning 'priests into workers' and smashing an established clericalism as it were on the factory floor as they strove to remain there on pain of forsaking what they now saw as a priestly vocation. For those on the outside or on the edge of such discussion it was all rather confusing, and only a deliberate apology by worker-priests for what they were about would begin to explain their particular position. As the debate continued towards the end of the 1950s, there was always the possibility that some form of auxiliary ministry might now develop. *A Report of the Working Party on Supplementary Ministries* was completed in 1961, and although this was never formally published on its own (Vaughan believes it was an internal report to the bishops' meeting, and that there was subsequent pressure not to publish) it admitted to the 'fears of parochial clergy'.[579] Nevertheless, ideas for some kind of non-stipendiary ministry were now being advocated – ideas that might even support what the worker-priests had begun. There was at least one bishop ready to put them into practice.

2. From theory to practice: making a start

(i) Episcopal vision on the South Bank

One of London's senior clergy is reputed to have remarked that he was 'thinking of having the Thames widened' when he heard of the elevation of Mervyn Stockwood to the diocese of Southwark. Stockwood, a man set against capitalism 'with its unscrupulous drive for profits', had become a member of the Labour party in 1946, and had also associated with Communists.[580] He had made his mark first in Bristol, and later in Cambridge as Vicar of Great St Mary's, the University Church. It would come to seem as if few other individuals in the Church of England could at once be the cause of such diverse views among clergy and people south of the river if not further afield.

But it was in Southwark that Stockwood would make his mark in terms of ministry. Determined that there should be a radically new approach to ministry and to the training of candidates for the ministry, he was the first bishop to establish a scheme which would allow men to be prepared for a 'part-time' or 'full-time' ministry while they remained in secular occupations during their training. It was a bold and brave move, in a diocese where, rather like Bristol, Stockwood believed the gospel was simply seen as irrelevant.[581] Stockwood's concern was that the church should 'get alongside those in society who had no inclination to go near the church'; and Southwark was full of them.

On a visit to Rome Stockwood found inspiration in Monsignor Cardinale 'living in a co-operative block of flats', a member of the Vatican staff, nevertheless '. . . anxious to remain rooted in the lives of the people'. The citizens of Rome – he suggested to Stockwood – were little different from the citizens of London, '. . . they were outside organized religion, and were unlikely to return'.[582] Stockwood was 'fascinated', and began to consider ways he could implement his ideas for 'auxiliary priests' and 'worker-priests', which he had hinted at during his enthronement sermon.

Stockwood had grown 'increasingly sceptical' about the value of the traditional theological college training, and directed attention to the millions who were unlikely to be approached by parochial strategy, believing it possible '. . . that if a priest worked among them and shared their lives he would be able to establish a Christian group'. One of Stockwood's ideas, for example, was to have a eucharist among dockers, presided over by a docker.[583] The Church of England, he once concluded, could no longer *de facto* write off the unchurched masses '. . . for years we have tried to approach them from the parochial base and have failed'.[584]

(ii) The Southwark Ordination Course

Stockwood's plan in 1959 to set up the Church of England's first part-time training scheme for clergy was announced at his diocesan conference the same year, and came to fruition with the Southwark Ordination Scheme, under the overall guidance of Bishop John A. T. Robinson, and the immediate direction of Eric James. Although Archbishop Fisher accepted the scheme, it was not enthusiastically received by fellow bishops. The course, it was hoped, would cater for three categories of men: (i) those already in established secular jobs who would train for the full-time stipendiary ministry; (ii) those in exactly the same position but who would train for a ministry 'within the sphere in which they were already working', that is, at their place of work, and who, by implication would remain there as 'part-time' priests; (iii) 'younger undergraduate ordinands who feel the need to do at least a part of their training in the context of the industrial world – in which they hope later to work'.[585] There is no hint that those in the second category, who in the later 1970s would become known as 'ministers in secular employment', would have a major role in the context of the territorial parish. It looked as if for the very first time in Britain, at the hands of an enterprising bishop, some kind of developing worker-priest movement might be made possible from 'the top down', '. . . a means of bringing new classes of ordinands to the church'.[586]

Yet from the very beginning there was ambiguity about the precise nature of this ministry: on the one hand it was a response to a shortage of money and manpower; on the other, a way of 'engaging with the work-aday world'. From the outset it had been the intention of Stockwood to train some kind of indigenous ministry. Judged by this intention SOC was clearly a success. But if Stockwood had hoped for workers from an industrial setting who would remain on the shop-floor after ordination, he was to be sadly disappointed. Virtually no shop-floor workers came anywhere near the SOC course. It is possible to argue that the academic demands of the course, locked as they were into London University's Extra-Mural Department, were simply too demanding. Indeed, had there been a sizeable working-class element with a vocation to ordination generally, then they would surely have already shown themselves as enquirers to the more traditional patterns of ordination training. As for the conventionally trained clergy – 'priests turned workers' – there were few at this time who had taken a conventional route. Only Ken Ramsay, already a member of the WCG and then working in Battersea, had made himself known to Stockwood.

Perhaps it was with some early foreboding that he might not get the workers he wanted that Stockwood wrote to Tony Williamson in Oxford making a somewhat surprising offer: 'I have a derelict parish in Camberwell which happens to be the Lancing Mission', and he continued:

> It is a large parish and has good amenities. The last Parson was overwhelmed by the situation and has cleared out. I wonder whether it would be possible to make it a base for worker-priests in London?[587]

If Stockwood was approaching a newly established worker-priest in the hope that he might be some kind of 'authentic' beacon in Southwark he was again to be disappointed. Williamson and the others were totally committed to staying put. Yet there could be no doubting Stockwood's sincerity. The SOC course would go on to train hundreds of gifted men, many of whom stayed in their occupations and became a presence themselves.[588] Yet the questions that Stanley Evans, John Robinson and Mervyn Stockwood all had to face was still just how to engage with the working-class world and with what kind of worker-priest. Perhaps for the first time it was pertinent to ask, what exactly was a worker-priest anyway, and who, precisely, fitted that title? Though answers were possible, the fact was that very few were asking the questions.

3. Practice to theory – shifting definitions

(i) What is a worker-priest?

(a) France's prêtres ouvriers

The first clergy to whom this title was applied were clearly the *prêtres ouvriers*[589] of France, whose story has been outlined in the second chapter of this study. Given the way in which the term has sometimes been rather loosely applied to a range of different ministries in Britain, with the French alone perhaps it should remain. The simplest definition of a French worker-priest was one who saw his vocation as a priest in the context of a working-class occupation in post-war industrial France. In an article which had greatly influenced Henri Perrin, Pierre Hamp, the socialist writer, had written:

> No priest has dared to re-establish the primitive law of Christianity and go to work alongside those he wants to convince. No one has founded an order of priest-workers. The tradition of Jesus the carpenter, of Paul the carpetmaker, has no continuity in the padded upholstery of the Faubourg Saint-Antoine . . . Overalls would have helped more than the cassock if he wanted to incorporate the influence of a corporate Christ into the customs and ideas of people who work . . . [590]

By December 1946 Perrin could simply say to friends that he would be in Paris in 1947, 'almost certainly to begin my life as a worker . . . But more than anything I feel moved by the thought that I'll be giving the whole of my twenty years of study, travelling, experience, and training to the working class, with the determination to live with it, move to its pulse, and be truly bound up with it.'

Thus could Perrin describe himself as *ouvrier* and not even with the prefix *prêtre*. It was French class-consciousness in opposition to capital, and the estrangement of the working-class from the church, that led the first worker-priests into the workers' milieu, not simply in some 'sympathetic identification', but in what they described as 'incarnation'. In the early 1950s, when serious questions began to be raised about what precisely worker-priests thought they were doing in taking secular jobs, one produced thoughts for discussion among his colleagues.

> Our ambition has always in practice been much humbler and less pretentious. It has simply been to become workers, to share totally the state and condition of workers until we little by little come to participate in the proletarian mentality. For, until the contrary is proved, that is the first and undisputed condition if our priesthood is to take on any meaning in the world of the workers.[591]

So the worker-priest cannot 'abstain' from the struggles of workers. It was a truth of their 'incarnation' into the proletariat that their priesthood could progressively 'make itself intelligible to the world of workers'. 'It is only thus that we shall be able to live it in the midst of this new race of mankind.'[592]

And if there were some who were afraid of priests being turned into something other than priests, the evidence seemed to come in open admissions. 'Some few of our number, in proportion as they share in working living conditions and the proletarian consciousness, are no longer able to take part in the priesthood in the form in which it finds expression in bourgeois civilisation.' No wonder that Cardinal Liénart in January 1954 had written in *La Semaine Religieuse de Lille*:, 'Being a priest and being a worker are two separate functions, two different states of life. They cannot be joined in one and the same person without derogating from the idea of being a priest.'[593] It was all that was feared by those who felt deeply that *worker*-priests could no longer be considered *priests*. Some had clearly become part of another world in which, at its extremes, the priestly acts of saying office or mass, or hearing confessions, for example, had simply fallen away, or so they thought, so that the priest, instead of transforming others, was himself being transformed into something other than a priest – or worse perhaps, something other than a Christian.

Siefer attempted a specific definition of the term *prêtre ouvrier*, to 'exclude at the onset all possibility of misunderstanding'. He admits that the term briefly emerged even before World War I when some priests, presumably those who had been mobilized had had to become wage earners in order to live. 'The term was only re-introduced in the sense normally accepted nowadays in the *Journal d'un prêtre ouvrier en Allemande* by Henri Perrin.'

> It was now understood to describe a priest who did not live in a presbytery or monastery, was freed from parochial work by his bishops, lived only by full-time labour in a factory or other place of work and was indistinguishable in appearance from an ordinary workman . . . The worker-priest in principle regarded as irrevocable his decision to live as a workman and saw, as a logical conclusion of his first step, no kind of limits, short of sin, to his commitment as a workman.[594]

Significantly, Siefer goes on to mention certain changes, especially in the use of the title 'priest-worker' in the foreign press, 'obviously meant to indicate an alleged diminution of the priesthood of the worker-priests' (though this is not explained). He concluded that '. . . none of these alternative titles won general acceptance'.

(b) Britain's first worker-priests: publications

Britain's first worker-priests were undeniably sympathetic to the French *prêtres ouvriers* and their incarnational theology, not to mention their explicit socialization and politicization, which gave expression to that. In their earliest references almost all of these early priests spoke of the 'gap' or 'gulf' between the church and the working classes in Britain. At first Michael Gedge and John Strong were only marginally aware of the French experiment. Later, Gedge felt vindicated in all he had attempted, and both were touched by the French admiration of what they were doing in Eyethorne. Those who followed soon afterwards, Rowe, Grubb, Williamson and Ramsay, experienced the 'gulf' too, though they saw little actual hostility to the church.

But Britain's first worker-priests were reluctant to describe themselves as a movement of worker-priests, though they often embraced a measure of publicity and certainly accepted and used the title 'worker-priest'. For them it had at least one distinct meaning: it described a priest generally from a middle-class background,[595] conventionally trained for the priesthood but who had chosen as a vocation to move into a world of exclusively manual labour directly on the shop-floor, skilled or unskilled, but never above the 'rank' of chargehand.[596]

The business of trying to produce some kind of explanation of their chosen life began almost as soon as the Worker Church Group was founded in 1957, and was expressed in the Group's Statement published privately in 1959, shown in full in Appendix 3. Although a relatively brief 'apology' and born also from arguments between catholics and evangelicals in the group, it remains the clearest testimony of their intentions, and its arguments were used in later publications.

The Statement opened with the sub-title:

> A Group of Churchmen Priests and Lay who have chosen
> to be wage-workers in industry
> as an expression of their faith.

The Group professed that while the conventional approaches on the part of the church to workers were made from the 'footholds' of the institution, they had chosen 'another level'. (They may indeed have felt it to be a 'deeper level', but the words were crossed out in a draft – for they had no wish to be unkind to parochial ministry, even if they recognized its limitations.) Their approach was to be made by 'binding up our salvation with that of the industrial workers . . . by working as they work and living upon the earnings of labour as they do'. For the church to be out of contact with workers was a 'sin':

> . . . the answer to this situation is for the church to enter with humility and sympathy into the life of the working people . . . [597]

And again this way of incarnation involved 'such identification with man, with his sin, his hopes and fears, his misery and needs, that we become his brother . . .', so that work becomes not some opportunity for ecclesiastical propaganda, 'but the means whereby we become one with working people'. Their biblical base was St Paul, who says 'that he has not made use of this right [to receive charity], but prefers to earn his own living by work'. There was, with this, a vocation to a level of poverty. Workers may not have been uniformly poor 'in material things, yet as a class, they are the lowest stratum in society', what Ken Ramsay would later call the 'sediment' that rests at the bottom.

> If we seriously intend to get over the Gospel to the people of our time, we must live it in the materialistic terms of money and work which they [the workers] most easily understand. For our part, this means that we must express our faith by sharing fully the life of the wage-earning class. In our opinion only on the basis of such a life is the preaching of the Word likely to carry much conviction in modern industrial society.[598]

They went on to maintain 'no classes in Christ', and what they described as a secular precedent, especially in the role of trade unions:

> We feel bound therefore to enter into the struggles for justice, brotherhood and industrial democracy which are already going on in secular terms, serving the gospel no less this way than in direct personal acts of love.[599]

In a later section they took up the specific issue of worker-priests. They use the very title, and although their understanding of, and even identification with, the French was personally clear, they (perhaps deliberately) avoided any direct reference. Rather, the attention of readers is drawn to Resolution 89 of the Lambeth Conference (1958), which had made it clear that there was no theological objection to a priest earning a living in secular employment.

But the 'mission' was never to be confined to worker-'priests', and this is an essential in understanding the Worker Church Group. Though those in the Group who were priests acknowledged that title, they saw the entire group – rather than any movement – as a fundamental expression of a Christian response to modern industrial society.

> That means clergy and a predominance of laity, men and women, married and unmarried, all alike responding to the call to glorify God in the lives of workers.[600]

It was almost a call to become part of a religious community. The worker-priest movement in France was virtually that; perhaps only in this way could they hold together in Britain.

For these first worker-priests, who had met the French and who saw their own life as a vocation, the issue was unequivocal. Though they had been drawn from the middle, even upper, class and had perhaps greater emotional, even financial, reserves somewhere in their backgrounds (though that might have been said of other clergy), they determined to live out a working-class life. A priest-member of the WCG might then be described as a worker-priest, that is one who identified totally with the world of working men and women, sharing their labour, wages, housing and expectations.

Anne Grubb's article in *Frontier* (1960)

In 1960, an article appeared in the winter edition of the periodical *Frontier* by Anne Grubb, describing 'English Worker-Priests'. This was the first time in any journal that specific details had been given about the small group and how it was organized. 'There are four worker-priests of the Church of England,' the article began, 'and one worker-deacon due to be ordained as a worker-priest next Trinity.' The latter, of course, was Tony Williamson, the others Strong, Rowe, Grubb and Ramsay. Anne Grubb quoted part of their Statement, and maintained that their *raison d'être* was an attempt to close the gap between the church and the world of industrial labour. She explained that this was not a formal movement, and that it was open to laymen and women. Indeed the prize for length of chosen service went to Tom Waldon – the first of the group to begin manual labour in 1949. But at this stage and apart from wives, there was only the one.

After a brief biographical note on each worker-priest, Grubb raised the inevitable question: 'Are we getting anywhere?' In her answer, she argues indirectly for being a presence in the work place. 'The worker-priests do not go out of their way to make themselves known as parsons, but the fact inevitably comes out . . .' There were no 'spectacular results', she says, but tells how individual people in the work place had visited a church, or the homes of worker priests, and generally proved a little more interested. On the political scene she accepts that most are active members of the Labour Party, though one (possibly Ken Ramsay) 'doesn't care a button for political labels'. She describes their union activity as shop stewards, her husband's sackings, and all that is '. . . determined by the needs of the human situation in which we are placed, that Christian love can lead to political action will not be a new idea to readers of Frontier!' Then, in the almost inevitable link to be made with the French worker-priests, she adds:

> This of course explains why so many of the French worker-priests considered political activities so essential – though in view of the communist tendencies of working-class politics in France, such involvement carried more heart-searching problems for them. Contact with several French worker-priests and others concerned in the French Industrial Mission has convinced us that the differences between our two countries are considerable, though intelligent comparisons can be very rewarding.[601]

Grubb continues with a note about their children, since there were those who felt that this chosen way of life might do damage to their future. This matter was later dealt with in the Statement, but here Grubb is adamant that '. . . our children will almost certainly benefit from being brought up in closer contact with "real life" than their parents were' . . . 'Living as ordinary families seems to most of us an important part of our calling . . .' Finally Grubb locates their work in the context of the 'whole church' and says that they were '. . . thankful that part of what we have done and hope to do is now being sponsored officially, notably by the Bishop of Southwark . . .'

She goes on to explain that though England's worker-priests did not see themselves as a formal group, they had nevertheless resolved to meet together every summer to 'exchange views and ideas'. Though this would remain a sometimes dispersed group, disadvantaged perhaps by geographical distance, different understanding and churchmanship, yet committed to sharing the lot of industrial workers, with the full approval of 'our bishop': '. . . we are all alike united by a deep conviction of "belonging" to the working class, and belonging to each other almost as a religious order'. It remained the clearest apology for worker-priests in Britain:

> As the French worker-priests said, *'C'est la presence'*, with them we feel our main business is to be present among people and to learn from the life around us.[602]

Ted Wickham and his 'Appraisal' in *Priests and Workers*

Anne Grubb's article in *Frontier* was reprinted in an updated version in the volume *Priests and Workers* (1961) edited by David L. Edwards, and was intended as a counter to the penultimate chapter written by Ted Wickham in the same book. While the Sheffield Industrial Mission was in full swing, Wickham had made no secret of the fact that he preferred industrial chaplains to worker-priests as a part of missionary strategy. Wickham would be answered later by John Rowe, who on behalf of the WCG composed a Rejoinder (1965), which argued fiercely against Wickham's judgment and which in the process further defined the worker-priests. To understand that answer, it is essential, first, to appreciate Wickham's criticism.

In his 'Appraisal' of the English scene, Wickham upheld the role of the French, and though moved by their conviction, had nevertheless come to the conclusion:

> . . . that there could not in fact be a worker-priest movement in this country that was in any sense an equivalent of the French movement, because of the vastly different concepts and contexts of the church in the national communities concerned. Were a 'worker-priest' movement to come to the English scene, comparison would still remain as impossible as that between a French surrealist and an English Munnings.[603]

Wickham admits an Anglican history in all this, even to Thomas Arnold's suggestions, though he doubts whether Arnold 'had in mind the ordination of the early nineteenth-century artisan'. He also admits to the existence of a handful of English worker-priests, but was anxious to distinguish them from others 'never very many, fortunately, who have taken "welfare jobs" or other white-collar jobs perhaps to eke out a stipend'.

But, Wickham adds, 'the handful of genuine worker-priests do insist that theirs is a strong case for the development of such a ministry and there are several bishops who would support such a development.'[604] Wickham preferred a strategy that aimed to place ordained men on the factory floor as chaplains, not workers, and he believed that it remained an 'overwhelming case'. The difference between England and France was substantial and could be seen in our 'class relationships', '. . . for our British Society, class-ridden though it may be, has not the deep social fracture of the French scene and the subsequent rise of communist agitation'.

At the same time there remained the deep rift 'between the Catholic Church in France and the working- class culture'. Yet Britain had its own panacea, its Labour Party 'non-Marxist, woven of many strands, but deeply marked by ethical and Christian idealism'. In France, by contrast, the worker is anti-clerical in an ideological sense, unlike the English, who, though estranged from the church, may in protest argue warmly that 'you can be a Christian without going to church'. With such an acute difference, argued Wickham, 'one can understand why the French priest seeking acceptance in a cultural group so radically disassociated from the church and the church culture has himself felt impelled to make a radical disassociation with the conventional Church and Ministry . . .'[605] By contrast the social changes in Britain had not left the working classes isolated or closed. France and England remained essentially different and the factors in France 'are not the factors that can be shown to be decisive in the British situation'.

Could a theological reason be given for worker-priests in Britain? Wickham argues this time that there might be priests in places of work ministering to their own group, but then this would be to tear up the secular community into the sacred and the profane, and so bring division among men:

> The mind boggles at the prospect of the lay-priests in all different groupings, departments and grades of say, a steel works of 10,000 men – for undoubtedly we need Christian men in them all, an apostolate, catalysts. However unselfconscious, however wise, however lay such ministries might seek to be, anyone who knows the structure and life of such an industrial organization can only be appalled at the prospect. Truth to say, in the English scene, it is hardly imaginable.[606]

Wickham looked to all kinds of situations – India, the red belt in Paris, the evangelical church in South America – but added, 'Britain is not like this and we cannot simply revert to an expression of the church appropriate to the Christian missionary situation'. He argued for a 'lay presence' in the world, and was clearly alarmed by the prospect of throwing up a supplementary ministry by ordaining ordinary laymen deacons or priests without abstracting them from their secular job.

But the problems of an industrial work force largely indifferent to the church would not go away, and Wickham argued for an expression of mission 'appropriate to the English situation and as radical as the English conditions impose'. Wickham's idea of specialists, under a bishop, with definite areas of deployment, was realized in the industrial chaplains then making their mark in Sheffield. 'Such mission,' he admitted, 'must appear less dramatic than in the French context, less costly, less courageous [and, in his own emphasis] . . . *But this is the qualitative, depth equivalent for the British scene . . .*'

John Rowe and *Priests and Workers – A Rejoinder* (1965)

Not so, argued John Rowe, in *Priests and Workers – A Rejoinder*, published some four years later.[607] If the working-class were less than hostile to the church, it did not mean they were not estranged. For Rowe and the rest of the WCG who supported his publication, the issue was class. It was about what it meant *'to share working-class* life' (Rowe's emphasis), and it was a vocation for all Christians, though priests had their own part in it.

> The worker-priests may be pardoned for being just a little tired of doubtful compliments. So often they seem to be told how admirable they are in their willingness to commit themselves so whole-heartedly to their vocation, yet how really uncalled-for the commitment in general is.[608]

In complete contrast to Wickham's suggestion that class division is less acute in England than in France, Rowe argued that the Worker Church Group was 'swimming against the tide of ideological assumptions'. Rowe attacked capitalist society, the upper classes who made alliances with those rising in the social scale, the private education system, from which a number of early worker-priests had clearly benefited. He rejected the idea, emanating, he claimed, from Michael Jackson, that 'the cultural cleavage is less pronounced here . . .'

The church itself, argued Rowe, had played its part in class divisions. It was not that the church was less estranged than in France – that much Rowe might have conceeded – but that it was essentially middle-class. As for the working class, it was not their church, yet this was a very large class '[and] the most neglected in our ministrations. This is a class of people which is characteristically collective in mentality, and yet whose characteristic collective is not the body of Christ but the trade union.' This class would not be amenable to any kind of educative approach, and the gulf between it and the church could only be bridged by 'sharing' – the most characteristic expression of Christian 'caring'. A parson, as Wickham had suggested, can eventually talk even man to man. But, argued Rowe in a spirited rebuff, 'talking is not the point':

> When you have worked a while in a factory and seen the unconscious arrogance of authority, even in good men; when you have experienced the situation of being under command day after day, knowing that it will always be so; when you have clocked your card late and taken a quarter-of-an-hour's pay less, next pay day; when you have seen what that pay means in terms of housing and necessities and comforts, and learned the lessons of overtime; and when you have looked out from the circle of your workmates and seen with their eyes that manner of life of the socially superior, including the clergy, a realization is borne in upon you with unmistakable force. You realize something which you might have known before but have been afraid to admit, that on the side you have relinquished lies privilege and on the side you have accepted resentment.[609]

There existed a class of men and women 'marked out' by the nature of their work. A class separated 'and not to be talked or discussed or sympathized out of existence'. And so before the Gospel could be taken to workers, there was the prior demand that the conditions of the worker must be shared.

> Thus there is no comparison of *virtue* between worker-priests, as such, and parish priests. Love must be lived wherever a man is, and love may glorify *any* setting. The argument is not at this level. The argument is whether or not a deep meaning of the Gospel is being ill served by a church which is unwilling to share, through the lives of a representative body of her clergy and laity, the conditions of life of the manual workers of our society. [610]

Rowe went on to challenge the notion that this was always the role of the laity alone. Indeed the WCG had always challenged this notion by establishing itself from the outset almost as a community of men and women, lay and ordained, with a joint vocation. Nor was there any overt sacerdotalism among the worker-priests, some of whom were evangelical anyway, and though not typically evangelical, might have shunned such sentiments. Still Rowe warns against patronizing attitudes towards the laity, and that easily exalted role of the clergy which in its very existence 'perpetuates the old relationship of clergymen (outside the world) = guide and inspirer – 'producer' – of laymen: layman (in the world) = workers'.

> 'Be ordained,' said the Director of the Sheffield Industrial Mission to theological students who had worked a time in factories, 'and produce the kind of laymen you have now discovered it possible to be.' Apart from the shallowness of the experience at the basis of this 'discovery', was this not to exaggerate both the actual and proper powers of the clergy?[611]

But Rowe generously commended the work of industrial chaplains – just as the Group had done in their Statement – and indeed went further, arguing that if 'achievement' was something to be measured, then in the

> . . . amount of pastoral care undertaken, numbers of people drawn into discussion groups, and the numbers of misconceptions corrected in one way or another, there can hardly be any doubt that the industrial chaplain, if he is any good, ought to achieve a great deal more than the lay priest . . . [Rowe's sudden interpretation of a priest 'at work'].[612]

Rowe concluded, however, that it is all achieved 'on the basis of the traditional status of a clergyman'. 'He is essentially an outsider who is *permitted* (Rowe's italics) to come into the factory to do his stuff . . .' The worker-priests were claiming theirs was a part in the mission to the working class and not a worker-priest movement as such, and the WCG, ordained or lay, had no leadership in that mission. Leadership was about the exercise of gifts and abilities (which might be talked of in terms of functions); for Rowe, priesthood, in a similar way to what Williamson had earlier argued in Oxford, was first about 'corporate being'. Here Rowe upholds an ontological notion of priesthood, as if the very core of what it means to be a priest is almost forced upon a worker-priest; for this reason the passage deserves to be quoted in full:

> He [the worker-priest] cannot now organize and administer a congregation in the midst of the secular sphere he moves in. He cannot make of religion a thing in itself, with its visible building and its separate activities of worship. He cannot hold a 'living'. But he does not for an instant divest himself of the character conferred upon him at ordination. His word on matters of doctrine and morality are no less the word of a priest. If nothing is said about the sacraments, in which he of course continues to play his part among the faithful though not overtly among the unchurched workmates, his part in the 'economy of the church and in the Christian impact on society' is in terms of his undoubted continuance as a focus of authority. Any who come forward, or are brought forward by the laity, may have confidence in his answer to questions and in his teaching, for he does not lack any grace which any other priest enjoys by virtue of his Order. Is this not a 'practical' role to play? Anyone who knows anything about the distortions and ignorances of unchurched people concerning the faith must appreciate the value of there being knowledgeable and authoritative officers of the church wherever people are, available for questioning at the moment when questions come up, or very soon after. Their usefulness would undoubtably increase if there were more and more active laymen in their workplaces. Meanwhile they remain as prophets of a future in which the church genuinely has come alive within the industrial environment and by its presence is posing questions and inciting men to a dialogue . . . [613]

The WCG found inspiration in Jesus of Nazareth, St Paul's tentmaking, Fr Charles de Foucauld and Voillaume's Little Brothers of Jesus, and their earlier Statement was quoted in full as an appendix. Rowe was careful, however, to say nothing specific about the French *prêtres ouvriers*. Perhaps to claim inspiration from their brothers across the Channel (with whom the WCG had contact) would simply have been to exacerbate the issue, making alarmed Anglicans retort 'I told you so'. For Rowe, and all other members of the WCG, there had to be a beginning at home, with a good British reason for doing what they did, not simply an aping of the French. A demonstration on the part of the church that it cared sufficiently, proofs that came by 'deed' that 'the church loves, that the church repents that the clergy do not really care about their social position . . .'[614] If those proofs were to be given, then ordained men too must enter the working-class world, and become workers. And even if the French were not mentioned, it mattered little;

the Rejoinder was eventually translated into French and published across the Channel.

A decade on, what Rowe had said had not been lost on Robert Martineau. In his study *The Office and Work of a Priest,* he accurately, and in some detail, described what worker-priests were about, and raised the question of the nature of that priesthood.

> There is in ordination a certain 'setting apart for the life and work of a priest', it is more than authorization to perform particular functions. On the other hand there is a need to be alongside those to whom one ministers, to sit where they sit and to speak the language they speak. . . . Over-emphasis on identification can lead to a playing down the distinctiveness of a man's vocation. A typical illustration of this was the chaplain in wartime who was so anxious to be seen as a man's man that his work as a priest suffered. There is no standard formula to resolve this tension . . . [615]

And Vaughan (*Non-Stipendiary Ministry in the Church of England*, 1990) also highlighted the importance of Rowe, contrasting him with Bickersteth in *Part-Time Priests?,* who, Vaughan says, 'launched into print after only a fortnight in the factory'. But of Rowe he reminds his reader:

> . . . the book is written by a practitioner who has devoted his life to his vision. He is a resident within the working class, not a passing alien visitor (like so many priests cited in this book).[616]

(ii) Who is a worker-priest?

(a) Britain's first worker-priests: membership and exclusivity

By the early 1960s the Worker Church Group, although it had a Statement, was already having to face the question of which clergy or laity might be eligible for membership of the group, and who therefore by implication could properly be described as a *work*er-priest. Even to highlight worker-priests (except for the purposes of this study), however, might be misleading, for there was never any great concentration on the term. Some members of the WCG happened to be worker-priests, others were wives or laity; all were full members, and it was their commitment that mattered.

Over the years they debated this 'full' membership, asking what the criteria might be. At times it seemed to dominate, even dog, their general discussions. As early as 1961, for example, they were having to ask whether agricultural workers should be able to join. After all, they had produced their Statement in 1959, they stuck by it, and the matter seemed settled; but it was not so simple:

> Basis for membership was discussed on Saturday evening. It was felt important to try to define this for three reasons. Robert Bell, whom we all felt to 'belong', does not work in industry in its narrow sense, but in agriculture. Secondly, we must have some guide as to whether we were or were not prepared to welcome office workers such as or not such as Charles Lambert, with whom we indeed have much in common; and finally our relationship with part-time priests such as the Southwark scheme envisaged was not clear.[617]

Here, for the first time, because of the mention of the Southwark course, is an indication that the institution itself was beginning to look more favourably on a range of innovative ministries, which, though no one knew it at the time, would raise all kinds of new questions, as ambiguity emerged. In 1964 there was further beating of breasts. On the Sunday afternoon of their main Whitsun Conference, John Rowe raised the possibility of 'forming ourselves into a definite organization'. Rather than developing into a strong worker-priest movement, Rowe wanted more committed laity on board, and favoured the idea of a membership based solely on wage-earning – for clergy or lay; but still there was a lack of consensus on this point, and the issue was dropped. They wanted more laity on board, yet were anxious to avoid any 'artificial attempts to make the group more lay'. For the next few years these discussions went on, and in 1965 (when full notes were not produced) some reflection by a Sister Christina, who had also been working in a factory and attended as a visitor for the weekend, reported:

> None of us seem to know quite what we're doing – only that we ought to be doing it.[618]

Nevertheless, for the first time, and apart from their Statement, they were able to produce a Constitution. It was relatively brief and to the point:

> 1. The Worker Church Group is an association of men and women who accept the life of wage workers as a Christian vocation.

2. Members must be either

(a) Manual workers who have the ordinary status of employees in industry, agriculture, the public services, etc, and who live upon the earning of their labour as their fellow workers do.

(b) Clerical and other workers who hold jobs which, in the opinion of the Annual Conference, are closely allied with manual labour and which do not involve a real difference in status.

(c) The wives of any members under (a) and (b), provided that their husbands' wages represent the principal sources of income in their families.

3. Members may be either clergy or laity.

The Constitution went on to talk about its purpose of (4) 'mutual strengthening and support . . . about the vocation', (5) the common basis of sharing the 'life of wage workers and their families', (6) meeting regularly for conference. Despite this, membership was again on the agenda the following year (1966), where it was agreed after Tony Williamson's suggestion that:

> . . . those who qualify under the constitution drawn up last year should form the worker-church group and organize the conference; they could invite anyone else to the conference at their discretion.[619]

It had taken some eight years to get this far. They desperately wanted to be open and welcoming, yet the establishment of their own 'gate-keeping' practice was a deliberate attempt not so much to keep others 'out' as a means to preserve their obligation, just as in a religious community a commitment is maintained through vows. Visitors were welcome, very welcome; joining the 'community' was a completely different step.

Yet of all the events which marked their resolve to remain workers on the shop-floor, none emphasized this more than the voluntary departure of Martyn and Anne Grubb from the Group in 1966. Having laboured on the shop-floor for over fifteen years, apart for a break for ordination training, Grubb had decided on a change of direction. His commitment as a Christian to fight racism, which had brought him into conflict with members of his union and a parish church, now gave him the impetus to change jobs. Martyn had found that there had been no backing for the voluntary Southall International Friendship Committee from church or trade unions – especially as the Communists were showing an interest.

Martyn believed that here was a calling to which he must respond. In 1965, Martyn and Anne corresponded with others in the WCG, explaining that Martyn had applied for a job as Secretary/Liaison Officer to the Ealing Community Relations Council. 'It goes without saying [wrote Anne] that this has meant a lot of heart searching, and in the popular phrase an "agonizing reappraisal" of all our ideas and beliefs, not least our commitment to the Worker Church Group.'[620]

John Rowe was unable to take this lying down. The Grubbs' departure might compromise the future of the rest of the Group, for John Strong was now too unwell to labour and, for the first time since becoming a worker-priest, was about to take on a couple of country charges as 'full-time' incumbent.

> . . . there seems a lot at stake now. A moment of truth, maybe, is here. John Strong is pulling out. He is virtually forced to do so, and does not seem to me to be offending against any position he has ever taken in doing so. His is an honourable defeat in battle, but it is a defeat for us nevertheless . . . our morale and our 'front' to the world is likely to be seriously undermined.[621]

However, in a further elaboration of what was at stake, and in one of the most striking declarations of what being a worker-priest means, Rowe wrote passionately, asking Grubb to reconsider, and to embrace and maintain this [a worker-priest's] most difficult witness on the shop floor. There may be some apparently good reasons for a move, people may indeed have encouraged this, but

> . . . do not allow yourself to be overwhelmed by a local need when the alternative is nothing less than rediscovering the Gospel and helping to replant the seed in its proper soil . . . (and in the context of working-class life) you will be retreating from this matrix if you take this job . . . [622]

Though there were several applicants for the job, Martyn Grubb was appointed, and, believing himself no longer worthy to be called a worker-priest, he prepared to leave the WCG. This, however, was not before Anne had made the point that, despite their constitution, ambivalence remained. How could John Strong remain 'a member', or Sherry Waldon (Tom Waldon's wife who was a secretary)? The truth was that here were friends trying to deal with matters of principle; no one had the heart to turn either 'out' and such ambiguities remained painfully evident.

But there was no animosity and, perhaps unknown to them at the time, the Grubbs had unwittingly demonstrated their own acceptance of the WCG's shop-floor commitment by actually upholding the working vocation of the others. The Grubbs would reappear as visitors and make a further contribution to the WCG many years later. Martyn was to serve as Officer for the Ealing International Friendship Committee (later ECRC), and would remain in that work for many years.

By 1972, when non-stipendiary ministries were already beginning to take off, Robert Martineau, in his *Office and Work of a Priest*, made mention of a range of settings where priests might appear. In a chapter entitled 'Ministry to Special Interests', Martineau mentions priests in shops, theatres, and holiday camps. But he singles out worker-priests and contrasts them with industrial chaplains, giving one of the briefest and most accurate accounts of what the WCG and its worker-priests were about.

> In contrast with the industrial chaplain, worker-priests deliberately accept the role of manual workers. Those who are so engaged see this as their life's vocation with no intention of accepting promotion above that of charge-hand. Thus they share the tensions and clashes of loyalty, the frustrations and fears of unemployment, that are part of the life of the weekly wage earner. The number of such priests in England at present is small, and most are members of a group of worker-churchmen; this group includes both priests and laymen. They recognize the great division between the organized church, with its middle-class emphasis, and the vast majority of manual workers. In their desire that the church should be present among these workers, they see the church as including both priests and laymen and so their aim is the presence of priest and Christian layman among the manual workers. The priests who accept manual employment do so not to save and rescue individuals nor to create some half-way church; as in the French worker-priest movement, it is the Christian presence that matters and that presence must be provocative by its holiness. The identification must be as far as possible real and permanent . . . [623]

It was a good summary, but in a sense, it was already history.

(b) South Bank visions and disappointments

In the most general terms, up to 1963, there was only one answer to the question 'Who is a worker-priest?'. Worker-priests were French, or, in the case of Britain, a handful of conventionally trained clergy who (though they never made a fuss about being 'worker-priests') had nevertheless opted for a vocation in manual labour on the shop-floor, and were likely to be members of the WCG.[624] But in 1963, Mervyn Stockwood's Southwark Ordination Course would produce its first thirteen ordinands[625] from what the bishop had clearly hoped would be mixed backgrounds. Some would be full-time stipendiary clergy, others were described in various ways, sometimes as worker-priests, who, having remained at their place of work as they studied, would now continue there. The whole idea was revolutionary. Stockwood, given the rhetoric of the time, had completed something no other bishop had even begun. Was this now the first chance for Britain to have a real worker-priest movement, now expanded on the South Bank, sanctioned by a bishop, coming possibly as some kind of relief column to a beleaguered WCG, which alone, surely, had sustained this radical ministry from Michael Gedge's beginnings in 1943? Would the men from SOC prove heirs to the WCG? Had the latter provided a foundation for this new ministry soon to be taken up the length and breadth of the church in Britain?

Despite all that Mervyn Stockwood may have said and hoped about worker-priests, it would surely have dawned on the ordinands in SOC – as John Rowe visited them to talk in the mid-1960s – that theirs was a perspective utterly different from Rowe's. In September 1963 the first ordinands to emerge as deacons from Southwark Cathedral were heralded in a variety of ways. 'Worker-priests', 'God's Late Developers', 'God's New Frontiersmen'. Their training had been a long and hard struggle, and for one reason or another, many had fallen by the wayside. Of an original ninety applicants for part-time training, thirty had been accepted, with only thirteen surviving the course. There are very few of that first year remaining at the time of writing who remember hearing of 'worker-priests' anywhere else. Dennis May, a surveyor, had apparently heard something about the French, and his wife at the time 'thought there was a course in Sheffield'. Oliver Whyman knew nothing of the French; Eric Normington had heard of them, but he saw them as 'mass priests only'.[626] As John Rowe had not yet visited SOC, none of them seemed to know anything about the situation at home either. By all accounts, little was made of becoming a worker-priest anyway, and Henry

Theobald, a stipendiary member of the first group who had heard of worker-priests 'mostly at that time I think in France', maintains:

> SOC was not set up specifically for those wishing to become 'worker-priests'.[627] It was born from the vision of Mervyn Stockwood and John Robinson that there were men in the church who had a vocation but for various reasons had not been able to pursue it . . . [628]

The first thirteen deacons from SOC were almost to a man professional or semi-professional white-collar workers who intended to remain that. They included a headmaster, solicitor, university clerk, property manager, London City Missioner, quantity surveyor, electrical engineer (who worked in a showroom), office manager, and the treasurer of the British Railways Board. In the press, a photograph of them outside Southwark Cathedral at the time of ordination and later 'downing a pint' in a 'local' (BISHOP GIVES A TOAST TO HIS WORKER-PRIESTS)[629] added to the novelty of the occasion. It gave little hint of the brave struggles so many had endured in order to complete the course while trying to maintain careers.[630]

In a sermon on the eve of their ordination, Stanley Evans gave a potted history of SOC and an account of its significance. The call to the ordained ministry did not simply come to boys and young men 'in a particular type of school or university . . . but the call must come to dockies [dockers], insurance agents, and schoolmasters, butchers, bakers[631] or who you will'.

In a *Church Times* article,[632] Hugh Gunning wrote of the 'Christ the carpenter' picture at the Wychcroft (SOC Conference Centre) – symbol of the thirteen men who were just completing the course: five would be clergymen 'while carrying on their ordinary working lives',[633] while the remainder would become stipendiary clergy. Dennis May, the quantity surveyor, beaming in a centre-page spread, in a surveyor's news-sheet the *Reporter*,[634] epitomized the group. He was one of 'God's New Frontiersmen' 'building the gap between the church and the working world . . .' 'The church has become a little detached from everyday life', he remarked, and, in a sense speaking for himself and his fellow ordinands, he added, 'we shall attempt to put that right'.[635]

At a press conference, Stanley Evans would use subtly different language before the press.[636] When asked, 'What is the good of a worker-priest?', Evans replied that the conception of the worker-priest sprang from an attempt to face the fact of a gulf between the church and the industrial working-classes. 'The clergy have to go right in with the workers by being one of them.' But there appeared an immediate discrepancy between what Evans was describing and what SOC had just produced. It was not lost on one reporter, who commented that all the men Evans was talking about were 'white-collar workers' whose jobs lay in offices or schools. Evans 'hastened to assure the questioner that since the original intake of men, a certain number of manual workers had been enrolled for the course and these included a factory worker and a baker'. As time would show, however, these two, David Wilson the baker and Tom Field, a bus driver, would prove to be the exceptions, not the rule. If there had been a 'factory worker' (and evidence makes it unclear as to whether this is Tom Field or another individual), there is no record that such a person finished the course.

The story of a 'white-collar' worker was certainly what Jack Lucas set out to tell in the *Herald*, where Jim Storey (a solicitor), one of the new 'night-school' parsons, was shown in a full-page spread whacking a golf-ball across his local course. 'People do not understand how a working life fits into the story of redemption. They think you become a Christian and then contract out of the activities of life as much as possible.'

And, as Lucas added:

> No contracting out for *him*. A handsome bachelor of 36, he golfs, skis, swims underwater and drives an Austin-Cooper.[637] He will carry on with all this, though he will do church work on weekdays as well as weekends.[638]

The same article introduced Harry Hill '. . . a parson's father. He is fifty-eight and earns a top salary as treasurer of the British Railways Board. When he retires he will work as a curate without a stipend'; presumably Hill could afford to do so.

It was clear that whatever hopes Stockwood, Robinson and Evans might have had for 'workmen turned priests' (and they may only have hoped for a handful), something very different had emerged from SOC, and would continue to do so. Ambiguity remained. For the Bishop of Southwark and his supporters, the notion of men carrying on in the working life while being priests seemed right, and they bravely made it real. But it also meant that a predominance of middle-class educated individuals, rather than 'entering the world of industry', or 'downsizing' themselves (to use a late-1990s expression), had just had their middle-class status in a sense reinforced, even enhanced, as they now joined the rather hallowed ranks of the Church of England's clergy. When a much later experiment in the late 1970s to ordain a group of four working men actually did take place south of the river, in the Brandon area under the priest there, Dominic Walker, Stockwood confessed to Walker, who was his chaplain, that this was what he had always hoped to have seen coming from SOC. [639] Despite Stockwood's vision to have 'an order of worker-priests – men who will stay on the ground floor, earning their living as factory hands',[640] there would be virtually no working-class 'shop floor' candidates on board the new scheme, and only as Stockwood's illustrated list of trades came to an end with 'shopkeepers and schoolmasters' did the good bishop begin to get it right. Despite the vision and the rhetoric, the Church of England's dynamic new course in Southwark would not only draw almost all its new clergy from exactly the same middle-classes as it had always done – it would keep them there.[641]

A gnawing disappointment became evident. Six years after SOC had begun, Stockwood wrote in Southwark's magazine *The Bridge,* confessing disappointment at a course that had not, it seems, come up to his full expectations in training worker-priests, and which in some respects 'disturbed me greatly'. By 1967, one of the early ordinands, Frank Hewlitt, was the first SOC man to be instituted to a benefice. But such moves into stipendiary ministry were slow, for some suspiciously slow. The year before, one ex-student, Eric Normington, argued that Stockwood's primary objective had been to train men for the stipendiary priesthood. But he had now 'caught Stockwood out' when the latter proved ambivalent about actually appointing his 'own' SOC men to stipendiary benefices. Stockwood was now suggesting that primarily the 'purpose of the course was to train men for priest-workers and not for full-time ministry', 'whereas,' adds Normington to the then principal of SOC, 'all the correspondence that I have places the first purpose as that of training men for the full-time ministry', adding in some frustration:

> No real policy has apparently ever been worked out with regard to SOC. It has been played 'off the cuff'. I can appreciate the disappointment of the Bishop of Southwark in that his dreams were never fulfilled in that 'workers' did not offer themselves. Of course they could not. They were precluded by the rigid requirements of the course and the strict ordinances . . . [642]

But then Stockwood himself had begun a partial retreat from his earlier stance by suddenly arguing that the term worker-priest

> . . . is misleading as it suggests a man who works in a factory, and nowhere else. In fact a worker-priest may work anywhere in the secular world . . . [643]

But that was Stockwood's own definition, born perhaps of his disappointment. As late as 1984 Stockwood wrote in reply to a query from the Revd G. Winterbottom about original intentions:

> I wish that more had come forward as worker-priests in the secular world. My main distress is that so few found their way into industries. There were too many professions and civil servants.[644]

The radical bishop and his senior clergy of Southwark had never been able to face the rather unpalatable fact that none of their new ordinands had any intention of 'moving' 'down' to the shop-floor, and, since academic standards were demanding (and perhaps more demanding than courses would subsequently become), the course was anyway unlikely to attract real working-class candidates. But there may have been a more significant reason; the fact was, that as there were few workers in the pews of Southwark anyway, there would be even fewer found seeking training for ordination from the Southwark course or – for that matter – anywhere else.

(c) An exception – David Wilson: commitment 'where you find yourself'

It was unlikely, however, that, given the tenor of the times, no attention would be paid to SOC by the Worker Church Group. Indeed the Group was interested in what was happening in Southwark, hopeful, happy and most enthusiastic at Stockwood's courage. Nevertheless, a few years before, John Rowe had proposed that the WCG 'must be defined as a group of "wage workers"'. It was essential, they believed, though it might sound uncharitable, to exclude those working but perhaps not 'manual workers'. Yet, with their rather rigid 'gatekeeping' practice in place, they were happy to admit, first as a visitor, one of the few priests from SOC who, according to their constitution, might meet the criteria for membership.

David Wilson, the baker alluded to by Evans, had joined the course in 1962, and, looking after his small family business in Brixton, appeared for the first and almost the last time at the Whitsun Conference of the

WCG in 1967. On meeting the Group he confessed a general interest in describing himself as a baker 'who virtually manages the family bakery'. Nevertheless, he was welcomed to the 1967 Conference with another visitor, Bill Millard,[645] a postal worker from Portsmouth, who had trained under his own bishop, using a Wolsey Hall Course, and together they took part in the meeting (including discussion wth a French worker-priest Daniel Bonnechère).[646] By the end, Millard was encouraged but Wilson less enthusiastic. When the visitors were asked to give their initial impressions of the WCG, Wilson admitted, as the record explains:

> This Group was not for him. He did not wish to be particularly associated with manual workers and did not agree with much of the Group's political and social thinking. He saw the largest problem for worker-priests in their relations with parish clergy, the poor communications between church and people could be improved, he thought by a large number of worker-priests. This he saw as a greater task than the role accepted by the Worker Church Group.[647]

So passed one of the earliest opportunities for a direct meeting of minds between the WCG and at least one of the first members of the Southwark course who could be described as a worker. It was not a hopeful sign. Ideology clearly separated the two, and just five years later, with NSM courses growing across the country, Bill Millard, himself trained part-time, confessed to his friends in the WCG:

> that . . . the idea of the various Auxiliary Pastoral Ministries might just be a way of getting priests on the cheap. Not so much a vocation like that of the worker-priests, but a convenience . . . [648]

And Anne Grubb has since reflected:

> I felt that if the worker-priests got mixed up with the idea (as it later became called) of non-stipendiary ministries . . . it would be the destruction of the heart of the worker-priests. As a group we were very aware that a lot of people would see the two as the same . . . whereas in fact they are different . . . [649]

But there was never ill-feeling. At the same meeting there was a suggestion that David Wilson might be one of those to return a French visit. David Wilson kept in touch with the WCG and his name appears later in a Report of the May Conference in 1974 when he wrote with news from Southwark.

There was, however, a much more outspoken analysis of these different perspectives several years later. Tim Justin in the *Guardian*'s 'Miscellany' column at the beginning of 1974 argued that the first worker-priests 'would not accept these priests [NSMs anywhere], as fully taking part in the spirit of what they, the original worker-priests, have undertaken . . .'

> . . . Although they would be chary of saying it publicly, they believe strongly that the whole point is not to take a professional job . . . It is here that the gap exists, and it exists precisely because the church has remained a largely middle class organization . . . the Southwark scheme has tended to attract professional men . . .'[650]

For the WCG, the term worker-priest (and worker church) meant identifying, as Anne Grubb had said, with the French, in being a presence (*c'est la présence*) among working-class people and learning from the working-class life around them, 'leaving God to produce what results he sees fit'.[651] For David Wilson and other working clergy from the Southwark course, being a worker-priest was simply about earning your own living alongside others, whatever it was and wherever you found yourself; even, it seems, if you were a senior executive, and treasurer of the British Railways Board.

By the late 1970s and early 1980s, when John Strong had been forced by ill-health to give up labouring, he was already a little anxious about the way non-stipendiary ministry might be affecting what worker-priests had been all about. In an undated paper from the end of the 1970s or the beginning of the 1980s, in which members of the WCG asked what they expected from the Group, John Strong maintained that the growth of non-stipendiary ministry might indeed have got some inspiration from the worker-priest idea. (It was certainly true of Mervyn Stockwood, who in a sense had stood alone as their one supporter.[652]) Strong recorded that people from Southwark had actually visited Eyethorne in 1957 and were 'agreeably surprised that the miners seemed to like us . . .' But on the differences between worker-priests and non-stipendiary ministers he was clear:

> If you believe that the Worker Church Group is committed to a stance within the working class . . . one must look very warily at members of

> the Non-Stipendiary Ministry who claim to be at one with the Worker Church Group. Very few of them, in their neck of the woods, have any real idea what the Worker Church Group, or worker-priests, are about, and do not want it anyway.

He added:

> But having said so, there are almost bound to be some of them, from time to time, who have a common concern. At least we hope so – we do hope that not all of them will be bank managers, lecturers, retired civil servants, etc.[653]

4. New worker-priests – new perspectives

(i) The Southwark priest-worker chapter

If David Wilson believed that the WCG was 'not for him' there was nevertheless an opportunity for him to help in the formation of a different group, located in Southwark. Discussions to this end among SOC's ordinands were already taking place in 1966 under the Cathedral provost, Ernie Southcott. In an undated memo possibly from about the same time, Bishop John Robinson suggested that the relationship of the priest-workers of the diocese 'should be given a more permanent structure' and he went on to recommend an 'extra-territorial deanery chapter with membership open to all men in regular full-time employment'.[654]

Those who joined the chapter stuck with the term 'priest-worker' to describe themselves, and it is impossible to determine when this was first used or the precise thinking behind that use, though Wilson suggests it was a deliberate attempt to put the emphasis on priesthood first, rather than relate it to manual labour.[655] From the beginning, however, the priest-worker chapter had a broad range of occupations among its membership, stating that it '. . . shall consist of those clergy in full-time secular employment . . .'[656] In an undated list (possibly 1967) of 'clergy in secular employment who have expressed a wish to join the proposed priest-workers' chapter' there are twenty-six names. Of this list, only one is described as 'factory worker'; this turns out to be not a 'SOC' man at all, but none other than Ken Ramsay, worker-priest and already a member of the WCG.

An inaugural meeting was held on 13 July 1968, where the chapter was given a quasi-formal structure with rules for membership. By October of the same year David Wilson had been elected dean in precisely the same way as any other chapter dean. At a successive meeting there was a report that 'members of the WCG had met the chapter and engaged in a fruitful discussion on problems of "worker-ministry"'. In the event, members of the WCG must have seen there was something very different here, and very few meetings of this kind ever took place again. It a sense, it signalled a parting of the ways. Later Wilson admitted that the WCG were nearer Mervyn Stockwood's idea of what worker-priests were about, but of the WCG he commented 'they didn't need us [SOC chapter] . . . they [WCG] never grew . . .'[657]

Besides the differences at home, a predictable contrast in views was also evident between the Southwark priest-worker chapter and the views and the positions of French worker-priests. David Wilson had taken a keen interest in the French and had made visits abroad. But this time differences were made explicit in a meeting with Belgian worker-priests in April of 1969, followed later by a visit from French priests – not worker-priests but JOC chaplains. In a report written by one of the chapter, contrasts were highlighted and the chapter's own minutes offer an appraisal of their own very different position:

> The chapter recognized that, from what the French priests had said, our own situation as priest-workers was entirely different from any existing in France. We believe our ministry is of a different nature from that of the French priests but that it nevertheless has a purpose.[658]

In the same note (possibly from April 1969), a further reference to the French appears, pointing to a different political situation in the two countries, and especially in France where:

> Passions run high, issues are much more distinct, and the priest who becomes a worker not only fights alongside the men for the rights they all want, but also discovers that in some cases the church he represents is on the management side. It is because the issues are so clear and the worker-priest has to take sides that the movement in France has thrown up a very militant group.[659]

That was clear enough for the WCG to agree with and live out even in Britain, but for the Southwark chapter there was a different perspective, and they saw little point in going to such lengths:

> In England, with the exception of a handful of men [and they presumably meant the WCG] the priest-worker movement has not sought to join the fight on behalf of the working class but in some measure has been an attempt to reopen the lines of communication closed for years among the working class.[660]

Here, then, they classify themselves with other worker-priests. Yet this was a different position and could have been claimed as a 'contradiction in terms' by the WCG. If you did not side with workers by actually becoming one and actually helping to 'fight on their behalf', there was surely a case for arguing *you were not a worker-priest at all.* Furthermore, the Southwark Group now talked about a priest-worker movement (a term the WCG refused to use) in which they saw essentially themselves. The fact was that the Southwark chapter saw things differently, and in a final paragraph, defending their middle-class status and values, they began: 'we cannot and ought not to try and copy what the French have done in this field'.[661]

It is difficult to avoid the conclusion that though the Southwark priest-workers had so appropriated the title 'priest-worker' for their own ministry – at a time when few other terms had come into common use – and had set themselves up as 'representatives' in England, yet they were now in a sense being forced to retreat from the whole notion of what a worker-priest actually was by effectively denying the very meaning given by the French and agreed by the WCG. Wilson effectively admitted that they appropriated, indeed reinterpreted, that title to describe a difference in approach, in his contribution to *Men for the Ministry*. Were they were now being forced to disengage themselves from the very interpretation which they had chosen?

> The situation in this country is very different. Few priest workers can earn less than parish clergy and some a good deal more. It is not clear how we can identify specially with the working class. Whether it is an economic class or whether it refers to a certain type of job or condition of employment . . .

He added:

> It looks as if we are middle-class in a middle-class church.[662]

Yet this was precisely how they had described the French church earlier, and what Britain's first worker-priests in their Statement had always admitted to being and yet challenging.

The Southwark chapter still faced the need for a more direct articulation of their role. David Wilson had done much in his contribution to an ACCM series on Men for the Ministry in which he advocated a role for the priest in his place of employment wherever that might be; indeed this would prove to be the only leaflet ACCM ever produced advocating a 'ministry at work'. Wilson also kept in contact with the French, despite the acknowledged differences, and opened up a significant correspondence with Swedish and American clergy on the topic of non-stipendiary ministries.

But members of Southwark's priest-worker chapter still believed there was some misunderstanding, even hostility, from stipendiary parish clergy.[663] In 1969 an ACCM working party emerged to begin a close examination of 'ministry in secular employment'. Generally, they found that the Southwark chapter was itself divided among those who, though they earned a living in secular work, still had their ministry focussed on the parish, rather than in the work place.

> Discussion revealed an immense diversity of opinion even among the members of the Worker-Priest chapter themselves . . . opinions ranged from those who are exercising a direct support to the parochial system . . . to those who find their secular work an expression of their priesthood.[664]

Towards the later part of 1972, about five years after the SOC priest-worker chapter had been in existence, a correspondence opened between David Wilson and the staff of St Augustine's College, Canterbury, a theological college.[665] All at once, it seems, there was new reason to discuss the meaning of the term worker-priest. In a rather remarkable move, four workers had just been ordained across the Thames in Stepney by Bishop Trevor Huddleston, under the direct supervision of their incumbent Ted Roberts. They were seen as having been 'called out' from the local congregation and were, for the first time, genuine 'workers turned priests' and included a docker. Their training was different from that undertaken by the SOC men, and was deliberately designed to make for an effective local ministry. Huddleston, it seemed, with all a missionary's understanding of the need for an indigenous ministry, had suddenly been prepared to give support. Perhaps a subsequent newspaper headline, 'Britain's First Worker-Priests', was a little too much for long-standing members of SOC's priest-worker chapter, who agreed that 'there was widespread ignorance regarding the priest-workers and their vocation'. But the WCG might have had as much cause to say something similar![666] Besides, the scheme, as Vaughan relates, 'did not flourish'. Local ministry schemes would later develop in other parts of the country, but never like that in Stepney, and there may be evidence that, in the end, the experience for the four was never entirely happy.[667] Later there were other separate arrangements in London's East End with working men being ordained: some of them made friends with the WCG. Fred Rollinson was ordained to Bow with Bromley in 1971 and Derek Waxman to Old Ford St Paul with St Stephens in 1979. By the spring of 1972 the Dean of Southwark's priest-worker chapter referred to two meetings with the staff of St Augustine's, where the object had been 'a theological appraisal of the work of the worker-priests in the Southwark diocese'.[668] In a précis of the issues to be raised the SOC representatives wanted to know: (a) What was a priest? (b) Could a priest-worker do more than a layman? (c) Was a priest-worker such by conviction or was it an 'easy way out' – (an 'easy way out' of what, precisely, is unclear). In 1973, however, and following about half a dozen visits to St Augustine's and the completion of several questionnaires, Ken Mason, sub-warden of St Augustine's, had prepared a paper. Mason began by distinguishing between SOC's idea of priest-workers and the WCG's notion of worker-priests, emphasizing that SOC contained businessmen and professionals and showed their overwhelming consensus that the latter too had a 'ministry at work'. In an outline of what he saw as the distinctive features of the SOC priest-worker chapter, Mason highlighted their ministry as having

(i) A ministry in the totality of life.
(ii) A ministry as identification. Many had spoken of a 'gap' to be bridged.

To do this, Mason added, the priest-worker[669] has not adopted a 'new style of living' (as the WCG had done), but rather 'stays where he is'. Mason's thorough paper on the nature of the priesthood, however, left no doubt about the rightness of any priest combining his vocation with secular work. He too stressed 'presence' where the word had gained a certain dignity, and concluded that the priest-workers of SOC were surely also right to pursue their role and to recognize it as an expression of their priesthood.

At least one important feature emerges from the St Augustine's paper. Unlike the WCG, the SOC priest-worker chapter had sought out others to examine the nature of their ministry. It may have been right to go to the staff of a theological college for an appraisal of their role, but it is sometimes hard to avoid the conclusion that, apart from the very significant contributions of David Wilson, or a brief paper they produced in 1971, they were not too good at it themselves. One of the results of Mason's paper was the emergence of a 'special group' within the chapter who would have a 'deeper commitment' to a rule of life and reflection upon their role. This would eventually develop as the 'Friday group', which gathered in strength in succeeding years as members sought a more considered reflection on their daily life and work.

Throughout the 1970s and 1980s, the SOC priest-worker chapter continued to meet and deal with a variety of subjects, and so continued the Friday group. In general, the Chapter remained in their middle-class occupations. Indeed, a list – possibly of chapter members – drawn from the early 1980s shows the SOC ordinands' occupations heavily weighted in the direction of middle management (Appendix 4). Yet SOC and the priest-worker chapter were a real success in their own way: of the training of men who might otherwise never have enjoyed any theological education there was much, of the establishment of professionals and semi-professionals as ministers in secular employment there was plenty. But of worker-priests in the sense in which Mervyn Stockwood had originally hoped, and which had been expressed earlier by the WCG, or the small number of workers turned priests and ordained by Trevor Huddleston, there would be almost none.

(ii) Development, individualism, fragmentation

In the decade following 1965, further courses training men (and later women) for the non-stipendiary ministry began to develop across Britain, following on from the 1961 unpublished Report, and later incorporating other Christian denominations. The style and the content of courses varied, though up to the late 1980s, most of the courses used the church's own General Ministerial Examination (GME, an examinable essay scheme) to assess candidates. There was a considerable expansion of the courses in the 1970s and 1980s,[670] but some cutbacks in the early 1990s as courses and theological colleges were closed or amalgamated in a broad cost-cutting exercise at a time when, once again, the numbers of those coming forward for stipendiary ministry began to fall.

It was, more than anything else, the *Welsby Report* of 1968 which encouraged the development of these courses, a report which Vaughan has judged as 'the foundation charter for non-stipendiary ministry in the

Church of England'. Between the Reports of 1961 and 1968, little had been developed, though Vaughan records that by 1966 'over 32 men (not including those trained on SOC), had been ordained in 21 dioceses . . . and a few dioceses had begun to establish courses to train them'. By 1968, then, the 'supplementary ministry' was 'an established fact' and the *Welsby Report* detailed the selection and training that should now be standardized.

From the outset, however, it was very clear that, as it stood, this would never be a support to a worker-priest ministry, as perceived by the Worker Church Group. Because 'the Church Assembly was judged likely to consider favourably the introduction of an auxiliary ministry which aided the parochial ministry' the Report deliberately avoided dealing with men 'who might be ordained to non-parochial situations such as chaplaincies or worker-priests'.[671] By 1969, the Church Assembly fully endorsed this new ministry, but the parameters were already firmly set:

> . . . everything about the plan was designed to strengthen the parochial system. The proposals thus played to the expectations of the dominant model. The very title proposed by the Report for this new ministry was 'Auxiliary Parochial Ministry' (APM), and it was perceived as being an assistance to parochial clergy – especially in regard to the increasing demand for celebrations of the eucharist . . . [672]

On the whole Vaughan's conclusion highlights both the rewards and the frustrations of those who completed training but who, for one reason or another, did not enter the stipendiary ministry. While new non-stipendiary clergy aiding the territorial parish flourished, a variety of ministries 'at work', which later by a kind of common consent were designated 'ministry in secular employment' (MSE), appeared with mixed reports. Vaughan highlights the fact that the candidates who before and after ordination seriously contemplated this role as their main focus of ministry (even when as always there was an attachment to the parish) were in a minority. There was, anyway, and there remains among some non-stipendiary clergy, a feeling of a dual role: a ministry 'at work', that is, a ministry in the context of daily living, and a ministry in a local parochial setting, precisely what Gedge and Strong had done in the mid-1950s.

But even while non-stipendiary ministry evolved its own patterns, first evident among the Southwark men, other unhappier features became evident. There emerged what Vaughan has called 'signs of discontent' among non-stipendiary clergy. First, it was sometimes perceived as a shortcut into stipendiary ministry, and there were not a few 'full-time' trained stipendiary clergy in many different dioceses who clearly despised those whom they saw as seeking entry 'by the back door'.[673] There were sometimes 'sly remarks' about 'second-class priests' and this, Vaughan has thought, even contributed to some NSMs abandoning their secular jobs to become stipendiary clergy. Secondly, there was sometimes less understanding of ministry-at-work anyway, despite its assumed relevance. Indeed there were a few ministers-at-work who gave the impression that they were unsure how to conduct themselves in their own settings and circumstances and gave accounts that might have made earlier worker-priests cringe. In *Working for the Kingdom,* John Hind recognized a 'sad reference to the difficulties faced by priests who feel they ought to be celebrating the eucharist in the context of their perceived focus of ministry'.[674] And there are recorded incidents of individuals suddenly appearing at the place of work in a clerical collar, to the astonishment of fellow employees. Such incidents, perhaps few in number, nevertheless demonstrated that some new ministers in secular employment were unfamiliar with the motivation, thinking and practice of earlier worker-priests whose own accounts of working life might have helped them.

Though the 1968 *Welsby Report* had effectively concentrated on non-stipendiary ministry as a support to the territorial parish, with the 'world of work' and 'mission' generally effectively side-lined from the discussion, there was some recognition that Ministry in Secular Employment, since it clearly existed in a variety of forms, ought to be examined. A further Report on *Priests in Secular Employment* (1972), which took evidence from a variety of sources including David Wilson and members of the Worker Church Group, was completed though never published. There proved to be disagreement among the working party themselves on the subjects of ministry and mission, and Ted Wickham, in a kind of minority report, remained scathing about efforts of this kind which did not seek a 'penetrative ministry in the secular world' but remained more concerned, one way or another, to 'prop up traditional church structures'. For Vaughan, the Report '. . . raised too many awkward questions, which the institutional church at the time was probably incapable of facing'.

Thus, although there were indeed priests already engaged in secular employment, and who despite parochial attachment believed their main focus of ministry was in the work place, the 1972 Report remained unpublished. And though the Report commended a kind of 'contemplative role' (what might be called a 'presence' in the work place, and which the worker-priests already lived out), there would be little major support or endorsement for this particular ministry. The overriding difference for most MSEs when compared with the first handful of worker-priests was that while the MSEs intended to remain in and focus their ministry in middle-class and professional occupations, the worker-priests remained committed to manual labour on the shop floor. As the SOC experience showed in the early 1960s, most candidates for the ministry on the South Bank were drawn from the same social categories (though perhaps slightly higher categories)[675] as stipendiary candidates who attended residential theological colleges; they had no intention of 'stepping down' from that, nor was there any evidence they were expected to do so.

As the new non-stipendiary ministries began to develop their own pattern and rationale in the late 1960s and early 1970s, there were still some Church of England stipendiary clergy simply fed-up with the institutional church, sometimes attracted by the story of the French worker-priests, but generally ready to forsake the territorial parish for a 'relevant' job and as far as possible from an 'irrelevant' church: teaching, social and community work were favourite occupations, though a number also sought a role in new 'sector ministries' as school, college, hospital and forces chaplains. The numbers who 'left' the institution – and the reasons why they left may never be known – were enough for Lloyd to comment on the drain, affected by the 1960s climate. For some, only a trial on the shop-floor would do.

It would be impossible to give a definitive list of all those later clergy who might be described as 'worker-priests'. For one reason or another, and with justification, many men never made public the facts of what they were 'about', and attempts to discover others for the purposes of this study have often been disappointing. It is possible, however – following the definition given in this study – to give some indication of the way in which some clergy, from different denominations, drawn from the ranks of stipendiary and conventionally trained clergy, specifically sought out manual labour.

There was, for example, the Revd J. H. Richardson, from Crawley, who, following a challenge in a house group, went to work in a local transformer factory. When the works manager claimed that clergy 'didn't know what it was like to work on the shop floor', Richardson, the local team vicar, decided to prove him wrong.[676] The work force proved 'very friendly and used to come over and talk to me'. So did the works director, who asked Richardson (surprisingly, if he thought the clergyman not very 'worldly wise') how he might get people to work harder. Richardson suggested that he tried talking to them, perhaps even arriving for work at the same time as they did. Richardson's team rector supported this experiment, but that is all it remained, and though it would be repeated early the following year, there was no intention to make it permanent.

The Revd Peter Langford spent longer on a gas-works site in his parish.[677] Inspired by a visit to Westcott House by John Rowe, he spent part of his time, while a curate, at the Beckton gas works in East Ham, where he was employed as a stoker between October 1962 and March 1963, and all with the full support of his incumbent, John Derrett. At one point he was invited to join the WCG. But there is no record that he did, and, feeling there was too much to do in the parish, he abandoned the works, returning to full-time parish duties after six months. Nevertheless he thought the experience invaluable. Like others, he was aware of feelings of dissatisfaction with the church as it was, and was conscious of a gulf between the church and 'the mass of working people'.

> Those among whom I came to work reacted for the most part with great friendliness. I did not advertise myself as a parson, and it was a few days before I was found out . . .

In his short and concise account, his reasoning is almost identical with that of the WCG, and he hoped after his first six months that there might be an opportunity to do it all again. But no further experiments in industry ever took place.

The Daily Telegraph among other papers told the story of the Revd Antony Clements, who resigned as curate-in-charge of St Edmund's, Kings Lynn, 'because he was not allowed to continue what he called a "worker-priest" experiment'.[678] Mr Clements, the paper explained, had gone into nursery work to make closer contact with ordinary people by doing manual work. 'What profits he made were deducted from his stipend.' But then the bishop gave Clements the choice of either concentrating on the nursery work and resigning his parish, or returning to full-time parochial duties. Clements chose the former. In a remark that echoed the problems of John Strong a few years before in Harlington, Clements suggested that the bishop might not be the 'prime mover', implying, perhaps, that some parishioners were at odds with his chosen way of life.

By the early 1970s, stories of clergy who had decided to take up a 'working life' were still sufficiently novel to keep the press interested. A Bedfordshire newspaper had a headline: I'M BORED – VICAR BOB QUITS TO BE A WELDER. Tired of the trivialities of a village priest's job, the paper went on, Vicar Bob Torrens had decided to quit. Torrens was in fact in correspondence with John Rowe. At first there was the possibility of Torrens joining the WCG, and his name certainly appears on at least one occasion. Between 1973 and 1975 Torrens remained outside the territorial parish in the St Albans Diocese, and together with another NSM hoped to take charge of a church under Runcie. It never happened, and he would later return to the institutional church.

There was a highly significant representation from the Roman Catholic Church which met up with the WCG in the late 1960s. Father Stephen Innes of the Capuchin Fraternity in Erith in Kent has explained that it was on the initiative of Michael Butler (Fr Everard, OFMCap) and with the consent of his religious superiors that the Capuchins in England became involved in the worker-priest ministry in the autumn of 1966.

Michael Butler had visited worker-priests in France and had even worked with them in Paris and Nanterre. In England he found acceptance and enthusiastic encouragement from Derek Worlock, then Bishop of Portsmouth, to begin the worker experiment in his diocese. It was Easter 1967 when he first found work in the Portsmouth dockyard, earning £11/15/0 per 40-hour week as an unskilled labourer. In mid-October 1967 he was joined by Frank Hickman (Fr Leopold, OFMCap), a Capuchin confrère who quickly got himself a job locally assembling heaters and refrigerators. Feeling the need to support the venture further, another Capuchin confrère was permitted to join the experiment in January 1968; he was James Durkin (Fr Cuthbert, OFMCap).

For a short time the three-man fraternity thrived and all appeared to be secure until Michael Butler began to experience a crisis in his vocation. In December 1969, he was given three months leave of absence with a view to laicization, which was later effected. Despite the special pleading of the Bishop of Portsmouth, the two Capuchins were transferred to Lache, near Chester, in July 1970. They lived in a presbytery with the parish priest, Fr Michael [McIntyre] OFMCap, and found employment locally.

The two years at Lache appeared to be settled and successful ones. But a further move came in December 1972 when under the leadership of David Johnson (Fr Boniface, OFMCap), Jim and Frank transferred with him to Swallownest on the A57 between Sheffield and Worksop. Within a month, all were employed: David Johnson as RE teacher at St Paul's

School, Frank Hickman as an 'inspector' at Woodhead Components, and James Durkin as a fitter's mate at Browne Bailey Steelworks – later he fulfilled his ambition and became a miner on the coal-face at Treeton Colliery. Whilst the employment aspect was strong throughout, sadly the investment in fraternity so faded that it was virtually non-existent. David Johnson asked for leave of absence in May 1975 and this put the experiment once again back to two men. In effect, this proved to be a death-blow and the experiment was closed down on 15 August 1975, Frank returning to a friary in Chester and James to Pantasaph. The Capuchin worker-priest experiment had failed, but lessons had been learned by all parties concerned.

Records show, then, that in the early stages Michael Butler had not only worked on the continent with the French worker priests, but in 1967 in Portsmouth had made contact with Ken Ramsay. He joined in several of the Worker Church Group meetings, and his name appears in some of the recorded notes alongside Frank Hickman, who joined him later. Michael Gedge had advocated a worker-priest ministry in his *Universe* article, and though there are few accounts of worker-priests developing among Roman Catholics, the Franciscan experiment is of considerable importance. Together with the Little Brothers of Jesus from Leeds, whose names appear in the records of the WCG in the early 1970s, their full participation in WCG meetings demonstrates the inclusion of Roman Catholics in the overall worker-priest enterprise, and the rather astonishing breadth of ecumenism that had developed among those who had chosen this way of life.

In Scotland, where the Iona community had long had an interest in industrial mission, and from where George McLeod had set off to visit Ted Wickham's Sheffield experiments, there were a number of interested clergy in both the established Church of Scotland and the Scottish Episcopal Church. Andrew Parker read theology at Edinburgh University and was ordained as an assistant minister of the Church of Scotland. In 1968 he went to work in France with the French Protestant Industrial Mission, earning his living first as a builder's labourer and then as a semi-skilled factory worker. In 1973 he was expelled from France (an expulsion later quashed) in consequence of his community activities arising out of this joining of theology and the world of work. He returned to Glasgow, where between 1973 and 1981 he worked as a hospital driver while active in community politics on the large housing estate where he lived. In London from 1981, he has been a porter at St Pancras Hospital. He has always wanted to understand the Bible form the point of view of people at the bottom of society. In the 1980s he joined up with the Worker Church Group before it became the Shop Floor Association. While in Glasgow he produced cartoon books on the parables of Jesus and latterly has been the author of *Painfully Clear – The Parables of Jesus* (Sheffield Academic Press 1996).

An Anglican priest, the Revd John Halsey, represents an important departure from those who simply 'opted out'. From the beginning of his ministry in the north, Halsey endorsed the need of the church to engage directly with the working class. Halsey – originally from a landed family – had been educated at Magdalene College, Cambridge, and Westcott House, and had begun his ministry in Sheffield with some training under Roland Walls. Walls had returned to Scotland to serve in the Episcopal Church and lecture in theology at the University of Edinburgh and the theological college, Coates Hall. He also led the setting up of an entirely new community which drew some of its inspiration from the Little Brothers of Jesus, and from what Walls describes as 'kingdom theology' '. . . around silence, solitude, but also an open house with hospitality and a "no label" humanity'. Walls found the ideal building for his community house – an old village library – in Roslin village just outside Edinburgh. Halsey joined Walls in 1965 and, together with the Revd Robert Haslam, began a community life.

Halsey, in a little ecumenical venture with the Church of Scotland, joined the team of George Wilkie in an industrial mission that took him to the railway yards at Haymarket on the western side of Edinburgh.[679] Unsure of his role at first, Halsey simply employed the 'Wickham' approach he knew from his days in Sheffield: 'we would wander around the railway yard talking to the men'. Later, and again under Wilkie, Halsey moved to the local coal pit near the community house at Roslin.

Although Wilkie had arranged everything with management, there was some mutual uncertainty about Halsey's role and he found himself facing a puzzled manager, Mr Hastie, when they both 'put their cards on the table'. The manager took him underground, Halsey suspected, in a deliberate attempt to put him off working there. But Halsey was not easily deterred and soon found out that some jobs lent themselves to the 'Wickham approach' more than others. Mining was not one of them. Men could not be interrupted underground, and the same kind of 'snap breaks' did not take place. Later, and after underground training (which was essential anyway just to make visits), Halsey effectively became a worker-priest, as he took a job underground, coming amongst the men at the 'level of humanity . . . basically that's what it was all about'.

Later, in 1969, when the pit had closed, Halsey began a spell of community work with the Cyrenians, before beginning his longest period in industry when he started work for an accident and repairs vehicle workshop originally run, he found, on 'Dickensian' lines. At the pit Halsey had been an active member of the NUM, and when in his new workplace he asked at one of his first tea breaks, '. . . if there was a union', the atmosphere, he remembers, could be cut with a knife. There had indeed been disastrous attempts to introduce a union, but it had been poorly supported by the workers, and virtually 'outlawed' by the management. But under Halsey's encouragement, union membership was achieved. The first shop steward, perhaps unwillingly, began the task of general negotiation, but he had no experience of procedures, let alone negotiation, and facing the management proved difficult. After a dispute over rates, the shop steward, on the advice of the union, withdrew an agreement to do overtime and was promptly sacked. The atmosphere in the shop reached its lowest ebb and Halsey himself was made shop steward. Beginning slowly to 'learn the rules', he attempted to negotiate on behalf of a sometimes lethargic workforce with a suspicious management. The shop-steward's job, as John Rowe and Martyn Grubb had found out before, could prove something of a thankless task. Men handed over their union 'subs' reluctantly, wondering what the TGWU was doing for them, though Halsey believed that in the end, membership proved more successful than many of them had appreciated. Management and men gradually came to learn the importance of negotiation, and Halsey was able to settle some disputes and keep tempers cool.

Working as a semi-skilled labourer, Halsey prepared vehicle body work for painting by cleaning, masking and priming. The skilled men mixed the paint and undertook the actual spraying. Throughout the Thatcher years Halsey saw the powers of the union gradually eroded, though the establishment and limited recognition of the union in his own workshop was a milestone in improved relationships. It was all very different from the pit, where union membership and general solidarity gave a traditional cohesion.

Not quite as far north was Tony Bell, who had originally studied at King's College, London, and St Augustine's, Canterbury, where Kenneth Mason was sub-warden.[680] After an initial curacy in County Durham, and because of personal difficulties, Bell, in 1975, 'opted out' of parish ministry and took a job as a fork-lift driver with a local Lyons tea depot, where a job 'for a fortnight' turned into more than seven years. At first, he admits, he thought he was 'the only one' doing such a thing, and had forgotten that while a student in Canterbury he had met John Rowe, who came to talk to students. After a while he wrote to Tony Williamson and was eventually invited to join the WCG, where he remained loyal until its structure changed in the early 1980s and he returned to stipendiary ministry. Understanding for his role as a worker-priest was not always forthcoming from stipendiary clergy to whom he was 'attached' for Sunday duty, and at least one incumbent could not grasp what Bell was doing, reminding him that people needed to 'look up' to a priest, and that they 'didn't want one working alongside them'.

A member of the GMB Union, Bell admitted that the experience helped to shape his theology more than any theological training, as he took his industrial experience into the church. Suspected at times of being a management spy, and repeatedly being reminded or simply aware he was over-qualified, Bell stuck it out, winning the respect and friendship of his work mates that lasted long after he left.

In 1979, Richard Syms' *Working Like the Rest of Us* was published.[681] It should be noted that in the context of this study Syms is different, because he wished to work in the theatre. It may be a little difficult to 'place' an actor among the working class – but what Syms says remains important. The title was a quotation from his local butcher, who made the remark that that was what Syms would now be doing when he heard Syms was giving up his job as a vicar and going to work in the theatre. It is a blunt little book, presented in a popular style, and it hit hard. In an early chapter, 'A Bunch of Last Straws', Syms reveals all the frustrations of community pettiness towards a clergyman. He recounts instances and issues which tended to blacken his name locally, adding:

> We are not interested in people. We are interested in principles, in services, in buildings, in having an good unruffled influence.[682]

He came to believe that the world knew more about caring than the church had ever done: he saw regular churchgoers as the 'sickest people in society', and clergy as 'the saddest professionals'. He was also able to draw attention to something then and since largely ignored, that the radical 1960s theology was effectively rejected by the established church.

> The names of Bultmann and Bonhoeffer and Tillich are not breathed in respectable church circles. Not because their theology is doubted, but because there is little theology of the organized church.[683]

In a passage that worker-priests would have warmed to, he talks of the 'blasphemy of the incarnation', of Jesus as an 'embarrassment', where the world is good and loved by God. 'We do not need to protect ourselves against it, we need rather to enter it.' And when it came to 'entering', Syms was not for the use of what he described as 'fraudulent ministries' like chaplaincies; he meant theatrical chaplaincies, but he implied them all.

Marcus McCausland might be described as a 'late-starter' worker-priest. After training at Mirfield and ordination in 1959, he served a curacy in Birmingham. He followed this by working in four parish churches in the Hereford diocese, but began to feel that the church had never really made 'contact' with the shop floor. After initiating a correspondence on such themes in the *Church Times*, McCausland decided that he wanted to remain a priest while earning his own living. He was aware of stories of worker-priests, found himself being encouraged by John Vincent and the Sheffield Urban Theology Unit, and in the early 1980s began a 'TOPS' course as a heavy goods vehicle mechanic – and all this in his early fifties. In 1983 he started work with a Citroën garage in London, eventually going north to Shropshire where he began working independently as Rev Up, a mobile car mechanic, concentrating on Citroën vehicles. In about 1984 McCausland, 'enrolled' by John Rowe, met up with the Worker Church Group members who had changed their name to The Shop Floor Association. Here he renewed acquaintance with John Halsey, whom he already knew. McCausland didn't feel there was much in the SFA at that time to hold him, though he remained interested in that and the Sheffield Urban Theology Unit, and at the time of writing has remained an 'independent' worker-priest, always welcome in the parish church, and always much impressed by those who have gone before him.

While such individual stories interested the press, they were usually about stipendiary clergy, traditionally trained, who, for a time, had decided to 'opt out' of the institutional church and move into working-class jobs. There may have been others who left the church for good, and found fulfilment in living in that 'other world' outside the ecclesiastical institution. A number of attempts to locate others who may have been worker-priests, for this study, have proved difficult,[684] but McCausland believes many may have given up on an institution which has never really endorsed worker-priests, and, it must be said, rather like some of the French, have simply 'disappeared'.

While the Sheffield Mission, Iona, the Roslin Community, the WCG and the RC Franciscan worker-priests and other industrial missions across the country all helped open up ecumenical dimensions in the early 1960s, there were a few individuals from other Christian denominations who began to experiment individually with secular employment. For example, in an early and what he believed was an isolated case, the Revd David Goodall, of the Congregational Church in England, trained for the ministry in the late 1940s before beginning work as a milkman. At Brill in Oxfordshire he bought up a milk round and, together with a partner, between 1951 and 1957 carried on the daily task of local delivery because he was 'driven to it';[685] there was little money for a free-church parish minister. Goodall only later became aware of the French worker-priests; they were not a direct influence, and though after a few years he returned to full-time ministry he found his days as a milkman 'something positive', if 'very hard work'.

The Revd Barry Parker was a Congregationalist minister, and a part of the Sheffield Mission in 1961–66.[686] On Michael Jackson's change of heart Parker had been one of those given notice to quit. Parker eventually left Sheffield, and – somewhat disillusioned – left the church at the same time. In 1966 he began work as a motor industry training officer at Linwood in Renfrewshire, and later took to bus driving. After twenty-five years he eventually returned to industrial mission as a United Reformed Church minister.

One of the most celebrated working ministers outside the Church of England was a Methodist, Jack Burton. He had been a full-time minister in Glasgow, who had moved back to his native Norwich to work as a bus driver in 1968, and by 1976 had published an engaging volume *Transport of Delight*.[687] Burton explains that it was after '. . . a tremendous battle, I was given reluctant permission by the church . . . to serve in this dual capacity'(minister and bus driver). First, however, he found himself and his family homeless, helped by an elderly couple. Like the worker-priests of the Church of England, Burton had 'come down' to a position where he was economically dependent on his own labour, 'exposed to the influences and situations that might overwhelm me. I have not escaped unscathed.'

Burton's book is a one-year diary in which he recounts blow by blow all the human thoughts, encounters, events and jokes which came his way day by day, while driving his bus, and while he was based 'in an ecumenical gesture at an Anglican church', where by all accounts he was perfectly at home.

> I have attempted to outline my daily routine as a 'worker-priest', hoping that some may understand better why it is I have found greater fulfilment in my present unorthodox role (combining the sacred ministry with bus driving), than the traditional pattern of ministry which I have abandoned.[688]

The diary begins in September 1974. No event, no incident, no part of the landscape is missed, as Burton reflects on people and places, and the wonder of the created order, in his delightfully engaging style in which he reflects on everything in life from experimental sex in air-raid shelters to the hilarious working life among bus drivers and conductors. He was particularly active in union affairs, and for two years was branch chairman, personally responsible for calling a one-day strike over the issue of deteriorating working conditions with at least one of the meetings held in his church vestry.

Yet Burton admits to a sense of 'failure'. 'To my immense disappointment I have not persuaded one person regularly to attend divine service. But I have discovered what I long suspected – that it doesn't matter very much.' In his introduction Burton had commented that modern Christians were divided between those who set the church against the world as a guardian and witness to truth, and others who saw that the church is a leaven in the world 'properly active in all human concerns . . .'[689] In the last words of his book he reflects on that same theme

> We say that the world needs the church and its gospel. I believe that it is equally true that the church needs the world. If we are content that our religion be a hobby and the church a club, then we shall decay in an isolated byway while the life of the world rushes past untouched and unredeemed. But the moment we venture deliberately into the world, eager to provide a Christian presence and willing for the gospel to be made flesh in us, our religion springs instantly to life because we are thrown back upon the Holy Spirit. Away from church premises and practices and regulations, we tread new ground. The doctrines at the centre of our faith – the cross and the atonement, the kingdom, the new birth, the Holy Spirit, the means of grace – all are thrown into clear focus and assume new vitality. In the context of the world, faced by the forces of evil and the needs of men and women, our religion comes into its own. None of this should surprise us, for is not ours the religion of the God who left the skies because he cared for the world, who left the quietness of temple and countryside to be with the masses . . .'[690]

5. Twilight years and the costs of commitment

(i) Ministerial pluralism

As the 1970s moved into the 1980s, what might be described as ministerial pluralism became evident among the British churches. Within the Church of England and the Scottish Episcopal Church the extension of non-stipendiary ministry continued in earnest, especially since the *Welsby Report* of 1968, and the Church Assembly's endorsement of that the following year. The free churches' experiences with forms of lay or non-stipendiary ministries – no necessary solution to a declining full-time ministry – were not always heeded.[691] The Roman Catholic Church introduced its permanent diaconate; men from ordinary walks of life received training after which they took on a new liturgical and pastoral role. Within the Church of England by the beginning of the 1970s, a variety of ministries had emerged, and may be delineated as follows:

(i) There was an 'original' group of worker-priests, 'priests turned workers' episcopally licensed, but in keeping with French worker-priests wholly committed to a working-class milieu. Their story had begun in the late 1940s and early 1950s.

(ii) There were priests in secular middle-class and professional employment; some, though licensed to a parish, specifically sought to focus their ministry at work. They would eventually become known as Ministers in Secular Employment.

(iii) There were others who, though engaged in secular middle-class and professional employment, focussed their attention on the territorial parish, sometimes known after the Welsby Report (1968), as Auxiliary Parochial Ministers (APM). They might also, however, declare some ministry at work.

(iv) There was a growing number of clergy from the 1960s on who 'forsook' (to use Lloyd's term) the territorial parish and had effectively become worker-priests in the sense that they took on manual labour. Others took to teaching, social and administrative jobs. Many had 'had enough' of the institutional church, and their abandonment of the institution, sometimes temporary, can be seen as a form of protest.

(v) There also evolved a new category: Local Non-Stipendiary Ministers, who, with the support of their local territorial parish, i.e. their own congregation, were trained within their diocese to serve their own parish. The pioneer here was the Lincoln diocese (1978), but other dioceses followed, and while there was often ambiguity about a role sometimes indistinguishable from NSM generally, it was easy for cynics to claim that this time it really was 'clergy on the cheap'.

(vi) Last but not least, there were, as there had always been, forms of 'secular' ministry in universities, schools, hospitals, forces and industrial settings. This growing 'sector ministry' of 'chaplaincies', sometimes stipendiary, that is, paid for by the church, but sometimes employed by institutions themselves, meant that there were clergy who saw themselves, with some justification, as having a 'ministry at work'.

Local Non-Stipendiary Ministry, (v) above, despite its rather radical implications, especially in the form of the 'Ted Roberts scheme' in Stepney, which Vaughan has argued brought 'structural confusion' to the whole area of non-stipendiary ministry, turns out to be an endorsement of conservative ministry. The very reason the scheme was generally accepted after the Lincoln experiment of 1978 had been fully endorsed, 'a recipe for the confusion which persisted in the following years',[692] was that it endorsed the ministry in the parish, and especially in rural areas where there was a fear of parochial collapse. It was from the local parish that men (and later women) would be drawn, 'older candidates with lower educational background',[693] and where they would remain.

For a time, (iii) above came into regular use in some areas. In the Oxford diocese, for example, an edition of the Diocesan Magazine for September 1975 devoted space in an attempt to clarify precisely what was involved in these 'new' ministries. In an introduction to a number of stories, it was made clear that:

> Auxiliary Pastoral Ministers are not exactly identical with worker-priests . . . the APM earns no stipend from the church; he follows his secular employment, and he is licensed by the Bishop to officiate as a deacon or priest in a particular parish or deanery . . .

but then it did add that for some:

> . . . the APMs will find their ministry in places the parish clergy normally do not penetrate.

Which might have begged the question: if some had a ministry in their place of work – which was implied – what kind of ministry was being exercised in the parish?

Up to and beyond the early 1970s, however, there was a lack of consensus about the nature and function of non-stipendiary ministry generally, save perhaps one common denominator: that a majority of bishops endorsed the new ministry which was already saving money, and presumably helping to save the territorial parish at the same time. Vaughan explains how in the early 1980s Mark Hodge, a professional social-science researcher, was commissioned by ACCM to undertake a survey to examine how NSM was functioning, with a view to changing regulations. In many areas Hodge saw confusion: at the point of selection, in the training schemes, and in a range of differing diocesan regulations. Interestingly for this study, Hodges found that the vast majority of non-stipendiary clergy were drawn from non-manual groups, 'teachers, members of the professions, managers . . .' and others. Indeed the largest group of his sample came from educational occupations, with only 4% from social categories III (M), IV and V. In short, there was very little representation indeed from the working-class, and Vaughan could conclude that 'the incidence of vocations to NSM may do no more than mirror the social categories of the male membership of the Church of England'.

The unpublished Report of 1972 which had looked at the role of Ministers in Secular Employment had been, perhaps, the one chance for a thoroughgoing discussion to commence on some of the principles on which the first worker-priests had embarked on their vocations back in the 1950s. If this was the nearest thing the Church of England ever got to seriously looking at worker-priests, it was too little and certainly too late. The evolution of non-stipendiary ministry essentially as a support for the territorial parish gave scant regard to any idea of 'ministry at work' either for worker-priests or those in 'higher' occupations. The truth was, that the Church of England, despite its apparent concern for 'mission' and its occasional forays into the 'sector ministry' of hospitals, schools or other institutions, could see no other way of the church being the church except in the context of territorial parochialism – something Ted Wickham had always known.

A variety of attempts were made to draw some of these disparate groups together. Ministers in Secular Employment, for example, many of them schoolmasters, came together for a Conference at the William Temple College beginning in October 1968, convened by Michael S. Allen of Birmingham and Len Tyler, Principal of the William Temple College. There were some seventy-seven individuals in correspondence about this first conference and twenty-three eventually attended. These conferences continued for several years, with David Wilson from the SOC priest worker chapter visiting and speaking.

In 1984 the first National Conference of Ministers in Secular Employment took place in Nottingham, under Bishop Kenneth Woollcombe,[694] the first bishop appointed to 'oversee' ministers in secular employment. Under the auspices of Michael Ranken, one of the results was the founding of a *Newsletter Among Ministers at Work*, which continues to be published, and serves in some respects as the only channel for discussion on 'working ministries'. Ranken, in an ACCM Publication, made a most valued contribution to writing on non-stipendiary ministry, including a helpful introduction to the French worker-priests, and drew the important distinction between the French and British early worker-priests on the one hand, and non-stipendiary ministry on the other.[695] The *Newsletter*'s general articles, however, have been judged by one commentator with an interest in non-stipendiary ministries, Jim Francis, of Sunderland University, as 'weak and anecdotal' when compared with the writing of the French worker-priests.[696]

Given such a variety of roles, and the slow but evolving 'history' of modern ministry now under analysis, claims and counter-claims were made for the origin, inspiration and theological foundations of these various ministries, especially where they involved a ministry-at-work. Apart from substantial studies being prepared by Patrick Vaughan and others, books, articles, letters and reports emerged attempting to pinpoint the true theological or historical origins of anything that was not stipendiary parochial ministry. Sometimes it was St Paul, sometimes Thomas Arnold or Roland Allen; more often than not the story of the French worker-priests was also appropriated to give a kind of authority or authenticity to new experiments.

Two things were clear. On the one hand, the established Church of England and other Anglican Churches in Britain had firmly endorsed a range of non-stipendiary ministries, though it has to be said generally in support of the territorial parish[697] and under the control of a diocesan bishop; for 'loose cannons' were always discouraged. On the other hand, initiatives following that early call by Michael Jackson and Stanley Booth Clibborn that clergy might be directly engaged with industrial society either as worker-priests or industrial chaplains were already slipping away. Vaughan comments that by the end of the 1970s, 'it was becoming increasingly clear that the churches had set their faces against any real "radical change" of almost any sort',[698] and Towler and Coxon admitted that some of the 1960s 'flush' had gone and that in the short term at least, conservatives reacting to earlier radicalism would win the day.[699] Throughout the 1960s and 1970s, individuals from a variety of ordination courses, or very occasionally from stipendiary ministries, would visit the WCG; very few ever stayed and became full 'members'. Many found the WCG's original commitment to the working-class too difficult to follow or now inappropriate, as the 'affluent worker' emerged in Britain,[700] and the group's social and political ideology was too much to take. After attending one or two conferences, most newcomers simply voted with their feet.

If the 'original' worker-priests ever felt left behind or snubbed by a growing number who favoured ministries in middle-class or professional secular employment, generally divorced from working-class life or any kind of politicization, they rarely showed it. As early as 1962 John Rowe had suggested in the opening of the *Rejoinder* that people should not confuse MSE's (as they would later become known) with the Worker Church Group's '. . . vocation to share the working-class life'.[701] But the *Rejoinder*, although it received a response in the church press, was soon forgotten, and any argument for the church being alongside men and women in some of the most lowly occupations was simply forgotten with it. There was little hope even by the mid 1960s that what the WCG had tried to stand for would ever be taken seriously by the institution, as the clamour for new ministries, including the ordination of women, new liturgy, human sexuality, and new synodical structures, began to drown earlier voices that had called for risky engagement with the very industrial society in which men and women lived and earned a living. One might hear little enough about worker-priests, now largely ignored, while the Sheffield Industrial Mission on which much hope had been placed would sometimes be dubbed as a 'failure'. Even auxiliary movements like Sheffield's Urban Theology Unit, which took most seriously the theological dimension in modern society, found itself often marginalized. It would not be enough to argue that 'society was changing', or in the 1980s that the West had already entered a post-industrial age, and worker-priests or movements like the UTU in Sheffield were therefore superfluous. The men and women who had laboured in the factories and mines of Britain did not 'disappear' as Britain's manufacturing base headed for demolition under Margaret Thatcher. Rather, they joined the ranks of unemployed, and in France, and occasionally Britain, worker-priests joined them too. Tony Williamson was well aware of changing practices and shrinkage in the car industry, John Halsey of the erosion of union power. More than any other groups, both the worker-priests and the clergy of industrial mission had much to contribute to understanding as they literally lived through those changes. It mattered not. Since neither worker-priests nor industrial chaplains could be seen to encourage growth in the pews of city, town or village, both were side-stepped as the institution continually moved on to 'achievable agendas'.

(ii) Ted Wickham – new protagonist

ACCM had, with a range of differing ministries evolving, decided on its study paper on *Ministry in Secular Employment.* Evidence was taken from a variety of sources, including members of the priest-worker chapter in Southwark, and the Worker Church Group itself. The deeper the paper went into ministry at work, the more was the evidence of an estranged world, yet the less it seemed to have to do with the institution's understanding of ministry and the nature of the church. A difference in ecclesiology was clearly a key to understanding, but precisely what that ecclesiology was, no one was yet sure. Despite the breadth of work, the paper was never made public. Yet the first worker-priests were not entirely forgotten, and in 1973, Bishop Ted Wickham, their former critic, suddenly began to sound like a protagonist. His comments deserve consideration.

These first appear as an end-piece to ACCM's paper, but since that was never published, Wickham's section was later published in another form as one of the *Audenshaw Papers* (February 1973). Wickham launched forth on the subject of the development of ministry in secular employment, and its significance for the mission of the church, using two 'benchmarks'. He categorized ministers in secular employment as entering either in 'strength' or in 'weakness'. The first he applied to clergy who had moved into secular occupations deliberately as a vocation to mission, the second to those who simply 'found themselves in a lay job' without any particularly missionary motivation were there 'in weakness'. Thus the French worker-priests could be described as those who had gone 'in strength'. Wickham then admits that once he had favoured industrial chaplains over worker-priests, whom he had seen as 'unnecessarily dramatic' . . . 'a kind of left-wing infantilism'. But now, suddenly, Wickham changes tune; '. . . there was more to it than that'. Indeed there was. More than a decade on, the first worker-priests had demonstrated a remarkable commitment to the working-class milieu, and Wickham was now forced to admit that the original consensus about being alongside working people – if indeed it ever really existed – either as industrial chaplains or workers-priests had been lost by the church at large. He had argued not only for active industrial chaplains but for a 'catalytic laity'; but it had not 'worked', and he went on to describe existing industrial mission as merely a 'token', and, because he continued later, church leadership '. . . becomes increasingly pre-occupied with the tasks of maintenance . . .' In a damning criticism of the status quo, Wickham argued that few Ministers in Secular Employment became 'genuine worker-priests, manual workers, engineers and factory workers. They are more likely to teach liberal studies in technical colleges . . .'

> Suffice it here to say that if the case for priests in secular employment 'in strength' is conceded for the mission task, it should refer *par excellence* to priest-workers. Granted all the transmutation of the working-class since the war, manual workers, industrial workers had remained the largest single social group most estranged from the Church. This at least we should learn from the *prêtres ouvriers* of France.[702]

That Wickham was not fooled by every argument thrown up for the adopted term non-stipendiary clergy, believing rather that 'economic necessity could be a compelling factor . . .' could have gone without saying. He drew attention to the Lambeth Resolution of 1968 (No.32), calling for 'a wider ordained ministry', and No.33, reaffirming the 1958 Resolution that there was 'no theological principle which forbade a suitable man from being ordained priest while continuing his lay occupation . . .',[703] but went on to argue that 'to deal with the issues raised by priests in secular employment, by implication they must support the idea without appraising it'.

'It is,' Wickham was forced to admit, 'a very confusing picture', and he finally conceded:

> . . . it looks as though the handful of genuine worker-priests, work-orientated in their ministry whatever their motivation and objectives, are likely to find themselves a very isolated group, swamped by the larger number of ordained men in secular employment who are auxiliary parochial ministers.

For all his earlier criticism, it was as if Wickham now felt acute sympathy for a group that had lived out its vocation in the context of an institution '. . . orientated toward the traditional parochial structures of the church', and where the aim of promoting priests in secular employment was essentially to 'secure ancillary parochial help in the face of shortage of clergy and money'. The plans for varieties of non-stipendiary ministries, he suggested, could really be seen as answers to questions about shortages. But were questions ever openly addressed? Questioning selection and training, Wickham argued that the whole subject was 'fraught with confusion' . . . 'zeal without knowledge', even at the highest levels of the church. Wickham longed for a movement in the church that faced the realities of a changing world, of developing a 'counter-society' which might enter once again into the 'secular world'. 'It is *this* (he concluded) we should be about, not priests in secular employment as a separate issue.'

Although he could not have known it, Wickham may have been effectively describing what the WCG had tried to be. By the early 1980s, while new non-stipendiary ministers came and went, the WCG, now rather few in number, suddenly found itself coming to a kind of end.

(iii) The end of the Worker Church Group

In the late 1970s John Halsey, together with a handful of others from Scotland and the north, met up with the WCG. Among the others were a young laywoman then working in Newcastle; John Miller, a Church of Scotland minister working in one of Glasgow's worst housing estates; and a committed and radicalized minister, Andrew Parker. This northern cohort, which had been meeting to share their experience of life among the working-class, some now rapidly becoming an under-class, began meeting with the WCG. Was a remarkable feature of the newcomers that they demonstrated a commitment to mission 'in the world' at a level which other newcomers, especially NSMs, for a whole decade before were quite unable to bring to the WCG? Among the newcomers, and of particular interest, were two Little Brothers of Jesus from Leeds, Guy Jarrosson and Xavier Chevillard, themselves French, who had been resident in a Leeds back street since as early as the 1960s. They had been noted at their first address by Geoffrey Moorhouse in his exploration of the monastic life. They were members of the very community which in the post-war years sided with the worker-priests in France, whose own commitment to industrial society and the poor in Western industrialized Europe had been one of the original inspirations for the community in Scotland of which Roland Walls and John Halsey were members.

Perhaps for the first time in over twenty years, the WCG had radicalized new blood and something of a new direction. The names of many of those recorded as being a part of this new body are shown in Appendix 1. At Ilkley in Yorkshire in 1982 the WCG changed its name to The Shop Floor Association, apparently emphasizing its continued commitment to men and women who remained in industry and in low status. Its constitution, shown in full in Appendix 5, included the following profession:

> We are followers of Jesus Christ who seek to live by and express our faith at the level of work on the shop floor or at home or in enforced unemployment.[704]

But within this newly formed group is it possible to see the seeds of its own destruction? Can it be argued that some of the radicalized newcomers succeeded in taking the WCG forward in a logical but radical direction, though that logic was sometimes lost to some? If the WCG had committed themselves – as Wickham had appreciated – to a class still low in status, that meant meeting that class wherever it was, now in the late 1970s and early 1980s on the run-down housing estates, among the unemployed, among the poor and disaffected, among the socially excluded. This much the newcomers understood.

In time, heated discussions on the nature of 'presence' in the work place, the case for liberation of the oppressed against a capitalist society, now with Margaret Thatcher at the helm, was sufficient to make meetings come alive. But John Strong was already unhappy about this 'socialist political involvement' and added in a paper of comments they shared in the very early 1980s that it was '. . . a knife edge on which we have to walk because we believe that socialist politics are more in keeping with the Gospel than other varieties'.

As the Worker Church Group had done earlier, the association went to work on a further statement, this time entitled a Manifesto, that spoke out for the poor and dispossessed of Britain (Appendix 6). It is easy to treat these aspirations as shouting in the wind at the time when left wing-politics and the Labour party were in disarray. The new association argued over a number of points, theological and ideological, including what was to happen when, because of widely different theological positions – traditional to neo-atheist – they felt they could not share the eucharist together. Perhaps it was a sign that the end of this association was near; though it came after nearly a decade.

It is not possible in the space remaining to give a full and adequate account of a new and very different association where significant differences of opinion still remain at the time of writing. The preceding impressions, gleaned from oral recollections and limited documentary material, must not be taken as a historical summery of this Association, let alone an attempt at analysis.[705] Suffice it to say that the WCG itself had lasted about twenty-five years when it came to an end. The 1990s were to find some of the worker-priests further radicalized. John Rowe resigned his licence, others went their way independently, but many were still committed to the world of work. In a sense it mirrored what was happening to the worker-priests in France where some of the original number felt dispossessed by the church. There were those who got married, others who went off to live among the unemployed, agitating for poor and immigrants; some left the church altogether, became atheist or agnostic, feeling the weight of an oppressive post-Vatican II church led by a conservative papacy and curia.

(iv) The first worker-priests – 'presence and failure'?

This study has essentially been an outline of Britain's first little group of worker-priests, their wives and lay associates, who resolved to live and earn a living alongside Britain's post-war working-class. And it takes the view that only priests engaged in manual labour and on a shop floor should be granted the title worker-priests. But worker-priests are modest men, and among them will be those who, with justification, may simply argue that such deliberate and precise definitions hardly matter. But the prefix 'first' is quite deliberate. There is no question that others followed who wished to style themselves 'worker-priests' or 'priest-workers' and who, like the first few, deliberately entered manual labour. And it must also be added that out of successful courses that followed SOC there has always been a committed body of MSEs who have understood themselves to have a ministry at work, and articulate that through their Newsletter. But when it comes to priests in manual labour, very few will have done so (like MSEs) in the context of official diocesan experiments. Most have simply abandoned parish work, even the institution, and are now generally unknown. Few enough joined the ranks of the Worker Church Group or its successor.

Consistently, however, two views emerge from this study. First, for Britain's first worker-priests and the wives and laity who sided with them in the Worker Church Group, this life was about making a commitment, living out a vocation to share the lives of ordinary working-class men and women in a post-war industrial society. Secondly, there was the view sometimes held by non-stipendiary ministers, that the life of a 'worker-priest' was essentially about remaining in ministry and priesthood, while 'earning your own living' in any secular job, albeit alongside other men and women. There have been relatively few anyway who have wished to style themselves Ministers in Secular Employment, when so many non-stipendiary clergy have seen the main focus on their ministry in the territorial parish. Whether you called yourself a worker-priest or not, may, as John Rowe has generously suggested, be 'splitting hairs',[706] but, as the documentary evidence demonstrates, there has undoubtedly been a world of difference between the two perspectives of those engaged in ministry in middle-class and professional secular employment from the mid-1960s, and those who up to a decade before had, like the French, committed themselves to the working class milieu and who would continue to do so up to the 1980s and 1990s.

Those who remained in the WCG and saw it develop into the SFA lived through the changes in the world of industry, and came to know at first hand some of the costs of a changing political scene at the beginning of the 1980s. Being committed to the working-class world, however, was still something of a stepping down, as others have suggested, into an alien world. The first working priests and working laity of the WCG were not working-class themselves and, as John Rowe admits, 'never became working-class'. Yet in them, as in France, an attempt had been made by some churchmen and women lay and ordained to engage directly with that world as a lifelong vocation. There was still an underlying sense of mission, not to make immediate converts, but simply to be alongside men and women on the shop-floor, so that forty years on, a non-churchgoing ex-miner could still sense Jesus Christ, present in the life of one of Britain's first worker-priests.

And was the WCG also about 'failure'? The original group never succeeded in 'taking off' in any measurable way, but then they never pretended to be about success. Vaughan has argued that the Church of England had no mechanism in 1965 where it could have offered the kind of affirmation John Rowe was looking for in his *Rejoinder*. But this may have been because the Church of England simply chose not to do so. Rather, the WCG struggled to maintain a commitment against a sometimes rising tide of their own anxiety, frustration, even sometimes self-doubt. Yet a commitment it remained. It is also possible to argue that the more traditional training which the first worker-priests received, what Towler and Coxon have called 'closed training', with its community life and the substantial theological education (most were graduates, and frequently in theology), perhaps ironically stood them in far better stead for a 'stepping down' into a working-class world. Later non-stipendiary candidates, undertaking their part-time education and training while 'at work', and having to relate their working life to their theological studies, often seem in contrast to have been less inclined to take any interest in what is now called Ministry in Secular Employment. Few have seen a real ministry 'at work', while others have sought the means to escape secular work and move into stipendiary ministry as quickly as regulations allow. Moreover, as is currently the practice, some dioceses, especially at ordination services, have deliberately avoided even mentioning the fact that some candidates have any secular work and might recognize a ministry there. In other words, a candidate's 'title' is to the territorial parish. No other ministry seems to exist.

For the first worker-priests there was often an underlying 'high' doctrine of priesthood which most held. It was to Catholic clergy that even the Evangelicals went for advice and support, and it was more often from among Catholic parochial clergy that the worker-priest found grassroots support. 'I have a worker-priest; a real worker-priest,' said Father Kirkby to two enquiring students who visited his Bow Common church in the mid-1960s.[707]

If there was sometimes ambiguity about what they were doing – and Ken Ramsay would write a paper 'What Have We Got to Offer?' in 1968, in which he highlighted the fact they were not growing – those uncertainties were often made explicit at meetings or in individual correspondence. Some of this is particularly evident in that mid-1960s correspondence between John Rowe and Martyn Grubb, following the latter's decision to leave the WCG for a new job that took him off the shop-floor. At the time (1966) they both faced something of a dilemma. In writing to Grubb, Rowe had admitted that there were frustrations in their chosen life, especially when no 'pattern' seemed to emerge, though, argues Rowe, he had always possessed the strong feeling that Grubb himself might have felt he could 'break-through' to the working-class world by finding some '. . . magic key which would transform things'. Rowe admits to similar feelings himself, and confesses that the previous year 1965, there had been amongst them all a 'feeling of defeat'.

> What can and does happen is that we can become frustrated because no pattern seems to emerge which shows us the Kingdom in the making as a result of our loving. No circle grows around us which seems to prove we've found the 'answer' or even that we have a recognizable clue.[708]

Unknown to them, perhaps, Rowe and Grubb were not alone in facing the ambiguity of the situation. When Roland Walls had left the environs of Sheffield to seek out a community life, he had visited the Mission de France and asked Fr Vinatier how they knew when a man 'was ready' [to work in the industrial world], Vinatier had simply said 'When he's ready to fail'. It was a perspective now echoed by Rowe to Grubb:

> How much are you unconsciously hoping to 'succeed' in the new vocation when you have 'failed' in this one?

Rowe was conscious that what members of the WCG hoped to be about might often be difficult for members to maintain. Perhaps it was more a process than a single vocation, easily defined, measurable, and always understood.

> The church needs this witness but it is an even harder witness to maintain than initiate . . . Christianity must not only (be) represented but even understood within our own minds in radically new ways. Our experience in the world has taught us this much as anything we have read . . . our milieu is the common people and it is our contact with them which gives us an advantage. The gospel belongs to them 'before' it belongs to anyone else.[709]

Grubb's answer was a robust one, taking up all Rowe's points one by one. He felt genuinely moved to make a 'next step' and for him that meant taking on a new role in vital race-relations work, which had grown from the work place, and which would inevitably involve his departure from the shop-floor and WCG. For all that, it remains a warm letter between close and understanding friends, caught up in the ambiguities of life and vocation in an industrial society.

In 1976, Edward Norman, Dean of Peterhouse, Cambridge, and with the 'South Bank' and John Robinson in mind, was one of the severest critics of the 'radicalized' church of the 1960s. Norman argued that 'the radicalism of contemporary churchmen has reproduced all the vicarious qualities which have characterized progressive attitudes in the church throughout the preceding hundred years. It is a talking shop, where consciences are displayed, but very little actually happens.' The emphasis on ideas, on the analysis of social problems, Norman believed, made radicals 'incomprehensible to working-class people'. Thus this ecclesiastical radicalism had been little concerned 'with the redistribution of wealth, industrial relations or wage policies – issues which have formed the substance of working-class politics', so that the church's 'class presuppositions are more or less completely out of touch with working-class and lower-middle-class society'.[710] There is much truth in this: but none of it could be said of Britain's first worker-priests. As this study has demonstrated, they met, often head-on, some of the most significant cultural and social features of the post-war years which were outlined at the beginning of this study. And they did so in ways that parish clergy could not. They knew the difficulties and drudgeries of shop-floor life, they might encounter petty crime and delinquency, problems relating to family and marriage, abortion and divorce. They might witness at close hand the ugliness of racism. They sometimes knew the threat of redundancy, or experienced unemployment. They could suffer the high-handedness of management, experience the indifference and sometimes lack of comprehension on the part of workers. They knew about stoppages and strikes, union power and union weakness. They felt for men and women who had lowly jobs yet were never likely to rise from that, and they surely knew and understood the attractions of a consumer society, where gambling and beer, cinema and television, gave enjoyment and escapism from work. They also surely came to understand the often profound irrelevance of institutional religion to the men and women among whom they spent their day.

Would it anyway have been an institutional religion that they would have wished to commend? The institutional church by the late 1960s had shown little or no interest in the endeavours of WCG over the previous decade, though over the years notable churchmen and women continued to visit the Group at their invitation. But the Group itself would show little change over the next twenty to thirty years. The WCG, in evolving into the SFA, remained as it had always done, a small and relatively insignificant group, making little impact upon the greater institution that was the Church of England. Indeed, a visitor to the Southwark priest-workers' chapter admitted in a report that 'they (the Southwark priest-workers) were not like the French worker-priests', explorers in a totally alien culture, and added in parenthesis: 'there are hardly any priests in this country as yet working on the shop floor as labourers'.[711] It was true enough; individual members of the Worker Church Group made more impact, perhaps, upon the men and women with whom they worked, but from whom, it must be added, we hear so little. Theirs was a lonely commitment, often made in obscurity, but for them a commitment none the less. It was a commitment to maintain a vocation in the face of what often amounted to institutional indifference, that could sometimes be interpreted as hostility. While in the mid-1960s the Worker Church Group's members and visitors began to realize they might be going nowhere, those who stayed, or even many who left, nevertheless remained committed to the nature of that incarnational vocation, rooted, they believed, in the story of Jesus Christ.

> We determined to love *this* way and loving in *this* way was our vocation which we cherished in the face of opposition.[712]

Conclusion: The Presence and Place of the Worker-Priests

A committed presence and its costs

Even after their efforts were highlighted in *Crockford's Preface* 1961–62, the publication *Priests and Workers* (1962), the church press generally, or the *Rejoinder* (1965), Britain's first worker-priests and their Worker Church Group failed to take off as a movement. It was Edward Carpenter, at one of their conferences (1964), who had remarked that if they became larger or more organized, they might lose their 'cutting edge'. Indeed, had the WCG been more acceptable to the institutional church, and had it somehow been drawn into its formal structures, who is to say what it might have become?

But there was never any danger of that. Britain's first worker-priests in the context of the institutional church remained a tiny and marginalized body. While the institution appeared generally indifferent to engaging with working-class society directly, and certainly at a major institutional level, the worker-priests and their lay brothers and sisters remained committed, as a vocation, to siding with that class, utterly estranged, they believed, from that same institution. The main layman and founding member of the Group, Tom Walden, lasted over thirty years as a labourer; John Rowe and Tony Williamson both worked for up to thirty years on the shop floor; and John Strong lasted some fifteen years from miner in Eyethorne to car worker in Oxford. Ken Ramsay spent over ten years on the shop floor, and Martyn Grubb over fifteen years in factories, much of that before he was ordained. Moreover after his time in race relations, Grubb ended his working days in the tough world of minicab driving. Many of the wives also worked, and kept home in working class environments. In Scotland, John Halsey lasted over twenty-five years on shop floors. Several remained in their working-class areas: Martyn Grubb in Southall, John Rowe in the East End of London, Tony

Williamson in Oxford and John Halsey in the mining village where he had begun.

One feature rarely discussed in this study, not least because it would be very difficult to do so, is the possible cost that this way of life had upon worker-priests' wives and their children. The parsonage house in the 1950s could on occasions be close to a kind of poverty; it was little different in the worker's house before the affluence of the late 1950s changed life-styles. With children usually being educated locally, and life around them just as it came, the worker-priests, their families and friends embraced a life studiously avoided by some clergy even today. It is simply not possible to say what the true human cost has been.

A presence in the face of hostility

This was a commitment made in the face of an indifference that could sometimes be interpreted as hostility.The *Crockford's* preface of 1958 did not believe that the worker-priest experiment had much to contribute to industrial evangelization or that it was an unqualified success, and argued that the 'one published account of it in English circumstances (it does not say what account) is most depressing . . .' As we have seen, the institution's report *The Task of the Church in Relation to Industry* (1959) seemed totally oblivious to the existence of the worker-priests. As early as 1955, Simpkiss had found his bishop's attitude to secular employment one of 'total incomprehension'. John Strong, while a worker-priest, was also a totally committed parish priest. Yet it did not save him from a bishop determined to destroy what he had achieved in Harlington and his Luton factory, to the amazement of Strong's employers and non-churchgoing villagers. Martyn's Grubb's first interview with a bishop had the response that it simply 'couldn't be done'. Tony Williamson and John Rowe's bishops were always approving but exceptions, and when Leslie Paul at a press conference for his *Report* in 1962 showed enthusiasm for worker-priests, the then Bishop of Lincoln was reported as being 'hot under the collar' at the very suggestion. Tony Williamson received correspondence from a number of unhappy individuals. One, an ordinand at Lincoln Theological College who wanted to be a worker-priest, found his bishop wholly unsympathetic; another, a Welshman, found his archbishop openly antagonistic. It is easy to accuse the institution's bishops (apart from Mervyn Stockwood, Harry Carpenter and Joost de Blank, who individually gave considerable support) of being indifferent to the vocation of worker-priests. The fact was that the majority of Anglican clergy – from whose ranks the bishops were inevitably drawn – were deeply attached to the traditional ways of 'being a priest' and 'being the church' in city, town and country. The very idea of worker-priests, if it ever entered their heads, had little hope of institutional sympathy or support. Robin Greenwood in *Transforming Priesthood* (SPCK 1994) has commented that the Church of England attracts to its leadership those who 'prefer it as it is'; in the 1950s and 1960s most bishops preferred a church without worker-priests or other eccentrics (including eccentric bishops) to irritate it. The British Council of Churches' publication *The Church and Industry* (which Paul Bagshaw has called 'an accomplished example of ecumenical double-speak') made much of the French worker-priests but totally ignored the British, condemning those who 'go it alone'. Had the Church of England seen fit to give a measure of recognition as happened in France with the development of a non-territorial diocese and a worker-priests' own bishop, then a movement of some sort – albeit 'institutionally' weakened – might have developed.

But even this would be to miss the essential point. The majority of clergy in the middle-class Church of England held to a received institutional ecclesiology that supported the territorial parish. Few were interested in the idea of worker-priests, industrial mission or even working-class communities allowing an indigenous church to somehow 'emerge'. 'The church', no matter how middle-class or irrelevant it might seem to 'outsiders', already existed in the parish, and could not possibly 'exist' anywhere else. Had there been a stronger commitment to working-class life especially in the north, to industrial mission and Wickham's broader understanding of a church beyond the church; had there been more interest in the religious life among men, from which such priests were sometimes drawn, then the worker-priests might have found more allies, if not active supporters. Finally, Ted Wickham, who could have been encouraging had, early on, set himself against worker-priests, favouring industrial chaplains instead – and history remembers him for that, though he later had a change of heart. But then even Wickham and his ideas would fall from favour, and had he supported the worker-priests, his 'downfall', and that of his own missionary methods, would have done them no favours.

A favourite criticism – still heard – and usually couched as a question was: 'What did a worker-priest have to offer in the workplace that a layman did not?' The simple answer might be an understanding of human and pastoral problems, substantial theological comprehension and a human face for a distant institution whose clergy he represented. But the question can be put the other way: 'What did an ordained priest have to offer the parish?' If the answer was obviously some kind of 'leadership', a focus of the community's understanding and celebration, why should he not provide the same for those who might one day ask for it somewhere else? To suggest that the working world was the right place for laymen or -women only, and the parish for the parson, was to suggest divided worlds where the parish existed in some other exclusive dimension 'not of this world'.

An organized presence

The first worker-priests, wives and lay associates remained committed to their informal organization, the Worker Church Group. Though that group from 1957 up to its changed form in the 1980s was sometimes insular and lacking in consensus, it remained a forum for vigorous discussion and debate. It was to this gathering that bishops, leading academics and churchmen happily came, among them John Robinson, David Jenkins, Ted Wickham and Edward Carpenter. The group also invited others like Len Murray, who played a part in trade union affairs and the political and social life of the country. Above all, it met French and Belgian worker-priests (Appendix 8), and the records of some of its meetings comprise detailed accounts of attempts to analyse many of the issues then facing church and society in Europe.

But the organization might also be described as having hidden fissures. Because they represented catholics and evangelicals, its members often lacked a common mind on a range of concerns: the nature of the church, the territorial parish, presentation of the gospel, or the form their 'presence' might take among working people. Yet, perhaps rather than being fissures, these were positive strengths, as members engaged in discussion to make themselves understood to one another. Though a worker-priest, John Strong was as singularly vigorous in his defence of the parochial system as John Rowe was ambivalent. Strong ended his days in a trio of country parishes, physically worn out by manual labour, John Rowe by resigning his orders, uncertain what had been achieved, but still committed to living in a working-class area, to the gospel and its interpretation. Martyn Grubb, whose faith had always been rooted in Jesus first, before any kind of institutional religion, asked to be released from his ordination vows and, leaving the Church of England behind, found a home among the Quakers; his growing understanding of other cultures and creeds led him to work for greater unity amongst all races, though, as we saw, he ended his working days as a minicab driver, back perhaps among working people where he had begun. Yet all members of the WCG held each other in the deepest respect, as their commitment to life among the working class – however that was interpreted – gave them an essential sense of solidarity and direction.

An articulate presence

While making some effort at organization, the WCG also took responsibility for articulating its members' chosen life. Though they came from middle- (very occasionally upper-) class backgrounds, with no pretence that they could themselves become working-class, they were at least ready to share that life and, sometimes, to make its hardships known to others. In some of the earliest writings, from those of Michael Gedge to those of the Grubbs and Ramsays, there is surprise, shock, even honest disapproval at the working-class life they see around them. But there is also a growing understanding of the enormous gulf between institutional religion on the one hand and the understanding and culture of ordinary working people on the other. More than any other member of the group, it was John Rowe, with his considerable theological gifts, who was able to gather ideas up into the Group's Statement of 1959 (in the composition of which they all shared) and the *Rejoinder*, of 1965, translated into French, which gave expression to their vocation to share working class life. But it may also be true to say that because they individually enjoyed a longer and more extensive theological training and community life than most later non-stipendiary ministers received – as evidence taken for ACCM later suggested – they were far better equipped to reflect theologically on their day-to-day presence in the work place.

A prophetic presence

Finally, there is a sense in which the WCG, especially in terms of their commitment to the working-class and the poorest, remained prophetic. At times they spoke for a church in deed, where individuals in that same institution could only talk with incessant sophistication about an 'engagement' with an industrial society, but which at an institutional level never actually took place. Apart from the relatively small numbers of men and women engaged in industrial mission, or the sometimes forgotten but dedicated parish clergy who ministered in slum or housing estates, the WCG, alongside unknown and often unacknowledged Christian laity, tried to be a believing presence in a post-war industrial society – by living and working at its heart.

It is difficult to see the first worker-priests as precursors of any later group, though they can still be aligned with radicalized French worker-priests today, whom Arnal believes '. . . represent a paradigm of liberation thought and praxis for the industrial West'. There may, it is true, have been some non-stipendiary clergy who found the French worker-priests an inspiration for their own secular employment, but that inspiration led few enough to join the ranks of their British counterparts. There was, and remains, a sizeable number of non-stipendiary clergy who have never heard of Britain's worker-priests, and it certainly looks as if few have been attracted to any kind of ministry in secular employment. Indeed, since the Church of England as an institution seems to have abandoned even talk of radical mission or ministry by the early 1970s, so industrial mission has become a kind of tokenism, and real concern for working-class and underclass only re-emerged when unemployment and inner city deprivation seemed to threaten society itself. The one body, for example, which might have made considerable use of members of the Worker Church Group's detailed knowledge and understanding of Britain's emerging underclass, seemed oblivious to the group's history or existence. The Faith in the City Commission (1986) – a bold and brave sign that Archbishop Runcie was ready to attempt something in the context of Mrs Thatcher's Britain – still represented institutionalism itself. What had been said by Roger Lloyd of *Towards the Conversion of England* in 1943, could easily have been said of the membership of the Faith in the City Commission appointed in 1983:

> It contained many people of high distinction, who were gathered from all walks of life save one. The whole working-class area of life was left unrepresented.

And despite all the good work that was undoubtedly done in the 1980s and 1990s, because of Faith in the City, the terms of reference resolutely stated an emphasis on institutionalized ecclesiology, as the Commission set out to examine, 'the strengths, insights, problems and needs *of the Church's life* and mission in Urban Priority Areas' (my emphasis); not it seems, the needs of ordinary humanity that might be served by and through the church.

While there can be little doubt that some of the earliest ideas of Roland

Allen and others came to pass in French and English worker-priests, non-stipendiary ministries in the Church of England have generally remained in middle-class occupations. It should have been no surprise that Tony Williamson, worker-priest in Oxford, was son of 'Father Joe' of Stepney: the WCG was perhaps a part of that earlier Anglican tradition which had its roots in workers' missions, Oxford Movement, Christian Socialism, urban and slum ministries, and at least two religious communities. It may have been for this reason that the WCG developed into the Shop Floor Association, attracting new members, like the old, who now sought to align themselves with Britain's growing underclass in the 1980s and 1990s. John Vincent, leader of Sheffield's Urban Theology Unit, has commented in correspondence that he believes that the first worker-priests were not precursors of any non-stipendiary ministries, which he has viewed as a kind of 'ecclesiastical invention', but rather part of a para-church which entered into under-class Britain.

Though an organization of apparently little significance, the WCG in its earliest stages had upheld the role of women and laity, demonstrated common ground and concern among Catholics and Evangelicals, and sought to establish and exercise a radical ministry directly alongside the working-class. If Fr Vinatier was right in his understanding – which he had shared with Roland Walls – that the readiness to 'fail' was an essential prerequisite of incarnational ministry in godless and de-Christianized areas of Europe, then, perhaps, the members of the WCG had understood that too. If – in response to what they earnestly believed was God's revelation in human existence in the story of Jesus Christ – ministry was as much about 'being' as 'being there', then Britain's first worker-priests and their Group demonstrated a radical 'invisible' commitment every bit as valuable as the more traditional but 'visible' ministry in the territorial parish. In the post-war decades, the institutional church spoke relentlessly about mission in an industrial society, and then assessed effort and measured success by filled pews and growing territorial parishes there for everyone – if only they would come in. For that same institution, still obsessed by an ecclesiology which more often disables it from engaging with a post-Christian culture it believes it can only cower from or counter, the story of Britain's first worker-priests, and those who supported them in and outside the parishes, was, and remains, a judgment and challenge.

Epilogue

In France and in Britain, in the twenty-first century, worker-priests, some still at work, many more now retired, continue to serve the communities in which they find themselves. You can search them out. But questions from publishers or readers about where the churches are today on this ministry and whether there can be any kind of revival of it, raise more fundamental questions of what we think we might be doing other than engaging in romanticism. There is undoubtedly a need for the Christian story to be expressed afresh in what is now reputed to be a godless Europe, one of the most de-Christianized continents in the world, and where the churches are said to be in decline.

There are, of course, some that continue to strive for a ministry at work. Though they have not been mentioned very often in this study, it is vital to acknowledge the life, work and theology of ministers in secular employment, one group at least who have tried to keep this ministry alive. Nevertheless, in Britain at least, important factors associated with our mission, ministry, theology, and our social and economic context would seem to mitigate against any revival of worker-priests as they have been defined and understood in this study.

Changing society, changing mission

In the post-war years, there was a growing recognition among some people both in and outside the institutional churches that a 'great divide' existed between the Christian churches – especially the Church of England – on the one hand and the working men and women of the country on the other; at times it was a recognition that approached consensus, a consensus that maintained that in the end, the Christian faith, the story of Jesus Christ, was for all men and women everywhere. In a number of small ventures, from Iona in the north to industrial missions in the south, it was this concern that saw ecumenism develop, where parish priests and ministers, catholics and evangelicals, industrial chaplains and, on the very edge, worker-priests, might share what could be described as a single vision: that because God had entered human existence and 'became in all things like unto men', so a concern to go beyond the boundaries of the territorial parish must shape engagement.

But that was the second half of the twentieth century. Now, beyond the year 2000, though a form of mission appears to be top of many agendas, all the evidence is that at least at an institutional level, the church has totally abandoned that front-line 'on the edge' ministry and mission which was essentially about working in other people's territory, where the risks of failure were acknowledged and accepted, and where being and doing among ordinary people was what it was all about.

As finances began to bite, as social theology and social action became taxing – and there was the best excuse, that industry was in decline and the working class 'disappearing' – so the criticism arose that little was being 'achieved', or that this was 'not what the gospel was really about'. And so the church seemed to lose its nerve. It gradually withdrew larger-scale support for industrial chaplaincy and a range of other rather odd ventures, and turned from that committed theology towards its own housekeeping. Now, the institutional churches, and especially the Church of England, have allowed themselves to be swamped by internal concerns: slowly but surely, and with *Faith in the City* an exception that proved the rule, canon law, liturgical revision, pastoral measures, ministry and the ministry of women, issues in human sexuality (shorthand for homosexuality) and changes to the internal structures of the institution, have often been top of the General Synod's agenda. The irony is that in origin, some of these issues were supposed to aid the church's outreach. Instead they have often driven it inwards. All that may be alarming enough: it has been made worse by the apparent abandonment of certain interpretations of lifelong ministry, and what can only be described as a growing departure from godly learning.

Costly lifelong priesthood

If it is true that the institutional churches (apart from some pockets of continuity) and as an institutional commitment have largely abandoned their declared attempts simply to 'be' in other people's territory and sometimes beyond the territorial parish, has the Church of England also abandoned some of its understandings of priesthood that made such front-line ministry possible? Priesthood – for that matter being a Christian – is not a job or a pastime; it is a calling, a way of being, and the genuine costly incarnational priesthood of the 1950s and 1960s, occasionally highlighted even in *Picture Post,* was often evident in its crippling stipends and neglected parsonage housing. Teased by a growing wealth around them, a poor parson and his family (without a working wife), living on a minimum stipend, could find it difficult to have even the most modest luxuries the growing 'affluent worker' might then enjoy. This was acknowledged to be a sacrificial calling, and many a young curate and his family in the late 1960s and perhaps even the early 1980s could find themselves on some kind of income support. Perhaps this costliness began to act (alongside the changing culture) as one of the deterrents to the priesthood, as the numbers of ordinands fell in the 1960s; no one likes to admit that possibility. The truth is that though individuals can choose to sacrifice themselves, it is much harder to drag your wife and children to the altar at the same time. Most of us will rightly argue against clergy and their families suffering the same hardships now – it would be inexcusable – yet those of us who are clergy, at every level, enjoy our 'differentials', and confidently expect to live in a way that can make us quite indistinguishable from other comfortably-off professionals. And we do this apparently without any recognition that somehow or other, when all has been said and done, we have to ask how our church and priesthood can be a simple, frugal and holy sign in a wasteful world.

There was also an assumption in the recent past that priesthood (including that of the worker-priest) was effectively for life, a life in which an individual could grow up and journey in his – perhaps changing – convictions, certainly developing reading and thinking and through pastoral care, an in-depth understanding of humanity. That 'men of experience' would make the best priests was generally acknowledged, but that didn't have to mean an emphasis on ministry in mid- or later-life. What is often forgotten is that the claim – especially in the immediate post-war years – that it was good to have experienced men 'from the forces' ignores the fact that many who had grown up quickly fighting a war were still in their twenties. 'Experience of life', it seemed, was everything. And there was much truth in that. Many young ordinands between the 1950s and early 1970s were quite rightly told to go away and get some work experience before they would be seriously considered for training. A number, with the encouragement of bishops and college principals, went to work in factories, including Sheffield's steel works. As for older men, the church and its theological colleges had always welcomed a number into their communities; they enriched college life, and for many it was indeed a costly change.

Beyond the 1960s, however, when the institution found the numbers of its younger ordinands dropping, there was a significant change, as the same institution positively encouraged higher numbers of more mature and experienced candidates. What else could it do? This move, prompted by a range of different motives, has positively helped to broaden the understanding of Christian ministry, drawing it from the very communities which it seeks to serve. But as developments have galloped ahead, and papers have been produced and rhetoric has been marshalled to sanction the latest localized developments, one person's vision of 'a strategy for the changed situation' may indeed be another's 'last ditch attempt to plug gaps'.[713] However they are interpreted, what were originally seen as a range of ministries, and especially the introduction of the part-time courses to prepare them, have turned out to be a mixed blessing and a major contributor to more fundamental changes in the very character of the Church of England and its priesthood. It is not that many good and gifted people, men and women, lay and ordained, have not learnt well and are not now serving and enriching the church's life and ministry, but that the negative aspects of this change (especially the condensed learning that leads to it) can be furiously denied. The fact is that some of these changes may yet prove to have a catastrophic affect on the church's ability to engage with our changing society and culture.

Godly learning

Beyond the Second World War the Church of England still used a two-fold training system. The first part, in the bad old days of the General Ordination Examination (sometimes following university education and always in residence), was expected to engage the ordinand with some of the intellectual tools that might assist his ministry in a growing complex and technological society. But not everyone could cope with biblical and historical criticism, systematic and pastoral theology, made worse if the college was seen as detached from the world and an out-of-the-way 'monastic retreat house'. There were many who saw the training as a woefully inadequate preparation for ministry. But it was not always bad; by the late 1960s much depended, as it had often done, on the principal's vision. But at least everyone was exposed – and at some considerable length – to those core disciplines which provided the initial foundations for future ministry, study, preaching and teaching and gave the young ordinand at least – especially the academically disadvantaged – the opportunity to grow in knowledge and to develop gifts and skills. The second part was a curacy where under the direction of a good incumbent (though they could often be bad) a curate learnt many more practical and pastoral skills. From the mid-1960s on, many curates, directed by good bishops, took on courses and further learning and training. The emergence of more formal Post-Ordination Training and Continuing Ministerial Education, while addressing inadequacies, were not so much inventions as an acknowledgment that in the best of circumstances this had always been done.

Today, however, there are those who argue that the training is everywhere better. But the truth is that it is a *different* training producing a very *different* ministry. What were once seen as the core subjects on a theological curriculum, for example critical biblical, theological and historical work, are sometimes deliberately shortened and subsumed, almost hidden under a list of broad and acceptable outcomes. On regional or local courses especially, the initial study of the Bible (to take but one example) is sometimes completed in a fraction of the time students once spent engaged with the text. For students without much academic background or experience in dealing with textual work, this could prove disabling, if not disastrous. It doesn't always help, when in an attempt to make up for this, such coursework is 'made relevant' by subsuming it under all manner of associated headings or by feeding the students the very connecting points with life, faith and other disciplines that it was once assumed they would search out for themselves. Creativity is essential in the design of any course, but it simply cannot make up for the reduction in contact time between learner and teacher and text, and the sheer lack of exposure to so much in-depth historical critical work. The word 'rigour' is a favourite word to use in course design, but it is perhaps not always used with rigour itself, and it is little wonder that some of the church's own documents question the amount of study of traditional theological disciplines, admitting to '. . . uncertainty about the quality and depth of a candidate's engagement with the traditions of the church'.[714] Though the numbers of ordinands were apparently 'rising' at the turn of the millennium, the pool of biblical, historical and theological comprehension may be ever shrinking. It is possible to argue that though more and more people are being trained for ministry, fewer and fewer are being helped to grasp in any real depth the building blocks that will help them engage with a sophisticated and fragmented society.

There are always those, of course, who would remind us that academic learning may be something of an anachronism; that the 'educated parson' can be seen as a kind of nineteenth-century invention, and a mistaken one at that. What we need to return to apparently is an older model of a local priest, rooted in the local community. The argument has its merits, especially when we are considering an engaged local ministry. But it was not for nothing that the idea of the educated parson was developed; to move into the future we need also need to own and understand our past. If that was true in the nineteenth century, it is even more true today. It is precisely at this point in our history that we also need the greater body of ministers to have a thorough grasp of core theological and historical resources which will help them engage with the complex world in which we live. But are we losing this in our apparent rush to fast-track some men and women into a diversified ministry? There is already evidence (albeit from the superficial level of the national press) that the consequences of withdrawing from substantial learning will prove utterly disastrous.[715] It is a rather terrifying prospect.

None of this is the fault of staff or students on courses, or the Ministry Division of the church working hard and creatively to address serious questions of validation and expectation in ministerial education. Condensed learning represents a conscious decision by the whole church that even if this is so, it must be so. Candidates selected for ministerial training may be on the increase from time to time, but circumstances, aims and serious economic restraints make it impossible to prepare them all full-time or on much longer courses even if that was thought appropriate. On a 'part-time' scheme, students must learn to engage their reading, reflection and thinking with what is happening in their everyday lives. Yet lengthy in-depth reflection on the tradition and its bearing on life (and life's bearing on the tradition) is so much harder when you haven't been given time and space for in-depth engagement with that tradition in the first place. Is this one of the reasons so many ordinands find it difficult to theologize about their life and work? The truth is – and surely we must learn to be truthful – that we are compelled by our circumstances to prepare men and women for a *very different kind of ministry* from the one inherited after the war. Preparing some on part-time courses, regional or local, may prove quicker, cheaper, and far less disruptive of life than the bad old days of residence. Yet the further we go, the greater the dangers. One of the Church of England's own documents on Ordained Local Ministry, for example, insists that this particular ministry was not introduced to plug gaps, yet it later admits that in some places there has been poor selection and training where national guidelines have not been followed and where 'ordination takes place after only cursory training'.[716] But why worry? When the initial training, residential, regional or local is over, there is adequate Continuing Ministerial Education is there not? Yes, there often is, and with many dedicated officers working at their best; but reports of clergy who feel under no obligation to do any are not uncommon. Today, it seems some clergymen and women have forgotten their solemn undertaking made to their bishop at ordination that they will continue to study. Their initial training over, they casually please themselves whether they attend a course, engage in exploration or ever open a book. Added to this is the growing impression of a decline in the numbers of university theological teachers and the amount of serious critical biblical and theological work being written and studied.[717] The bad old days may indeed have been bad. But were they ever as bad as this?

The demise of modern theology

But if it is acknowledged that the church must learn to survive with a very different kind of core stipendiary ministry, sharing and working with a much broader range of self-supporting lay and ordained local ministries which need not be as biblically or theologically resourced as ministry tried to be in the past, that itself is a symptom of something deeper still. A third and critical factor which may make 'front-line' ministries (never mind worker-priests) so difficult is the avoidance of the kind of critical thinking that shaped so much post-war modern theology.

In the decades that followed the war many parish clergy, industrial chaplains and a handful of worker-priests with them, including catholics and evangelicals, found their work and ventures supported and fuelled by radical theologies that took seriously the evil of the first half of the twentieth century, theologies in which some were particularly competent. It was unspeakable inhumanity that had driven so many to stop and take honest account of the sheer impossibility of engaging the world with religious thought and language isolated and incomprehensible in the face of human suffering. The ongoing work of biblical criticism, and the issues raised in systematic theology, sometimes came from those had suffered in the latest conflict, and who had themselves witnessed and reflected at first hand on the horror so recently unleashed on Europe.

But since the early 1970s some of the radical European theologies, '... tolerated but not welcomed', [718] have been superseded by a kind of theological fragmentation. Some of the more reductionist theologies have been interpreted as a form of liberalism which has failed the Church of England. There may indeed be a variety of 'liberal' theologies that deserve to be challenged. But then there are also those who will use this as a licence for dubbing all ambiguity and all critical inquiry a 'failure', in order to embrace the 'success' of some of the more closed and conservative theologies now in evidence. This can easily become a slippery slope where some of Europe's best theological minds – other heirs of radical post-war thinking – are dismissed out of hand and remain simply unread. At its worst, those of an extreme fundamentalist and literalist variety give succour to often good, caring, but incredulous people outside the Christian community, who can still attack it for its often high-handed incomprehensibility. This narrow perspective can encourage a kind of closed theological system where truth is defined by itself, where self-righteousness turns the church into an associational ark, where inclusion is strictly conditional, and where outreach is limited to forms of liturgical entertainment.

On the catholic side it is sometimes difficult to avoid the conclusion that some of the underlying theological principles about what it meant to be a catholic priest, radically engaged with humanity and supported by an equally challenging theology and spirituality, are already slipping away. Some of these principles, still alive among radical European Catholic theologians and clergy today, seem to be demoted by others in favour of a different approach: a chilling new clericalism, supported by a kind of ecclesial purity that isolates and elevates some aspects of order and gender. Today it is not difficult to find some catholic clergy, including those new to priesthood and to the tradition, and who may describe themselves as conservative or traditionalist, who have learnt that it is their opposition to the ordination of women that defines their catholicity rather than that older and deeper understanding of a priestly life, holy, learned and rooted in incarnational commitment.

Yet that earlier post-war radical theology which challenged an earlier liberalism was often rooted in critical New Testament scholarship, and struggling with philosophical and historical issues, attempted to address and deal head-on with the realities of Christian faith and ministry in its relationship to human existence.

The greater and overriding changes that would make a revival of worker-priests difficult if not impossible have been in society and culture itself. The wholesale reduction of Britain's manufacturing base, the rise of service industries, the growth of part-time insecure jobs, religious diversity, community and social disintegration, and the current relentless decline of the institutional churches raise fundamental questions about the future of the Christian faith in Britain and Europe. They also raise questions about the kind of mission and ministry that can be afforded to address that. Christian parishes, which will inevitably be driven together, will hopefully remain among the most important bases for Christian expression. Some ministries, however, whatever the financial cost, and thoroughly rooted and supported by a critical history and theology, must surely work at and beyond the very edges of society, and far removed from the traditional territorial parish. Occasionally writers on mission come tantalizingly close to suggesting such things, yet this can still be seen as the business of 'getting out there' in 'challenging outreach' because the accepted ecclesiology suggests that the Christian church as 'a prevailing church' is sole guardian and purveyor of all truth, rather than accepting the fundamental recognition that our knowledge is partial, that God is already a part of his creation, and that in mission and in Christ he somehow goes ahead of us into Galilee.

How often we hear that above all things the church must be 'counter-cultural'? Always? What are we to do when in the prevailing culture we see things that are good and enriching and waiting to be affirmed? 'Welcome them in' is often the answer. But it will not be enough, as some have suggested, to be an 'open church' with doors and facilities thrown wide to all comers; the whole point is that some people, even those who might be touched by the story of Jesus Christ, will never *want* to come in, and the institution needs to learn again to be a *permanent, engaged and holy presence* and sometimes a *failing presence* in territory that will never be its own. Yet such ministries cannot be encouraged by a church pre-occupied by its internal problems, weakened in its intellectual base, and sometimes served by a new generation of lay and ordained ministers some of whom seem to know little of its priesthood and less of its history and theology.

Society and fragmentation

Recent polls and studies seem to suggest that Europe is less Christian than it has ever been, a darkling corner of the world. If this is so, then perhaps we have come full circle, and the Abbé Godin's argument that a mission 'is something that reaches out beyond [the parish]' needs to be heard afresh. The story of Jesus Christ drove priests in France and a handful in Britain to do just that, and in France at least they were no failure; rather, there has been a general acknowledgment that they helped to change the Catholic Church in Europe and the working population's attitude to it, and can still do so today. In Britain there were just too few to have that broader impact, though at a local level and in a sense supporting industrial chaplaincies the same thing has often happened. But, 'we've moved on from all that' is sometimes the cry; 'the world has changed and those days are behind us'. Yet it is also possible to argue that at an institutional level the Christian churches seem to have learnt little from some of these more radical ministries, full of energy, full of enthusiasm, full of hope. With massive change in our society and culture and in our understanding of ministry and priesthood, we cannot live in the past and expect to have worker-priests in precisely the same way, but their stories can engender enormous hope; perhaps we can learn from their engagement, and have something as courageous. Indeed there is good reason for optimism. If we can recover some understanding of that costly, spiritual vocation into the heart of humankind; if we can understand the need to meet men and women where they are, in their territory, and use some of the critical intellectual tools that will help to support us to minister and teach and engage with a new and sometimes frightening world, we will have every hope of living and engaging others with the transforming story of Jesus Christ.

The worker-priests of Britain, a tiny little group though they were, more often than not eschewed the media that sought them out. They valued the hard-edged simplicity of life, just as the Little Brothers and Sisters of Jesus have greatly valued the word 'little' in their title. Only now, some fifty years after their beginnings, have they been ready for part of their stories to be heard. Today, of all the lessons to be learnt from them, perhaps the very hardest is that godly and spiritual humility, a humility expressed in a quiet and holy presence among ordinary people where they are, not a presence that demands we seize and occupy the space in-between. The Church of England, among Britain's other churches, is often like a well-meaning chatterbox; even our liturgies reflect a 'wordy' church which likes the sound of its own voice, seems to have an opinion on every subject and cannot bear to be still. It is not surprising, and not always its fault; the media damn it when it speaks and damn it when it is silent. But this is where courage and nerve must not fail. As we face our fellow men and women in the world, we need to learn that perhaps we have sometimes said enough to frighten and hurt and make people angry. Perhaps our ceaseless rhetoric, our claims to what sometimes seems like absolute truth, our rallying cry to 'prevail' and 'go for growth' need to be replaced by a kind of contrite silence before the God who meets us daily in blessed word and sacrament and in the lives of frail humanity. Not the passive silence that retreats into a private and disengaged piety, but a disciplined silence that goes hand in hand with a praying, and action and loving in the world, where we learn to have faith and learn to have hope. What if we are being called to be small again, to be marginalized as Jesus Christ once was, to be pushed to the edge to stay there and learn awhile? Perhaps *we* are the ones who need to go out and be humbled; changed and transfigured, rather than always demanding it of others first.

St Ninian's Mid-Craigie mentioned in the Preface is still there on Dundee's East Kingsway, surrounded by factories, stores and DIY centres. The exceptionally close ecumenical work undertaken by the Church of Scotland and the Scottish Episcopal Church means that St Ninian's and its house may be demolished to raise funds for new joint enterprises on the Church of Scotland's adjacent site. But the demolition of the house may be more significant than the demolition of the once historic little church. The building of the house said as nothing else could say, '*here* among the people, a pastor will live and minister'. It is something that the Scottish churches and all other churches in Britain must grapple with when some anxious clergy ask not to be placed in Urban Priority Areas, or when ministers of the gospel are understandably tempted to live somewhere more convenient, safe and comfortable.

Today, many of the old tenements on the estate have been demolished and new housing has been built complete with paths and gardens, yet sometimes still I wander its streets near the church, searching for a part of myself I seem to have left behind. There, in a place I so often detested, my parents in laughter and sorrow poured out their love for very ordinary men and women. There were few worker-priests or committed laity in Britain to live the gospel on the country's factory floors. Consequently there were never enough for one to come to work in the engineering works opposite our house, to secretly visit my dad (as I would later dream), to share our eucharist, perhaps a cigarette, and engage him, not only in arguments – which I'm sure there would have been – but also in the stimulating conversation he had to do without. He deserved better. The worker-priests were his contemporaries, but they were elsewhere when he might have valued one, because that's the way it was. Though many of them are still with us, we may never see their like again, and the Christian church will be the poorer for it. Perhaps, one day, someone will grant them just a few lines in the *Oxford Dictionary of the Christian Church*.

Appendices

Appendix 1: WCG – names of founding members

Name	Approximate Year of Joining
Martyn and Anne Grubb	1957
Don Heap (Canada)	1959*
Ken and Isobel Ramsay	1958
John & Isobel Rowe	1957
John & Veronica Strong	1957
Tom Quigley	1959*
John Wilcox	1958*
Tony & Barbara Williamson	1958

The names of visitors and potential new members appear in 1967 and include: Michael Butler, David Wilson, Bill Millard and visitors from France: D. Bonnechère, P. Valet, G. Estorino.

* Dates simply indicate the formality of joining, or when names first appear in reports of WCG meetings. Since the group had at an informal structure at various stages, it was often the case, as it was with the Ramsays, that an association had gone on for many years before names appeared on reports. At the same time, when individuals or couples 'left' they might return later as visitors, or keep firmly in touch with others.

Sources: Minutes/Reports of the Worker Church Group 1957 on. See John Rowe and Tony Williamson, Papers.

Appendix 2: WCG and SFA conference locations from 1957

1957–1962	Harlington, Dunstable, Bedfordshire
(1958 August	Stoke Newington*)
(1959 August	Harlington*)
1963	St Katharine's Foundation, London
1964	St Peter de Beauvoir, Hackney
1965	Bobbingworth,* Essex
1966	Bobbingworth, Essex

1967–1979	Marsh Baldon, Oxfordshire
1980–1981	Holy Island, Northumberland
1982–1983	Ilkley (WCG/SFA)
1984	Newcastle (SFA)
1985–1986	Rydal Hall, Cumbria
1987–1988	Bishop Mascall Centre, Ludlow, Salop
1989	Chisworth, Derbyshire
1990	Ludlow

Sources: WCG/SFA Reports: John Rowe, Papers
*From inked notes in Tony Williamson's Papers

Appendix 3: The WCG Statement – in full

Statement of a group of churchmen, priests and lay who have chosen to be wage-workers in industry as an expression of their faith.

This is a provisional statement. It has been prepared primarily for our own use and only secondarily for distribution. It is not for publication in any public journal, but may be circulated among those who can be expected to discuss its contents seriously. We would be particularly glad of constructive comments and criticism.

February 1959

Introduction

It is now widely recognized that there is a serious and deep-rooted estrangement between the Church and the industrial wage-earners of this country henceforward referred to as 'workers' or 'working people' (the terms by which they describe themselves). Committees, missions and projects of all sorts are springing up to tackle the problem.

Most of these efforts are addressed to the workers from conventional footholds in the Church – chaplaincies, parishes, and formal missions. The Church may be expected to gain much from these, providing they are inspired with humility and patience and willingness to re-examine traditional assumptions.

We ourselves, however, feel called to answer this challenge at another level, by binding up our own salvation with that of the industrial workers. This, we feel, can only be done by working as they work and living upon the earnings of our labour as they do. Substantially, therefore, we speak as a group of men and women, with their families, all committed by this decision to a certain form of life, addressing the working people primarily by involvement rather than by propaganda. What we espouse is not primarily a 'technique of evangelism' but a form of obedience.

We may further clarify our position as follows:

1. *The Way of the Incarnation*

The Church is out of contact with the lives of most working-class people. It is not a natural growth within their kind of life but stands without. Speaking generally, it does not understand them and their problems and they have little confidence in it or its representatives. This separation is primarily regarded in the Church as a technical rather than a spiritual problem. We think it should be clearly recognized that for the Church to be out of contact with the people is sin. Technique is no answer to sin.

It seems to us that the answer to this situation is for the Church to enter with humility and sympathy into the life of the working people and build up the Church from within, that is, by Christians who are called to it becoming or remaining workers. Even on the human level this seems the obvious way to grow in understanding of the workers and to win their confidence. But beyond this, it is surely right for a faith founded on the Incarnation. The Christian minister or missionary must be, and must be felt and known to be, one with his people. 'It is not enough for the Church to speak out of its security. Following our incarnate and crucified Lord, we must live in such identification with man, with his sin, his hopes and fears, his misery and needs, that we become his brother and can witness from his place and condition to God's love for him. Those outside the church make little distinction between faith and works' (World Council of Churches, *Evanston Report*, Section 11). Work is for us not an opportunity for propaganda, but the means whereby we become one with the working people.

This is not a wasteful use of the Church's manpower. It is a proper exercise in faith. In the midst of a world which believes in salvation through money, technique and force, Christians believe in the power of the 'foolishness' of the Cross.

2. *The Meaning of Evangelism*

All evangelism is the work of the Holy Spirit. Successful evangelism is not pimarily the result of organizations and plans, but it follows from lives inspired by the Holy Spirit. Evangelism is not just getting people to church. Nor is it merely altering people's opinions. To evangelize is to convey the love of God to people in any way possible – by word and by life. It is to make men know and feel that they are loved, that behind our feeble love lies the absolute Love of God seen in the Cross of Christ. In that experience lies the possibility of response, and therefore of salvation. Thus the first step in evangelism is not one of controversy, but always one of love. We ourselves feel bound to express this spirit of love by becoming one with the workers. 'There are varieties of gifts but the same Spirit, and there are varieties of service but the same Lord' (I Cor. 12.4 RSV).

3. *The Gospel Free of Charge*

Our feeling is similar to that of St Paul as expressed in 1 Cor. 9. He recognizes clearly that the preacher of the Gospel has a right to get his living by the Gospel: but he goes on to say that he has not made use of this right, but prefers to earn his living by work, in order to make the Gospel free of charge (v. 18), i.e. in order the more fully to express the love of Christ, by seeking no material gain in return for his preaching.

Further, the completeness of this self-giving love makes him want to become 'the slave of all' (v. 19) and become 'all things to all men that I might by all means save some' (v. 22).

We think this applies to both laymen and clergy. It is merely accidental that most of the Church's paid agents are clergy.

4. *Vocation to Poverty*

Throughout the ages Christians have been called to show forth Christ's love by sharing the lot of the poor. We also feel this impulse. And though in England today the wage-earners are not uniformly poor in material things, yet, as a class, they are the lowest stratum of society: suffering a 'poverty' which is a complex of conditions – the very wage-status itself, the impersonal nature of much of the work, the deprivation of responsibility, job insecurity, educational under-privilege, and low social status.

5. *The Gospel in Material Terms*

If we seriously intend to get over the Gospel to the people of our time, we must live it in the materialistic terms of money and work which they most easily understand. For our part, this means that we must express our faith by sharing fully the life of the wage-earning class. In our opinion only on the basis of such a life is the preaching of the Word likely to carry much conviction in modern industrial society.

6. *Re-discovering the Gospel*

We wish to learn, even while we live it ourselves, what the Gospel should mean for industrial workers and their families, and how to express it so that it may be understood. We must not only humbly learn the outlook and conditions of life of those so long estranged from the life of the Church, but also, with them, allow our grasp of the faith to be deepened. Our purpose is not to 'translate the Gospel into terms which simple people can understand ', but to discover again what the Gospel of Love means for today, in life as well as in word.

It follows that we must learn the practice of prayer, worship, and the priestly vocation (in its particular and general sense) in the life and work of those with whom we have to do.

7. *Dignity of Labour*

We believe that manual labour, the necessary support of the material fabric of society, partakes, like other forms of work, of an intrinsic nobility conferred by the Creator. The status of worker has therefore a godly dignity in itself. We seek to make it manifest. It is only by seeing it in this way and recovering the sense of a divine vocation in such a life that the fatigue, boredom, and apparent triviality of labour in industry may be freely borne and given its true significance.

8. No Classes in Christ

We believe that most social benevolence as commonly taught and practised gives all aid short of equality of essential status and that this is repugnant to the will of God and falls short of Christian love. The Incarnation of God is with man as simply man, and whatever in the structure and practice of society demeans one class of men in relation to another is a virtual denial of the Incarnation.

9. Secular Precedents

In the Lord's own words, the Gospel is the good news of the Kingdom of God. To preach the Gospel among the workers is therefore to stand for the Kingdom in industry, that is, for a re-ordering of industrial relations, and even of the economic structure of society. But we are by no means first in the field. We are preceded by various secular and partial expressions of the human desire for brotherhood and justice. Among such are the Trade Unions. We feel bound therefore to enter into the struggles for justice, brotherhood and industrial democracy which are already going on in secular terms, serving the Gospel no less in this way than in direct personal acts of love.

10. Church Finance

We are uneasy about the present financial policy of the Church of England. We believe that the Church, more than any other body, should be self-supporting, and that the clergy, if they do not earn their own living by secular work, should be dependent on the giving of Church members. Although this is gradually being realized in the Church and efforts are being made to implement it, the official financial structure of the Church does not accept its implications. The charge often made by working men that the Clergy are state-paid is far too near the mark. Although they are not actually state-paid, the fact remains that in practice most of them are living very largely on 'unearned income' (i.e. the interest from past investments). This, to the working man, is as bad as being state-paid. With some justice he may regard the clergy as living on the fruits of his labour, and without his consent.

11. Relation to the Conventional Ministry

We would emphasize that we are in no sense in competition with the paid ministry, although we believe the clergy should not partake so much of the character of a profession in the secular world as they now do. We are anxious to work in co-operation with the parochial ministry in every way, and with any specialized ministries with which we may come in contact. Some of us prefer to exercise a primarily parochial ministry, being committed as priests on the staff of or in charge of parishes, while others of us desire to be clear of parochial responsibility in order to have greater freedom to experiment in whatever way seems best. We think that there is a place for worker-priests in both of these situations.

12. Worker-priests

The Lambeth Conference (1958) has said plainly that there is no theological principle which forbids a man being ordained priest while continuing in his lay occupation (Resolution 89). We wish to take this further: the expression of religion in daily life in the world is not an extra, but is of the essence of Christianity. It therefore seems right that some clergy – the accredited leaders of the Church – should be fully in the strains and stresses of daily life to the extent of earning their living at secular work. The laity are frequently told to exercise Christian leadership in their place of work and to work out a pattern of Christian discipleship there, and so they should. But it seems both unreasonable and unkind to expect them to do this effectively in a sphere of life in which their appointed spiritual leaders are not engaged, particularly when the problem of witness in that sphere (the sphere of industrial work) is acknowledged to be one of the most intractable problems facing the Church today.

13. The Wholeness of our Mission

Our mission is not confined, even at present, to worker-priests, nor is it conceived as a 'Worker-priest Movement'. It is rather, we believe, a fundamental expression of the Christian response to modern industrial society, and as such the whole Church needs to be adequately represented in it. That means clergy and a predominance of laity, men and women, married and unmarried, all alike responding to the call to glorify God in the lives of the workers. Some who have grown up in this life will feel called to surrender the chance to escape from it. Others, who enter from without, will surrender claims to privileged status and security. (Signed)

SHERRY WALDON,
TOM WALDON
28 Pigott Street, London, E14

VERONICA STRONG,
JOHN STRONG (The Revd)
The Vicarage, Dunstable,
Beds

ANNE GRUBB
MARTYN GRUBB (The Revd)
100 Queen's Road, Southall,
Middlesex

ISABEL ROWE
JOHN ROWE (The Revd)
28 Pigott Street, London E14

BARBARA WILLIAMSON
TONY WILLIAMSON
359 Iffley Road, Oxford

The following, who are also of this vocation, are in general agreement with the above statement, though for reasons of distance they have not been able to take part in the conferences which have produced it.

DON HEAP (The Revd),
ALICE HEAP,
1 Manor Road, Toronto,
Canada

TOM QUIGLEY (The Revd)
125 Shaw Street,
Upperby, Carlisle

Appendix 4: List of SOC ordinands' occupations in the early 1980s

Education	
Headteachers	
Deputy Head	
Lecturers	
Teachers	16
Miscellaneous	
Meteorologist	
Salesman	
Writer	
Librarian	
Printer	
Clerk	
Engineer	7
Banking/Finance/Insurance	
Accountant	
Insurance Agent	
Stockbroker	6
Medicine	
Medical Superintendent	
Doctor	
Psychologist	
Psychiatrist	
Consultant	5
Administration/Middle-Management	
Quality control	
Asst in HM Patent Office	
Administrator to SLIM	
Computer Executive	4
Management/Director	
Director of Social Services	
Managing Director	
Head of British Council	
Director of a Housing Association	4
Civil Service/Police	
Civil Service Officer	
Local Government	
Police Inspector	4
Social Services	
Senior probation officer	
Careers officer	
Youth leader	4
Legal	
Solicitor	
Barrister	2
Workers	
Baker	
Office Messenger	2
[*Bus driver	1]

*Tom Field may have died before the list was made.

This is certainly not a definitive list of ordinands from the Southwark Course – there will have been many more since this list was produced. It dates from the early 1980s – possibly 1982 – and demonstrates the almost total lack of 'working men' that Mervyn Stockwood hoped might join. Although the actual numbers of each profession have been omitted, of the 54 names, only two might be described as 'workers'.

The list not only represents what was happening in Southwark, but was a clear reflection of what was happening in Non-Stipendiary Ministry across Britain.

Source: List of Southwark Ordination Course (possibly 1982); David Wilson, Papers.

Appendix 5: Names of WCG/SFA in the 1980s

Bell, Pat and Tony
Chevillard, Xavier
Comber, Tony
Gardiner, Barry
Grubb, Martyn
Halsey, John
Harwood Jones, Susan
Jarrosson, Guy
Keevong and Ivan
Kessler, Ed
Lloyd, Ann and Selwyn
Miller, John and Mary
O'Leary, Patrick
Parker, Andrew and Pat
Peel, David
Rita
Rowe, Isobel and John
Rowe, Annette
Rollinson, Fred
Shaw, Andrew
Smith, Caroline
Sneddon, Pat
Strong, John and Veronica
Vanthournout, Roger (from Belgium)
Waldon, Tom and Sherry
Williamson, Barbara and Tony

The list includes names of those who actually took part in founding the Worker Church Group in the late1950s, but it does not include David Wilson, or names of those associated with any alternative group like the Priest-Worker Chapter in Southwark. By this time, the SFA was already becoming radicalized (Andrew Parker and John Strong's names appear together) and the draft 'manifesto' had already indicated their change of direction. The list also includes the names of the two Little Brothers from Leeds, Guy Jarrosson and Xavier Chevillard.

Source: Worker Church Group Papers, Tony Williamson Papers

Appendix 6: WCG/SFA Manifesto

First draft of a WCG Manifesto (February 1981)

THE WORKER CHURCH GROUP

1. The group consists of men and women from all parts of Britain. It is committed to the field of manual work and to solidarity with the working class. This commitment the members of the group see as an expression of their commitment to the Gospel of Jesus Christ. Members of the group are of all ages and sexes and from Christian and non-Christian backgrounds.*

2. Basic to the WCG are the facts that for most of his life Jesus lived and worked in the working world of the Nazareth family business joinery; that his Gospel was good news to the poor; that the common people heard him gladly; and that it was through them that both the earliest church and subsequent renewals in church and society have come about.

As in the days of Jesus, so now the 'poor' include not only the destitute and deprived, but the powerless, those alienated by the 'powers that be' in Church and State, and those vulnerable to the whims of the governments, bureaucracy and officialdom of political, industrial and religious life. It is with these that the members of the Worker Church Group aim to enter into solidarity by their work, their economic conditions and their lifestyle, in the conviction that it is here that the Gospel may be heard and shared, and that the new life which Jesus promises to the poor may be experienced.**

* Some found the inclusion of this sentence hard to accept – others that its exclusion would be equally hard to accept. We believe it to be controversial.
** Some thought that the manifesto should end here; others thought that it would be incomplete without some recognition of the controversy (however small) that members' presences among their workmates provokes.

3. Some of our workmates find it a puzzle that someone of the middle class (as most, though not all, of us are), with the benefits of higher education and the possibilities of 'advancement', should *choose* a way of life characterized by hard work (sometimes!), boredom, restriction, and most of all indignity; or they may understand it as an 'opting out' of 'responsibilities' (for they often associate responsibilities with middle-class jobs) and a failure to use the gifts and opportunities with which their privileged background has provided them.

Our workmates often seem to feel that if the factory floor is where people are manipulated, exploited and demeaned you either escape from it, if you can, into a better job or you fight for your interests by establishing your own power structures or you use the existing structures to do social good works.

The group believes that the Gospel shows another way by which human dignity may be recovered. This is by use of a different kind of power – a human power within individuals and within their communities.

We believe that this is the only way whereby a really significant change can take place by which the evils of the system as well as the destructive forces in ourselves may be overcome.

4. Others of our workmates may ask 'are you with us all the way? Or only for a limited time or objective?'

To this we would reply that we have not chosen to enter the life of working people lightly or romantically. We realize that the experience will severely test us as we try to adjust not least to unrealistic thoughts of what we are missing. On the other hand we know that we do not maintain solidarity simply by an act of will. So we make no promises. However, we believe the basis of our solidarity with the life of working people is the life and work of Jesus by whom we believe God enters into the fullest solidarity with man in man's condition of alienation as victim to the forces of sin and evil. The commitment of Jesus to man has no conditions or limits; it is a movement of love which has no ulterior motive. This solidarity, already given by God, to restore the society of man in justice and dignity, the group enters convinced that such a restoration awaits to be discovered and won.*

5. Again our mates may ask 'What have you to offer?'; in reply we make the following points:
– We don't pretend we have ready made solutions.
– We believe this is the right place for us to be.**
– We believe that society can be different.
– We offer ourselves.
(a) Not in the sense of mere addition as one more to the ranks; rather as of a chemical reaction involved in the process of human solidarity.
(b) Offering the Gospel includes offering ourselves, as the nature of the Gospel is that of a life lived and shared by Jesus Christ with us. The Gospel is discovered as well as offered in this solidarity. This has power to transform ourselves and our society.***

* This is a composite work not necessarily agreed to by the sub-group.
** Some would prefer that the 'for us' be removed. We believe that this also is controversial.
*** This whole section has only been put forward in note form – due to lack of time.

This document is a first draft of a manifesto of the group of people who up to the present have called themselves the Worker Church Group. It was drawn up by a sub-group designated by the WCG at its meeting in Ilkley in 1980.

This document is meant for discussion and involves the responsibility only of the sub-group itself. The sub-group worked from the agreed basic stance (agreed at Ilkley) that the manifesto should be turned towards that working world rather than the church.

This document will be the basis of discussion at the May meeting of the WCG in Holy Island in February 1981.

Note: 1981/82 was a period of much heart-searching, in which the WCG evolved into the SFA. Some of the new 'statements', be they 'manifesto' or something else, indicate a deliberate effort to articulate their understanding of themselves.

Source: Tony Williamson, papers, but may be found in other collections.

Appendix 7: A Worker-Priest Questionnaire

This questionnaire was designed at a very early stage of research to help in establishing some basic questions relating to the lives and labour of worker-priests, and most of the questions were drafted for those who were members of the Worker Church Group. In the event, only a handful of forms went out. Clergy, who sometimes described themselves as worker-priests, and who were given questionnaires on request, found themselves unable to fill the forms up and might, in an enclosure, admit that they were a 'different kind of worker-priest', which usually meant they were not employed in manual labour.

The questionnaire appears in its original form, though for the purposes of this appendix, the spacing has been altered.

A Worker-Priest Questionnaire

This questionnaire is for the purposes of sociological and historical research, and the contents will be kept strictly confidential.

I would be most grateful if you could try to answer the questions by giving your answer ON the question sheet. However, where there is insufficient space, please feel free to use the back of the question sheet or use additional paper.

PERSONAL

NAME:
PRESENT ADDRESS:
DATE OF BIRTH:
DATE OF ORDINATION:

Training

1. Where did you study for the ministry?
2. Was your training full-time or part-time? Did it include University?
3. For how many years? Dates of training
4. Were you in paid employment before you began your studies?
   YES/NO
5. What was your job or jobs? Dates?
6. Did you go on a Church's Selection Conference with CACTM or ACCM?
   YES/NO Where and when?
7. Did you begin your training for ministry with the intention of becoming a worker-priest? YES/NO
8. If the answer is NO – When did the idea of becoming a worker-priest emerge; during you training or after?
9. Can you explain, in your own words, why you wanted to become a worker priest? Were you for example inspired by (a) Others (b) Reading (c) Other means? [AT THIS STAGE A BRIEF ANSWER WILL SUFFICE]
10. Was your training for the Ministry 'geared' generally for parochial ministry – or, were there any 'worker-priest' elements? That is, was there any specific content about ministry IN the workplace?
11. Did you at any time consider 'sector ministry', that is, hope to become a chaplain in any institution or situation, perhaps in an industrial mission?
12. Before 'becoming' a worker-priest did you serve a full or part-time curacy of any kind? For how long?
13. How was this 'choice' made?
14. Where was your curacy?
    What was the name of your Vicar or Rector?

Working life

15. As a worker-priest were you full-time or part-time in secular employment?
16. What type of work did you do?
17. Were you apprenticed? Time-served? Skilled? Other? Please give details.

18. What company or companies (firms) did you work for? (Can you please try to supply full names and addresses – even if the company or companies no longer exist.)
19. For how many years did you work there?
20. If you changed jobs, or moved to different work(s), can you give dates and reasons for the change?

Diocesan and parochial

21. Did your diocesan or local bishop offer you a 'position' at a local church – or did you find it for yourself?
22. What was your bishop's reaction to you becoming or wishing to become a worker-priest?
23. In terms of your 'parochial role' were you fully licensed, or did you have permission to officiate, or other?
24. Did your licence state that you were in secular employment – or did it only mention your church (parochial) responsibilities?
25. Were you attached to one or more parish churches? Can you give dates?
26. Name(s) of the churches – the Vicars/Rectors? Their dates?
27. Did you have a written contract for your parochial responsibilities?

Life as a worker-priest

28. At your workplace, can you describe in your own words how you looked on your role as a worker-priest? e.g. In what sense did you 'merge' with workmates – at what point (if at all) did you say who and what you were?
29. In what sense (if at all) did you 'minister'? Did you ever have any liturgical function? e.g. prayers in the workplace, occasional celebration of Holy Communion – Or were those functions confined to 'the parish' ?
30. Did you have any political interests? Were you a member of a political party?
31. Were you a member of a Trade Union – an official of a Trade Union – if the answer is 'yes' what Union, and how did you serve?
32. If you were a member of a Trade Union, did this at any time create apprehension or anxiety among other clergy? Church members? Your Bishop?
33. Did you enjoy your work – do you think it was important for worker-priests in any way to feel 'fulfilled' 'at work'?
34. Did you have any notable encounters, pleasant or unpleasant, with management about your work, or your 'other' interests – social, political or religious?
35. With fellow workers – on social, political or religious matters?
36. Are there any special moments of 'pastoral encounter' that you especially remember? That is, were you ever asked in your capacity as a worker-priest to officiate at an occasional office for another worker?
37. When (if at all) did you stop being a worker-priest, and why?
38. Did you ever meet formally or informally with other worker-priests? Were you a participant in any worker-priest 'network' or association?
39. Were there any other worker-priests living near you? Can you give their names? Parishes? And of another denomination?

40. Do you feel overall that:
    (a) The Church of England (or other Church) understood the worker-priest's role? Did your bishop, Vicar or local congregation understand?
    (b) Your 'Diocese' or 'Province' understood? Was any visible support shown to you through synods, councils, conferences, local meetings of any kind?
    (c) Was your opinion sought at any times in the question of relations between church and industrial society?
41. Were you ever asked to speak about your place as a worker-priest at conferences or meetings? Can you give notable instances?
42. Was there ever a 'works committee' or similar group which ever sought your advice 'at work'?
43. Do you believe that your role as a worker-priest was fulfilling, that you achieved whatever it was that you set out to achieve?
44. Do you believe there is a place for worker-priests today?
45. Do you have any comments to make on todays NSMs (Non-Stipendiary Ministers) or MSEs (Ministers in Secular Employment)?
46. Are there any questions which you have not been asked which you feel are important?
    Please indicate the question(s) and your answer(s)

Most important

(a) Do you have in your possession any documentary material on worker-priests? i.e. letters, magazine articles, old *Church Times*, newspaper cuttings, minutes of meetings?
(b) Do you know of any documents (printed or otherwise) from PCC minutes, chapters, synods or ANY other meetings which relate to worker-priests generally, and your personal role?
(c) Did you ever keep a diary or journal?
(d) Do you know the whereabouts of any laypersons with whom you worked?
(e) Can you give the names of other worker-priests you knew of in the 1950s and 1960s?

If any of your answers to (a), (b), or (c) is 'YES', I would be most grateful for an opportunity to make or receive copies of such material, or at least to 'search through' what exists. I will reimburse ANY copying expenses – but would prefer to see original material first, if that is possible.

Even if your answer is 'NO' to most questions, would it please be possible for me to visit you to take an historical oral record (tape-recorded) of your memories/stories?

When you have completed this form, would you like me to send you a full copy with your completed answers? YES/ NO

Appendix 8: Belgian and French Visiting Worker-Priests

The surviving list below, from the Worker Church Group papers, indicates the names and some of the occupations of just one group of Belgian and French worker-priests who visited the Group in the Spring of 1974. The list was originally intended as a guide to those who were to offer hospitality to the visitors.

Jacques Brouckaert: Seminarian, living in Marchienne-Dochérie (Charleroi). Once lived with Roger for nearly four years.

Roger Vanthournout: 'Leader' of the worker-priests (Friendly; speaks da* English). Living with Roger.

Bernard Melot: Worker-priest – lives with Roger.

Michel Patternotte: Deacon on way to priesthood. Works as storeman.

Jean-Claude Brys: Seminarian. Lives with Roger.

Janine Coulon: Works in Council Service for elderly people.

*as written

At the meeting itself visitors would give more detail of their occupations as discussions began on general topics. 'Living with' here indicates a clergy house which is shared by this particular group of worker-priests. It should be remembered that the revival of the worker-priests after Vatican II continued to encourage priests living in groups to avoid the isolation which it was believed hindered their work in the early 1950s.

This was only one group which visited the Worker Church Group – there were others from France in the 1950s and 1960s – though the records of all in the visiting parties are fragmentary.

Source: Tony Williamson, and others: papers.

Notes

1. Raymond Williams, *The Country and the City,* Paladin 1975.
2. *The Task of the Church in Relation to Industry*, CIO 1959.
3. *Faith in the City,* CIO 1985, 75.
4. Michael Sissons and Philip French (eds), *Age of Austerity 1945–1951*, Penguin Books 1963, 29. The words were actually spoken at the beginning of April 1946, on the third reading of the Government's Trade Disputes and Trade Unions Bill.
5. Such points are not only made by recent commentators like Alan Sinfield, *Literature, Politics and Culture in Post-War Britain*, Blackwell 1989, but by the occasional admission of a wretched wartime past. *The Guardian*, 25 April 1995, told the story of Margaret Britton, who was about to visit West Midlands schools to talk about the Second World War. 'One story,' the paper commented, 'she will not tell is that of her own childhood in war and of the toll it took on the next fifty years of her life,' adding: 'Her story (of a broken home), like millions of stories in her generation, is Hitler's fault.'
6. Graham Sergeant, *A Statistical Source Book for Sociologists,* Macmillan 1972; also A. H. Halsey, *Trends in British Society Since 1900,* St Martins Press 1972, 47.
7. Edward Norman, *Church and Society in England, 1770–1970,* Clarendon Press 1976, 40. Indeed from time to time newspaper reports related commonly sad stories. See *The Argus* (Brighton and Hove), 11 July 1995, which in its '50 Years Ago' column retold the story of a soldier who had appeared before Eastbourne magistrates 'in answer to an application from his wife for a separation order and custody of three children on the grounds of cruelty'. Much was then blamed on the war, and the fact that women, being in the 'front line' at home, had grown accustomed to 'running the house by themselves'.
8. *Annual Abstract of Statistics*, HMSO, No 91, 1954. Some parts of Britain, such as the North East of England and the Scottish Lowlands, which had known depression in the 1930s, had actually benefited from the war. The steel works at Consett, for example, had gained, and the overall demand for steel was demonstrated in the rebuilding of the Port Talbot works in 1947. But raw materials, especially those essential for its manufacture, were in short supply. The coal industry was low on manpower, and output rarely met demand, especially in 1947–48, when the country would suffer one of the worst winters in living memory. By 29 January1948 the entire country was paralysed, with over two million men out of work. For further information on the percentage rate of unemployment (in 1947 at a relatively high figure of 3.1%, which then dropped to 1.8%

in 1948) see, 'The Percentage Rate of Unemployment in the United Kingdom', in George Sayer Bain, Robert Bacon and John Pimlott, 'The Labour Force', A. H. Halsey (ed.), *Trends in British Society* (n.6), ch.4.

9. W. Johnson, J. Whyman and G. Wykes, *A Short Economic and Social History of Twentieth-Century Britain*, Allen and Unwin 1967, 112f.
10. Alan Sked and Chris Cook, *Post-War Britain. A Political History*, Penguin Books 1983, 100.
11. *The Guardian*, 24 March 1959.
12. Sked and Cook, *Post-War Britain* (n.10), 189.
13. Ibid., 191.
14. William Temple, *Christianity and the Social Order*, Penguin Books 1942, 10: 'The varied forms of suffering which bad housing causes are easy to imagine in part, but few who have had no personal knowledge of it are able to imagine the whole – the crushing of a woman's pride in her home through the ceaseless and vain struggle against dirt and squalor; the nervous fret; the lack of home comforts for the tired worker; the absence of any space for children to play.'
15. The 'mod cons' included a form of central heating through an open fire, a cooker, refrigerator and a bathroom. When some residents from Finnermore Road in Hainault were moved off to adjoining estates, or some to new flats in Redbridge in 1967–68, though the new properties were good and contained modern amenities, they lacked a sense of privacy and of being 'detached' (which the prefabs often were), and gardens. Interview with Mrs Gwen Armstrong, January 1995.
16. Quoted by Adrian Hastings, *A History of English Christianity 1920–1990*, SCM Press ^{3}1991, 422.
17. Quoted by Norman, *Church and Society in England* (n.7), 376.
18. *Theology* LV, No. 390, December 1952. Only eight years later another contributor would add that it was sad how some clergy spoke 'wistfully' of days when slums were really slums, 'and contemptuous references are so often made to the welfare state that it is quite evident that many people are unaware of the things that have come to pass – things for which our fathers fought all their lives', *Theology* LXIII, No. 481, July 1960.
19. Sissons and French (eds), *Age of Austerity* (n.4), 336.
20. There had been much pre- and post-war criticism of popular writing, not least by Q. D. Leavis in *Fiction and the Reading Public* (1932), who showed alarm at a commercial culture which had come to dominate the literary scene.
21. A. Marwick, *Class – Image and Reality*, Collins 1980, 294f.
22. The ultimate sign of affluence was the car. Increased production with new techniques brought prices down, and the 'affluent worker' of the car industry (Goldthorpe) at Ford's Dagenham, or the Cowley works in Oxford could enjoy special purchase rates for employees. Using licence rates as an indicator, the number of cars registered in 1954 was 3,100,000. In only six years this had risen over 100% by 1962, bringing the total to 6,556,000, and by a further increase to over 8 million in 1964: see HMSO *Abstract of Statistics*, 1965, Table 82.
23. John A. T. Robinson, *Honest to God*, SCM Press 1963, 112.
24. Anne Grubb, 'English Developments', in *Priests and Workers, An Anglo-French Discussion*, edited by David L. Edwards, SCM Press 1961, 154.
25. Marwick, *Class – Image and Reality* (n.21); cf. also id., *Class in the Twentieth*

Century, Harvester Press 1986
26. Quoted by A. Marwick in *British Society Since 1945*, Penguin Books 1982, 111.
27. Sinfield, *Literature, Politics and Culture in Post-War Britain* (n.5), 21.
28. Marwick, *Class – Image and Reality* (n.21), 239. See also John de Satge, 'Mission and Unity in France', *Parish and People* 30, Trinity 1961: '... it was the war of 1939–45 which speeded things up. The experience of priests and seminarists in the Resistance, in the prisoner-of-war camps and forced labour camps, brought them in to touch with the attitudes of the unchurched'.
29. Marwick, *Class – Image and Reality* (n.21), 296.
30. J. H. Goldthorpe, *The Affluent Worker in the Class Structure*, Cambridge University Press 1969, 158f.
31. Ibid., 165.
32. J. H. Goldthorpe, *Social Mobility and Class Structure in Britain*, Clarendon Press 1978.
33. Marwick in *British Society Since 1945* (n.26), 47.
34. Letter of John Rowe, worker-priest, to Martyn Grubb, worker-priest in 1966, in Rowe, private papers.
35. Sinfield, *Literature, Politics and Culture in Post-War Britain* (n.5).
36. Norman, *Church and Society in England* (n.7), 380.
37. *Picture Post*, December 1953.
38. G. Stephen Spinks, *Religion in Britain Since 1900*, Andrew Dakers Ltd 1952, 216f.
39. Ibid., 223.
40. Roger Lloyd, *The Church of England 1900–1965*, SCM Press 1966, 463.
41. Less kind was a reference in the editorial of the new series of the *Modern Churchman*, X, no.3, April 1967, which commented: 'In the years since the war the Church of England has hardly moved at all. The time spent on the revision of Canon Law will come to be seen as a most scandalous waste of effort and a refusal to face the real issues of a post-war period.'
42. Hastings, *A History of English Christianity* (n.16), 437. William Purcell's work on Fisher, *Fisher of Lambeth. A Portrait from Life*, Hodder 1969, '... produced with the full approval and active co-operation of Archbishop Lord Fisher' and, after Lloyd, remains a somewhat disappointing benevolent affirmation of his work.
43. Grace Davie explains that in the diocese of London, 'only 70 out of 100 churches remained unscathed', *Religion in Britain since 1945*, Blackwell 1994, 30.
44. Lloyd, *The Church of England 1900–1965* (n.40), 484. And there could be other 'problems'. The Revd George Meek, who returned to his parish (from war service at the front as a padre in Italy) which had been looked after by another clergyman with sons, found some items 'missing' from his vicarage. Interview with G. Meek, 24 October 1996.
45. Lloyd, *The Church of England 1900–1965* (n.40), 487.
46. Spinks, *Religion in Britain Since 1900* (n.38), 224.
47. See *Towards the Conversion of England*, quoted in R. P. Flindall, *The Church of England 1815–1948 – A Documentary History*, SPCK 1972.
48. Lloyd, *The Church of England 1900–1965* (n.40), 473.
49. Alan M. Suggate, 'The Christian Churches in England since 1945. Ecumenism

and Social Concern', in Sheridan Gilley and W. J. Shiels (eds), *A History of Religion in Britain. Practice and Belief from Pre-Roman Times to the Present*, Blackwell 1994.

50. Lloyd, *The Church of England 1900–1965* (n.40), 521.
51. Paul Welsby, *A History of the Church of England 1945–1980*, Oxford University Press 1984, 12.
52. Robin Gill, *The Myth of the Empty Church*, SPCK 1993, 202.
53. Spinks, *Religion in Britain Since 1900* (n.38), 224.
54. Sinfield, *Literature, Politics and Culture in Post-War Britain* (n.5), 8f. Sinfield's pictures of human loss are well described, and there are certain common themes reiterated in Mass Observation's questions about 'belief' and 'loss'.
55. David Martin, *A Sociology of English Religion*, Heinemann 1967, 69.
56. Copies of the surveys by *News Review*, *British Weekly* and *Daily Graphic* used in this study were located among the material relating to Mass Observation in its archives at the University of Sussex. MO was used by the press from time to time to collect material, though the papers liked to make their own analyses and interpretations. MO clearly had a policy of filing copies of material that resulted from their initial research, especially when this covered a popular topic.
57. *News Review*, 30 October 1947: 'The answer was clear. They are moving away from the churches – becoming less frequent in their attendance.'
58. *Puzzled People – A Study in Popular Attitudes to Religion, Ethics, Progress and Politics in a London Borough*, Victor Gollancz 1947, 11.
59. *Religious Broadcasts and the Public*, BBC 1955.
60. Ibid.
61. W. S. F. Pickering, 'Religious Movements of Church Members in Two Working-Class Towns in England', *Archives de Sociologie des Religions* 11–12, 1961, 129f.
62. Ibid., 138.
63. Tom Harrison, paper in Mass Observation Archives (n.56), entitled 'For God's Sake'.
64. Richard Hoggart, *The Uses of Literacy*, Penguin Books 1957, 117: 'Most people in the working classes appear therefore not merely unfanatical but unidealistic, they have their principles, but are disinclined to reveal themselves in their pure state. For the most part their approach is empirical, they are confirmed pragmatists.'
65. Robert Graves and Alan Hodge, *The Long Weekend, A Social History of Great Britain 1918–1939*, Reader's Union Ltd. In this the authors chart church controversy including the matter of the 1928 Prayer Book.
66. K. B. Smellie, *The British Way of Life*, Heinemann 1955, 172
67. Pickering, 'Religious Movements of Church Members' (n.61), 138.
68. Antony Sampson, *Anatomy of Britain*, Hodder and Stoughton 1962.
69. J. W. C. Wand, *The Church Today*, Penguin Books 1960.
70. Robert Currie, Alan Gilbert and Lee Horsley, *Churches and Churchgoers – Patterns of Church Growth in the British Isles since 1700*, Clarendon Press 1977. For church growth and decline see graphs, p.30; for arguments about 'secularization' see 122.
71. Paul Johnson, *20th Century Britain*, Longman 1994, 429.

72. Davie, *Religion in Britain since 1945* (n.43), 106.
73. E. R. Wickham, *Church and People in an Industrial City*, Lutterworth Press 1957.
74. Norman, *Church and Society in England* (n.7), 425, quoting Wand in *Anglicanism in History and Today*, London 1961.
75. Robin Greenwood, *Transforming Priesthood – A New Theology for Mission and Ministry*, SPCK 1994, 32.
76. Kenneth Hylson-Smith, *Evangelicals in the Church of England*, T. & T. Clark 1988, 107.
77. Antony Russell, *The Clerical Profession*, SPCK 1980, 233.
78. B. G. Worrall, *The Making of the Modern Church*, SPCK 1988, 19.
79. Georgina Battiscombe, *John Keble – A Study in Limitations*, Garden City Press 1963, 176.
80. Worrall, *The Making of the Modern Church* (n.78), 42f.
81. E. Norman, *The Victorian Christian Socialists*, Cambridge University Press 1987, 26.
82. Ibid., 1.
83. S. Mayor, *The Churches and the Labour Movement*, Independent Press 1967, 323.
84. Alan Wilkinson, *The Church of England and the First World War*, SPCK 1978.
85. William Purcell, *Woodbine Willie*, Hodder & Stoughton 1962, 118.
86. See Siegfried Sassoon, *Memoirs of an Infantry Officer*, Faber & Faber 1930: '. . . the dressing station was a small underground place crowded with groaning wounded. Two doctors were doing all they could for men who had paid a heavy price for their freedom. My egocentricity diminished among all that agony. I remember listening to an emotional padre who was painfully aware that he could do nothing except stand about and feel sympathetic. The consolations of the Church of England weren't much in demand at an Advanced Dressing station' (169). This situation had changed by World War Two, but perhaps only a little. In writing on the D-Day landings (1944), Max Hastings says: 'Good chaplains were greatly prized by their units, but bad ones – of whom there were many in the allied armies – were detested and avoided for the hypocrisy with which they offered their blessings from the rear echelon.' Max Hastings, *Overlord*, Guild Publishing 1984.
87. Greenwood, *Transforming Priesthood* (n.75), 20.
88. Ibid., 25.
89. Fr S. Bedale, at the SSM London Reunion, SDSMQP Christmas 1922. Quoted by A. Mason, *SSM History of the Society of the Sacred Mission*, Canterbury Press 1993, 137.
90. Ibid., 65.
91. Ibid., 66.
92. Paul Ferris, *The Church of England*, Penguin Books 1962, 45.
93. *Picture Post*, 23 October 1948.
94. Ferris, *The Church of England* (n.92), 100.
95. *Picture Post*, 2 January 1954.
96. Horton Davies, *A Mirror of the Ministry in Modern Novels*, New York: Oxford University Press 1959.

97. Ibid., 140.
98. Raymond Durgnat, *A Mirror For England – British Movies from Austerity to Affluence,* Faber 1970.
99. See *Halliwell's Film Guide,* Paladin [7]1989.
100. Ibid.
101. Lloyd, *The Church of England 1900–1965* (n.40), 521.
102. L. G. Tyler (Rector of Bradford), 'The Church and Industry', *The Modern Churchman*, September 1954, 185.
103. L. Erlander, *Faith in the World of Work*, PhD thesis published by the University of Uppsala, 1991.
104. *The Times*, 30 June 1950. Quoted by Patrick Vaughan, *Non-Stipendiary Ministry in the Church of England,* Mellen Research University Press, San Francisco 1990.
105. Quoted in the leader of *The Modern Churchman*, New Series III,2, March 1960.
106. Cyril Garbett, *The Claims of the Church of England*, Hodder & Stoughton 1947, 125f.
107. J. W. C. Wand, *What the Church of England Stands For*, Mowbray 1951, 29f.
108. Ibid., 28.
109. *The Times*, 11 July 1947.
110. Colin A. Roberts (ed.), *These Christian Commando Campaigns – New Men for a New World,* Epworth Press 1945. The reference to Arnhem was timely. In September 1944, the Parachute Regiment had captured Arnhem bridge, but ground troops, in an armoured column, failed to reach them before they were overrun by enemy SS troops.
111. Ibid., 84f.
112. 'Christian Commandos Strike Again', in *Picture Post,* 3 May 1947. The French had at least one worker-priest working *in* the film industry, Fr Jaques Riosse. See Oscar Arnal, *Priests in Working-Class Blue*, Paulist Press 1986, 115.
113. Abbé Michonneau, *Revolution in a City Parish,* Blackfriars 1949, 15.
114. Joseph Williamson: *Father Joe – An Autobiography of Joseph Williamson of Poplar and Stepney*, Hodder & Stoughton, 1963. Williiamson's photograph appeared in the *Daily Mail*, kneeling in front of a slum that was being demolished: 'and when I saw all these filthy hovels coming down I just fell on my knees and said a Gloria' . . . 'people accused me of specially posing for the picture, of trying to be a sensation. But the only thing that was in my mind at that moment was a great surge of thankfulness to God that this foul place was at last being done away with' (166).
115. Personal interview with Kenneth Mason, Coates Hall, Edinburgh, 18 December 1995.
116. Tim Gorringe, *Alan Ecclestone – Priest as Revolutionary,* Cairns Publications 1994, 79, 99.
117. Ibid., 79.
118. John de Satge, 'Mission and Unity in France', *Parish and People* 30, Trinity 1961, 7.
119. Mention of the church and housing estates appears, especially in *The Times*, from June 1953.

120. Ronald Frankenberg, *Communities in Britain – Social Life in Town and Country*, Penguin Books 1966.
121. Ibid., 201.
122. Lloyd, *The Church of England 1900–1965* (n.40), 522.
123. Colin Rushbridge, 'The Stresses for Ministers in New Town Churches', *Churches in Industrial Areas*, 21.
124. C. Morrison and Trevor Beeson, 'Training for the Mission', *Theology* LXIII, 478, April 1960, 478.
125. G. Cutcher, 'Housing Estate Church', Parish and People, New Series 1, April 1955. For E. R. Wickham's views see *Church and People in an Industrial City* (n.73), 265.
126. Lloyd, *The Church of England 1900–1965* (n.40), 525.
127. See in particular the work of Margaret Kane, *Theology in an Industrial Society*, SCM Press 1975; *Gospel in an Industrial Society*, SCM Press 1980.
128. John A. T. Robinson, *On Being the Church in the World*, SCM Press 1960, 6f. and Chapter 5, 'The House Church and the Parish Church'. Also see Robinson's 'kingdom' theology spelt out in Chapter 1, which was originally the first of the Stafford Cripps Memorial Lectures, delivered in St Paul's Cathedral in October 1959.
129. Norman, *Church and Society in England* (n.7).
130. Ibid., 16, and see the Preface, 7–8.
131. de Satge, 'Mission and Unity in France' (n.118).
132. An example of this is Ved Mehta, *The New Theologian*, Weidenfeld & Nicholson1966. The idea was that Ved Mehta would use Robinson's *Honest to God* 'as a springboard' to talk about other theologians including Bonhoeffer, Bultmann, Tillich and Robinson himself.
133. *The Lambeth Conference 1968, Resolutions and Reports*, London and New York 1968, 'A Message from the Bishops', 23.
134. Dom Gregory Dix, *The Shape of the Liturgy*, Dacre Press 1945.
135. M. Grundy, *An Unholy Conspiracy – The Scandal of the Separation of the Church and Industry Since the Reformation*, Canterbury Press 1992, 63.
136. For French sources see Adrien Dansette, *Destin du Catholicisme Français 1926–1956*, Flammarion 1957. For the most recent comprehensive study in English see Arnal, *Priests in Working-Class Blue* (n.112). For knowledge of the worker-priests in Britain, see John Fuller and Patrick Vaughan (eds), *Working for the Kingdom,* SPCK 1986; Rod Hacking, *On the Boundary*, Canterbury Press 1990; Grundy, *An Unholy Conspiracy* (n.135). For earlier material on the French worker-priests themselves, see *The Worker Priests*, Collected Documents translated by John Petrie, Routledge & Kegan Paul 1956; Stanley Windass, *The Chronicle of the Worker-Priests*, Merlin Press 1966; Gregor Siefer, *The Church and Industrial Society – Complete History of the Worker-Priests – and the Present Dilemma,* Darton, Longman and Todd 1964.
137. Henri Godin and Yvan Daniel, *France Pagan*, Sheed and Ward 1950. This publishing house in particular, because of the great enthusiasm of Maisie Ward and Rosemary Sheed, gave English readers the opportunity to read these modern 'classics' which would include the first autobiographical material from Henri Perrin (see below).

138. Siefer, *The Church and Industrial Society* (n.136), 23.
139. Ibid., 24.
140. Cardinal Ferrata, *Memoirs,* quoted ibid., 25.
141. Ibid., 26.
142. Arnal, *Priests in Working-Class Blue* (n.112), 17.
143. From W. Gurian, *Die politischen und sozialen Ideen der französischen Katholizismus 1789–1914* (1928), 14, Quoted by Siefer, *The Church and Industrial Society* (n.136), 35.
144. Ibid., 38. See also Arnal on the JOC: 'Throughout the 1930s it spread rapidly in the industrial centres of France, so much so that by the outbreak of war it was the single most important proletarian youth group in the nation' (*Priests in Working-Class Blue,* n.112), 27.
145. Siefer, *The Church and Industrial Society* (n.136), 38.
146. Leo Zander (from Eckhart, January – March 1955), 'The Tragedy of the Priest-Workers in France', *Church Quarterly Review*, July-September, 1955. Some caution should be exercised over what might be described as a romanticization of the workers and their relations with the Resistance. Siefer paints a glowing picture of priests united against the Germans. Thus: 'The solid front formed by all who pledged themselves to the Resistance formed the basis of that new, and at first strong, sense of solidarity which was now manifest.' But in general terms the involvement of the French clergy in the Resistance might be uneven, even though Michael Foot comments favourably: 'Although the Vichy regime was supported by the bulk of the popish hierarchy, and had a strong popish flavour, a large majority of the country priests of France put their duty as compassionate human beings before their duty of obedience to their bishops. Allied aircrew shot down over France, or allied commandos left behind on raids, were recommended to apply for advice on how to escape to any village priest; and there can hardly be any instance when this trust was misplaced.' Or, there is strength in his negative, '. . . that there is nothing new in the theory that only the communists and the priests really resisted . . .' M. R. D. Foot, *SOE In France,* HMSO 1966, 135, 178.
147. Père Loew, *Mission to the Poorest*, Catholic Book Club 1951, 22.
148. Godin, *France Pagan* (n.137), 71.
149. Ibid., 87.
150. Ibid., 92.
151. Ibid., 97.
152. Ibid., 155. It would have been difficult to find such a radical comment anywhere in Britain at that time, though later Ted Wickham would be noted for his scathing comments on parish ministry. Daniel and Godin were not, of course, opposed to parish ministry like some, but were issuing their own warning.
153. Siefer, *The Church and Industrial Society* (n.136), 63.
154. Godin, *France Pagan* (n.137), 191.
155. Arnal, *Priests in Working-Class Blue* (n.112), 57.
156. H. Perrin, *Priest-Workman in Germany*, Sheed and Ward 1947.
157. Ibid., 106. There were few equivalent groups in Britain (apart from Rover Scouts). These were militant lay associations and though the worker-priests would later work alongside them, they were never thought of after the war as

having been militant enough.

158. At the beginning of March 1944, and after disappointing hold-ups, during which Perrin used the time for a self-imposed 'retreat', he heard he would be sent home to France. But as delays came and went, he wrote to his mother to prepare her for his possible deportation to a concentration camp. 'We had so often been lied to,' he admitted, 'that it would not have surprised me to be sent to Buchenwald or sent back to France the next day.' Perrin, *Priest-Workman in Germany* (n.156), 216.
159. Ibid., 230.
160. Arnal, *Priests in Working-Class Blue* (n.112), 60.
161. Petrie, *The Worker Priests* (n.136), 10.
162. Ibid., 11.
163. Perrin, *Priest-Workman in Germany* (n.156), 66, 83. It is clear that Perrin was thought well of by local clergy both in Paris and later at the Isère-Arc Dam. It would be true to say that in making contacts with local clergy he kept his head down. But making contact was one thing; he clearly had no intention of becoming embroiled in parochial life.
164. Ibid ., 77. Training for a skilled or semi-skilled job was one of the features of the movement. The notion that worker-priests were sent 'disguised' as workers into Germany or back to France, as if they were simply 'dressed up', fails to credit a number with real skills which they had developed. See Perrin, *Priest-Workman in Germany* (n.156), 2 .
165. Ibid., 101.
166. Ibid., 102.
167. Ibid., 105. In the earliest days there were reports of worker-priests making themselves very obvious, and on some rare occasions by actually wearing the soutane. Such obvious displays of priesthood, as Arnal suggests, quickly evaporated, and working overalls became the norm. See Wickham, in Edwards, *Priests and Workers* (n.24).
168. Ibid., 110.
169. Ibid., 120f.
170. Ibid., 116. Again this was precisely what was found by Mass Observation in Britain in 1947. Less antagonism with Christianity's core story, more with the way it was lived or not lived by those who laid claim upon it.
171. Ibid., 121.
172. See E. R. Wickham's 'Appraisal' in Edwards, *Priests and Workers* (n.24), 124.
173. Perrin, *Priest-Workman in Germany* (n.156), 142.
174. Ibid., 154.
175. Ibid., 161.
176. Olivier de la Brosse OP (ed.), *The Responsible Church, Selected Texts of Cardinal Suhard*, Geoffrey Chapman 1967, 127. There was a broad movement anyway in favour of reform of the liturgy which had evolved in France some time before the war. It was in much of this that the adherents of the Parish and People movement in England had taken an interest. See also evening mass as advocated by Perrin himself, in *Priest and Worker. The Autobiography of Henri Perrin*, Macmillan 1965, 70.
177. This indeed happened, and apart from the romanticized view taken by G.

Cresbon in the novel *Saints in Hell* (*Les Saints vont en enfer,* Laffont 1952), disliked by worker-priests as there was no mention whatever of a priest's factory life, there is also an account of an evening mass given by Violet Welton in 'Two Tables', in *Priests and Workers* (n.24), Chapter 1.

178. de la Brosse, *The Responsible Church* (n.176), 130.
179. Siefer, *The Church and Industrial Society* (n.136), 55.
180. Ibid., 58.
181. Ibid., 56.
182. de la Brosse, *The Responsible Church* (n.176), 131.
183. *Le Monde*, 15 April 1952. This was, in fact, a far greater blow than may have been realized at the time, weakening the voice of the worker-priests. Suhard had been able to act as an intermediary between the spiritual needs of the worker-priests, which he well understood, on the one hand and the anxieties of the Vatican on 'spiritual activity' and the implicit interpretations of the nature of this new priesthood on the other.
184. A commentary in Perrin, *Priest and Worker* (n.176), describes how '. . . an extremely complex situation had arisen in Paris and its suburbs, where there was a tendency for priest-workers (or those who believed they had a vocation) to proliferate. They included secular priests, regular priests, and above all priests 'who were more or less in an irregular position' (165). Perrin admitted to being up against difficulties including the fact that 'the Archbishop, overwhelmed with requests from priests who have broken off from their diocese and orders, is at the moment adopting a strict negative policy' (168).
185. In March 1952, Perrin confessed that through some 'indiscretion of the police', it became known that I was a priest. '. . . and today on the occasion of the funeral of the seventh of our work mates killed within a year on the site, I performed my first religious act.' Later he wrote: '. . . all the workers were present when I appeared all dressed up and ornamented . . . half of them came into the church, the other half stayed outside. When we emerged some of them came up to me and said in full view of all, or nearly all, that the ceremony had increased the trust they felt in me', *Priest and Worker* (n.176), 193.
186. Ibid., 225.
187. Siefer, *The Church and Industrial Society* (n.136), 71.
188. Zander, 'The Tragedy of the Priest-Workers in France' (n.146), 293.
189. Siefer, *The Church and Industrial Society* (n.136), 73 (see his footnote on the same page).
190. 'Letter from the worker-priests of Limoges to Monseigneur Rastouil, 14 February 1954', in Petrie, *The Worker Priests* (n.136), 187.
191. Ibid., 80.
192. Arnal, *Priests in Working-Class Blue* (n.112), 154. Arnal writes the history of the first stage of the worker-priest movement. But, as he explained in the text, this was not, of course, the end of the worker-priests – though at the time it would have been difficult to think otherwise.
193. S. Windass (ed.), *The Chronicle of the Worker-Priests,* Merlin Press 1966, published just after the worker-priests were revived under Pope Paul VI.
194. Petrie, *The Worker Priests* (n.136), 203.
195. *The Times*, 15 September 1959. This kind of interpretation worked two ways.

On the one hand it confirmed for the more conservative at home and abroad that the Vatican was firming up its understanding of the priesthood; on the other, those who advocated radical ministries were convinced of a totally different understanding of what it meant to be a priest.

196. André Dupière, Report, Montreuil (1949) quoted by Arnal, *Priests in Working-Class Blue* (n.112), 115f.
197. E. R. Wickham, 'Appraisal', in Edwards, *Priests and Workers* (n.24), 126.
198. Perrin, *Priest and Worker* (n.176), 137.
199. 'Letter from the worker-priests of Limoges' (n.190), 188.
200. Père Robert, 'Rapport sur mon engagement de prêtre ouvrier', Paris, 22 January 1949, quoted by Arnal, *Priests in Working-Class Blue* (n.112), 131.
201. 'Letter from the worker-priests of Limoges' (n.190), 188.
202. Perrin, *Priest and Worker* (n.176).
203. Ibid., 240.
204. Interview with French worker-priests from the Lille and Arras areas in the Nord de Calais, October 1993 (interview recorded with British theological students).
205. John Cogley, 'They are Priests and Workers Both', *The New York Times Magazine*, 26 December 1965.
206. Arnal, *Priests in Working-Class Blue* (n.112), 171.
207. E. Lurkins, *The Origins, Context and Ideology of Industrial Mission 1875–1975*, unpublished PhD thesis London School of Economics 1981; Shigeko Masumoto, *A Critique of British Industrial Mission as a Response of the Church to Modern Industrial Society*, unpublished MPhil thesis, University of Leeds 1983; Erlander, *Faith in the World of Work* (n. 103); Grundy, *An Unholy Conspiracy* (n.135).
208. W. Temple, *Christianity and the Social Order*, Penguin 1940, was reprinted very quickly. For the publishers this was a book which faced the gravity of the world's crisis '. . . yet which presented with the spirit of hope the teaching of Christ . . . which can yet save Western civilization'. C. Garbett, *The Claims of the Church of England*, Hodder & Stoughton 1947, was rooted in institutionalism; the title said it all.
209. Temple, *Christianity and the Social Order* (n.208), 74.
210. Mass Observation for the *British Weekly*, 20 January 1949.
211. Interview with Simon Phipps, Sussex, May 1996.
212. M. Atkinson, 'A Sort of Episcopal Fly on the Walls of British Industry', in Gordon Hewitt (ed.), *Strategist for the Spirit – Leslie Hunter Bishop of Sheffield 1939–1962*, Becket Publications 1985, 164.
213. Ronald Ferguson, *George Macleod – Founder of the Iona Community*, HarperCollins 1990.
214. For a study of Bishop Hunter, see Hewitt (ed.), *Strategist for the Spirit* (n.212).
215. From 'Towards a New Age', late typescript by Leslie Hunter, quoted by Atkinson, 'A Sort of Episcopal Fly' (n.212), 156.
216. Report of the Anglican Congress, 1954, 163, quoted by Norman, *Church and Society* (n.7), 396.
217. P. Bagshaw, *The Church beyond the Church – Sheffield Industrial Mission 1944–1994*, Industrial Mission in South Yorkshire 1994.

218. Mary Walton, *A History of the Diocese of Sheffield 1914–1979*, Sheffield Diocesan Board of Finance 1981.
219. E. R. Wickham, *Audenshaw Papers*, date uncertain: possibly 1973.
220. M. H. Atkinson, 'The Sheffield Industrial Mission', 3–4, an undated paper from the mid-1960s which gives a detailed account of how the clergy went out to meet men directly on the shop floor. The dating may be significant; though Michael Jackson is mentioned as senior chaplain, there is no hint of an impending break-up.
221. Report by Philip Bloy from Interviews, a paper dated July 1984.
222. Ibid., 2. Bloy conducted his interviews with 'past associates' of the Mission, and included the material in a retrospective view.
223. Interview with Clive Everett-Allen, 30 January 1997.
224. Bagshaw, *The Church beyond the Church* (n.217), 15.
225. Interview with Roland Walls and John Halsey, 18 December 1995, see also Bagshaw, *The Church beyond the Church* (n.217), 17.
226. Jeremy Morris, 'Church and People Thirty Years On: A Historical Critique', *Theology* XCIV, March/April 1991, No.758, 92.
227. Wickham, *Church and People in an Industrial City* (n.73), 227.
228. Norman, *Church and Society* (n.7).
229. Wickham, *Church and People in an Industrial City* (n.73), 234.
230. Atkinson, 'The Sheffield Industrial Mission' (n.220).
231. Wickham, *Church and People in an Industrial City* (n.73), 247.
232. Ibid., 265.
233. One young ordinand was Clive Everett-Allen, who, between 1965 and 1966, and straight from school, was sent by Sydney Evans (Dean of King's College, London), 'who thought it was a good idea for us to go and get our hands dirty'. Everett-Allen worked alongside several other ordinands at Firth Brownstone of the biggest steelworks, but not as missioners: 'I was a crane driver . . . Margaret Kane came round to visit the men and we had basic lectures from different members of the team. "Tha 'll never be a f***ing Vicar thee" was often the usual reaction . . . from workers. I lived in a "Coronation Street house" up in the attic . . . the landlady had been somehow involved with the mission; there was no great resentment [at being in such a house] but there was a certain loneliness.' They were encouraged to read Ted Wickham and Richard Hoggart. 'The snap break was so novel – they were quite intrigued; really it didn't get beyond . . . like talking to people at a bus stop . . . it was where the people were at . . . they saw the church was so distant, that the idea that someone from the church should come and talk to them was astonishing – people didn't want to talk about the gospel but what we thought about the archbishop or David Sheppard or the pope and birth control – the headline issues rather than some fundamental aspect of the gospel, but that's OK . . . that's where the people were . . .' Interview with Clive Everett-Allen, Sussex, 30 January 1997.
234. M. Atkinson, 'A Sort of Episcopal Fly' (n.212), 165.
235. 'A brilliant man', interview with C. F. D. Moule, Sussex, 28 June 1997.
236. Interview with Roland Walls and John Halsey, Roslin, March 1993. Simon Phipps is uncertain about the occasion of the meeting in Cambridge with Leslie Hunter.

237. Correspondence and discussion with R. Walls, May, 1996.
238. *The Church and Industry*, British Council of Churches 1958. Its cover suggests 'an interpretation of each to the other', though the reader is hard pressed to believe that this view of the importance of industry to the churches and the nation is anything other that the churches' view, and certainly not that of industry, even if it was in any way sympathetic to such a document.
239. Grundy, *An Unholy Conspiracy* (n.135), 69.
240. Correspondence with P. Bagshaw, February 1997.
241. Bagshaw, *The Church beyond the Church* (n.217), also correspondence with Margaret Kane, 3 January 1996.
242. Interview with Roland Walls and John Halsey, 18 December 1995.
243. Ibid.
244. Bagshaw, *The Church beyond the Church* (n.217), 59.
245. Ibid., see also *The Times*, 21 June 1966; *The Guardian*, 23 July 1966.
246. Bagshaw, *The Church beyond the Church* (n.217), 66.
247. 'No New Gospel', *Theology* LXIX, no 558, December 1996, 539f.
248. H. P. Forder, *The Future of the Sheffield Industrial Mission, Report by a Working Party,* May 1967.
249. Ibid., 7.
250. Walton, *A History of the Diocese of Sheffield 1914–1979* (n.218), 69.
251. Bagshaw, *The Church beyond the Church* (n.217), 69.
252. Bloy (see n.221), 4.
253. Ibid., 5.
254. Ibid., 9.
255. Bagshaw, *The Church beyond the Church* (n.217), 25, talks about the Thursday celebrations, open to all, where there was some innovation: '. . . they avoided the book of Common Prayer, and used a form of service tailored to the group'. But Bloy (se n.221), 10, says of the Thursday celebrations of the 'Lord's Supper': 'no new liturgical imagination was put into this celebration but there was a warm simplicity'. Bloy explains that there was this celebration which was later moved to the Cathedral, at which, Bagshaw admits, some of the workers held back, and which Bloy says, was later abolished.
256. Interview with Roland Walls, December 1995.
257. E. R. Wickham, *Encounter with Modern Society*, Lutterworth Press 1964, 69.
258. A. J. Drewett, 'England – A Field for Mission', *The Modern Churchman*, New Series VI, No 1, October 1962
259. Edwards (ed.), *Priests and Workers* (n.24), 5.
260. Ibid., 131.
261. John Rowe in a letter to Martyn Grubb, 28 March 1966. John Rowe Papers.
262. S. Booth-Clibborn and M. Jackson, 1955, quoted by Vaughan, *Non-Stipendiary Ministry in the Church of England* (n.104), 163.
263. There will be some discussion of these particular issues at a later point in this study, though it should be noted here that throughout Europe there were Catholic, Orthodox and other clergy who in a variety of traditions and contexts did earn their own living.
264. Vaughan, *Non-Stipendiary Ministry in the Church of England* (n.104). See also John Fuller and P. H. Vaughan, *Working for the Kingdom. The Story of*

Ministers in Secular Employment, SPCK 1986. Also Rod Hacking, *On the Boundary – A Vision for Non-Stipendiary Ministry*, Canterbury Press 1990.

265. Vaughan, *Non-Stipendiary Ministry in the Church of England* (n.104), 150.
266. For a period of several years starting in 1993, and for the purposes of this study, advertisements were placed in the *Church Times* and in some diocesan magazines, asking for the names of clergy who 'even for a short time' may have been employed in secular work, and who might describe themselves as 'worker-priests'. The handful of names obtained, many of whom were simply later NSMs, reveals not simply that numbers may have been low, but that some anyway may not wish to give reasons why they left the full-time employment of the church.
267. Worker-priest questionnaire, partly completed by Simpkiss's wife – both now deceased. This questionnaire (see Appendix 7) was prepared for this study as a systematic way of attempting to determine common features in the background, motivation and employment of some of the first worker-priests.
268. Simpkiss diary 1955.
269. John Bickersteth, 'Factory Interlude', *Theology* LXX, January 1959.
270. Worker-priest questionnaire (Appendix 7), response from M. Gedge, 1993.
271. Ibid.
272. Michael Gedge, *Priest-Workman in England – A Study in Life*, SPCK 1951, xi. This was published anonymously to prevent any libel action, as Gedge mentioned work-mates in a variety of industrial settings.
273. Ibid., xi.
274. Gedge gives no record of who this was, though it is possible that it was one of the 'few priests who had deliberately decided to earn their living as a factory manual worker', possibly E. J. Lister. See Vaughan, *Non-Stipendiary Ministry in the Church of England* (n.104), 150.
275. Gedge, *Priest-Workman in England* (n.272), xiii. Gedge has described these reasons as 'purely pastoral: everyone said, "You can't be a Christian at a place of work." I decided to find our for myself', questionnaire (see n.267), 3. And in the text of his book he adds: 'At this time my mind was moving, unknown to me, along the same lines as those of several priests in France. Again unknown to me, God was working events so that I, and other Priests, not only in France, but in England as well, could and did find employment in ministry' (xiii).
276. M. R. Loew, *Mission to the Poorest*, Catholic Book Club 1951: 'In the struggle to get behind this poverty to the people themselves, there is, in fact, only one way which so far the sociologists haven't tried: Living it themselves. Consequently, I concluded, it was no good wasting time on paper theories; the thing to do was to buy an overall on the old-clothes market, get a job like everyone else, and then, at the end of the day's work, go off and live with the very dregs of the population – the dockers in the ports' (22). Simply going to work 'as a docker' was nothing like so simple for an individual in Britain who would attempt this some ten years later. See Martyn Grubb in Chapter 4 below.
277. Gedge, *Priest-Workman in England* (n.272), 50–1. The whole question of the need for workers to have their own tools would later become a highly contentious issue on the shop floor, and one into which Gedge would unintentionally be drawn.

278. Ibid., 25. See also John Bickersteth, who in 1959 after a fortnight in a factory admitted: 'I am certain I have never looked at a clock or watch so much as I did during the working hours of that fortnight' ('Factory Interlude', n.269).
279. Ibid., 52. The men had their own agendas for discussion. 'What is today's subject for talk? Love? No. What did George say to me earlier? "Man turned down by tribunal because his objections to the war were political, not religious." That is a good one to get us going.'
280. Ibid., 56.
281. Ibid., 34.
282. Ibid., 49. There are also similar sentiments in Henri Perrin, *Priest-Workman in Germany* (n.156).
283. Ibid., 50. Some of these sentiments were being expressed by Bishop Leslie Hunter at almost exactly the same time, and would lead him towards his fundamentally different approaches, through Ted Wickham's efforts on the shop floor.
284. Perrin, *Priest-Workman in Germany* (n.156).
285. These can be extremely short, consisting of part of a psalm, a prayer and a collect. In the monastic tradition (learned by Gedge at Mirfield), work and prayer were interlocked so that short moments of set prayer gave the whole day a reflective structure. Gedge later admits that a worker has a routine, a timetable, so his life is very much like a religious life.
286. Alan Sillitoe, *Saturday Night and Sunday Morning*, W. H. Allen 1958, 26.
287. Gedge, *Priest-Workman in England* (n.272), 57.
288. Ibid., 137.
289. Ibid., 63f.
290. This was the process of watching for incendiary bombs dropped by enemy aircraft, either in the course of a full-scale raid or in random attacks.
291. Gedge, *Priest-Workman in England* (n.272), 77.
292. Sinfield, *Literature, Politics and Culture in Post-War Britain* (n.5), 8.
293. Interview with M. Gedge, Canterbury, February 1993.
294. Gedge, *Priest-Workman in England* (n.272), 134. 'I often wonder if it is the devil who has made us pay so much attention to the question of bad language; it would be like his usual strategy, for it draws away attention from more serious sins, so that men will call themselves too wicked to go to church because they swear . . .'
295. In a later publication first produced in 1956 by the West Yorkshire Printing Co Ltd, Wakefield, under the title *The Seven Sacraments*, and written and illustrated for children by Enid Chadwick, all the sentiments of the time are present. A good communion cannot be made without fasting from midnight on, and must be received at least three times a year, 'of which Easter [in red letters] must be one'.
296. Gedge, *Priest-Workman in England* (n.272), 178.
297. For information on the founding of these communities, which have had relations with worker-priests, see René Voillaume, *Seeds of the Desert*, also *Brothers of Men – Letters to the Petits Frères*, Darton, Longman and Todd 1966. See also details of the orders in Kathryn Spink, *The Call of the Desert*, Darton, Longman and Todd 1993.

298. O. Chadwick, 'Tent-Makers', *Theology* LIV.368, February, 1951
299. Gedge, *Priest-Workman in England* (n.272), 233.
300. Ibid., 237.
301. This is a question which will be addressed in due course, when a worker-priest will be defined as one committed to skilled or unskilled manual labour.
302. Gedge, *Priest-Workman in England* (n.272), 187.
303. Michael Gedge, in a worker-priest questionnaire, 1993, 3.
304. Interview with Michael Gedge, Canterbury, February 1993.
305. John Strong, papers: untitled papers on work at Eyethome, possibly dated mid-1960s.
306. Bickersteth, 'Factory Interlude' (n.269).
307. *Guardian*, 4 January 1974. Comment from John Strong in an article by Tim Justin Robinson, 'Blue Collar Priests': an appraisal of worker-priests and their past history.
308. *Crockford's Clerical Directory*, 1961–62.
309. John Strong papers (n.305), 3.
310. *Guardian*, 4 January 1974 (n.307). Strong says that the Archbishop did 'express some misgivings'.
311. 'The Bishop (Bishop Rose at the Eyethorne PCC) explained that it was proposed that Rev. M. Gedge and another younger priest should take over the parish as priest-in-charge and assistant priest respectively. They would at the same time work at the pit as ordinary miners on 8 hr shifts, but one would always be above ground. They would be free on Saturdays and Sundays and would receive £5/15/0 (£5.75) per week and would not receive the stipend' (PCC Minutes of Eyethorne Parish, 27 February 1951).
312. Ibid.
313. John Strong, 'A True Vocation – Role of the Worker Priest in Industrial Society', *The Church Times*, 2 October 1959.
314. *The Guardian*, 4 January 1974 (n.307).
315. Gedge, interview, February 1993.
316. Strong, papers, 4.
317. Ibid., 5.
318. Goff Hares, Interview, 28 February 1996.
319. Strong, papers, 8.
320. There were many strikes, sometimes at what seemed the slightest pretext, perhaps for a few hours or just for a day or so. Hares, Interview (n.318).
321. *The Frontier* I.11, November 1950, 'Notes for the Month'.
322. Strong, papers, 12.
323. *Picture Post*, July 1954.
324. This has been echoed by Goff Hares some fifty years later. He claimed Gedge was a 'good worker'. On one occasion when a vast amount of coal, dust and rubble, more than usual, collected at the end of a belt, Hares and his fellow miners passed it, remarking that Gedge 'would never shift that lot': but it was shifted, '(Gedge) worked stripped to the waist to clear it' (Interview, n.318).
325. Strong, papers, 13.
326. See *Crockford's Clerical Directory*, 1961, 'Priest-Workmen': 'There has been some ill informed comment on the wages paid to these men, and comparison

has been made between what they would have received as curates. Such talk is as ungenerous as it is unjustified. It fails to take account of such things as the cost of buying or renting a house, the fixed hours of work, shortness of holidays, and other factors which make the two kinds of life radically different' (ix).

327. Strong, papers, 15.
328. Ibid., 20.
329. Minutes of Eyethorne PCC, 26 August 1954. A Mr Hampshire suggested the building of the lych-gate.
330. The end of the year also brought to an end the worker-priest experiment which had been running for 3 years. '(Gedge and Strong) are continuing the experiment in other spheres. We are grateful to them for their work here,' Minutes of the Eyethorne Parish AGM, 13 April 1955.
331. Michael Jackson, 'The Character and Functions of the Non-Professional Ministry', *Theology* LVIII, 424, October 1955, 367: 'It is obvious that the weakness of the church and the shortage of full-time men requires a drastic reorganization of parishes on a territorial basis. This is true both in industrial and in rural areas.' Already the spectre of a shortage of manpower was leading on to questions of how to 'man' parishes.
332. Strong, papers, 12.
333. Ibid., 13.
334. Patrick Vaughan also highlights the 'bathhouse experience', quoting from John Strong's article 'Into a Thick Wood', *The Franciscan* 17, 32–36, in *Non-Stipendiary Ministry* (n.104).
335. Ibid., 167.
336. Ibid., 176.
337. Vaughan quotes p.16 of Convocation's Report (1955) relating to non-parochial ministry, where the whole tenor of the debate is about alternative ministries which would be there to support the parochial, and in which the new ministry '. . . will wish to be attached to a parish church to which they can direct their "converts" . . .', *Non-Stipendiary Ministry* (n.104), 172.
338. *Guardian*, 2 January 1974.
339. Hares, interview (n.318).
340. Ibid. It is very easy to ask what Hares meant by this. But the statement was made without further comment and with no attempt to unpack it. It seemed right at the time of the interview to leave it there rather than impose interpretation, or to seek something more 'sophisticated'.
341. See Michael Gedge's article: 'How can the clergy know about the rat race unless there are PRIEST WORKERS HERE . . . ?' Gedge argued that 'The question of priest workers is in danger of going by default. The subject is too serious to be casually dismissed', *The Universe and Catholic Times,* 23 December 1966.
342. Another worker-priest is uncertain of this: 'John was always available to people – John wanted me to join him. John believed in the parochial thing – I admired his single-mindedness – I could never believe in the parish, but I could respect him,' John Rowe, Interview,1993.
343. John Strong, 'A True Vocation – Role of the Worker-Priest in an Industrial Society', *Church Times,* 2 October 1959.

344. Conversation with Jim Oliver, January 1997.
345. In an article over thirty years later, in *Contact,* the Harlington village magazine, February 1991, the vicarage was described by a contributor as 'an imposing two-storied structure brick residence . . . alas, this graceful residence was demolished in the 1960s'. This prompted a response (April 1991) from the late John Strong's wife, detailing the awfulness of life within, while a still later article by a local man (May 1992) admitted, 'The Old Vicarage was a cold old building and home to bats and owls.'
346. Conversation, January 1997.
347. Bill Bryce, 'Old Harlington', *Contact*, May 1992.
348. Strong was committed to improving the liturgy, and in keeping with changes already taking place all over England (see Southcott at Halton) was prepared to argue for and explain changes and would contribute articles about them to the quarterly magazine that he produced. See the article, possibly by him, '1662–1962', in *St Mary's Harlington Parish Quarterly,* summer 1962.
349. Strong, papers, 11.
350. Peter Young, 'Worker-Priest in Harlington' *Prism* 8, December 1962.
351. *Luton News*, 13 September 1962. The fact that most of these statements are selected and quoted by Strong himself and interpreted out of bitterness should not detract from their value, though the compiled material must be read with caution. The bishop would later be given an opportunity to refute Strong's account.
352. Strong, papers, 8.
353. Strong, 'A True Vocation' (n.343).
354. *The Daily Herald*, 14 September 1962, 'Prisoner in the Pulpit'; Strong, papers, 25.
355. Strong, papers.
356. Ibid.
357. Ibid.
358. Letters to the Bishop of St Albans, 11 November 1959: Strong, papers.
359. See the story of Alan and Rita Hart, 'We went to the vicarage on Thursday to make our final arrangements only to find the house empty and the vicar flown, panic set in . . .', 'Parish magazine Memories', *Contact*, February 1996.
360. *Luton News*, 13 September 1962; Strong, papers 27. See also Minutes of the Quarterly Meeting of the Harlington Parish Council, 5 October 1962. 'Mr H. P. Whiskin moved a resolution . . . approved unanimously that a record should be made in the minutes of the recognition of the council of the many services rendered by John Strong and Mrs Strong to the village, not only as vicar and wife but as members of the community.'
361. See 'Letters' [uncertain origin], possible a 1961 edition of *Prism*: 'Perhaps it is time to offend at least some of the old ladies then perhaps the worker-priests should be put under someone else's authority.'
362. There has always been some doubt as to whether this really was the 'Manor House' and the occupant a 'Lady' at all. See John Rowe's papers and interview.
363. It must be born in mind that John Strong's account – the only one that exists – is personal and composed some time later for a group he helped to found. Nevertheless, the collated material, which has all the hallmarks of a care for

precision and accuracy, was sent to the bishop, who was surprised that his correspondence with Strong (which he thought with some justification was private) should be circulated. Yet the bishop challenged none of what Strong had said, though he claimed it was 'one-sided'. Strong, papers.

364. See Young, 'Worker-Priest in Harlington' (n.350), 56.
365. Ibid., 57.
366. It was the Lady of the 'Manor' who seems to have been concerned that Strong did not put 'one word' over to the men alongside whom he worked: 'he never preaches to them nothing at all'. That was before she berated him for his lack of visiting, though she admitted he did visit people in 'ordinary houses'. *News Chronicle*, 4 August 1959.
367. Strong, papers, 23.
368. Strong, 'A True Vocation' (n.351).
369. One of the first historical claims that this group represented 'the first real English worker-priests' was made by Tim Justin Robertson, *Guardian*, 4 January 1974.
370. For oral historical work attention was given in the earliest stages to the work of historians such as Robert Perks and Alistair Thomson, whose most recent publication *The Oral Historical Reader*, Routledge 1998, provides some essential background to the 'practice of oral history, from the creation of oral evidence, through to data analysis'. Among the points made in this and similar studies is the way in which oral history brings with the collection of 'events' an interpretation of these same events. It also highlights one of the difficulties present in the collection of such material, as those interviewed will understandably question interpretations made of their material or even that they ever 'said' such things. One chapter in the above publication by Katherine Borland is actually entitled: '"That's not what I said": Interpretive conflict in oral narrative research'.
371. Questionnaire (see n.267) on worker priests completed by John Rowe, December 1992, and personal correspondence. Rowe read philosophy and English, 1945–48, and theological subjects, 1948–1951.
372. See the mention of Joost de Blank, above.
373. Interview with John Rowe, 2 November 1993.
374. Rowe began as an 'unskilled labourer' in 1956 and left in 1986 a few months short of a full thirty years, as a skilled and highly experienced electrician: questionnaire (1992) and interview (1993).
375. There would occasionally be the suspicion (perhaps since there was no public awareness that the established church approved and supported such a role, as had been the case originally in France) that worker-priests had committed some misdemeanour or 'failed' in their work as clergymen. See John Halsey's story of the 'stickit' minister (Chapter 5), or Ken Ramsay's activities as described in this chapter.
376. 'Time served' is an expression which denotes a period of time – up to five years or more – in which an apprentice (and an apprenticeship is legally binding) would learn from a skilled man – a 'journeyman' – by accompanying him in his responsibilities, watching and learning 'on the job', with or without 'day release' or evening classes as a back-up. It was, and remained, the basic method

of labourers and younger men becoming 'skilled' in British industry.

377. Interview with John Rowe.
378. John Rowe in *Reynolds's News*, August 1959.
379. Interview with John Rowe.
380. Martyn Grubb, *Truth and God – One Person's Experience*, Quaker Home Service 1989, 3. Grubb comments that the booklet 'was originally written in . . . haste'.
381. Ibid., 3.
382. Ibid., 3, 4.
383. See Michael Jackson in Chapter 2 above.
384. 'University colleges' are mentioned here because Martyn Grubb does not remember it being *theological* colleges to which they invited Hunter, though he and Jackson were students of theological colleges later. It is possible that this may in some way relate to the meeting Hunter had with deans and chaplains remembered by Roland Walls: see Chapter 2 above.
385. Conversation with C. F. D. Moule, 1997.
386. Martyn and Anne Grubb, Letters to friends, from 85 Beaconsfield Road, Southall, Middlesex; Grubb, Papers, December 1951 to February, 1952, 1.
387. Interview with Martyn and Anne Grubb in Southall, November 1993.
388. Letters to friends, to February 1951, 3f. See also Sillitoe's 'Arthur Seaton': 'Without affecting the quality of the work you were turning out you forgot your past conflicts with the gaffer and turned to thinking of pleasant events that had some time happened to you, or things that you hoped would happen to you in the future', *Saturday Night and Sunday Morning* (n.286), 31.
389. Letters, from papers: Queen's Road, Southall, May 1954, 5f.
390. Letters to friends, May 1954.
391. Ibid.
392. Interview (n.387).
393. Letters to friends, August-September 1956, 3.
394. Sillitoe, *Saturday Night and Sunday Morning* (n.286), 25.
395. Letters to friends, 1956, 4.
396. Ibid., 7.
397. Ibid., 4.
398. Address to the Southwark Diocesan Conference, 2 November 1961: Grubb, papers.
399. Letters to friends, August-September 1956, 5.
400. Ibid., 5.
401. Interview with Martyn Grubb, 1993.
402. Letters to friends, December 1957, 1.
403. It was the very subject of abortion which was of the greatest concern when it was featured in *Saturday Night and Sunday Morning* – especially in the British Lion film version directed by Karl Reisz. A British Board of Film Censors' script-reader's report comments when considering categories: '. . . quite apart from anything else, the language would not do for "A". Neither would love scenes, to say nothing of the discussion of abortion and the fact that the abortion is actually carried out (though not seen).' See OU Popular Culture/Film booklets, Film, Appendix 5, AOF 20.11.59.

404. Letters, from personal papers, Beaconsfield Road, Southall, 1952–53, 3f.
405. See F. R. Leavis and Denys Thompson, *Culture and the Environment – The Training of Critical Awareness*, Chatto & Windus 1933, 1–2: 'What we have lost is the organic community with the living culture it embodied . . . Relics of the old order are still to be found in remote parts of the country, such as Yorkshire dales, where motor-coach, wireless, cinema and education are rapidly destroying them – they will hardly last another decade.' The book enjoyed a strong traditional following, with a seventh impression in 1959 and an eighth the following year.
406. Ibid., 3.
407. D. Bonhoeffer, *Letters and Papers from Prison*, Letter of 16 July 1944, SCM Press 1953. The standard English text is now The Enlarged Edition, SCM Press 1971, 357ff.
408. John Rowe, 'Faith on the Shop Floor', *Trade Union Affairs* 2, Spring 1961, 21f.
409. Ibid.
410. Letters to friends, August – September 1956, 1.
411. Letters to friends, 1952, 3.
412. See Chapter 2 above, for Hunter's thoughts on the degrading nature of work, also Hewitt (ed.), *Strategist for the Spirit* (n.212), Chapter 6.
413. Letters to Friends, 1956, 2.
414. Martyn Grubb, Address to the Southwark Diocesan Conference, 2 November 1961, 2: Grubb papers.
415. Letters to Friends, 1956, 4.
416. *Father Joe, the Autobiography of Joseph Williamson* (n.114).
417. Interview with Tony Williamson, 16 May 1996.
418. Kenneth Woollcombe, Chaplain and Lecturer at St John's College, Oxford; Lecturer at General Seminary, New York; Principal of Edinburgh Theological College; and Bishop of Oxford, 1971.
419. The Statement first appeared in 1959 in a quality printed format and was sent to friends and sympathizers. It will be studied later (Chapter 5), when a detailed examination will be made of the document and its intended readers.
420. Interview with Williamson (n.417).
421. Ibid.
422. Letter from Bishop Carpenter to Tony Williamson, 11 March 1959: Williamson, papers.
423. Bishop Carpenter to Tony Williamson, 11 June 1959.
424. Tony Williamson to Bishop Carpenter, 16 June 1959.
425. Bishop Carpenter to Tony Williamson, 13 July 1959.
426. Tony Williamson to Bishop Carpenter, 14 July 1959.
427. Tony Williamson, essay entitled 'Priest-Workman – Why?' (precise date uncertain): Williamson papers.
428. Williamson describes how the news was handled locally: '24 hours after the ordination service had ended, the *Oxford Mail* filled half a page with pictures and write-up of me as the new worker-priest; this story was then printed in six national daily papers and the *Church Times* sent a special reporter, who later filled over half its front page; several other newspapers wrote or tried to contact me in vain, and later I was interviewed for an early morning radio programme

and a religious programme on Sunday ITV.' See: Williamson, papers, 'The Pastoral Opportunity in a Secular Setting', undated paper, possibly 1960 or 1961.

429. *Daily Telegraph*, 28 June 1960.
430. *Daily Mail* and *Guardian*, 28 June 1960.
431. *Christian Herald*, 30 July 1960.
432. There was a cartoon, 'Varney's View', showing two workers facing each other, one holding a newspaper indicating Williamson's ordination to the workshop – 'DEACON CLOCKS ON'. The other worker, oblivious to this event, remarks to his work mate: '. . . Wot's going on around 'ere? Alf just dropped a cylinder block on Sid's foot and Sid says, "Gracious Alf – that was exceedingly careless of you!"', *Daily Mail*, 29 June 1960.
433. *Oxford Mail*, 27 June 1960.
434. Williamson, papers, 1960.
435. Letter from the Revd Fr Francis of the Ancient Catholic Church, 4 July 1960: Williamson, papers.
436. *Church Times*, 1 July 1960.
437. Ibid.
438. Address to the Southwark Diocesan Conference, 2 November 1961: Williamson, papers.
439. Ibid., 4.
440. Ibid., 5.
441. Ibid., 4a.
442. *Oxford Mail*, 17 April 1961.
443. *Daily Express*, 17 April 1961.
444. Letter from Jean Canninade, Noisy-le-Grand, 28 July 1961: Williamson, papers.
445. Interview with Williamson, 1996.
446. Interview with Veronica Strong, May 1996.
447. Ibid.
448. Interview with Williamson, 1996.
449. Ibid.
450. Interview with Veronica Strong 1996.
451. Notorious 'noose trials' took place in the 1960s in which some workers held a 'mock trial' of work mates who had refused to participate in industrial action. But this was happening at the Morris plant, and nowhere near the section in which John Strong worked. Nevertheless, an angry and rather conservative member of the Diocesan Synod had asked what their worker-priest 'was doing about it'. Williamson made it publicly clear (since he was a union official) that this was happening in an entirely different plant, away from the 'other worker-priests anyway'. This resulted in the rather odd headline in the local press, 'Why I am Silent – says worker-priest.' Interview with Williamson (n.417).
452. *The Sun*, 11 February 1971.
453. Questionnaire (see n.267) from Tony Williamson, 1993.
454. 'The Pastoral Opportunity in a Secular Setting': Williamson, paper.
455. Ibid.
456. Interview with Tony Williamson, 1996.

457. *Daily Express*, 26 June 1961.
458. Interview with Williamson.
459. The question of the children of worker-priests also having to attend local schools was, of course, no different from other dedicated parish priests whose children might attend locally, though this was in contrast to Williamson's father, who insisted that his son enjoy the best education possible (interview with Williamson). While many of these first worker-priests had enjoyed private or more exclusive education, questions were asked about their insistence that their families 'went with them'. The Worker Church Group was forced to answer this question in a revised edition of the Statement, but it remained a contentious issue with clergy generally, and was certainly not exclusive to worker-priests. It would be true to say, however, that clergy horrified by any state education might have been equally horrified by ministry in industrial areas or housing estates anyway.
460. Questionnaire completed by Williamson, 1993.
461. Letter from Vera, 25 March 1959: Williamson, papers.
462. For an example, see the invitation to speak at the Canterbury School of Ministry's Summer School, St Stephen's House, Oxford 1984: Williamson, papers.
463. Ruth Etchells, *Set My People Free*, Fount 1995, 62: 'for it is the laity who are in the front line, needing to be supported by their clergy – not the other way round.'
464. 'Priest Workman – Why?' (undated): Williamson, papers.
465. Ibid., 2.
466. Ibid., 3.
467. Cowley *Chronicle* (parish magazine – precise date uncertain), 1960.
468. Ken Ramsay, interview, 9 September 1996.
469. Worker-priest questionnaire (see n.267), completed by Ken Ramsay, December 1992.
470. Ken Ramsay, *Newsletter*, 12 February 1953: Ramsay, papers.
471. Ibid.
472. Ibid., December 1956.
473. Ibid., December 1958.
474. Ibid., December, 1960
475. Ramsay, Factory log, 13 December 1960: Ramsay, papers. Ramsay adds later: 'I remember a leather tag on my bike with "Rev. K. Ramsay" on it. Had it been spotted? . . . Of course I had no wish to remain incognito for ever.'
476. Ibid.
477. Ibid., 20 December 1960.
478. Ibid., January 1961.
479. Ibid., 23 January 1961.
480. This applies essentially to small hand tools: spanners, screwdrivers, files and so on. In any workshop these remained precious, not only because of individual costs, but because anyone could 'appropriate' the items and build up their own set for home. In the late 1960s and 1970s, like other firms, Ford's car works at Dagenham, for example, had 'gate checks' to ensure that workers were not carrying tools and material out.

481. Ibid., 20 February 1961.
482. Ibid., 10 March 1960.
483. Ramsay, *Newsletter*, December 1963.
484. Factory log, Easter 1966.
485. Factory log, Christmas 1968.
486. 'Ken and I have been offered a trip to visit the worker-priests there, next Spring we hope. One of the Portsmouth group (an RC) hopes to take us; he speaks good French and has been before.' By 'worker-priests' in the Portsmouth area Ramsay means English Roman Catholic worker-priests, Franciscans.
487. Interview with K. Ramsay, 1996.
488. Ibid. Quite who this may have been is uncertain. Relatively little had been published in the late 1950s, apart from Henri Perrin's *Priest-Workman in Germany* (1947) or Michael Gedge's *Priest-Workman in England* (1951).
489. *Newsletter*, February 1953.
490. Ibid., December 1953.
491. It will be shown later that the Statement (1959) could only be signed by those who accepted the way of life it proposed. At the point of its production, Ramsay was not yet a worker-priest.
492. *Newsletter*, January 1963.
493. Ibid., Easter 1963.
494. Ibid., Easter 1966.
495. Ibid.
496. Notes for factory log, 21 February 1961.
497. Letter to Bishop Mervyn Stockwood, 16 January 1961: Ramsay papers.
498. *Newsletter*, February 1962.
499. Interview with Ramsay, 1996.
500. Ibid.
501. Interview with John Wilcox, 2 March 1993.
502. Ibid. On Fridays, when students were addressed on the subject of ministry, Wilcox met Ted Wickham, Ernie Southcott, and even Michael Gedge, and it was from the latter that he first learnt about the French worker-priests. 'At Warminster I felt so far removed from the world of industry from which I had come that I decided to return to it for a time in a shop floor job and this led me to being ordained in that job.'
503. Notes on Tom Quigley from a miscellaneous paper on the Worker Church Group, May 1965, Williamson and Rowe, paper. There are, regrettably, no further notes on Tom Quigley. After he moved abroad, contact with him was lost and my efforts to make contact with him again for the purpose of this study proved unsuccessful.
504. Ibid.
505. Ibid., on Tom and Sherry Waldon. Waldon remained utterly faithful to the Worker Church Group and the Shop Floor Association to the very end, and was the only layman to remain for so long.
506. See *Trade Union Affairs*, Spring 1960, 17; in a paper entitled 'Faith on the Shop Floor' a subtitle 'A "worker-priest" plays his part as a shop-steward' is headlined above the title. The words 'as a brewery steward' are underlined with 'not claimed' scribbled alongside, presumably by Rowe himself. Rowe, papers.

507. Ibid.
508. Grubb, Letters to friends, 1954, 8.
509. Martyn Grubb, Address to the Southwark Diocesan Conference 1961, 3.
510. Letters to friends, December 1962, 1.
511. Interview, 1993.
512. Letters to friends, 1956, 5.
513. 'Pastoral Opportunity' (n.454).
514. *Oxford Mail*, 19 January 1961.
515. GPO telegram, from Jack Pleasant: Williamson, papers.
516. 'Pastoral Opportunity' (n.454).
517. Ibid., 4.
518. Williamson claims that he learnt a terrible lesson then about conducting funerals without having determined something about the deceased: interview, 1996.
519. Interview, 1996.
520. M. Gedge, *Priest-Workman in England* (n.272).
521. Interview with Williamson,1996.
522. *Oxford Mail*, 8 February 1971, and *The Sun*, 11 February 1971.
523. Interview with John Rowe, 1993.
524. This was a society founded in 1939, 'a society of priests and laypeople in the Anglican Communion', which had its origins abroad, and which Rowe, because of his Canadian connections, was able to use as a basis for sharing his ideas. See *Society for the Catholic Commonwealth,* Vine Press, Oratory of St Mary & St Michael, Gloucester, Mass. 1939, revised, 1958.
525. Interview with John Rowe, 1993.
526. Grubb, Letters to friends, May 1954.
527. Interview with Martyn Grubb, 1993.
528. Letters to friends, September 1956.
529. This would become a venue for a Worker Church Group meeting in 1964, see Appendix 2.
530. Letters to friends, December 1957.
531. Interview, November 1993.
532. Letters to friends, December 1957, 3.
533. Ibid., December 1959, 2.
534. Interview with Tony Williamson, 1996.
535. Ibid.
536. One of the first of what might be called 'historical claims' that this group represented 'the first real English worker-priests' was made by Tim Justin Robinson in *The Guardian*, 4 January 1974.
537. See John Rowe's papers, Report 1982, also id., *Priests and Workers: A Rejoinder*, Darton, Longman and Todd 1965.
538. Strong, 'A True Vocation' (n.313).
539. Ibid.
540. Letter of Alexander Jacobs to John Rowe on behalf of Rediffusion Television, 30 September 1959: Rowe, papers.
541. *Church Times*, 4 August 1959.
542. Ibid.
543. Interview with Veronica Strong, 1996.

544. Vaughan, *Non-Stipendiary Ministry* (n.104), 167.
545. See Statement, written by the WCG (1959), which later appears in other forms, and the arguments which Anne Grubb would use in 'English Worker Priests', *The Frontier*, IV.3, Winter 1960, and the Grubbs' later contribution to Edwards, *Priests and Workers* (n.24).
546. *Church Times*, 2 October 1959.
547. Bickersteth, 'Factory Interlude' (n.269).
548. John Bickersteth, 'Not Workmen Turned Priests but Priests Turned Workmen', in Robin Denniston (ed.), *Part-Time Priests? A Discussion*, Skeffington 1960, 122.
549. E. Knapp-Fisher, 'Training for Ministry', *Theology* LXII.464, February 1959.
550. See Bagshaw, *The Church Beyond the Church* (n.217).
551. Anne Grubb, 'English Developments', substantially a reprint of her *Frontier* article (n.545) with revisions, which appeared in Edwards, *Priests and Workers* (n.24).
552. Nick Earle, *What's Wrong with the Church?*, Penguin Books 1961, 62.
553. Ibid., 64.
554. See *Crockford's Clerical Directory*, Preface, 1961, viii-ix, and the reaction in *Prism*, December 1962, no.68.
555. 'England is not France and the Church of England is not the Church of Rome, but a lesson from France can be learned regarding the necessity for hierarchical supervision and the maintenance of strong ties with the local church', *Church Times*, 2 October 1959.
556. Michael Gedge, in *Priest-Workman in England* (n.272), argued for the support of bishops, while for fear of 'separatism' Michael Jackson, in 'Character and Functions' (n.331), called for an 'episcopate numerous enough to exercise pastoral oversight of the life of their dioceses' .
557. See the contributions by F. R. Barry, Bishop of Southwell, and H. W. Bradfield, Bishop of Bath and Wells, to Denniston (ed.), *Part-Time Priests?* (n.548), Chapters 1 and 2.
558. *Facts and Figures about the Church of England*, prepared by the Statistical Unit of the Central Board of Finance, 1962, 26.
559. Ibid., p.41, Diagram XIV.
560. *The Times* reported on the shortages of clergy from 1948 on into the 1950s, and there had been particular mention of 'older incumbents' increasing in number: see, for example, *The Times*, 25 January 1945, and of servicemen coming forward, 1 January 1945; 22 March 1946; 13 March 1947; 3 February 1948, and so on into the 1950s.
561. *Crockford's Clerical Directory*, 1961–62.
562. *Theology* LI. 342, December 1948.
563. Ibid., LIV.368, February 1951.
564. Ibid., LIV.370, April 1951.
565. Ibid., LIV.372, June 1951.
566. Ibid., LV.384, June 1952: '. . . it seems to not a few that the only hope of salvation for the Church of England . . . is to recognize without further delay . . . that the coming pattern of ministry is bound to be largely non-professional.'
567. *The Modern Churchman* V, October 1961: 'It is true to say, with D.

Bonhoeffer, that we have come into the age of maturity of mankind. where men are required for the first time in history to be adult, to bear the responsibility, and where submission to authority is not possible any more.'

568. *Parish and People* 1, Michaelmas 1961: Lt Col. Hubert Madge drew attention to anomalies in figures of large numbers of clergy ministering in some dioceses to few people. 'Can it really be said,' he asked, 'that this is full-time employment for a priest?'
569. Leslie Paul, *The Deployment and Payment of the Clergy*, Church Information Office 1964.
570. Vaughan and Fuller (eds), *Working for the Kingdom* (n.136); Vaughan, *Non-Stipendiary Ministry in the Church of England* (n.104); Hacking, *On the Boundary* (n.136).
571. Vaughan, *Non-Stipendiary Ministry in the Church of England* (n.104), 23; id. and Fuller, *Working for the Kingdom* (n.136), 171.
572. Vaughan and Fuller, *Working for the Kingdom* (n.136), 172.
573. Robin Gill, *The Myth of the Empty Church*, SPCK 1993. Gill has argued against the notion that the First World War was largely responsible for a decline in churchgoing. See 9f.: 'Before the First World War a majority of churches in Britain were more empty that full' and '. . . a report on "The Army and Religion" had shown that men from their adolescence onward knew practically nothing of the real life of the churches from within' (181).
574. Quoted in Vaughan and Fuller, *Working for the Kingdom* (n.136), 173. I am particularly grateful to Patrick Vaughan for pointing out that traditional views of priestly vocation can actually mask an important sociological phenomenon – that full-time clergy have made themselves potential victims of sanctions if they step out of line. In other words, through stipend, and particularly housing, which laity may view as a 'perk', clergy are effectively controlled by the institution. John Strong (Chapter 3) learned what that meant when he and his wife and child were forced out of Harlington by their bishop.
575. Ibid.
576. Interview with John Rowe, November 1993.
577. Interview with Simon Phipps, formerly Bishop of Lincoln, and of the Coventry Industrial Mission, May 1996.
578. John Strong recalled that one man said [at the mine at Eyethorne] that he did not think Strong ought to have been there. '"Stick to your proper job." He admitted that he had no use for the proper job even in its "right place". I said, "Suppose one of the men here got ordained?" He snorted, "I wouldn't think much of it. He'd only be changing a hard job for an easy one." "But if he went on earning his living here, what then?" "Ah now, that would be different."', 'Into a Thick Wood' (n.334).
579. Mentioned by Vaughan, *Non-Stipendiary Ministry in the Church of England* (n.104), 220.
580. Mervyn Stockwood, *The Chanctonbury Ring*, Hodder & Stoughton 1982, 58.
581. Southwark consisted of 'hundreds and hundreds of drab streets housing a working-class to whom the Church of England means next to nothing, to whom a bishop is as relevant as an Ethiopian ambassador, to whom our literature and our gospel are meaningless mumbo-jumbo'. See Michael De-la-Noy,

Mervyn Stockwood – A Lonely Life, Mowbray 1996, 101.

582. Stockwood, *The Chanctonbury Ring* (n.580), 105. There is a contrast in the way Stockwood chose to live, in a rather grand house complete with able staff, the centre of parties in the 1960s, where even royalty were entertained.
583. Interview with the Revd David Wilson, from SOC, and subsequently first Dean of Southwark Priest-Worker Chapter, September 1993.
584. Notes from a sermon preached in Great St Mary's in the early 1960s: Ken Ramsay Papers, 1993.
585. Southwark Ordination Training Scheme, introductory outline document, undated, possibly early 1960: Rowe, papers.
586. *Crockford's Clerical Directory*, 1961–62.
587. Mervyn Stockwood to Tony Williamson, 18 July 1962: Williamson, papers.
588. Southwark set the pattern for a variety of new courses across the country, until in the 1990s and at the direction of ACCM, it was forced into an ill-judged cost-cutting marriage with the Canterbury School of Ministry. SOC, with the longer tradition, was the greater loser.
589. A literal rendering of this in English would be 'priest-worker', but given the placing of the verb in English, 'worker-priest' may be said to be a correct translation. Subsequent attempts to suggest that the term 'priest-worker' may be used for some other subtle meaning are unsubstantiated by any primary French source, and are, one might simply say, an invention. Indeed, Siefer, *The Church and Industrial Society* (n.136), suggests it was only the foreign press which used the title.
590. Perrin, *Priest and Worker* (n.176), 89–90.
591. Ibid. 144.
592. Ibid.
593. Petrie, *The Worker Priests* (n.136), 42.
594. Siefer, *The Church and Industrial Society* (n.136), 4.
595. There was, of course, one exception in this little group, and that was John Strong, who not only recognized the value of the parochial system but felt that 'he had to be a worker priest running a parish', Tony Williamson, interview, May 1996.
596. This point about not rising above chargehand was made by John Wilcox, worker-priest questionnaire (n.267), 1992, and by Robert Martineau in his *The Office and Work of a Priest*, Mowbray 1972.
597. The Statement (1959), Section 1: The Way of Incarnation.
598. Ibid., Section 5 (complete).
599. Ibid., Section 9.
600. Ibid., see 13: The Wholeness of Our Mission.
601. Anne Grubb, 'English Worker Priests' (n.545).
602. Ead., in Edwards, *Priests and Workers* (n.24), 156.
603. Edwards, *Priests and Workers* (n.24), 125.
604. Ibid. It is doubtful in fact if there were very many bishops like Mervyn Stockwood, Harry Carpenter or Joost de Blank willing to have worker-priests. Most were dubious, and the latter two, in practice, only ever had to deal with two or three individuals.
605. Ibid. 138.

606. Ibid., 143.
607. Rowe, *Priests and Workers* (n.537).
608. Ibid., 12.
609. Ibid., 21–2.
610. Ibid., 26.
611. Ibid., 29. Here Rowe quotes Wickham, who, speaking of ordination candidates, had written: 'At least he should learn on his pulses what it might mean to be a good layman. Indeed, students have come to me urging this as a good reason for not proceeding to ordination, fearing that they should be cut off from the world in which, for the first time in their lives, they have discovered the real significance of being a layman. Such men have invariably been amongst the best theological students – and to such my advice has invariably been the same: "Be ordained, and produce the kind of laymen you have now discovered it possible to be,"' *Priests and Workers* (n.537), 148.
612. Ibid., 30.
613. Ibid., 36–7.
614. Ibid., 41. Also at a Whitsun Conference of the WCG (1960), Martyn Grubb had suggested they ought perhaps to call themselves 'voluntary priests' rather than worker-priests. Although there was some sympathy for this idea, it was never used.
615. Martineau, *The Office and Work of a Priest* (n.596).
616. Vaughan, *Non-Stipendiary Ministry in the Church of England* (n.104), 202.
617. WCG Whitsun Conference, Harlington 1961: Williamson, papers.
618. Ibid., Sister Christina's notes (1965): Williamson, papers. It is earlier notes from the previous year that indicate Sister Christina's work.
619. Report of the Whitsun Conference (Bobbington, Essex) 1966: Williamson, papers.
620. Letter from Anne Grubb to all members of the WCG, 1965: John Rowe, papers.
621. John Rowe to Martyn Grubb, 28 March 1966: Rowe, papers. John Strong had suffered serious rupture problems, made worse by underground work at Eyethorne. The manual labour in the north-west made them more serious still, and by the time he came to Oxford, his back was giving him problems so that on at least one occasion the WCG was forced to hold a meeting by his bedside. Strong's labouring days were over. It is easy in hindsight to argue that he could have 'gone sick' or 'on benefit' (if he was to remain alongside the working-class) rather than make the move that took him into Oxfordshire country parishes for his remaining days. Neither John Rowe nor any other members of the WCG saw it like that, and with some justification. John Strong had been the one member of the Group consistently to uphold the importance of the territorial parish, a view from which he never once wavered. And all his labouring days he remained a conscientious and hard-working parish priest, noted by at least one young Oxfordshire parish priest who described him as one of the most 'saintly men he had ever met'. Conversation with the Revd John Joyce, May 1996.
622. John Rowe to Martyn Grubb, letter, May 1966: Rowe papers.
623. Martineau, *The Office and Work of a Priest* (n.596), 122.
624. Britain's first worker-priests became such because they had opted for a life on

the shop-floor. They never demanded to be called 'worker-priests' or argued they were Britain's equivalent of the French. This study, however, is arguing that that is precisely what they were. On the matter of knowledge about worker-priests little had been translated on the French movement apart from Petrie, *The Worker Priests* (n.136), or Edwards, *Priests and Workers* (n.24). There was enough, however, with a smattering of other articles, to make others aware of a movement started just after the war, condemned in 1954 and again in 1959. The British contribution, meanwhile, was sometimes seen as some kind of alternative strategy to industrial mission.

625. There is some discrepancy. The number is generally mentioned as thirteen and the photographs of those outside Southwark cathedral on the day of the ordination shows thirteen. But a printed text of Stanley Evans' sermon on the eve of the ordination mentions 'fourteen': Wilson, papers.
626. Questionnaire (n.267) and correspondence, November 1996.
627. This would eventually be directly contradicted by Mervyn Stockwood in an article in Southwark's magazine *The Bridge*, an article which Eric Normington, one of the first candidates, would fiercely attack in 1966: Normington, papers. Later, questioned again on the matter, Mervyn claimed 'It was about both'. The fact was that Mervyn Stockwood could be exasperatingly inconsistent.
628. Henry Theobald in correspondence with the author, November 1996.
629. *Daily Express*, September 1963 (precise date uncertain).
630. The course was extremely demanding, not only because CACTM insisted on it, but because Mervyn Stockwood and John Robinson were most anxious to ensure that this should never be seen as a 'back door' to the ordained stipendiary ministry. The ordinands could feel rightly proud of their course with London University. But there was a price to pay for difficult studies, and the drop in numbers from the original intake said it all.
631. This was a significant inclusion on the list – not an aside. A baker, who had just joined the course, would prove to be almost the only one who took any interest in the WCG.
632. 'Part-time Ordinands – Southwark Experiment Nearing its Climax', *Church Times*, 13 September 1963.
633. This number conflicts with H Theobald's 'three' (see correspondence, November 1996) and may simply be a case of straightforward confusion, or the fact that one or two later entered stipendiary ministry.
634. Dennis May, surviving papers, see below.
635. Ibid. May's is in fact a sorry story of a man, who in later life sought entry into the stipendiary ministry, and who for unknown reasons was rebuffed. When illness overtook him, he and his wife felt abandoned by the institution, and with a sense of bitterness lived out their remaining days in some obscurity in Ashford, Kent, abandoning even churchgoing. Constance May in correspondence with the author, November 1996.
636. A newspaper cutting – origin unknown, possibly the *Church Times*: Wilson, Papers.
637. The Austin-Cooper or Mini-Cooper (named after the racing mechanic John Cooper) was a souped-up version of the Mini, which had its engine capacity increased in size. It was the sporty version of the Mini, and very much a status

symbol at the time – hence its mention.

638. *The Herald*, Monday 14 September 1963.

639. Bishop Dominic Walker, then Chaplain to Mervyn Stockwood. Walker claims that they were able to learn from the mistakes of the 'Robert's scheme' in Stepney. The men were not given charge of churches, but were under the authority of the local parish priest. Nevertheless, they remained in a parochial ministry and they did not see themselves as having a ministry 'at work'. Conversation, November 1996.

640. 'I think it's likely that in addition to the parochial system we need a more flexible type of church organization – and that in addition to the parochial priesthood we need an order of worker-priests – men who will stay on the ground-floor, earning their living as factory hands, bus drivers, railwaymen, trade-union officials, shopkeepers and schoolmasters . . .' (November 1958). From a sermon at Great St Mary's Cambridge, De-la-Noy, *Mervyn Stockwood – A Lonely Life* (n.582), 131–2.

641. Eric James would later ask the question that could have been addressed years before but never was: 'How can you get a working-class ministry out of a middle-class church? If they are not in the pews they cannot be in the theological colleges'. SOC essay, 1966.

642. Letter, Eric Normington to Frank Colquhoun, 1966.

643. Mervyn Stockwood, in *The Bridge*, Southwark Diocesan Review, September 1966.

644. Stockwood in a letter to G. Winterbottom: papers, 1984.

645. Bill Millard was one of the few priests who in the late 1960s had given up his trade union work to train for ordination on a part-time basis. Following his ordination in the Portsmouth diocese, he returned to union work. He was a popular member of the WCG, and there is a common belief that the 1969–70 postal strike and the active part he played in the union fight, before its defeat, were partly responsible for his breakdown and premature death.

646. See David Wilson, *A Priest-Worker Ministry*, ACCM and CBF 1968. This was Wilson's account of life as a priest-worker, working in his bakery, as part of a series of ACCM publications on the nature of new ministries.

647. Report of the Worker Church Group Spring Conference 1967: Williarnson, Papers.

648. Bill Millard, in a letter to the Group Conference, May 1973, when they briefly discussed the growing NSM courses. Report of WCG, 1971 Conference.

649. Interview with the Grubbs, 1993.

650. *The Guardian*, 4 January 1974.

651. Anne Grubb, in *Priests and Workers* (n.24), 157.

652. David Wilson has commented in correspondence, and rightly, that '. . . one day someone will write about Mervyn that in 1960 he changed the whole concept of ministry . . .'

653. John and Veronica Strong in an undated paper – possible a section of minutes – from the Worker Church Group, about 1980: Williamson, papers.

654. John A. T. Robinson, undated memo, 'Priest-Workers', possibly 1966–67: David Wilson, papers.

655. In his *A Priest-Worker Ministry* (n.646), Wilson had written: '. . . l am an

ordained priest, but continue in a secular job. For want of a better title such people . . . are known as worker-priests. The title is a bad one and those of us to whom it applies would all disown it if we could erase the underlying implications of the words. The title has actually been taken over from the French situation where the priests in question really were workers. In England the term basically means a priest who earns his living in a secular occupation and receives no stipend from the church' (ibid.).This, of course, was David Wilson's personal definition, which applied to the Southwark Chapter – but which he was admitting was at variance with the understanding of the Worker Church Group and the French. It is also possible to argue rather negatively that 'priest-worker' was simply a deliberate appropriation, since the term by now had radical kudos.

656. SOC priest-worker chapter, 13 July 1968: Wilson, papers.
657. David Wilson, interview, 1993.
658. Southwark priest-worker chapter Minutes, 17 April 1969: Wilson, Papers.
659. Ibid., 3 May 1969 (date uncertain).
660. Ibid.
661. Ibid., 17 April 1977.
662. Ibid., 12 November 1969.
663. 'At present many clergy are uncertain about the work of the priest-workers . . . [whose] ministry should be presented as one existing in its own right and not simply as an auxiliary stop-gap ministry.' See Chapter Minutes, 12 November 1969: Wilson papers.
664. Notes of a meeting between SOC priest-worker chapter and two members of the ACCM working party (E. A. J. and R. M. M) Wilson: papers. A rather interesting feature of these notes (it is unclear whether they were written by an ACCM visitor or a Southwark member) is the way in which they quite casually describe the Southwark chapter (even in the title) as 'worker-priests'. It may not have been so much a slip as an apparent lack of understanding of the 're-arrangement' of the title to 'priest-worker' of which David Wilson had earlier made so much. There is no existing evidence that the Southwark Chapter sought to 'correct' this and it may therefore be concluded that they were perfectly happy to accept the title.
665. St Augustine's College had been established originally as a missionary training college, but later became an important adjunct to King's College, London, where theological students received a further period of training. It was closed in the early 1970s as other residential colleges, too, were closed, and its place taken by the Canterbury School of Ministry, one of the new non-residential part-time courses.
666. 17 December was the date set for an ordination when a 'former docker and 3 companions will be ordained'. They included Jack Page (former docker), William Harrap (telephone engineer), Henry Watson (business machine engineer) and Gordon Kendall (roofing specialist). Newspaper cutting, origin uncertain: Wilson papers. There followed comment at the Southwark chapter: 'Stepney Ordinations. The dean reported communication with the media on reports on those ordinations. He had been in touch with Nationwide, PA, and *The Times*, and had received a reply from *The Times* expressing regret at the

lack of space to print his letter. The Chapter agreed there was widespread ignorance regarding priest-workers and their vocation.' Chapter minutes, Business meeting, April 1972: Wilson, papers.

667. For the purposes of this study attempts to communicate with the remaining three proved difficult.

668. Southwark priest-worker chapter Business meeting, April 1972, Wilson papers.

669. Mason gives the definition that the Southwark chapter presumably wanted: '[T]he Priest-Workers who share in these discussions would wish to distinguish themselves, not only from the stipendiary minister on the one hand, but also on the other from those men (Worker-Priests) who like their French counterparts, see the main line of their ministry in identification with industrial workers'. 'Priesthood of Priest-Workers', K. Mason: Wilson, papers.

670. Details of the growth of new courses, and the different experiments undertaken across Britain, can be found in Vaughan, *Non-Stipendiary Ministry in the Church of England* (n.104), 229.

671. Ibid., 229.

672. Ibid., 241.

673. Even the gathering of evidence on worker-priests or ministers in secular employment has occasionally been frustrating when letters from those trained on courses occasionally reveal a lack of interest in a non-stipendiary role: e.g. 'I began to fill in your questionnaire but then I found I could be of little use to you because I went into full time parochial ministry when I was ordained.' Correspondence to the author from an early SOC student, 1996.

674. John Hind, 'Varieties of the Priesthood', in Fuller and Vaughan (eds.), *Working for the Kingdom* (n.136), 90.

675. 'An analysis of the 1979–83 enrolments using the Registrar General's 1961 classification was produced in 1983 for the second review of the course . . . Towler and Coxon [in *The.Fate of the Anglican Clergy*] found a marked over-representation of classes I and II, and under-representation of classes Ill, IV and V compared with the general population. SOC candidates show even more representation of classes I and II than Towler and Coxon's late group, greater under-representation of class II and no representation at all of classes IV and V.' See the essay on the history of SOC by Antony Hardy.

676. Correspondence from J. H. Richardson, 1993, on his factory work in May 1966.

677. Peter Langford, 'A Short Experiment in Living as a Priest-Workman', *Christian Witness* XVIII. 1, March 1964.

678. *Daily Telegraph*, date uncertain – the cutting had been kept by John Rowe and others.

679. Interview with John Halsey, 24 May 1996.

680. Worker-priest questionnaire (n.267) and interview with Tony Bell, March 1993.

681. Richard Syms, *Working Like the Rest of Us*, SCM Press 1979.

682. Ibid., 33.

683. Ibid., 47.

684. In the course of research for this study, several attempts were made through the *Church Times*, over a period of years, to contact any clergy who 'even for a

short time' were engaged in manual labour. Some of the accounts here are drawn from ensuing correspondence, but either the numbers were in practice very low, or those who left the institution have little interest in retelling their stories, if indeed they still read the church press.

685. Conversation with David Goodhall, 24 January 1997.
686. Bagshaw, *The Church Beyond the Church* (n.217), and conversation with Barry Parker, 23 January 1997.
687. Jack Burton, *Transport of Delight*, SCM Press 1976.
688. Ibid., Introduction.
689. Ibid., viii.
690. Ibid., 198.
691. Free-church experiments in lay ministry and certain types of non-stipendiary ministry have not always gone well. In the mid 1990s the Methodist church was seen to be suffering from the closure of churches as well as a serious shortage of ministers – despite its history of varieties of ministry.
692. Vaughan, *Non-Stipendiary Ministry in the Church of England* (n.104), 279. In fact the Lincoln scheme envisaged a trained team of laity with one or more who might subsequently be ordained as a 'sacrament leader'.
693. Ibid., 283.
694. This was simply a role 'added' to other duties, and should not be seen as an attempt to do what the French church had done in setting up a 'non-territorial' diocese with its own bishop for worker-priests. Woollcombe was followed by the Rt Revd David Smith, Bishop of Maidstone, who later became Bishop of Bradford.
695. Michael Ranken, 'Ministry in Secular Employment and the Church's Mission', in *Ordained Ministry in Secular Employment,* ACCM Occasional Paper No 1, February 1989.
696. Correspondence with Dr J Francis, University of Sunderland, October 1996.
697. Vaughan, *Non-Stipendiary Ministry in the Church of England* (n.104), see his mention of the 1969 endorsement of the Welsby Report: 'Although the 1969 Report envisaged an extension of ordination, everything about the plan was designed to strengthen the parochial system' (241). A variety of students, men and women from the Canterbury School of Ministry on a study visit to France (1993), were struck by the importance that French worker-priests placed on a simple 'presence' and not some kind of traditional functionalism – like celebrating the eucharist or supporting the territorial parish – which the British thought important.
698. Vaughan, *Non-Stipendiary Ministry in the Church of England* (n.104), 308.
699. R. Towler and A. P. M. Coxon, *The Fate of the Anglican Clergy,* Macmillan 1979, 198f.
700. J. Goldthorpe, David Lockwood. Frank Bechhofer and Jennifer Platt, *The Affluent Worker in the Class Structure*, Cambridge University Press 1969, questioned assumptions about working-class *embourgeoisement,* but endorsed specific views about choices by the political leaders of the working class.
701. Rowe, *Priests and Workers: A Rejoinder* (n.537), Introduction.
702. Ibid.
703. Wickham specifically mentioned: *A Supporting Ministry*, CIO 1968; *Ordained*

Ministry Today, CIO 1969; the Church Assembly Report on *Selection and Training for the Auxiliary Parochial Ministry* (CA 1123, December 1968); *Bishops Regulations for the Selection and Training of Candidates for Auxiliary Pastoral Ministry* (August 1970). Since then, a whole range of new documents and updated regulations have emerged, including those for the latest local non-stipendiary ministries, for example: *The Report of the Church of England Working Party concerned with Local Non-Stipendiary Ministry*, ABM Publications, Church of England CBF 1991.

704. Constitution of the Shop Floor Association: John Rowe/Williamson, papers. For the first time the term unemployment comes to be used by those who were members of the WCG, and were now co-founders of the Shop Floor Association. The 1980s had arrived, and those who had decided to side with the working class would now come to see unemployment, as the French worker-priests in the 1980s did, as a cause against which they too must side. Jean Bertho, French worker-priest, correspondence with author, 1987.
705. The evolution of the Shop Floor Association rightly falls outside the scope of this study, though a mention of its existence has been essential. A mere account of the contents of meetings, or an attempted outline analysis of the subjects then under discussion, might prove difficult, and would do no justice to the strong differences of opinion which appear to remain.
706. John Rowe in conversation with the author, 18 February 1997.
707. This comment was actually made to the author in July 1965.
708. Letter from John Rowe to Martyn Grubb, 28 March 1966.
709. Ibid.
710. Norman, *Church and Society in England, 1770–1970* (n.7), 472.
711. Paper on Southwark priest-workers, author and date unknown, in Wilson, papers.
712. John Rowe to Martyn Grubb (n.708).
713. *Stranger in the Wings – A Report on Local Ordained Ministry*, CHP 1998, 4.
714. *Mission and Ministry* – The Churches Validation Framework for Theological Education, CHP 1999, 33.
715. 'We love to go to church, but only when it's empty. The number of regular worshippers is plummeting. Mary Killen blames trendy vicars and their nonsensical sermons', *Daily Telegraph*, 25 January 2000.
716. *Stranger in the Wings* (n.713), 4.
717. Editorial in *Theology*, January/February, 2000, WM Jacob.
718. Gerald Parsons (ed.), *The Growth of Religious Diversity in Britain* (2 vols), OUP and Routledge 1993.

Index